The EEC and the Mediterranean Countries

EDITORS:
AVI SHLAIM AND G. N. YANNOPOULOS

The EEC and the Mediterranean Countries

CAMBRIDGE UNIVERSITY PRESS
CAMBRIDGE
LONDON · NEW YORK · MELBOURNE

Published by the Syndics of the Cambridge University Press
The Pitt Building, Trumpington Street, Cambridge CB2 1RP
Bentley House, 200 Euston Road, London NW1 2DB
32 East 57th Street, New York, NY 10022, USA
296 Beaconsfield Parade, Middle Park, Melbourne 3206, Australia

Library of Congress catalogue card number: 75-3858

ISBN: 0 521 20817 3

First published 1976

Photoset and printed
by Interprint (Malta) Ltd

CONTENTS

BIOGRAPHICAL NOTES

Avi Shlaim is a lecturer in the Graduate School of Contemporary European Studies and the Department of Politics, University of Reading.

George N. Yannopoulos is Deputy Chairman of the Graduate School of Contemporary European Studies, University of Reading.

Matthew McQueen is a lecturer in the Graduate School of Contemporary European Studies and the Department of Economics, University of Reading.

Mordechai E. Kreinin is professor in the Department of Economics, Michigan State University.

Dietrich Kebschull is professor at the Institut für Wirtschaftsforschung, Hamburg.

J. S. Marsh is reader in the Department of Agricultural Economics and Management and the Graduate School of Contemporary European Studies, University of Reading.

G. J. Kalamotousakis is associate professor of Finance in the Graduate School of Business Administration, New York University.

John N. Bridge is lecturer in the Department of Economics, University of Durham.

Roberto Aliboni is professor at the Istituto Affari Internazionali, Rome.

George V. Vassiliou is managing director at the Middle East Marketing Research Bureau, Nicosia, Cyprus.

Juergen B. Donges is lecturer in the Institut für Weltwirtschaft in the University of Kiel, Germany.

Sergio Minerbi is in the Israeli Foreign Ministry.

Gian-Paolo Papa is a member of the External Relations Directorate of the Commission of the EEC.

Jean Petit-Laurent is a former member of the External Relations Directorate of the Commission of the EEC.

Stanley Henig is lecturer at the Civil Service College, London.

David Robertson is reader in the Department of Economics and the Graduate School of European Studies, University of Reading.

ACKNOWLEDGEMENTS

We wish to acknowledge the generous grant awarded by the European Educational Research Trust and the supplementary grant by the UACES which helped the writing of this book. The Small Grants Committee of the Nuffield Foundation supported part of the research work upon which the chapter on Migrant Labour and Economic Growth is based. We also wish to acknowledge the encouragement given by the Chairman of the Graduate School Professor Hugh Thomas throughout the preparation of this volume.

We would like to thank all the participants of the conference held in December 1973 in Reading for their valuable contributions in the exchange of views on early drafts of the chapters of this volume.

Finally, our warmest thanks to Mrs P. Sales, Secretary of the Graduate School, for her efficient co-ordination of the whole effort – from the initial stages of approaching potential contributors to the preparation of the conference and the final typing of the manuscripts. Her response to this challenge was not only efficient but also skilful and intelligent.

G. N. Yannopoulos
A. Shlaim

1

Introduction

AVI SHLAIM AND G. N. YANNOPOULOS

Historical links, geographical proximity and a degree of interdependence in a number of crucial areas combine to make the Mediterranean region an area of special interest and special responsibility for the European Economic Community (EEC). The countries bordering on the Mediterranean take 12 per cent of the Community's world trade, which makes them a market comparable in importance to the United States. In addition, the Community is vitally dependent on North Africa and the Middle East for its oil supplies. For the countries of the Mediterranean themselves the link with the Community is of even greater importance because it provides a market for some 52 per cent of their exports; it is a source of technical and financial aid and it employs the overwhelming majority of their migrant workers. Thus, in economic terms, the Mediterranean countries, taken together, represent a principal trading partner for the EEC, while to their own prosperity and prospects of economic development the Community is a factor of the highest magnitude.

This high degree of real and potential economic interdependence is further enhanced by historical and cultural affinities and by the political dimension that pervades this relationship. As the Commission's first President, Walter Hallstein, used to say, 'we are not in business; we are in politics', and the desire to promote a stable regional order which would safeguard the security of its southern and south-western flanks has played a part, albeit not a determining one, in shaping Community policies towards this region. Not wishing to emulate the patterns of influence exercised by the traditional super-powers and not possessing the diplomatic and military means with which this influence is underpinned, the Community has preferred to rely on trade links as a key factor in enabling it to play a balancing role and promoting conditions of lasting social and economic and hence political stability in this region. However, there is a strong school of thought within the Community that goes further, in advocating that the

Mediterranean basin should deliberately be cultivated as a political sphere of influence[1] or, more modestly, that regional interdependence should be institutionalised within the framework of a 'sphere of association'. For the Community's partners, many of whom had to choose in the past between the two super-powers who dominated the scene – Russia and America – this offers the alternative of alignment with a new type of great power that has been deliberately projected as a 'civilian power', or, at any rate, the possibility of reducing their dependence by diversifying their links.

Given the stakes involved and the existence of unique conditions for regional co-operation, the apparently random and almost absent-minded manner in which the EEC's policy towards the Mediterranean evolved is most striking. Indeed, the importance of the problems was almost matched by the incoherence of the policies. Lacking an agreed overall conception of its own, the Community simply reacted to the requests of its neighbours by taking little steps of scant economic and political significance. Beginning with the Athens accord, which came into force in 1962, the EEC concluded a series of association agreements, trade agreements and preferential trade agreements with practically all the countries bordering on the Mediterranean Sea by the end of a decade.[2] The end product was a mosaic of agreements that had little relation to one another, complex and divergent commercial content, an assortment of institutional modalities and different provisions regarding the political future of each bilateral relationship.

This improvisation and step-by-step approach is in part explained by the flimsy foundation that the Rome Treaty provided for dealing with the countries of the area. The Treaty does not envisage any arrangements for the Mediterranean region as a whole; only the possibility of association with the countries that had been historically linked to member states is referred to in the annexed declarations. Article 237 does stipulate that 'any European State may apply to become a member of the Community', but, although in

1 The case against such a policy is eloquently argued by Wolfgang Hager, 'The Community and the Mediterranean', in Max Kohnstamm and Wolfgang Hager (eds.), *A Nation Writ Large?* (Macmillan, London, 1973) pp. 209–15.

2 For an account of the evolution of the Community's policies and an analysis of the agreements see Stanley Henig, *The external relations of the European Community; association and trade agreements* (Chatham House/PEP European Series no. 19, 1971), as well as his chapter in this book; Joseph Loeff, 'La Communauté elargie et l'Espace Mediterranéen' in *The external economic policy of the enlarged European Community* (College of Europe, De Tempel, Tempelhof, Bruges, 1973), and Horst Günter Krenzler, 'Die Beziehungen der EWG zu den Mittelmeerländern', *Europa-Archiv* IV (1971).

theory this covers the countries of the northern shore, in practice their economic under-development and the undemocratic nature of their regimes has precluded full membership. Consequently, all the association agreements concluded by the Community have been based on Article 238. In the case of trade agreements, the Community has had to rely on Article 113, which concerns the common commercial policy.

The effect of the frail treaty bases was reinforced by the fact that the agreements were negotiated at different stages in the evolution of the Community, when the process of economic integration was in a formative stage and at a time when dealings with third countries were severely hampered by the absence of common agricultural and energy policies. The so-called Mediterranean policy consequently evolved not out of a clear role that the Community defined for itself but as a response to the array of external pressures to which the original member states had to react as best they could given the limited means at their disposal for collective action.

The Community's system for making foreign policy constitutes a further factor that is not simply of historical interest but also has a continuing bearing on the Mediterranean policy. The salient feature of this system is the artificial but insistently applied division between external economic relations ('low politics') which fall within the jurisdiction of the Community organs, and 'pure' foreign policy ('high politics') which remains the jealously guarded province of the member states who have set up a loose inter-governmental framework of political co-operation outside the Community machinery. The extremely tenuous links that connect the Community institutions with the Davignon framework of political co-operation militate against the formulation of a coherent and integrated external policy which encompasses the economic and the political dimensions and the translation of impulses for co-operation among the Nine into effective action by the Community's institutions. It is largely this deficiency of the institutional system for handling external relations that makes the Community appear on the international stage as a 'fettered giant' (in Ralf Dahrendorf's phrase).[3] In the Mediterranean sphere this bicephalous policy-making system has hampered the evolution of a political role commensurate with the Community's vast economic power, and has permitted the growth of a policy the component parts of which were not always compatible.

By the early 1970s it became obvious that disjointed incrementalism would have to give way to a more systematic and coherent approach and

3 Ralf Dahrendorf, 'Limits and Possibilities of a European Communities Foreign Policy', *The World Today*, XXVII, no. 4 (April 1971).

that the collection of association and trade agreements which had accumulated in the course of the previous decade would have to be superseded by a comprehensive framework which would take into account the problems and needs of the region as a whole and balance the claims of this region in terms of aid and trade against those of the Community's other partners, notably the African associates. The prospective enlargement of the Community lent urgency to this task because the agreements with the Six had to be extended to the Nine, and some of the Community's Mediterranean partners made their agreement to the technical adaptations contingent on an improvement in the content of the accords.[4] The nature of the relationship was in any case bound to be affected by the changing balance of self-sufficiency in food that was occasioned by the accession of three new members – Denmark, Britain and Ireland – with their large population and by the arrangements that were to be worked out with the Commonwealth 'associables' regarding the access of their agricultural products to the European market.

All these factors converged to put pressure on the EEC to combine the revision of the agreements in force with an attempt to lay the foundations of a new global policy towards the Mediterranean. In October 1972, the Commission submitted its proposals for the progressive establishment of free-trade areas linking all the Mediterranean countries as well as Jordan with the European Community.[5] In November, the Council of Ministers agreed on the adoption of a global policy that would include within its scope the following principal categories of agreements:

the Association Agreements with Greece and Turkey, which are intended to lead to full membership at an unspecified future date (although the agreement with Greece was 'frozen' after the colonels' *coup* in 1967);

the Association Agreements with Morocco and Tunisia, the origin of which goes back to the declaration of intent annexed to the Treaty of Rome – Algeria originally enjoyed member status as a French *département*, but its position after independence was not formally defined and Algeria remains a juridical anomaly;

the Association Agreements with Malta and Cyprus, the second stage of which calls for the establishment of a customs union;

the preferential trade agreements with Spain, Israel, Egypt and Lebanon.

4 Mario Levi, 'La C.E.E. et les pays de la Méditerranée', *Politique Etrangère*, VI (1972) 806.

5 *'Note d'Information'*; *Les relations entre la Communauté et les pays du basin mediterranée*, Commission des Communautés Européennes, Bruxelles (Oct. 1972).

The global policy was to be pursued in three principal directions: free trade in industrial goods; the removal of restrictions from a substantial part of agricultural trade; and co-operation. The policy envisaged the progressive dismantling of all tariffs on industrial goods leading to a free-trade area in this field by 1977. Although this was not matched by the provision for a free-trade area in agricultural goods, the policy was calculated to grant concessions on some 80 per cent of the Mediterranean countries' exports to the Community. The third and, in the Commission's view, the most important element was development co-operation encompassing technical co-operation, schemes for environmental protection, financial aid and the provision of freer access and better conditions of employment for migrant workers.

In June 1973, the Commission was given a mandate to open talks with Spain, Israel, Morocco, Tunisia and Algeria. When negotiations opened in July, all five, with varying degrees of vehemence, criticised the Community package. Their dissatisfaction related principally to the agricultural component of the package. The Maghreb countries and Spain were also disappointed with the EEC offer for the treatment of migrant workers.

In the second round of negotiations held in the winter, the Commission improved the terms offered for the treatment of refined petroleum products from the Maghreb countries as well as making more generous concessions in the agricultural field. But the deadline of 31 December 1973 which the Community had optimistically set itself for completing the implementation of the global policy fell by the wayside – not least because of the Community's nervousness over pursuing trade negotiations with this part of the world in the wake of the Middle East war and the energy crisis.

Many months of intensive wrangling between the member states elapsed before the Council of Ministers, in July 1974, reached agreement on a new mandate for the resumption of negotiations with the Mediterranean countries. These countries were not responsible for the delays. On the contrary, all of them repeatedly urged the Community to resume discussions, and the Maghreb countries went as far as to threaten the Community representatives that the projected Euro-Arab dialogue would be jeopardised by continued procrastination in the Mediterranean negotiations. The difficulties sprang largely from the conflict between the consumer-oriented approach of the British and the producer-oriented approach of the Italians and the French, who see imports of cheap farm goods from the Mediterranean as a boon and a threat respectively. Paradoxically, the Italians and the French, who are foremost advocates of a Community sphere of influence in Mare Nostrum, also feel the most threatened when it comes to offering concrete concessions simply because they grow similar products; Britain, on the other hand, although advocating a liberal trade policy, has great reservations about proceeding along the road to a major regional role and urges a cautious approach that carefully considers all the possible political and strategic consequences and especially the reaction of the United States. In the absence of agreement on a meaningful set of policy guide-lines of a political nature, it is hardly surprising that the Community's approach to the Mediterranean has been marked by preoccupation with minutiae. Thus agreement on a Community package was obstructed for some time by differences of view as to whether the EEC customs reduction of 55 per cent would apply exclusively to tinned fruit salads weighing more than 1 kg or also to those of a lesser weight.

As this book goes into press, the future of the much-vaunted global policy remains uncertain. At the reopening of negotiations in October 1974, the new Community package attracted critical comment. In view of the difficulties overcome to arrive at a definition of the Community's position, the prevailing political paralysis and the deterioration in the economic situation of the majority of the member states, it is unlikely that large additional concessions would be forthcoming. If the Community's Mediterranean policy is not substantially called into question and negotiations with the six priority states (Morocco, Tunisia, Algeria, Spain, Israel and Malta) are successfully concluded, then another round of negotiations will take place with Egypt, Syria, the Lebanon and Jordan, who have expressed their interest in being included within the scope of the EEC's global policy. A further factor of uncertainty relates to the dialogue between the Nine and the oil-producing countries of the Middle East. Although this Euro-Arab dialogue is conducted at the level of governments and not by the Community and although it constitutes a separate area of policy, relevant developments are bound to affect the progress of the Mediterranean policy and *vice versa.*

This volume is not primarily concerned, however, with the future of the relations between the European Community and the Mediterranean countries. The purpose of the foregoing remarks was simply to outline recent policy developments and to place them within a broad historical and political perspective. The present volume examines in a systematic way a number of the most important aspects of the economic relations between the EEC and the Mediterranean countries as these relations have developed under the impact of the bilateral association and trade preference agreements concluded by the EEC. The emphasis is primarily on trade links, although the interdependence between the two groups of countries through labour movements is also examined. One aspect of the economic relations between the EEC and the Mediterranean area which is not examined, because of the lack of comprehensive and reliable statistical sources, is foreign direct investment.

The examination of the economic relations between the EEC and the Mediterranean area focuses on two major issues. The first is the impact of the Common Market association and trade preference agreements on the countries of the area and on third countries. The second is the implications of the Community policy on association for the world trading system. The book thus tries to answer two questions which have hitherto received scanty attention in the literature of international trade and international economic relations. The first relates to the evaluation of the actual effects of association and trade preference agreements between countries which are at different stages of economic development. The second relates to the study of the feasibility of a global EEC policy towards the Mediterranean area that, hopefully, will enable the Community to exert a balancing and stabilising influence round its southern flank and the effects of the regional arrangements worked out by the Community and its partners for third countries and for the General Agreement on Tariffs and Trade (GATT).

The book is divided into four parts. The first part gives an overview of the way in which the agreements have influenced trade flows. An attempt to quantify the impact of Common Market preferences for the Mediterranean countries is made in the second chapter by M. McQueen. His approach follows a path different from that suggested by traditional customs-union theory. His concern is with the Mediterranean countries alone rather than with the whole area covered by the quasi-customs unions created by the association treaties. In his paper, M. McQueen tries to establish that part of changes recorded in the share of EEC trade held by the Mediterranean countries which can be attributed to the special trade preferences granted to them. The method as such does not measure the total trade diversion within the customs union and does not aim at indicating the amount of trade creation in the form of EEC imports supplanting domestic production in the associated states. But, although conventional customs-union theory considers the latter as a gain, a developing country with infant industry to protect can hardly adopt the same view.

Professor Kreinin uses the conventional approach to estimate in the third chapter the possible effects on third countries and, in particular, on the United States. He finds that trade diversion against the United States is rather negligible – a view also reiterated in Professor Kalamotousakis' contribution in chapter 7. Professor Kreinin concludes that the resistance of the US Administration to the EEC policy towards the Mediterranean is determined not by the size of the trade diversion effects against American exports but by concern over the implications that it has on the world trading system as this evolved under the impact of GATT.

In the fourth chapter Professor Kebschull argues that only a disaggregated, product-by-product approach can produce any meaningful results as to the relevance of tariff preferences on trade flows. He shows that factors other than prices are more important in explaining changes in the shares of particular countries and products in world markets and that tariff concessions exert only a small influence in the evolution of these shares.

The second part of the book deals with two special problems the analysis of which is vital in understanding the nature of the economic interdependence between the EEC and the Mediterranean countries. The first concerns the Common Agricultural Policy (CAP) and the problems that it raises for the agricultural producing countries of the area. The second concerns the dependence of the EEC on the surplus labour of the area. It is extremely difficult to go through the maze of the CAP in the short space of a single article, but J. Marsh shows how the Community tried to regulate the export of Mediterranean agricultural goods to the EEC in order to protect its own producers. This restrictive attitude of the Community is also unfavourably commented upon by several contributors in the country studies of part 3 – particularly by G. Vassiliou and Professor R. Aliboni. Several contributors thus feel that such restrictions and regulations on agricultural imports from the Mediterranean area are hardly conducive to the promotion of economic development in the countries of the region. In chapter 6 G. N. Yannopoulos shows that without migrant labour the export-led growth of the economies of the pre-enlargement EEC would have run into capacity constraints. The EEC countries have relied upon the pool of surplus labour of the Mediterranean basin – a pool that was ingeniously tapped during periods of strained labour markets and 'topped up' again during periods of economic recessions.

Part 3 contains six country studies, which examine in detail the impact of the agreements on individual or groups of countries. Some of the studies, where data were fairly easily available, attempt an export analysis. In other studies, where the recently concluded agreements have not yet been given time to show up their results, attempts were made to look into the future and to predict possible results on the basis of the knowledge of the agreements and the analytical insights offered by economic theory and the history of economic development. The study on Greece by Professor Kalamotousakis starts by developing an analytical framework adapted from the conventional theory of customs union among developed economies to fit the special conditions that prevail in the formation of a customs union between an underdeveloped country and a group of highly industrialised countries. The author shows that the 'privileged' associate member status granted to Greece mainly because of political considerations has become a strategic factor in the growth and changing structure of Greece's exports and an important contributory factor in the acceleration of its industrial development. However, in the next study, on Turkey, Dr J. N. Bridge demonstrates that arrangements similar to those with Greece produced rather disappointing results both on export performance and growth acceleration. It thus seems that the ability of the indigenous economic agents to mobilise and re-direct the domestic resources of an associate country is a necessary condition to make the association beneficial to the developing country. The next chapter, by R. Aliboni, discusses the 'development associations' that exist between the Maghreb countries and the EEC. After examining the nature of these associations, Professor Aliboni explains why the concessions on agricultural products are far from generous and how these concessions are further undermined by the interpretation given in practice by the Community officials to the already complicated Community rules on agriculture. The case of Cyprus – discussed by G. Vassiliou in the next chapter, together with the agreements with Lebanon and Egypt – illustrates and reinforces the same point. The last two chapters of part 3 examine in some detail the effects of two trade preference agreements – namely, those with Spain and Israel, particularly from the point of view of the industrial sector of the two countries. Dr J. B. Donges finds in the agreement with Spain many examples of what he calls 'the neo-mercantilist philosophies' within the Community. Spain's exports of cotton and some petroleum products enjoy only limited preferences, while its exports of iron and steel products, cork manufactures, cotton yarn and thread are excluded altogether from the agreement. Israel – as Dr Minerbi shows in his contribution – similarly has a list of 'sensitive' products whose export growth is curtailed presumably to protect some sectoral Community interests. For many of these products, export expansion prospects have been adversely affected following the enlargement of the EEC.

Part 4 draws upon the previous chapters in order to evaluate the

'Mediterranean' policy of the EEC in its totality. G.-P. Papa and J. Petit-Laurent give in chapter 13 a comprehensive review of the evolution of the commercial relations between the EEC and the Mediterranean countries and examine the conflict of interests and perspectives among the member states which is essential to the understanding of the Community's Mediterranean policy. The penultimate chapter, by S. Henig, looks at the EEC Mediterranean policy in the context of the external relations of the European Communities. Whereas Papa and Petit-Laurent see the need to evolve an 'overall' or 'global' strategy and a move from empiricism to a total concept, Henig argues that in terms of the importance of the Mediterranean to the Community from the economic viewpoint 'the amount of time expended by the Community on reaching bilateral agreements has been misspent'. He argues that this is particularly true at present, when various bodies such as the United Nations Conference on Trade and Development (UNCTAD) and GATT are promoting the idea of schemes of generalised preferences. However, one should not forget that the EEC–Mediterranean relations have both an economic and a political basis.

The last chapter, by D. Robertson, pulls together the main points that emerge from the various contributions in this volume in an effort to see how the system of multiple trade discrimination that evolved through the Community initiatives stands in relation to the multilateral trading system promoted by GATT. The Community's formal commitment to the principle of a 'global' policy towards the Mediterranean countries is bound to intensify the controversy of multilateralism versus regionalism in international economic relations. Although the author recognises the importance of political objectives in the formulation of the Community's policy towards the countries of the Mediterranean basin, he nevertheless finds that 'very little attempt appears to have been made to ascertain the economic implications of the complex series of piecemeal bilateral trade agreements'. Perhaps the most important conclusion emerging from the examination of the EEC–Mediterranean economic relations is the need to establish a comprehensive Community strategy on international trade relations.

1

GENERAL ASPECTS

2

Some Measures of the Economic Effects of Common Market Trade Preferences for the Mediterranean Countries

MATTHEW McQUEEN

1. Introduction

The European Economic Community (EEC) has so far concluded seven preferential trade agreements with the Mediterranean countries, and is now in the process of drawing up proposals for the co-ordination of these separate agreements into a coherent arrangement that will create a Mediterranean free-trade area.

From the point of view of the Community, these agreements primarily fulfil the political purpose of contributing towards the greater stability and harmony of relations with an area directly affecting the security of the EEC. This, it is hoped, will be brought about by the acceleration of the agreements of the economic and social development of the Mediterranean countries through trade and capital flows and, in doing so, creating an increasing identity of interest over major policy issues between these countries and the Community. However, one of the principal constraints governing the extent of trade preferences granted is a conflict of interest between the desire of primary producers and some manufacturers of consumer goods (for instance, textiles) in the Mediterranean countries to expand their exports to the EEC, and producers of these products within the Community who fear the consequences of such an expansion of imports and consequently press for strict quotas and the maintenance of relatively high prices. This problem is exacerbated by the fact that many of these producers are in the relatively less developed regions of the Community and therefore face little prospect of being able to move into alternative lines of production. This conflict of interest can be resolved in the long run only by the Community's pursuing a vigorous policy aimed at changing the structure of employment in these regions.

The purpose of this paper is to present a series of estimates of the commodity trade effects of agreements concluded with Greece, Turkey, Morocco, Tunisia, Spain and Israel. Possible gains and losses are considered only from the point of view of these countries, and the chapter does not consider the effects of the agreements either on the Community or other less developed countries.

Section 2 outlines the theoretical basis for the measures used in the analysis of exports and imports subsequent to the conclusion of the agreements, and presents a series of estimates of the possible extent to which exports to and imports from the EEC are greater than would have been the case in the absence of the Agreements. Next, in section 3, an analysis is made of changes in the commodity concentration of exports. Finally, in section 4, some indication is given of the importance of international trade to the economic growth of the countries considered.

2. Estimates of the Effects of the Agreements on Total Commodity Exports and Imports

A number of reports published on the operation and effects of the agreements draw their conclusions directly from such measures as the growth of exports and imports with the EEC before and after the negotiation of the agreement, the change in the proportion of total exports and imports of the Mediterranean countries with the EEC, and changes in the balance of trade between the partners to the agreement. However, taken in isolation, these measures are subject to problems of interpretation and in general are of limited use unless set in the context of some, albeit simple, model of the determinants of trade flows.

For example, a look at the exports of the six Mediterranean countries to the EEC reveals that they have all recorded an acceleration in the growth of these exports subsequent to the signature of the agreements. Greece recorded an annual decline of 10 per cent in the value of its exports to the EEC in the period 1958–61 and a 32-per-cent annual increase in the period 1963/4–1971/2. Similarly, Morocco and Tunisia recorded a substantial acceleration in the growth of their exports to the five EEC countries (excluding France, as they already obtained preferential access to this market) after the agreements of 1969. More modest but still positive increases in the growth of exports to the Community occurred for the other three Mediterranean countries. This tendency is of course encouraging, but the acceleration is not simply attributable to the agreements. It may have been merely the result of an increase in the rate of growth of demand for imports by the Community, that would have taken place irrespective of trade preferences. It may also have been caused by the improved ability of the Mediterranean countries to compete both in world markets and in the EEC.

With regard to the latter point, it might be argued that it is more useful to consider the change in the proportion of total exports to the EEC. In this case the position is, if anything, reversed. Turkey's exports to the EEC in 1961–3 were between 37 per cent and 40 per cent of total exports, but this proportion actually declined considerably in 1964 (the date of the association agreement) and only recovered their former proportion in 1969. Morocco and especially Tunisia recorded quite strong increases in the proportion of their exports to the five EEC countries before the agreements, and no noticeable improvement occurred after 1969. However, it cannot be concluded from this that the trade agreements had little effect, for changes in exports to the EEC will be reflected in a commensurate change in total exports, the magnitude of this effect depending on the initial proportion of exports to the EEC in total exports. Analogous arguments apply to changes in the growth rate and proportion of imports from the EEC to the Mediterranean countries.

Another apparently useful indicator of the effects of the agreements is the balance of trade between the Mediterranean countries and the EEC. A comparison of the average level of imports and exports for the two years before the signature of the agreements with the average for 1971/2 shows that, with the exception of Spain, Morocco and Tunisia, the balance of trade has moved against the Mediterranean countries. Taking the exports to the EEC by the Mediterranean countries as a proportion of imports from the EEC, the picture is one of near stability, ranging from one-third in the case of Greece to almost equality for Tunisia. Spain has succeeded in raising the proportion of imports from the EEC covered by exports to the EEC from just over 40 per cent to just over 60 per cent in the three-year period 1968/9–1971/2. Morocco has shown some deterioration, from 98 per cent to 89 per cent, in the period 1967/8–1971/2. However, by itself a deterioration in the balance of trade between the EEC and the Mediterranean countries is of no particular significance and does not imply that these countries have suffered a loss of welfare. It is to be expected that a developing country will increasingly require resources that cannot be produced domestically and that, in the short run, may be covered to an increasingly smaller extent by exports of goods. This will present no problem of adjustment if the deficit is financed by invisible receipts, such as shipping and tourism, and by inflows of capital from foreign private investment, remittances from nationals working abroad, foreign aid and borrowing (provided that the terms of the loan match the ability of the recipient directly or indirectly to transform these resources into sufficient foreign exchange receipts to repay capital and interest). The important questions are firstly, whether the agreements have on balance (for example, as a result of granting reverse preferences) caused the Mediterranean country to import from the EEC on less favourable terms than if the resources had been acquired from the rest of the world, and to import goods from the EEC because of the elimination of a domestic producer that had a potential comparative advantage (infant industry argument). Secondly, we wish to know the extent to which the Mediterranean country has been able to increase its exports to the EEC to a level greater than could be expected on the basis of changes in its general competitive position in world markets. Whether the country has made a trade loss or gain from the agreement will depend on the net result of answering these two sets of questions. Even if it is concluded that the Mediterranean country has made a net loss on trade, it could be argued that this may be more than offset by other benefits from the agreement. For example, the agreement may provide for capital and technical assistance to enable the country to change its structure of production and thereby obtain greater future benefits from preferential access to the EEC. Perhaps more importantly, the very existence of the agreement and the promise that it holds for greater stability and harmony of political relations between the EEC and the Mediterranean country may induce significant flows of foreign private direct investment, bringing not only foreign exchange but also technical and marketing expertise and facilities. The agreements may also encourage governments in these developing countries to introduce policies with the objective of producing a better allocation of resources based on actual or potential comparative advantage, without fear of retaliation by the EEC countries if these policies are successful in substantially raising exports.

Clearly, to answer these questions even for one country would require a considerable programme of research not only on the commodities imported and exported but also on the consequences of the agreement on the structure of production of the Mediterranean country and the effects of this on income and employment. The objective of the author in this short paper is simply to indicate in a general sense whether there exists the possibility that the Mediterranean countries' exports to and imports from the EEC are different from the level that could be expected from the growth of demand for imports by the two groups of countries and the change in the ability of exporters to supply the goods at a competitive price.

Two interesting studies have been published by Kreinin (1973) and by Young (1972) on the effects of the Yaoundé Convention negotiated by the

EEC with eighteen African countries and Madagascar, under which they receive preferential access to the EEC while the EEC obtains preferential access to the markets of thirteen of the eighteen associated states (reverse preferences). The study of Kreinin[1] concentrates on the effects of reverse preferences, and argues that French firms operating in the former French colonies exercised a monopoly or semi-monopoly power in the years before the Yaoundé Convention, and consequently the granting of reverse preferences simply led to a further transfer of resources from the Associated African States to the French exporter, equal in value to the loss of tariff revenue. The gradual extension of preferences to other EEC members did not change this situation, because the French firms remained dominant suppliers either as a result of the continuation of close trading and monetary links or because EEC suppliers operated an effective cartel arrangement. Clearly, this analysis would appear to have at least some relevance to Morocco and Tunisia, although, because the agreements have been in operation only since 1969, we must obviously wait a few more years before analysing the evidence. However, it is doubtful if EEC producers could exercise the same degree of monopoly power in the other four Mediterranean countries in which the links with the EEC are not founded on the same strong economic and historical base, and whose economies are considerably more advanced and diversified than the Associated African States.

The study by Young[2] considers the total commodity trade under the Yaoundé Convention, and estimates that the maximum cost of reverse preferences to the Associates was 2 per cent of the total import bill, whereas the gain from preferences was probably about 1.9 per cent of total AASM (Associated African States and Madagascar) exports. Young's method of analysis can be easily adapted for the six Mediterranean countries in the following way.

To identify the extent to which the growth of exports to the EEC was due to the growth of demand for imports by the EEC, the rate of growth of exports to the EEC by countries receiving preferences was deflated by the rate of growth of imports by the EEC from other LDCs (excluding oil-exporting countries). The extent to which this ratio exceeded unity indicated that the countries receiving preferences increased their share of EEC imports from developing countries. However, this could have been due solely

1 M. Kreinin, 'Some economic consequences of reverse preferences', *Journal of Common Market Studies* (March 1973).

2 C. Young, 'Association with the EEC: economic aspects of the trade relationship', *Journal of Common Market Studies* (December 1972).

to an increased ability of preference-receiving countries to supply goods on a competitive basis. This was tested by deflating the rate of growth of exports from the preference area to the rest of the world (that is, by excluding the EEC) by the rate of growth of exports by other LDCs to the rest of the world. If this were the sole influence on the increased share of the preference area of EEC imports, then the two ratios will be equal. The extent to which the first ratio exceeded the second will be an indication of the beneficial effects of the agreement on the exports of the preference-receiving countries.

Similarly, the effect of reverse preferences on diverting imports from other developed countries in favour of higher cost suppliers in the EEC can be assessed by comparing the ratio of the rates of growth of imports by the preference area from the EEC relative to the imports from the rest of the world; to the ratio of 'other LDCs' rates of growth of imports from the EEC relative to imports from the rest of the world. The extent to which the first ratio exceeds the second indicates the degree of trade diversion from lower-cost third-country suppliers to higher-cost EEC sources.

The results of applying this method are summarised below. In view of the short period of operation of the agreements for four of the six countries, the results obviously indicate only the very short-run effects.

From the results shown in Table 1, it would appear that all six countries have recorded growth rates of exports to the EEC substantially higher than could be expected either from the growth of imports from developing countries as a whole or from any improvement in their competitive position in world markets. Indeed, it appears from the method of analysis that Greece and Turkey have suffered a small deterioration in their ability to compete in world markets relative to other developing countries. This

TABLE 1 Effects of the agreements on the imports and exports of the Mediterranean countries using growth rates

Country and time period of agreement	*Export coefficient*	*Import coefficient*
Turkey, 1965–71	1·9	0·2
Greece, 1963–71	3·8	1·1
Morocco, 1970–2	4·1	0·8
Tunisia, 1970–2	6·6	1·46
Israel, 1970–2	2·8	3·1
Spain, 1970–2	3·3	1·2

substantial residual element in the growth of exports to the Community is therefore attributed to the third potentially important determinant – namely, the beneficial effects of the agreement. As far as imports from the EEC are concerned, it would appear that Israel and, to a marginal extent, Greece, Spain and Tunisia have imported more goods from the EEC during the period of the agreements than can be explained either by the greater competitive ability of the Community to supply goods to the less developed countries relative to the rest of the world (although this was positive for all time periods considered) or by the general growth of imports by these Mediterranean countries.

This method can of course be criticised on a number of grounds – for example, that it operates at too high a level of aggregation and that, if the commodity composition (defined as precisely as possible to avoid the problem that apparently similar products may have small but important differentiating features) of trade between the Mediterranean countries, the EEC, other LDCs and the rest of the world is taken into account, entirely different conclusions may result. Indeed, the categories 'EEC', 'other LDCs' and 'RW' could be better defined at an individual country level. In reply to this counsel of perfection, one can also say that such a detailed microeconomic study may indeed be superior but that it would also involve severe methodological and statistical problems as well as considerable resources, with the problem remaining at the end of aggregating the results into valid general conclusions. Probably the best compromise is to combine aggregate studies with detailed studies of the most important traded goods. Secondly, the method can be criticised for assuming that the whole of the residual element in the growth of the Mediterranean countries' trade with the EEC can be attributed to the agreements. Again, this is a potentially valid criticism, and more detailed work could certainly be carried out to isolate the determinants of trade flows. However, it could be argued that the values of the coefficients are such that the magnitude of these unknown influences would have to be considerable to alter the general conclusions. Thirdly, Young's method could be criticised because the results are sensitive to the time period of measurement and because this is particularly important when dealing with countries in which primary product exports, that are notoriously volatile, account for a significant proportion of total exports. However, testing this possibility by selecting different time periods and using averages did not produce substantially different results for Greece and Turkey. The time periods of operation of the agreements with the remaining four countries are of course too short to test the significance of this criticism directly, but the magnitude of the coefficients are such that it would need a very considerable (though not impossible) degree of variability in export earnings to reverse the conclusions.

I would, however, criticise this method for not posing the 'alternative case', that is, what would have been the most likely level of exports to and imports from the EEC by the Mediterranean countries in the absence of an agreement. Thus it may appear from Young's method that all six Mediterranean countries were able to raise the level of their exports to the EEC as a result of the agreements. However, if at least some of the Mediterranean countries were already successfully exporting to the EEC and the rest of the world in the period prior to the agreement and one can observe no deflection in this trend after the signature of the agreement, then it would be more difficult to argue that these countries had obtained any noticeable benefit to their exports.

To obtain an estimate of the level of exports of the Mediterranean countries that would have occurred in the absence of the agreements, the trend share of exports in the imports of the EEC and the rest of the world (RW) prior to the Agreement was linearly extrapolated to 1971/2. By taking the share in imports, the problem of different growth rates of income and therefore imports of the EEC and RW affecting the export performance of the Mediterranean country concerned was eliminated. By considering the trend of exports to the rest of the world as well as to the EEC, we can estimate the extent to which exports to the EEC were higher or lower than predicted due to changes in the general competitive position of the Mediterranean country's exports. Thus, if XE and XR represent the actual level of exports to the EEC and RW respectively and $\widehat{XE}$ and $\widehat{XR}$ the predicted level; then, if XR is less than $\widehat{XR}$, it is assumed that the Mediterranean country has become less competitive in world markets during the period of the Agreement. The extent of possible beneficial effects of preferences on exports is therefore equal to the difference between:

$$\frac{XE - \widehat{XE}}{\widehat{XE}} \quad \text{and} \quad \frac{XR - \widehat{XR}}{\widehat{XR}}$$

Clearly, this method rests on some rather 'heroic' assumptions – for example, that trade was not substantially affected by cyclical factors, that autonomous shifts in the pattern of demand did not play an important role and that supply constraints did not significantly affect the results (probably this assumption is the most suspect). A particular problem arises from the fact that a significant proportion of the exports of these countries are primary products and therefore subject to considerable fluctuations in market shares. A series of projections is therefore presented covering all trends considered reasonable on the basis of available information. Trends were fitted where possible by two methods. The first method extrapolates the linear trend from two base years to predict the share in imports in 1971 and 1972, whereas the second method was to fit a regression line to the pre-agreement annual shares.

Imports by the Mediterranean countries were treated in a similar way; in this case, the share of imports from the EEC and the rest of the world in the GDP of the Mediterranean countries were extrapolated to produce the predicted level of imports.

The actual shares of exports by the Mediterranean countries in the imports of the EEC and RW are shown in Table 2, so that the validity of the trends used in Table 3 may be judged independently.

The results from this method shown in Table 3 indicate that the exports of Greece, Morocco, Tunisia and Spain are substantially higher than could be expected on the basis of the trend in the pre-agreement share of their exports in the imports of the EEC and the change in their competitive position in the markets of the rest of the world. This large residual growth of exports to the EEC subsequent to the negotiation of the agreements is considered to be predominantly attributable to the existence of the agreements, although not necessarily the result of the margin of preferences granted. As was pointed out earlier in the chapter, the agreements have for the most part a primary political objective, and the consequent promise of stable political relations between the EEC and the Mediterranean countries may be a more important determinant of trade and capital flows than the detailed provisions of quotas, tariff preferences and reference prices. It appears possible that Israel has obtained some benefit for its exports to the EEC in the short period of the operation of the agreement. The results for Turkey suggest that there has been a sharp deterioration in the ability of its exports to compete in world markets since the period 1959–67 when an increasing share of the 'rest of the world's' trade was recorded. The period 1956–70 shows a fairly steady decline in its share of EEC imports, although some improvement has occurred in the last two years. In view of this mixed evidence, no clear conclusions can be drawn on the effect of the Association Agreement on Turkish exports. As far as imports are concerned (as shown in Table 4), only Greece and Turkey show any clear possibility of imports from the EEC being greater than could be predicted from the pre-Agreement trend in the average propensity to import from the EEC and the rest of the

TABLE 2 Exports of the Mediterranean countries as percentage shares of the total imports of (*a*) the EEC, (*b*) world trade–EEC imports

		Exports									
		1954	*1955*	*1956*	*1957*	*1958*	*1959*	*1960*	*1961*	*1962*	*1963*
Greece	XEC	0·4329	0·4995	0·4044	0·3919	0·4284	0·3330	0·2250	0·2106		
	XRW	0·1215	0·1208	0·1269	0·1457	0·1538	0·1329	0·1339	0·1485		
Turkey	XEC			0·4582	0·4339	0·3677	0·5741	0·3615	0·4006	0·4302	0·3465
	XRW			0·2588	0·2826	0·1869	0·2304	0·2080	0·2077	0·2127	0·2433

		1960	*1961*	*1962*	*1963*	*1964*	*1965*	*1966*	*1967*	*1968*	*1969*
Morocco	XEC	0·3000	0·2846	0·2307	0·2367	0·2450	0·1974	0·1855	0·1821	0·1972	
	XRW	0·1384	0·1378	0·1359	0·1591	0·1527	0·1431	0·1361	0·1276	0·1173	
Tunisia	XEC	0·0771	0·0548	0·0848	0·0789	0·0516	0·0569	0·0743	0·0800	0·0747	
	XRW	0·0393	0·0344	0·0291	0·0406	0·0424	0·0532	0·0493	0·0550	0·0585	
Spain	XEC	0·9453	0·8288	0·7706	0·6903	0·8258	0·7042	0·7832	0·7783	0·6953	0·7780
	XRW	0·4383	0·4239	0·4315	0·4882	0·5492	0·5231	0·6646	0·7157	0·7647	0·7775
Israel	XEC	0·2076	0·2126	0·1979	0·2632	0·2315	0·2494	0·2672	0·2800	0·2591	0·2322
	XRW	0·1512	0·1675	0·1950	0·2605	0·2508	0·2688	0·2866	0·3005	0·3169	0·3301

TABLE 3 Predicted and actual shares of the exports of the Mediterranean countries in the imports of the EEC and rest of the world

		Base years for extrapolation	$\frac{X - \hat{X}}{\hat{X}}$ (%) 1971/2
Greece	EEC	trend 1955–8	+69%
		trend 1954–9	+123%
	RW	trend 1954–61	−14·4%
		trend 1956/7–1960/1	+5·6%
		trend 1959–61	−3·3%
		regression 1954–61	+12·5%
Turkey	EEC	trend 1957–61	−4·3%
		trend 1956/7–1962/3	+0·8%
	RW	trend 1957/8–1962/3	− 6·3%
		trend 1959–1963	−22.4%
Morocco	EEC	trend 1961/2–1967/8	+20%
	(5)	trend 1961–7	+71%
		regression 1960–8	+65%
	RW	trend 1962/3–1967/8	+3·5%
		trend 1963–7	+9·2%
Tunisia	EEC	trend 1961/2–1966/7	+44%
	(5)	trend 1961–7	+41%
	RW	trend 1960–5	−12·3%
		trend 1963–8	−28.3%
		trend 1961–8	−28·0%
		regression 1960–8	−26·0%
Spain	EEC	trend 1961/2–1968/9	+59%
		trend 1962/3–1968/9	+53%
		regression 1960–9	+58%
	RW	regression 1960–9	+6·0%
		trend 1962–8	−2·5%
		trend 1960/1–1967/8	+2·3%

Table 3 (*continued*)

		Base years for extrapolation	$\frac{X - \hat{X}}{\hat{X}}$ (%) 1971/2
Israel	EEC	regression 1960–9	−10·5%
		trend 1963–8	−1·6%
		trend 1962/3–1968/9	+2·7%
	RW	regression 1960–69	−17·5%
		regression 1963–69	− 6·4%

TABLE 4 Predicted and actual shares of the EEC and rest of the world in the imports of the Mediterranean countries

		Base years for extrapolation	$\frac{M - \hat{M}}{\hat{M}}$ %
Greece	EEC	trend 1955–61	+30 (1972)
		trend 1955–61	+17·7 (1971)
		trend 1955–61	+23·8 (1971/2)
	RW	trend 1956–61	+4·3 (1972)
		trend 1958–61	−6·5 (1971)
		regression 1955–61	+12·5 (1972)
		regression 1955–61	+9 (1971)
Turkey	EEC	trend 1956–63	−21·7 (1971)
		trend 1956–63	−34·0 (1970/71)
		regression 1956–63	−42·0 (1971)
	RW	trend 1956–63	−41·1 (1971)
		trend 1956–63	−51·7 (1970/71)
		regression 1956–63	−46·0 (1971)
Tunisia	EEC	regression 1962–8	+1·3 (1971)
		trend 1962–6	+1·3 (1971)
		trend 1963–7	+0·6 (1971)

Table 4 (*continued*)

		Base years for extrapolation	$\frac{M - \hat{M}}{\hat{M}}\%$
	RW	trend 1961–7	+1·5 (1971)
		trend 1961/2–1967/8	+13·2 (1970/1)
Morocco	EEC	trend 1962–8	−1·7 (1972)
		trend 1962–8	+8 to 14 (1969–71)
		trend 1962–7	+15·3 (1971)
	RW	trend 1960–7	+3·4 (1972)
		trend 1960–7	+12·8 (1971)
Israel	EEC	trend 1964–8	−4·3 (1972)
		trend 1962–9	−9·2 (1972)
		trend 1962–9	−3·2 (1971)
	RW	trend 1963–8	−7·8 (1972)
		trend 1963–8	+1·8 (1971)
		trend 1960–8	+2·4 (1972)
		trend 1960–8	+11·5 (1971)
		regression 1960–9	+2·5 (1972)
Spain	EEC	trend 1962–7	−11 (1972)
		trend 1962–7	−17·4 (1971/2)
		trend 1962–9	−7·1 (1972)
		trend 1962–9	+1·4 (1971/2)
		regression 1960–9	+12 (1972)
	RW	trend 1961–8	+14·4 (1972)
		trend 1961–8	+8·62 (1971/2)
		trend 1963–8	+13·0 (1972)
		trend 1963–8	+5·3 (1971/2)
		regression 1960–9	+9·3 (1972)

world. Morocco, Tunisia, Israel and Spain show no clear evidence of imports from the EEC being greater than predicted. Taking imports and exports together, it appears possible that in the short period of the agreement, Morocco, Tunisia and Spain have made quite substantial gains from the agreements for their exports to the EEC, at little or no cost in terms of higher than expected imports from the EEC. Greece appears to have made substantial gains in its exports to the EEC (pre-agreement shares were on a sharply declining trend which was reversed in the period 1962–72) at some possible cost in terms of a higher share of imports from the EEC. The evidence for Turkey is so mixed that it is difficult to draw conclusions with any degree of confidence.

One criticism that could be made of this method is that it fails to distinguish between the trade creation and trade diversion effects of the agreements; however, it is not the purpose of this chapter to decide whether Mediterranean exports to the EEC are higher as a result of trade creation effects replacing domestic producers within the EEC or as a result of trade diversion effects reducing EEC imports from their country sources of supply, although these factors are clearly of importance in a more general context. In addition, it must be remembered that the static analysis of trade creation and trade diversion are of limited significance to a developing country, where, for example, in the case of exports, an important long-term benefit from the agreement could be to enable the developing country to export goods that at present are produced only for domestic consumption or may not be produced at all. Similarly, in the case of imports from the EEC, if reverse preferences had the effect of replacing a higher-cost domestic producer in the Mediterranean with lower-cost EEC imports, then this 'trade creation' is treated as a welfare gain in traditional static analysis. However, from the point of view of the future development of the country this is a clear loss of welfare if the displaced domestic producer had a potential comparative advantage. Existing techniques of analysis of trade creation and trade diversion, which are of considerable value when analysing the trade flows of developed countries, are of limited use for developing countries where the dynamic effects are of central importance.

3. The Commodity Concentration of Exports

In addition to considering whether the Mediterranean countries have benefited from the trade preferences for their exports by looking at total export earnings, it is also of interest to see whether the agreements have enabled the countries to lower their dependence on a few primary products, because there is reason to believe that this dependence may lead both to a slow growth (given the low-income elasticity of demand for these products in world markets) and to instability (given variations in supply) in export earnings.

One approach to this is to consider the percentage of export earnings accounted for by the largest 2, 3 or 4 (and so on) commodities, but the problem with this measure can be seen illustrated in fig. 1.

A and *B* represent two countries at a given point in time or a single country at two points in time, and so on. In this case we cannot say whether *A* or *B* has the highest concentration of export earnings by the top '*n*' commodities method because it depends upon the number of commodities selected. It is therefore essential to consider the whole distribution. One summary measure is the Gini Hirschman coefficient, defined as

$$C_{jx} = 100\sqrt{\sum_i \left(\frac{X_{ij}}{X_j}\right)^2}$$

where C_{jx} = exports of country j
X_{ij} = value of country j's exports of country i
X_j = total value of country j's exports

The lower this coefficient, the larger will be the number of goods exported and the more evenly exports will be distributed among these goods (though the coefficient cannot distinguish between these effects). One criticism of this measure is that it is sensitive to the *number* of commodities in the total distribution, so that even if a few quite insignificant commodities are now exported in the second period of time considered, the coefficient

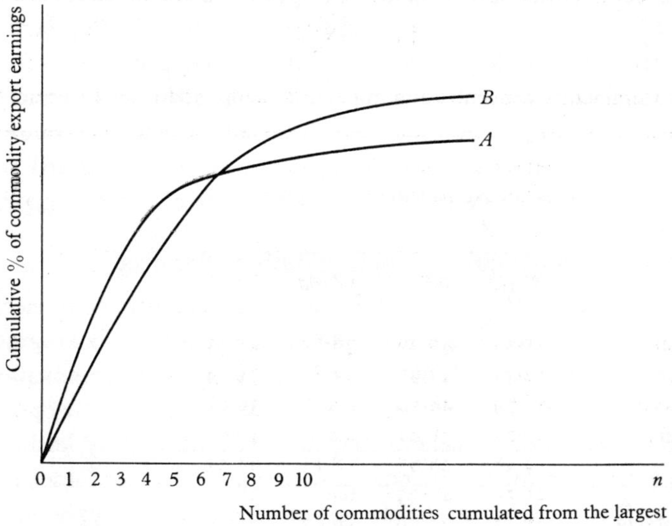

Fig. 1

will decline even though one could hardly argue that the change was significant. To some extent this sensitivity is reduced by squaring the shares. For convenience the results are expressed as percentages.

Statistics on the commodity composition for total exports (world) were not readily available for Morocco, Tunisia and Israel for 1971/2, as the latest *UN Yearbook of International Trade Statistics* was published in 1969. Figures for the other countries were calculated from OECD 'Commodity Trade Statistics' Series B and C. For Morocco and Tunisia, the coefficient was calculated from the imports of the six EEC countries, as shown in Series C. The definition of a 'commodity' is, of course, crucial, and the convention was adopted of taking the three-digit SITC level of aggregation.

It would appear that, with the exception of Spain, the agreements have not had any marked effect in lowering the commodity concentration of Mediterranean exports to the EEC. To some extent the overall assessment must be qualified by detailed examination of the commodity structure of exports. This is particularly true of Greece, where raw tobacco has declined from about 38 per cent of total exports to the EEC to just over 9 per cent. Similarly, raw material exports have declined from 30 per cent of exports to the EEC to 10 per cent. Conversely, manufactured goods exports have increased from a mere 3 per cent to 34 per cent (significantly greater than the increased proportion of manufactured exports to the rest of the world), 'miscellaneous manufactures' have increased from practically zero to more than 5 per cent. Other less dramatic exceptions to the general conclusion

TABLE 5 Commodity concentration of exports before and after agreements

	Average 2 yrs before Agreement 1971/2			
	World	*EEC*	*World*	*EEC*
Turkey	35·57	40·29	38·12	41·43
Greece	42·41	43·91	23·24	24·74
Morocco	36·79	38·28	n.a	36·69
Tunisia	30·25	38·61	n.a	40·62
Spain	19·38	28·65	18·15	21·33
Israel	41·38	40·75	n.a	38·00
Yugoslavia	21·14	25·49	19·92	23·55

are that, in the case of Morocco and Tunisia, manufactures and 'miscellaneous manufactures' exports to the EEC have increased from about 5 per cent to 10 per cent (Tunisia) and 13 per cent (Morocco). Tunisia has also shown a marked shift away from exporting the raw materials for fertilisers and towards manufactured fertilisers. In the case of Spain, the five years 1968–72 have shown substantial shifts in certain categories of exports, notably in the case of food, where exports to the EEC as a proportion of total exports to the market declined from 40 per cent to 28 per cent. Conversely, the proportion of manufactured exports increased from 19 to 23 per cent, machinery and transport equipment from 5 to 19 per cent (mostly cars, ships and boats) and miscellaneous manufactures from 7 to over 12 per cent (mostly footwear). This shift in the last two SITC categories of exports to the EEC was appreciably in excess of the change in these categories of exports to the rest of the world.

4. International Trade and the Growth of the Mediterranean Countries

To analyse the effect of the agreements on the structure of production, employment and incomes of the Mediterranean countries would be a fascinating but obviously complex task. The purpose of this short section is simply to provide some evidence of the possible effect of an increase in the capacity to import on the level of investment, assuming that five of the six countries studied (excluding Israel) are operating in a period of trade-constrained growth. By this is signified that there are a large number of investment goods that, for economic or technical reasons, cannot be domestically produced and that are required in some complementary relationship with capital goods produced in the importing country. A shortage of these capital goods imports will frustrate potential domestic investment and hence lower the growth rate of the economy. In other words, it is assumed that the economy is faced with structural factors which considerably limit its ability to transform domestic resources into exports or import substitutes. In Maizels' model,[3] the relationship is assumed to operate through two separate sub-relationships; imports of capital goods are assumed to depend on the capacity to import, while the level of investment in fixed capital is taken as dependent on the volume of capital goods imported. Ideally these relationships should be tested separately, but adequate data on capital goods imports as opposed to goods for consumption are not readily available for the

3 A. Maizels, *Exports and economic growth of developing countries* (Cambridge: Cambridge University Press, 1968).

TABLE 6 Results of regression of gross domestic fixed capital formation on the capacity to import and the level of reserves

Country	Z_{t-1}	R_{t-1}	I_{t-1}	R^2
Greece	1·27			0·88
1956–72	(0·23)			
	−2·7	1·13		0·98
	(1·31)	(1·61)		
	−2·5	1·05	0·14	0·98
	(1·53)	(1·38)	(0·35)	
Spain	1·02			0·98
1961–72	(0·06)			
	0·19	0·27		0·99
	(0·41)	(0·27)		
	0·25	0·19	0·19	0·99
	(0·45)	(0·31)	(0·63)	
Turkey	6·94			0·65
1962–70	(4·07)			
	1·3	0·29		0·98
	(1·55)	(0·05)		
	2·85	0·86	−2·3	0·99
	(1·4)	(0·3)	(1·2)	
Morocco	0·51			0·87
1960–72	(0·09)			
	0·25	0·12		0·92
	(0·16)	(0·06)		
	0·26	0·05	0·26	0·94
	(0·14)	(0·07)	(0·16)	
Tunisia	0·89			0·65
1960–71	(0·34)			
	0·65	0·23		0·84
	(0·27)	(0·08)		
	−0·82	0·08	1·16	0·93
	(0·53)	(0·08)	(0·04)	

TABLE 7 Marginal propensities and elasticities of investment with respect to the capacity to import

	M.P.I.	$\frac{Z_{t-1}}{I_t}$	*Elasticity of investment demand with respect to a unit change in* Z_{t-1}
Greece	1·27	0·625	0·794
Spain	1·02	0·647	0·660
Turkey	2·85 0·86	0·435	1·24 0·374
Morocco	0·51	2·460	1·255

countries considered. Investment in period '*t*' was therefore made to depend upon the capacity to import in the previous period – the 'capacity to import' being defined as the sum of export earnings (in national accounts sense), net factor payments abroad, and private and government transfers and capital. Investment was deflated by the most appropriate price index available, and the capacity to import by the import price index. The foreign exchange reserves position was included as a possible short-run factor that might influence investment behaviour. The results are summarised in Tables 6 and 7. The magnitude of the marginal propensity to invest (MPI) in this model depends to some extent on the relative size of gross fixed capital formation (I) in relation to the capacity to import (Z). Because this relationship varies considerably from one country to another (see column 2 of Table 7, which gives the average value of the relationship during the period covered), the elasticity is also given. It appears that both values are quite high for four of the five countries, indicating that the beneficial effects of trade preferences would probably have an appreciable effect on growth rates (depending of course on the incremental capital–output ratio), although to be more certain of this one would ideally wish to specify a more sophisticated model. In the case of Tunisia, it appears that I_{t-1} is a more significant explanatory variable of I_t.

However, the assumptions of such models have been strongly criticised recently, in particular the assumption that the structure of less developed economies is so inflexible as to be unable to reallocate domestic resources in such a way as to eliminate a 'trade gap'. The blame is placed, rather, on the unwillingness of governments to reduce domestic consumption, or their desire to foster industrialisation through over-valued exchange rates. It is also questioned whether an increased supply of foreign capital is directly additive to domestic savings and argued that it may well depress savings by pre-empting profitable investment opportunities or simply by reducing the need to save. This, however, is still a matter of considerable controversy (Griffin,[4] Papanek,[5]), because firstly it may be politically unacceptable to depress consumption; secondly, an argument can be made for operating over-valued exchange rates in the special circumstances of LDCs; and thirdly, foreign capital may increase savings as the trade gap model of course implies – that is, by increasing incomes.

4 K. Griffin, 'Foreign capital, domestic savings and economic development', *Bulletin of the Oxford Institute of Economics and Statistics* (May 1970).

5 G. F. Papanek, 'The effects of aid and other resource transfers on savings and growth in LDCs', *Economic Journal* (September 1972).

3

US Trade Interests and the EEC Mediterranean Policy

MORDECHAI E. KREININ

US Policy Towards the EEC

Throughout the past decade the United States has displayed continual interest in the special trading arrangements contracted by the European Economic Community (EEC) with African and Mediterranean countries. The American attitude towards these agreements has been adverse, and US representatives rarely missed an opportunity to express their displeasure with the nature and the extent of these arrangements. The intensity of US official feelings on the matter may be illustrated by the following episode. In 1970, between the third and fourth open wars in the Middle East, there developed intense artillery and air combat between Egypt and Israel, over and around the Suez Canal. Because these activities threatened to develop into a full-scale war, the United States exerted all the influence at its disposal to restore the cease-fire in the area. Towards that end, Assistant Secretary of State Joseph Sisco was dispatched to the area in an attempt to cool off the fighting. Yet, despite the real threat of a general conflagration, he found it necessary and desirable to spend the lion's share of his limited time in Israel talking about that country's preferential trade agreement with the EEC. Or so press reports indicated. Such is the intensity of the American interest in the problem under discussion.

Before turning to a detailed analysis of the US interest in EEC Mediterranean policy, the issue should be placed in a wide context of transatlantic policy. Disregarding relatively unimportant issues, there were three major economic bones of contention between the US and its trading partners that dominated the international economic landscape in the 1960s: the Common Agricultural Policy (CAP) of the EEC and its restrictive effect on the import of temperate-zone foods into the Community; the US balance of payments deficits and the attendant European surpluses; and the special trading arrangements contracted or contemplated by the EEC with African and Mediterranean countries, most in violation of the General Agreement on Tariffs and Trade (GATT) Most Favoured Nation principle and all discriminating against American exports.

Assuming that the present supply inadequacies of materials and food products is more than a temporary aberration, the conflict over the CAP may diminish in intensity during the coming years although the debate over the principles governing such a policy is likely to continue. Undoubtedly, the nature of the CAP would remain a point of controversy also within the EEC, between the producing and the consuming nations. However, in all likelihood it would generate less heat in the Tokyo Round of trade negotiations than it did during the Kennedy Round. Indeed, for several important commodities such as soybeans the point of contention may be shifting from how to dispose of accumulated surpluses to how to assure adequate distribution of available supplies. And special commodity agreements may be proposed as one method for doing so.

The US balance of payments deficit is in the process of being reversed following two devaluations of the dollar and the substitution of floating currencies or groups of currencies for the Bretton Woods system. This area of controversy is likely to shift to the question of reforming the monetary system and the disposition of the overhang of dollars held by non-US central monetary institutions. With the relative decline in importance of these two problems, the preferential trading arrangements of the EEC would loom increasingly important in future trade negotiations.

In analysing the US government position, it is important to keep in mind that, from its inception, the official American attitude towards the EEC has been governed largely by political rather than economic considerations. It was clear from the start that European integration would discriminate against the exports of outsiders, causing some trade diversion. Indeed, recent studies place the annual 1969/70 trade diversion effect of the original EEC at around $2 billions[1] for manufacturing and at $1·3 billions for agriculture – note, however, that trade creation in manufacturing is estimated at around $9 billions.[2] A large share of this diversionary impact was sustained by the United States. Yet the US attitude towards the creation of the Community was certainly positive and encouraging. The prime motivation appears to have been a desire to see a strong partner across the Atlantic, strong in political and even military terms. In other words, the US was willing to pay a certain economic price to build a strong ally in Europe. The fact that the EEC was intended to go far beyond a mere customs union, and eventually was expected to lead to a political union,

1 'Billion' is used in this chapter to mean 1,000 million.

2 See M. E. Kreinin, 'Effects of the EEC on imports of manufactures', *Economic Journal* (September 1972). Section A of the article offers a survey of previous estimates. Reprinted with some modification in: M. E. Kreinin, *Trade relations of the EEC – an empirical investigation* (Praeger, New York, 1974).

motivated the supportive US attitude. Within that policy the US did its best to induce the Community to pursue an 'outward-looking' policy; hence its exceedingly critical posture towards the CAP, and its pressure to lower the Common External Tariff (CET), and avoid or minimize special association agreements. Because the European Free Trade Association (EFTA) did not purport to go beyond the commercial arrangements of a free-trade area, its formation did not receive the same American support. The attitude of the United States towards EFTA integration can be described as lukewarm at best.

When it came to the enlargement of the Community from six to nine countries, American interests became somewhat more complex, although the American attitude towards that move became considerably less important in view of the economic and political stature that Europe had achieved by the 1970s – in other words, the US had lost much of its leverage with the Europeans. First, it may be anticipated that the enlargement of the Community, with the attendant creation of a free-trade area with the non-acceding members of EFTA, would have a strong diversionary effect on outside countries whose exports to Europe would be 'retarded' as a result – that is, they would be less than they would have been in the absence of enlargement. This would be further intensified by the special association agreements or preferential treaties with the associable members of the Commonwealth in Africa and the Caribbean. Trade creation in the manufacturing sector caused by EEC enlargement has been estimated at \$5·3 billions, while trade diversion would be \$3·9 billions.[3] Thus, although the world taken as one unit, including both member and non-member states, would experience an improvement in allocative efficiency as a result of enlargement, non-member countries would lose export markets. Table 1 gives details of the estimates, with the summary columns being 11–13. The substantial interpenetration in the EEC–EFTA markets can be seen in columns 11 and 12, while column 13 shows that the US would be a major loser in terms of industrial exports, with losses estimated at \$2 billions[4] or about one-fifth of the base period exports to the enlarged Community (other developed countries and the Commonwealth countries in Asia would be the other main losers). In addition, non-member countries are estimated

3 M. E. Kreinin, 'The static effects of EEC enlargement on trade flows', *Southern Economic Journal* (April 1973). Reprinted in *Trade Relations of the EEC, op. cit.*

4 This figure does not imply an actual reduction in exports. It means that US exports have been \$2 billions higher without enlargement than they would be with enlargement of the EEC.

TABLE 1 Estimated effects of EEC enlargements on trade flows in manufactures and semi-manufactures combined

	1970 imports ($ Billions)				
Exporting country	*Enlarged EEC (10 countries)* (1)	*UK* (2)	*Continental EFTA* (3)	*EEC* (4)	*Denmark Norway Ireland* (5)
World	88·29	11·34	20·73 (16.18)[a]	55·13 (21·62)[a]	7·42
Developed countries	80·21	9·39	19·45 (14·90)[a]	50·28 (16·77)[a]	7·05
USA	9·42	2·09	1·44	5·82	0·47
EEC	46·89 (15·40)[a]	3·35	9·81	33·51	2·40
UK	6·74	—	2·78	3·27	1·67
Continental EFTA	12·30 (9·03)[a]	2·15	4·55	5·25	2·17
Developed Commonwealth	2·01	1·15	0·13	0·72	0·04
Other developed	3·12	0·65	0·74	1·71	0·30
Developing countries	5·44	1·33	0·68	3·43	0·20
Commonwealth in Africa and Carib. Br. dep. ter.	0·95	0·39	0·16	0·41	0·05
Other developing Commonwealth	1·16	0·47	0·17	0·52	0·05
Yaoundé + Morocco and Tunisia (EEC dep. ter.)	0·88	0·05	0·03	0·80	0·02
Other developing countries	2·44	0·42	0·32	1·70	0·08
Socialist states	2·64	0·62	0·60	1·42	0·17
Change in area imports as a per cent of the total imports					
Change in trade balances of three areas $\Delta(X\text{-}M)$					

[a]Excluding intra-trade.
[b]This figure includes a gain to Ireland.
Minor inconsistencies are due to rounding.

…ated changes in UK imports ($ Millions)					*($ Millions)*			
…ge in …K to the … plus …al of …ariff …-vis …EC	*Discrimination against non-members (7)*	*Removal of discrimination in favour of Commonwealth (8)*	*Removal of discrimination against EEC (and its associates) and in favour of EFTA (9)*	*Total effect in the UK market (cols. 6–9) (10)*	*Estimated change in imports of Continental EFTA and Ireland (11)*	*Estimated change in EEC imports (12)*	*Total change (cols. 10–12) (13)*	*Change as per cent of total exports to the enlarged EEC (14)*
58	0	0	0	+1,058	+1,661	+2,187	+4,906	+5·6
92	+208	+62	+25	+1,387	+1,796	+2,857	+6,040	+7·5
01	−457	+57	–	−299	−246	−1,506	−2,051	−21·8
12	+885	+90	+571	+2,559	+2,359	–	+4,918	+31·9[a]
	–	–	–	–	−201	+2,042	+1,841	+27·3
	–	+66	+546	−480	+24	+2,872	+2,416[b]	+26·7[a]
51	−91	−169	–	−311	−17	−123	−451	−22·4
30	−130	+18	–	−82	−123	−428	−633	−20·3
59	−135	−81	−25	−300	−51	−362	−713	−13·1
	–	+13	−35	−22	+16	+75	+69	+7·2
	−91	−109	–	−280	−29	−125	−434	−37·4
80	+12	+2	+10	+28	+2	–	+30	+3·4
	−56	+13	–	−26	−40	−312	−387	−15·5
4	−73	+19	–	−29	−84	−308	−421	−15·9
7				9·3	9·6[a]	10·1[a]		
25				+783	+755	+2·731		

Source: Mordechai E. Kreinin, 'The static effects of EEC enlargement on trade flows', *Southern Economic Journal* XXXIX, no. 4 (April 1973), 567; reprinted in M. E. Kreinin, *Trade relations of the EEC – an empirical investigation* (New York: Praeger, 1974).

to lose about $1·4 billions in farm exports to the Community. Because these would be mainly temperate-zone foods, US supplies would weigh heavily also in this area. However, the agricultural estimates may be moderated or even nullified by a sustained long-run change in the world's food situation.

In addition to the commercial losses, American policy makers may have another reason to be lukewarm towards EEC enlargement. If the motivating force behind the originally favourable US attitude was the political viability and strength of the continent, then enlargement is likely to dilute the political content of the integration movement. Not only does it add three additional countries, making it more difficult to reach a consensus on important matters,[5] but it adds considerable diversity to the countries making up the Community.

On the positive side, the accession of the three new members, and particularly of the UK, may have the effect of exerting pressure inside the Community towards more liberal or 'outward-looking' economic policies, which would minimise commercial losses to outsiders. This may be particularly true in agriculture, because Britain is a net importer of food products, and because the accession treaty has forced a change in the domestic UK support programme that resulted in a substantial rise in food prices. Also the traditional 'special ties' between Britain and the United States may help shift the Community's policy in various spheres in a direction more desirable or acceptable to the US, thus cementing to some extent the Atlantic partnership.[6]

This short balance sheet of US gains and losses from EEC enlargement should not obscure the fact that even if they were counter to its interests, the US as an outside power cannot object to the major provisions of the accession treaty. Neither the enlargement itself nor the free-trade area with the non-acceding members of EFTA violate any international treaties, as customs unions and free-trade areas have long been recognised as exceptions to GATT's Most Favoured Nation rule. And in any case, with the emergence of Europe as a major economic power, there is little leverage that the US could exercise contrary to what the Europeans consider their major interests. For that reason American policy seems to be directed at making the Community's overall policy more liberal towards outsiders, and towards disputing the special association and preferential agreements

5 The political cohesiveness of the EEC has recently come into serious question in connection with the need to share the increasingly scarce oil supplies.

6 The recent transatlantic dispute over Middle East policies signifies a rupture in these relations that would require cementing in the coming years.

whose conformity with GATT's Most Favoured Nation rule can be questioned. This is the context in which the US views its stand towards the EEC Mediterranean policy, and that is why this policy may become a major bone of contention in the Tokyo Round of trade negotiations. It might be added that these negotiations would have a major role to play in stemming the tide of protectionist sentiments on both sides of the Atlantic. If progress is not made in the liberalisation of trade, the Atlantic Community could easily slide backwards towards protectionism.

EEC Mediterranean Policy

Enlargement of the EEC has been accompanied by far-flung Association and preferential trade agreements, of which the Mediterranean policy is but one component. Although US policy is directed towards the entire spectrum of these agreements, this section deals only with the Mediterranean policy. One general point needs to be made, however. The United States has voiced special objections to the reverse preferences feature of the association treaties, for it discriminates against American exports and in favour of EEC exports. In fact, the Trade Reform Act of 1973 would deny US GSP treatment to countries discriminating against the United States.

In recent pronouncements, the EEC seems to have weakened its insistence on reverse preferences with respect to the African countries, as in the Lomé convention of 1975. The only countries that would continue to grant reverse preferences, incurring the wrath of the United States, would be the Mediterranean countries, in particular Spain and Israel. For that reason the EEC Mediterranean policy is likely to hold special significance for the United States. There follows a short description of that policy.

The agreement with Spain envisages two stages, the first of which is to last at least six years beginning in 1970, covering reciprocal reduction in duties in successive stages. The agreement with Israel also took effect in 1970 and provides for reduction of up to 50 per cent of the CET on imports from that country of products covered by the agreement. Israel's return concessions include varying duty reductions on specified products imported from the Community. Under the five-year agreement with Egypt and Lebanon (1972) the Community will reduce the CET on most industrial goods by 55 per cent. Preferential duty reductions are also granted for nearly half of exports of agricultural products from these two countries into the Community. In return, Egypt and Lebanon will grant tariff reductions, reaching 50 and 70 per cent respectively, on certain products imported from the Community. Certain import quotas will also be partly liberalised. All these trade agreements will be subject to renegotiations and revisions in the light of changing conditions and the evolving economic interest of the participants.

The two-way discriminatory feature of the preferential agreements are held by the United States to be in violation of the Most Favoured Nation clause of GATT. American exporters would be discriminated in the Mediterranean markets against EEC exporters, and in the EEC market against exports from Mediterranean countries. However, it is the first effect (namely, the reverse preferences) that is most objectionable to the United States – and that for several reasons. First, whereas the direct preferences can be justified as a policy that supports economic development, and GATT's waivers have generally been granted for preferences in favour of developing countries (although the special preferences are also discriminatory between the developing countries themselves, for they favour tropical Africa against other exporters of tropical foods such as Latin America), no such claim can be made with respect to reverse preferences. In fact, reverse preferences are harmful to the developing countries that are suffering discrimination as suppliers to the markets of the Associated and Mediterranean states, and may be harmful to the developing countries that grant them. Secondly, in most manufacturing industries the EEC is a major competitor of the United States in third markets, although the range of competition between the US and the Mediterranean countries in the EEC market is rather limited. Even where it exists, it is doubtful whether the moderate protection applied by the Community would place American suppliers at a competitive disadvantage vis-à-vis suppliers from developing countries. Thirdly, the level of protection in the developing countries is rather high and therefore the degree of discrimination by granting the EEC special reverse preferences outside GATT is so much the greater.

Effect of Reverse Preferences on the Developing Countries

Reverse preferences discriminate in favour of the EEC not only against developed country suppliers, but also against suppliers from the developing countries. It is true that the Association Agreement with the Yaoundé countries permits the Associated African States (AAS) to grant low tariff or even free entry to whomever they wish, thereby eliminating discrimination in favour of the EEC. But in practice this is not likely to happen. Even within Africa, each of the existing customs unions covers no more than four to five countries. As a result, the preferential trade agreements discriminate against developing countries supplying the associated states.

To be sure, the volume of trade involved in this discrimination is relatively small, for the traditional trade partners of the developing countries are the developed ones. Table 2 shows that only one-fifth of the developing countries' exports are destined to go to other developing countries, and less than one-tenth goes to Africa and West Asia – the regions containing the countries that grant preferences to the EEC. These figures suggest that the quantitative impact of the discrimination against the developing countries is small. Yet this may change in the future. The annual growth rate of intra-developing countries' trade in manufacturing (SITC 5-8) has been very high in the later 1960s (part b of Table 2), even considering the low base figure. For various reasons, not the least of which is the restrictionist policy of the developed countries towards imports from less developed countries (LDCs), many observers believe that in the foreseeable future the LDCs' exports in manufacturing have limited prospects for expansion. And it is precisely in manufacturing trade that the reverse preferences would hurt the most. Instead of granting each other preferences[7] (beyond the current integration schemes among LDCs), LDCs find themselves discriminated against, in each other's markets. In a dynamic sense, therefore, reverse preferences may become an important impediment to the expansion of LDCs manufacturing exports. After the Lomé convention, this applies only to the Mediterranean countries.

Equally important is the effect of reverse preferences on the countries that grant them. In this case there is *a priori* reason to believe that the Yaoundé case differs considerably from the Mediterranean case. And, because past observations are restricted to Yaoundé, that experience will be surveyed first[8] and from it inferences drawn concerning the Mediterranean case.

Thirteen of the AAS grant preferences to the EEC. To analyse their effect distinction is made between two cases. In the first place it is assumed that there is one major firm (mainly French) that supplies each of the African countries and that has a monopoly power in that market, backed up by some degree of monopoly in France. This was a common situation before the mid-1960s, when France and Belgium alone received reverse preferences in the markets of their respective colonies or former colonies. Moreover, a strong residue of such ties remains even now, for the AAS are

7 See M. E. Kreinin, 'The Generalized System of Preferences – A Proposed Variant', *Journal of World Trade Law* (Summer 1973).

8 The discussion is based on: M. Kreinin, 'Some Economic Consequences of Reverse Preferences', *Journal of Common Market Studies*, March 1973, reprinted in *EEC Trade Relations*, *op. cit.*

TABLE 2a. Exports of developing countries to the market of developing Africa and West Asia, 1970 ($ millions, f.o.b.)

Exporting region	*Exports to:* *World*	*Developing countries*	*Developing Africa*	*West Asia*	*Africa and West Asia as a % of total exports*	*Annual percentage rate of growth in exports to:* *Africa* *1960–7*	*1967–9*	*West Asia* *1960–7*	*1967–9*
Developing countries	55,000	11,210	1,640	1,150	5·1	4·7	11·7	6·5	9·9
Developing Africa	12,690	1,290	730	140	6·9	6·4	9·5	4·4	1·8
Latin America	15,040	2,970	87	58	1·0	0·5	−8·3	9·4	18·5
West Asia	9,980	1,900	395	620	10·2	.			
South and East Asia	14,190	4,060	400	325	5·1	4·3	15·8	6·8	10·4

b. Exports of all developing countries by commodity groups, 1969 ($ millions, f.o.b.)

	Exports to:				Africa and West Asia as a % of total exports	Annual percentage rate of growth in exports to:			
						Africa		West Asia	
Commodity group (SITC)	*World*	*Developing countries*	*Developing Africa*	*West Asia*		*1960–7*	*1967–9*	*1960–7*	*1967–9*
Food, beverages and tobacco (0,1)	11,820	2,180	390	385	6·6	2·4	4·8	6·4	6·4
Materials (2,4)	9,700	1,450	155	105	2·9	3·2	21·5	6·6	–
'Other' manufactures (6,8)	9,890	2,040	400	305	7·1	6·7	12·7	10·3	25·1
Machinery and transport equipment (7)	1,080	510	61	50	10·3	19·6	32·0	10·4	38·7
Chemicals (5)	830	415	54	30	10·1	12·1	16·2	15·9	46·4
Fuels (3)	16,260	3,610	455	345	4·9	4·7	11·7	4·7	2·3

Source: UNCTAD, *Handbook of International Trade and Development Statistics, 1972.*

linked to France by language and cultural ties, business, banking and currency links and a general tradition of close relations. When a monopolist such as the one described here is given reverse preference, its profit maximising behaviour would be to raise the price of each product that it supplies to the level of the *world market price plus the tariff* (or the tariff rate implicit in a quota restriction) imposed by the African state. The monopolist cannot go above that level, for then it would face competition from outside suppliers. The higher the African tariff (and therefore the higher the degree of discrimination in the monopolist's favour), the higher the price it would charge. The reverse preferences would then have a unique effect: unlike a tariff, which is a transfer from the consumer to his own government, and unlike a quota, which is a transfer from the consumer to the importer in the same country, reverse preferences give rise to an international transfer – from the African consumer to the European exporter. Being a transfer from the relatively poor to the relatively rich, it is also inequitable.

Suppose, on the other hand, that the EEC suppliers to Africa have no monopoly power, and compete vigorously among themselves to supply the African markets. In that case, they would charge the prices prevailing in the EEC (plus transport cost). There would be no 'monopoly exploitation' of the Yaoundé countries. Still, the price charged can be higher than alternative sources (such as the US or Japan) would charge, because the latter must pay the African duty. The loss to Africa would then be in its commodity terms of trade, and would be confined to those products in which the EEC is not competitive worldwide.

In the case of AAS, both conventional institutional wisdom and empirical findings suggest that a considerable monopoly power exists among the supplying EEC firms. Empirical analysis for 1969 shows that: French f.o.b. prices charged to the countries granting reverse preferences are considerably higher than French prices charged to other African countries; and French f.o.b. prices charged to the Yaoundé countries exceed by a large margin the prices charged by other suppliers, especially those outside the EEC. These comparisons, done on a product-by-product basis and then aggregated over total trade, strongly suggest the existence of monopoly power among the firms supplying the Yaoundé countries, with the attendant transfer of resources from the African consumer to the European supplier.

To what extent does the Yaoundé experience apply to Mediterranean countries? Two main differences should be noted between the two groups of states: the existence of trade creation as well as diversion, and the lesser likelihood of monopoly exploitation in the Mediterranean case. They will be examined in turn.

In contrast to sub-Saharan Africa, certain Mediterranean countries have come a long way towards industrialisation, largely by the route of import substitution. This is certainly true of Israel and Spain. Consequently, whereas reverse preferences granted by the Yaoundé countries essentially divert their industrial imports from non-European to European sources, reverse preferences granted by semi-industrialised countries would have two influences: the *trade creation* effect, which occurs when imports from the EEC displace inefficient production within the country itself; and the *trade diversion* effect, which occurs when preferences cause diversion of imports to preferred (EEC) from non-preferred sources. When hardly any domestic industrial production exists before the introduction of preferences, there can be only trade diversion, for there is no local production to be displaced.[9] This was the case in most of the associate or associable African countries. But in some of the Mediterranean countries both effects can exist.

The relative strength of these two effects in each Mediterranean country can be determined only several years after the full implementation of the preferences, once their production and consumption structures have become fully adjusted to the preferences. For each industry, a comparison would need to be made between the pre- and post-preferences situations, for two crucial ratios: the change in the ratio of total imports (that is, imports from all sources) to consumption would be a measure of trade creation, while the change in the ratio of imports from non-preferred sources to consumption would measure trade diversion. Care would have to be taken to remove influences on the two ratios other than that of preferences.[10] The only thing that can be said *a priori* is that, because preferences to the EEC are granted selectively on a product-by-product basis, the internal political process in the Mediterranean countries will generate

9 Trade diversion caused by reverse preferences should be distinguished, in its economic effects, from trade diversion of a customs union among a few developing countries. In the first case the effect on the developing countries is clearly negative, for they lose in their terms of trade. In the second case it may be positive if the domestic resources drawn into the trade-diverting activities were formerly unemployed or under-employed, so that their opportunity cost is zero. There is another sense in which trade diversion of a customs union among LDCs may on occasion be welcome as the 'least of two evils'; namely, if the alternative to high-degree import substitution (under very heavy effective protection) by the customs union is the same policy pursued by individual members of the customs union, with much smaller domestic markets.

10 See M. E. Kreinin, *Economic Journal* (September 1972), *op. cit.*

pressure to minimise trade creation (displacement of domestic output) and maximise trade diversion. On the other hand, where industrialisation has reached a reasonably advanced stage, any meaningful preferences (on which the EEC is likely to insist) would involve at least some trade creation. This is attested to, for example, by the insistence of some Mediterranean countries on a long transitional period to allow the domestic industry time to adjust.

The implication of this difference is that for some Mediterranean countries, where trade creation exists, the reverse preferences carry some hidden benefits. For they force the country gradually to lower its tariffs on manufactured goods to a point of partial if not complete elimination. In other words, they force the country to do what is good for it, but what it finds politically impossible to do for itself – namely, to expose its industry to the fresh winds of competition from a highly industrialised part of the world. For a country industrialising under a maze of import restrictions in all forms – high tariffs, import quotas, exchange control and so on – wreaking havoc with production and allocative efficiency, such European competition may be highly useful in rationalising production. (Of course, non-preferential duty reduction would have been even better.)

Additionally, the semi-industrialised Mediterranean countries can take greater advantage than the Yaoundé countries of the direct preferences offered by the EEC as a part of the trade agreements, especially in the manufacturing sector. The example of Portugal, which derived considerable benefits from its EFTA membership, is brought to mind.

The next difference between the Yaoundé and Mediterranean cases concerns the existence of monopoly power among the supplying European firms. The only Mediterranean countries that may be subject to conditions similar to Yaoundé are Morocco and Tunisia, with their traditional ties to France. Certainly, countries like Spain and Israel are wide open to competitive supplies from all members of the Community. The competitive rather than the monopoly model is more applicable for them. Because the nine-country Community represents a major portion of worldwide industrial production and exports, and because in most products the Community is reasonably competitive with American and Japanese products (especially when transport cost differentials are allowed for), the terms of trade losses are not likely to be severe. Thus *a priori* reasoning suggests that, although the Mediterranean countries would incur some losses from granting reverse preferences to the EEC, such losses would not be large in most cases – certainly not as large as those sustained by the Yaoundé countries. On the other hand, the preferences would have the effect, desirable or not, of redirecting these countries' trade towards the EEC and away from other trading partners.

In sum, the effect of reverse preferences on the Mediterranean countries would vary from one country to another. It would be most adverse on the least developed among them and on those with strong traditional links to French suppliers. And it would be least adverse, and may even be beneficial on balance, to the semi-industrialised states among them.

US Commercial Interest in EEC Mediterranean Policy

It may be expected that the trade diversion caused by EEC Mediterranean policy will affect US exports adversely. Some American exports to the EEC will be displaced by Mediterranean supplies, while some American exports to the Mediterranean countries will be displaced by shipments from the EEC. The question is how large this displacement is likely to be.

Table 3 presents American and EEC exports to the Mediterranean

TABLE 3 US and EEC exports to Mediterranean countries ($ millions)

	US exports			*EEC (9 countries) exports*		
	1969		*1969*	*1972*		*1972*
Country	*Mfr. exports*	*All exports*	*All exports*	*Mfr. exports*	*All exports*	*All exports*
Greece	132	255	250	692	809	1,458
Turkey	108	299	300	383	435	833
Algeria	36	64	98	596	695	1,063
Morocco	29	53	58	284	338	415
Tunisia	14	52	54	131	150	308
Malta	n.a.	4	5	n.a.	98	112
Cyprus	3	5	13	92	123	190
Spain	343	601	972	1,525	1,762	2,842
Israel	205	457	558	565	631	987
Egypt	n.a.	67	76	n.a.	281	312
Lebanon	71	89	130	201	253	452
Total		1,946	2,514		5,575	8,972

Source: International Monetary Fund, *Direction of Trade, Annual, 1968–72.*

countries in 1969 and 1972. It shows the EEC as the dominant supplier, with exports to the area nearly triple those of the United States. Exports from the US in 1972 added up to \$2·5 billions, and to \$1·75 billions if Greece and Turkey are excluded (for comparision, total US merchandise exports in 1972 amounted to \$49 billions). Spain and Israel account for the lion's share (87 per cent) of the latter figure. Thus, if Greece and Turkey are treated as potential members of the EEC, and therefore not presenting an issue in the transatlantic dispute, then the two main American markets affected by the EEC Mediterranean policy are Spain and Israel. About half of US exports in 1969 were in the manufacturing category (SITC 5–8). The preferences granted to the EEC include varying degrees of tariff reduction, as well as some liberalisation of certain import quotas. In an attempt to get an idea of the tariff rates facing the non-preferred suppliers, some rough calculations are presented in Table 4 of representative unweighted averages of the *ad valorem* tariff rates for each of three broad commodity categories. The structure of protection reflects an escalation of tariff rates by degree of processing, familiar from the industrial countries, and a phenomenon that may be expected in countries attempting to industrialise by import substitution. This implies that effective protection (that is, protec-

TABLE 4 Unweighted average tariff rates (%)

Country	*Raw materials*	*Semi-manufactures*	*Finished manufactures*
Greece	15·8	24·7	32·9
Turkey	21·8	31·9	52·3
Algeria	n.a.	n.a.	n.a.
Morocco	31·7	37·9	76·7
Tunisia	9·3	23·7	39·0
Malta	3·5	5·2	30·3
Cyprus	5·2	7·9	22·4
Spain	13·2	23·2	30·6
Israel	6·0	15·2	29·1
Egypt	n.a.	n.a.	n.a.
Lebanon	5·4	9·3	15·6

Source: Computed from *The International Customs Journal*, published by the International Customs Tariffs Bureau.

The three-way classification of commodities is similar to the one used in the GATT Tariff Study.

tion accorded the domestic value added) on finished manufactures far exceeds its nominal counterpart.

Considering the relatively small size of their markets, it can be assumed that the Mediterranean countries face infinitely elastic export supply curves from both the EEC and the US. This means that the tariff discrimination in favour of the EEC would be fully reflected in the supply price differentials. The value of US exports (of differentiated products) displaced by the EEC would then depend on the elasticity of substitution, and on the degree of tariff discrimination. In the case of homogeneous products, US exports would be totally displaced, or their price would have to be lowered by the full margin of the discrimination.

Recent econometric studies yield estimates of the long-run (8–10 years' adjustment) elasticity of substitution between suppliers from any two industrial countries to a third market in the range of $3\frac{1}{2}$–4 for finished manufactures,[11] (and of lesser values for semi-manufactures). Intermediate-run (3–4 years) estimates are probably around 2. However, in order to determine the degree of discrimination, a product-by-product study must be pursued, first, because not all US exports are even potentially vulnerable to EEC competition – especially outside the finished manufacturing categories there are products which the EEC does not export – and secondly, because some US exports are financed by American grants rather than shipped commercially. Thirdly, the preferential treatment does not cover all commodities.

Two approaches were adopted to cope with this problem. As a first approximation, it is assumed that preferences were granted on all finished manufactures (but not on non-manufactures). In these products the US and the EEC are in direct competition; but because no exceptions were made, this procedure would yield an upper limit estimate of the displacement. Because Israel's preferences for the EEC range from 10 to 25 per cent and Spain's preferences from 25 to 60 per cent, a margin of preferences of one-third was assumed. With tariff rates averaging 30 per cent for finished manufactures, this assumption translates into a 10 per-cent price differential. And with a substitution elasticity of 4, a US export displacement of 40 per cent would be expected, after 8–10 years' adjustment period.

11 See H. Junz and R. Rhomberg, 'Price competitiveness in export trade among industrial countries', *American Economic Review* (papers and proceedings) (May 1973); D. Richardson, 'On improving the estimate of the elasticity of substitution', *Canadian Journal of Economics* (August 1972); M. E. Kreinin, 'Price elasticities in international trade', *Review of Economies and Statistics* (November 1967); and M. E. Kreinin, 'A further note on the export elasticity of substitution', *Canadian Journal of Economics* (November 1973).

Applied to the \$687 millions US manufacturing exports in 1969, this yields a displacement of \$275 millions. Allowing for only 3–4 years' adjustment, the substitution elasticity is around 2 and the estimated displacement of American exports \$137 millions.

A more precise method of measuring the displacement effect is a product-by-product approach. This involves identifying the commercially shipped products that are supplied by both the US and the EEC, and then excluding the duty-free items (on which there can be no preferential treatment) as well as items on which no preferences were granted. For each remaining product, it is necessary to multiply the preferential margin by a reasonable substitution elasticity to arrive at the final result.

Such a procedure was undertaken by a recent study on behalf of the US Department of State.[12] Most of the products on which displacement of US exports is indicated are in the manufacturing categories (SITC 5–8), and therefore the elasticity parameter of −4 would seem most appropriate for long-run estimates. The diversion of US exports is estimated at about one-tenth of total American exports to the countries concerned. In other words, American exports to the Mediterranean countries would be 10 per cent less than what they would have been without the preferential agreements. Part of this shortfall could be offset by possible acceleration in the growth rate of the Mediterranean countries caused by their greater exposure to EEC competition. Applying the above ratio to the 1969 US exports to the Mediterranean countries (excluding Greece and Turkey), an estimated export loss of \$140 millions is obtained. This loss could increase if subsequent renewal of the agreements would involve expansion of product coverage and/or increase in preferential margins. But it is not likely to exceed the previous estimate of \$275 millions which assumes preferences on all manufactures, unless the preferential margins are increased substantially.

Next is considered the possible displacement of American exports to the EEC. Here the range of 'vulnerable' commodities is narrow, because there are very few 'overlapping' exports between the US and the Mediterranean basin. Even in the 'vulnerable' cases, it cannot be assumed that Mediterranean supply is infinitely elastic. Thus only part of the preferential margin would be reflected in the price differential. Furthermore, for some products the supply potential in the Mediterranean basin may be limited, whatever the price. Allowing for these factors, and using the aforementioned State Department estimates as a benchmark, the US export loss is likely to

12 'The preferential agreements between the EEC and Tunisia, Morocco, Spain and Israel: implications for US commodity exports', mimeographed (July 1971).

approximate 1·0–0·25 per cent of the base period American exports to the EEC, or $125 millions.

The total estimated US export loss because of the preferential agreements is rather small. At $265 millions, it is around 0·7 per cent of 1969 US exports. Of course certain industries, such as preserved fruits and fruit juices, may be severely affected. But the overall effect, in a regime of fluctuating exchange rates, would merely translate into a small depreciation of the dollar (namely, a small loss in the US commodity terms of trade) and its effect on US real income would be negligible. Thus the American attitude towards the Mediterranean policy of the EEC must be based on matters of general principles (of the type discussed in the first section of this chapter), rather than on its direct commercial interest. The latter are only marginally involved. However, concentrated political pressure from specific industries – such as citrus – may be a factor in determining U.S. policy.

4

The Effects of EEC Preferences to Associated States on Trade Flows

DIETRICH KEBSCHULL

I. Effects of Association and Trade Preference Policies

The Problem Defined

The association and trade preference policies of the European Economic Community (EEC) have often been criticised both by the developing countries which are not favoured as well as by industrial states outside the EEC. After the association of the African states there were above all the EEC's Mediterranean policy, the expansion of the preference-granting area to Denmark, Great Britain and Ireland, as well as the inclusion of Commonwealth states in the preferential zone, which have strengthened the suspicion of the creation of a new bloc in world trade through an 'enclosure strategy'. The future of these association and trade preference agreements will presumably be an important topic of the negotiations currently taking place within the General Agreement on Tariffs and Trade (GATT) round.

The EEC does not pretend that its policies do not involve discrimination against third developing countries, but stresses the benefits of the association agreements and preferential trade agreements to development policy. Although in principle there is agreement that the EEC policy of trade preferences can theoretically lead to a discrimination against third countries, the views about the real effects are heavily diverging, due to the lack of adequate empirical research. Only empirical work can answer unequivocally questions like the following:

how far can a trade creation for the favoured countries or a trade diversion against the developing countries which are not favoured be demonstrated?

can any discrimination be found against industrial countries which are not EEC members, resulting primarily from the grant of reverse preferences? Which are the implications of the effects of the present association and trade preference policies for the EEC's position with regard to the GATT round?

Organisation of This Chapter

In order to discuss these issues systematically, the rest of this chapter is divided into four sections. In section 2, the substance and objectives of the association and preferential agreements concluded by the EEC are shortly summarised.

The rest of the paper tries to establish the extent of trade creation, trade expansion and trade diversion. In this connection, the crucial point is the proportionate variation of the trade flows over time, rather than their absolute value as would have been involved in a comparison of growth rates. On its own, however, a change in the market share at the expense of third countries not covered by preferential treatment need not necessarily mean that a trade diversion has taken place. This may also be traceable to an above-average increase of the demand for productions of the favoured country, following price reductions initiated by tariff reductions. Only if an absolute or relative decline of the demand for imports of the country granting preferences from the non-favoured third countries can be ascertained, may trade diversion be inferred. On the other hand, trade expansion exists if – the development of the demand for imports from non-favoured third countries remaining roughly constant – the demand for imports from the favoured country has grown faster than the average rate of increase of all imports. Finally, trade creation (in the range of finished and semi-finished goods) can be deduced, if part of the demand of the EEC member states – demand which so far has been met by the domestic production – is, after a shift of production, met by imports from the associated areas, given again the demand for imports from non-favoured third countries.

The basic parts of the study are sections 3 and 4, which contain the actual analysis of the effects of the association agreements. First, the chapter examines the consequences of the preferences granted by the EEC to the Yaoundé countries, to Greece and Turkey on its total imports from these countries in comparison to imports from non-favoured third countries. This global analysis is followed by the investigation of single representative products.

The final section discusses the question whether the findings of the analysis are transferable to the association and trade preference agreements of the recent period whose consequences cannot yet be estimated correctly, due to the lack of adequate statistical data. Furthermore, an evaluation of the agreements is undertaken with regard to the objectives of the EEC and the criticisms raised by third countries.

2. Nature and Objectives of the Agreements

The Agreements

Political but also special economic relations had been existing between Belgium, Italy, the Netherlands and, above all, France[1] on the one hand and their overseas colonies on the other long before the Rome Treaty was enacted. Generally, there were neither customs duties nor quantitative restrictions in the trade of the above countries with their colonies. The removal of these advantages would have had far-reaching consequences for the exports and thus the economic development of the – for the most part African – colonies. In order to make allowance for these relationships, the EEC Treaty (Articles 131 seq. and 238) provided for the possibility of an association.[2]

The Convention (Yaoundé I) was signed on 20 July 1963 by representatives of member states' governments, and entered into force after its ratification by the parliaments on 1 June 1964. As agreed upon, the first Yaoundé Convention ended on 31 May 1969. After that, on 29 July 1969 an additional Convention (Yaoundé II) was signed in Yaoundé again, which became effective after its ratification on 1 January 1971[3] and was to run until 31 January 1975.

Almost parallel with the negotiations for the first Yaoundé Convention there were talks taking place for an association of Greece and Turkey. In conformity with Article 237, both states aspired to a complete membership in the long run.

Apart from the mentioned agreements, the following five conventions of association[4] were signed and put into force:

1 Of the French colonies in Africa, only Tunisia had already gained its independence (date of independence: 20 March 1956).

2 See, among others, P. Agarwal, *Die Assoziierung der überseeischen Staaten und Gebiete der Europäischen Wirtschaftsgemeinschaft und die Auswirkung dieser Assoziierung auf die Ausfuhr der nicht assoziierten Entwicklungsländer in diese Gemeinschaft* (The association of the overseas states and regions with the European Economic Community and the effect of the Association on the non-associated developing countries' exports to the Community) (Tübingen, 1966), pp. 11 ff.; and H. Hasenpflug, J. Jägeler, *Grundfragen der Welthandelspolitik vor einer neuen GATT-Runde* (Fundamental questions of world trade policy before a new GATT round), (forthcoming).

3 Between Yaoundé I and the entering into force of Yaoundé II the relations were regularised by a transitional convention.

4 A further convention of association was signed with Nigeria on 16 July 1966. This convention, however, has, due to the Biafra war, not been ratified.

on 1 September 1969 with Tunisia,
on 1 September 1969 with Morocco,
on 1 January 1971 with Kenya, Tanzania and Uganda (Arusha Convention),
on 1 April 1971 with Malta, and
on 1 January 1973 with Cyprus.

With Algeria, to which the advantages of an associated state have been granted by tacit agreement without a formal legal basis, negotiations have been carried on since 10 July 1972, aiming at the conclusion of a formal convention. Furthermore, preferential agreements with Spain (1970) and the UAR-Egypt (1973) came into effect. At present, similar agreements are being discussed with the Lebanon and Jordan.

Contents of the Agreements

The basic parts of the association agreements are the provisions concerning trade and financial aid. The member states of the EEC committed themselves in all conventions to removing the customs duties and quantitative restrictions – totally or partly, immediately or gradually – for goods originating in the associated states. The difference between the Yaoundé and the single conventions lies primarily in the extent of the preferential arrangements.

The associated states for their part have undertaken to grant preferences to the EEC. Because the economies of the associated states are still in initial stages of development, the preferences are usually granted only on a limited scale and only for certain products which often are specified in exhaustive lists, 'Provided always that, each Associated State may retain or introduce customs duties and charges having an effect equivalent to such duties which correspond to its development needs or which are intended to contribute to its budget.' In cases of disturbances within an economic sector or an unfavourable balance of payments position of one party to the Convention, special protective measures can be taken. However, these provisos are not applicable to the associates outside the Yaoundé group.

3. Global Analysis

A first attempt to evaluate the effects of the association and trade preference agreements was made by means of a global investigation of the EEC imports from the associated and non-associated states. However, the examination of the associated countries' shares in the EEC markets yield results which are as difficult to interpret as the results of an analysis of the growth rates. Although the investigation was limited to states where association agreements were in operation over a longer period, the impact of the preferences did not come out distinctly. A reason can be found in the numerous separate factors which may have been operating in addition to the effects of the preferences.

The general analysis of the growth rates shows that between 1960 and 1971 only the Greek exports to the EEC have grown faster than the Community's total imports. In spite of preferences and association respectively, Turkey and the Associated African States and Madagascar (AASM) fell short of the average. Even if one supposes that the average import value becomes distorted by the explosive growth of EEC trade, there remains little evidence of the export-promoting effect of the preferences.

Only for Greece, whose market share increased – relative to the EEC foreign trade with developing countries – from 1·02 to 2·06 per cent, 'trade-creation effects' caused by tariff reductions can first be deduced. However, an additional examination over the same period of the Greek export structure both from the point of view of product composition and geographical destination shows clearly that the principal cause of this growth was the rapid expansion of Greek industry and its reorientation towards the fast expanding and geographically close EEC markets rather than in the relatively small tariff preferences accorded to the Greek products imported by the EEC.

This hypothesis is supported by the fact that Turkish exports, in spite of the tariff preferences, declined during the same period from 1·72 to 1·58 per cent of the EEC foreign trade. It is characteristic that the proportions of exports of semi-finished and finished industrial goods – in contrast to the development in Greece – remained nearly on the same low level.

The shrinking of the AASM share from 11·10 to 8·94 per cent cannot be attributed to one uniform cause covering all Associated African States. The analysis, however, gives support to the hypothesis that the different countries' dependency on the export of single products and their sales opportunities might have played a decisive role. In this connection it is surprising to note that countries which have been able to improve their EEC market shares (Ivory Coast, Togo) are dependent on their exports of primary commodities (coffee, cocoa) similar to those of countries whose market shares have decreased (Cameroon, Madagascar). In the case of Greece and Turkey also heavily diverging tendencies are observed, and the developments in the levels of their market shares have been very different. For these reasons it did seem necessary to examine the effects of preferential and association agreements in more detail for selected associates and third countries as well as for special representative commodities.

This analysis had to be limited to Greece, Turkey and the AASM because only for these countries significant time series were at hand. All other agreements were signed or became effective such a short time ago that an interpretation of the effects of preferences by means of the available figures was not possible. The criteria for the selection of products to be studied were that the commodities took a high share in the producer countries' foreign trade, that they had been subject to preferences over a fairly long period and that they were in competition with products from third countries. Thus the discussion included the following products as typical:

for the AASM – coffee, cocoa and bananas;
for Greece and Turkey – tobacco.

In order to make allowance for processed goods, whose importance for the foreign trade of the developing countries might rise in the long run, cocoa-paste, cocoa-butter and peanut-oil products were included in the analysis. The development of the production of such commodities is characteristic of the diversification policy of the countries of the Third world.

4. Evaluation of Analysis

In the field of primary commodities it is impossible to gain uniform, consistent results concerning the effects of the EEC preferences. Characteristic are the heavily diverging developments in the individual EEC sub-markets. Whereas coffee imports of the Federal Republic of Germany and the Netherlands have increased tenfold between 1960 and 1971 and grown much faster than imports from third countries, coffee imports of Belgium and Luxembourg decreased by 51·5 per cent. In Italy and France there were slight increases that, however, fell short of the expansion rates of the imports from third countries. Thus a connection between the grant of preferences and the development of imports may be established – although by no means conclusively – only in the cases of the Federal Republic of Germany and the Netherlands.

It must, however, be noted that this expansion of imports from the AASM has taken place from a very low level. So the AASM's market shares increased only to 6·6 per cent in the Netherlands and to 12·1 per cent in Germany. The high expansion rates have little indicative value and might probably fall off slightly in future. This opinion gets support from consumer habits. In the Federal Republic of Germany and in the Netherlands – as well as in Belgium, Luxembourg and Italy – consumers prefer Arabic coffee which the AASM states are able to deliver only in very limited quantities. Only in France there exists demand for the slightly bitter Robusta coffee which is typical for the AASM (market share in 1971 almost 63 per cent). In this case, the traditionally close relations with the former African colonies have very probably had an overwhelming influence on consumer tastes, whereas in the other EEC states a stronger expansion of the demand for Latin American produce could be noticed. The fact that a heavy expansion of imports from the AASM did not take place can be explained by the removal of quotas for third countries in 1964.

An additional explanatory factor for the improvement of the AASM's position in the Federal Republic and the Netherlands is the demand, which is comparatively strong in these countries for instant coffee. Because the production of this coffee is more profitable if the cheaper Robusta coffee beans are used, there have arisen additional opportunities for the sales of this type of product. In the other EEC states, however, the demand for instant coffee remained comparatively insignificant.

Although the preferences have been of importance at least for the demand for the Robusta variety of coffee, nevertheless the method of taxing coffee at least in Germany tends to undermine the advantage gained through preferences. Because coffee is taxed on a quantitative basis, the cheaper Robusta coffee is burdened relatively more heavily than the Arabic varieties. Altogether, it can be stated that the granting of preferences has very probably not led to an improvement in the competitive position of the AASM and thus not to discrimination of third producer countries in any of the EEC markets.

The research on the development of trade with raw cocoa in the individual EEC states has shown that the AASM shares of the total imports of this product have – with the exception of France – substantially grown. In the aggregate, the AASM share of the EEC imports of raw cocoa rose from 33·9 per cent in 1960 to 60·7 per cent in 1971.

The rise of shares has been progressing steadily with the gradual realisation of the preferential system. Here there seems to exist, in contrast to all other examined products, a case of trade diversion. Whereas the EEC imports from the AASM more than doubled, the imports from the non-favoured third countries decreased by over a third. This considerable trade diversion has been possible because raw cocoa is a comparatively homogeneous product. A further important element might have been, though, the Community's financial and technical aid which enabled the AASM countries to increase their production of cocoa by new plantations and by pest control, and to improve the quality of the exported cocoa.

Similar effects may have emerged from the fact that the AASM, in contrast to other producer countries, have had wide areas at their disposal which could be used for the planting of cocoa, so that their supply was – at least in the long run – relatively elastic. The sharp decreases of the shares of single third countries (Ghana, Brazil) may, at least partly, be traced back to special influences like unfavourable atmospheric conditions, deterioration of quality, deficient marketing and higher transport costs.

The preferential system has had no influence on the member states' imports from Ecuador and Venezuela, because they deliver primarily superior qualities which are not offered by the AASM.

That the AASM were not able to improve their market position in France substantially may on the one hand be traced back to the fact that their share was already very high (roughly 85 per cent) at the beginning of the observed period; on the other hand, an increasing share of the French cocoa imports consists of semi-processed produce.

With semi-processed cocoa products (cocoa-paste and cocoa-butter) AASM had substantially improved their shares in the product total imports of four of the six member states (Germany, France, Italy, the Netherlands). Their share in the total imports of the EEC increased from 19·3 per cent in 1960 to 41·1 per cent in 1971. In contrast to the development of raw cocoa, however, this development can to a great extent be attributed to trade creation at the loss of the home production of the above four Community countries.

Brazil's considerable losses of shares in the EEC markets between 1960 and 1963 were not connected with the granting of preferences, because the imports from the AASM remained nearly constant, in relative as well as absolute terms, until 1964. A negligible trade diversion can be ascertained only in the French market. The heavy fluctuations of the Brazilian share in the Community's total imports since 1964 might almost completely be traceable to shifts in the import structure of the Netherlands, for which no unambiguous explanation could be found.

Apart from the strong expansion of the EEC's imports of cocoa-paste and cocoa-butter from the AASM, Ghana and Nigeria also succeeded in gaining a part of the EEC market. These countries efforts to establish processing industries based on domestic agricultural products have been supported by the Community through the reduction of the Common External Tariff

(CET) for cocoa-paste from 25 to 15 per cent and for cocoa-butter from 20 to 12 per cent. The resulting trade-creating effect was not as powerful as in the case of the AASM, because these countries have been put into a much stronger competitive position by the preferences and the financial and technical aid that has been granted to them.

In West Germany, besides the AASM, the Netherlands has also managed to expand its market share which had already been very high before. The most important explanatory factor for this development is the gradual tariff reduction within the EEC. Already, before the creation of the Common Market, there was keen competition between Germany and the Netherlands – the two most important processors of cocoa within the EEC. That the AASM could not derive advantages from their preferential treatment in the market of Belgium-Luxembourg is also attributable to the traditionally strong market position that the Netherlands has there.

The poor results of the policy of preferences that association confers are demonstrated most clearly in the case of trade in bananas. Although in this case high preferences had been existing for long (20 per cent since 1 January 1970), the AASM market share declined from 27 per cent in 1963 to 13 per cent in 1971. The cause of this development was above all the comparatively high price of the AASM products in connection with their inferior quality. There has been no attempt on the part of these countries to improve quality through the plantation of better varieties. At the same time, demand for Latin American bananas, partly as a result of a vigorous advertising campaign, has been rising. In this connection it is important to note that the world banana market is to a great extent dominated by international fruit companies, which – compared to the AASM – have a good financial standing and dispose of their own sales channels and plantations, especially in Latin America. They registered a substantial success in the Italian market, which had been protected until 1965. Only in France sales possibilities are still limited by market regulations. This is why in France the AASM have a relatively high (nearly constant) market share of roughly 33 per cent.

Apart from this, the effect of the preferences is to a considerable degree limited by the fact that the Federal Republic of Germany is granting tariff-free import quotas to third countries, which altogether are higher than the actual imports. So far, the EEC preferences have by no means led to a discrimination against their countries.

No improvement of the AASM market position could be noticed also with regards to processed peanut-oil in spite of reasonable preferences. The AASM market share, that in 1960 still amounted to 65·3 per cent, declined to 63·5 per cent until 1970 and then shrank to 40·7 per cent in 1971. Specially affected were Senegal and Niger, the two main supplier countries among the AASM. Also on the most important EEC market, the AASM market share declined from 95·4 to 72 per cent between 1960 and 1971 although it had still amounted to 94·7 per cent in 1970. In the rest of the EEC countries, the AASM managed to realise significant market shares only since 1968.

The main cause, however, for the fluctuations of imports during recent years and their heavy decline in 1971 has been the lasting aridity in West Africa and the resulting bad harvests, rather than an improvement of the third countries' competitive position. The fact that the AASM's shares in the markets of the Federal Republic of Germany, Italy and Benelux have been growing since 1968 might be traced back primarily to the establishment of new mills in Senegal and Niger and to the efforts of the producer countries for market diversification following the withdrawal of the French price support programmes.

In none of the cases could a trade diversion produced by the preferences be ascertained. The possibility of discrimination against third countries can thus be eliminated.

In order to determine the influence of preferences in the cases of Greece and Turkey, a special study of tobacco was carried out. The EEC imports of raw tobacco have risen between 1960 and 1971 by roughly 70 per cent. With the exception of the United States, the above supplier countries have to an approximately equal extent participated in this growth. An examination of market shares showed that the countries which were favoured by preferences (Greece, Turkey, Brazil) have hardly changed their positions during the observed period. In contrast with this, Bulgaria's market share expanded heavily until the mid-sixties, but then reverted to its former level. The position of the United States hardly altered from 1960 to 1969, but then deteriorated in 1970 and 1971, primarily because the Federal Republic of Germany imported less US tobacco during that year.

A further analysis of the variations of market shares in the individual EEC member states reveals clearly that the grant of tariff preferences has not exerted any influence. Apparently, other factors were decisive for the growth of tobacco imports. The temporary decrease of the market share of US tobacco in the Federal Republic of Germany can, among other things, be traced back to commercial considerations of the importers who made use of the advantages of the quasi-revaluation. In addition, US tobacco price increases were registered, which affected its competitive position. In

Germany, there were also remarkable shifts of consumer preferences for the benefit of tobacco varieties with low nicotine which are not so much grown in the United States.

The causes of the decrease of Bulgaria's market share were the termination of the post-war compensation transactions as well as delivery obligations to Council for Mutual Economic Assistance (COMECON) countries. The decline of the Greek market share in 1971 might be due to EEC market regulations and the resulting advantage of the Italian competitors. Turkey was able to hold its position, above all, because of the substantial devaluation of the Turkish currency.

The development of market shares in France has unambiguously been determined by consumer preferences for domestic and Latin American tobacco. Thus Turkey, Greece, the United States and Bulgaria – in contrast to Brazil – registered losses of their market shares.

Although with the Benelux imports no remarkable developments could be noticed, in Italy the development of market shares showed high increases of US imports to the loss of the associated states. The principal causes were the change of the competitive situation due to the implementation of the customs union on 1 July 1968, and the change in the Italian tobacco-monopoly in product strategies with emphasis on 'light' American cigarettes.

To sum up, it can be stated that the tariff preferences did not have either a long-lived or a striking effect on trade flows. In cases where structural changes actually occurred they were usually caused by factors specific to the products concerned.

The over-estimation of the preferences in the international discussions is very noticeable in the global analysis of the reverse preferences, which have often been criticised. It is extremely difficult to establish that any substantial discrimination against third countries has directly resulted from the preferences granted. To the extent that a shift of supply sources away from third countries can be established, it is most likely to be traceable to other promotional measures of the EEC states (for example, industrialisation policy in Italy) and, above all, to the EEC's Common Agricultural Policy (CAP).

5. Summary

EEC tariff preferences granted for the benefit of the associated states produced practically no discrimination against third countries in the cases illustrated above. The explanation of this is simply that the margin of preference represents only one element of the price, and that the price is just one determinant of the demand for a product. Any trade diversion noticed in the product studies above can be attributed to factors such as consumer habits, qualitative requirements, fluctuations of harvests, traditional relations between exporting and importing countries, market power of the importers or the removal of quantitative restrictions. Another essential, though hardly quantifiable, determinant might have been the Community's development aid. In so far as the association is connected with a favoured treatment of the countries concerned relating to the grant of development aid, and in so far as special measures are taken for the direct sales promotion of the goods enjoying preferences, development aid can become a decisive factor. By looking at the projects that benefited from the European Development Fund (EDF), one can trace such an impact of development policy in the case of cocoa.

The product-by-product analysis detailed in this chapter has been linked to a few commodities. But the analysis may be also applicable to other products having the three basic characteristics of the products examined. It may also be applicable to other association and trade preference agreements. With slight modifications this might also apply to processed agricultural products[5] and to semi-processed and processed industrial goods. However, it must be pointed out that in cases of almost homogeneous goods where price competition between associated and non-associated countries is very strong, a considerable margin of preference may well have some influence on the competitive position. For such cases raw cocoa can be regarded as a typical example.

If, however, the preferences (as they usually do) apply to more differentiated goods and their margin is low, then such preferences miss their real aim – the creation of competitive advantages for the associated states vis-à-vis the third countries. Thus, the removal of this one-sided preferential treatment in favour of generalised preferences to all developing countries would in most cases bring no decisive deterioration in the market position of the associates. Such a shift of policy towards generalised preferences will bring additionally a political advantage to the Community in that it will cease to be exposed to the accusation of building up a system of multiple trade discrimination directly opposed to the GATT principle of multilateralism.

5 An exception are agricultural products which are competing with products of the Community. In these cases substantial advantages could be granted to the associated states by reductions of price adjustment levies and/or the removal of quantitative restrictions.

The introduction of a system of generalised preferences is also advisable for the following reasons:

zero tariffs have already been introduced for important exports of the associated countries included in this study (for example, rubber, cotton, sisal, tea, tin, cobalt, copper, calcium phosphates, skins and furs);

the expansion of the preference area to include the Commonwealth countries means that the previously associated states will have to share their preferences with a larger number of competitors;

general tariff reductions can be expected as a result of the present GATT round;

the EEC members have committed themselves to extend their system of generalised preferences.

All these factors might result in the further decrease of the importance of the preferences that association policy offers.[6] They thus suggest the introduction of generalised preferences[7] in place of the present system.

6 See Kommission der Europäischen Gemeinschaften, 'Memorandum der Kommission an den Rat über die künftigen Beziehungen zwischen der Gemeinschaft, den gegenwärtigen AASM sowie den im Protokoll Nr 22 der Beitrittsakte genaunten Ländern in Afrika, im Karibischen Raum, im Indischen Ozean und im Pazifischen Ozean, Luxemburg', 4 March 1973, p. 15.

7 The Community should also place greater weight on technical and financial co-operation. In this connection, special measures for marketing, diversification and compensation for fluctuations of export income would have to be considered.

Table 1 EEC imports of raw coffee from selected areas in metric tons and in percentage of total imports, 1960–71

Year	EEC countries	EEC internal trade	EEC import	AASM Total	AASM Per cent	Third countries Total	Third countries Per cent
1960	618,507	6,476	612,031	179,972	12·4	432,059	70·6
1961	647,645	9,029	638,616	188,407	29·5	450,209	70·5
1962	677,355	10,340	667,015	188,955	28·3	478,060	71·7
1963	707,148	7,881	699,267	199,350	28·5	499,917	71·5
1964	756,927	9,394	747,533	207,317	27·7	540,216	72·3
1965	764,447	11,213	753,234	188,243	25·0	564,991	75·0
1966	770,227	7,915	762,312	194,497	25·5	567,815	74·5
1967	797,248	8,833	783,415	181,265	23·0	607,150	77·0
1968	363,089	9,459	853,630	225,406	26·4	628,224	73·6
1969	888,140	11,757	876,383	216,965	24·8	659,418	75·2
1970	880,595	8,875	871,720	239,317	27·5	632,403	72·5
1971	940,651	7,048	933,603	239,784	25·7	693,819	74·3

Source: Computed from Europäische Gemeinschaften, *Analytische Übersichten*, Import.

TABLE 2 Percentage distribution of EEC imports of raw cocoa by selected countries/areas, 1960–71

	AASM					*Third countries*					
Year	*Total*	*Ivory Coast*	*Cameroon*	*Togo*	*Others*	*Total*	*Ghana*	*Nigeria*	*Ecuador*	*Brazil*	*Others*
1960	33·9	7·8	17·0	2·2	6·9	66·1	30·3	17·9	2·0	8·5	7·4
1961	35·1	12·2	15·1	1·9	5·9	64·9	30·8	17·6	2·0	6·9	7·6
1962	36·5	15·1	16·3	2·3	2·8	63·5	31·8	18·0	2·3	5·1	6·3
1963	41·0	17·3	17·9	2·5	3·3	59·0	30·0	17·9	2·2	2·2	6·7
1964	41·0	18·1	17·5	2·7	2·7	59·0	25·2	21·5	2·2	1·5	8·1
1965	45·3	22·0	17·6	3·8	1·9	54·7	20·0	23·4	2·0	1·3	8·0
1966	41·1	21·1	14·0	3·7	2·3	58·9	27·0	20·2	2·1	1·6	8·0
1967	48·8	25·3	16·4	4·3	2·8	51·2	12·8	22·6	2·3	4·2	9·3
1968	48·1	24·1	16·7	4·3	3·0	51·9	17·6	17·6	2·2	4·1	10·0
1969	54·0	25·4	18·4	5·9	4·3	46·0	13·4	13·7	2·2	2·8	13·9
1970	61·7	27·6	21·5	6·5	6·1	38·3	13·4	10·9	2·0	1·1	10·9
1971	60·7	25·8	22·3	5·5	7·1	39·3	14·4	16·9	2·2	0·5	7·5

Source: Computed from Europäische Gemeinschaften, *Analytische Übersichten*, Import.

TABLE 3 Percentage distribution of EEC imports of cocoa-butter and paste by selected countries/areas, 1960–71

		AASM				*Third countries*				*EEC*	
Year	*World-imports*	*Total*	*Ivory Coast*	*Cameroon*	*Others*	*Total*	*Ghana*	*Nigeria*	*Brazil*	*Total*	*Netherlands*
1960	100	19·3	—	19·2	0·1	80·7	1·1	0·1	42·2	30·5	25·9
1961	100	23·2	1·1	22·1	–	76·8	0·4	0·2	31·9	37·6	30·9
1962	100	21·2	1·0	20·2	–	78·8	–	–	30·1	41·7	33·1
1963	100	21·5	0·2	21·3	–	78·5	2·4	0·3	14·7	51·5	37·0
1964	100	20·9	0·5	20·4	–	79·1	5·7	–	14·5	46·0	34·4
1965	100	30·8	13·0	17·7	0·1	69·2	6·4	–	5·8	45·9	35·2
1966	100	25·9	14·9	11·0	–	74·1	2·3	0·1	14·0	44·3	32·9
1967	100	30·5	14·9	15·5	0·1	69·5	4·5	–	19·7	37·2	26·8
1968	100	48·3	26·3	22·0	–	51·7	3·1	5·3	8·9	30·9	25·4
1969	100	37·8	18·9	18·9	–	62·2	4·1	10·0	5·5	38·2	32·2
1970	100	42·2	25·8	16·3	0·1	57·8	4·4	5·3	9·2	36·6	29·6
1971	100	41·1	25·5	15·6	–	58·9	2·2	3·9	8·9	39·3	31·4

Source: Computed from Europäische Gemeinschaften, *Analytische Übersichten*, Import.

TABLE 4 Percentage distribution of EEC imports of bananas by selected countries/areas, 1960–71

		AASM					*Third countries*					
								South America		*Central America*		
Year	*World imports*	*Total*	*Ivory Coast*	*Somalia*	*Cameroon*	*Others*	*Total*	*Total*	*Ecuador*	*Total*	*Honduras*	*DOM*
1960	100	20	6	8	3	2	80	40	23	5	3	23
1961	100	20	9	7	5	2	80	41	23	4	2	23
1962	100	23	10	7	5	2	77	35	21	14	1	22
1963	100	27	11	8	5	3	73	41	23	11	1	18
1964	100	23	8	6	7	2	77	50	33	9	1	13
1965	100	25	8	8	8	2	75	46	28	8	3	16
1966	100	18	6	6	4	2	82	48	30	11	7	18
1967	100	17	8	5	3	1	83	46	31	18	15	17
1968	100	17	8	5	3	0	83	37	24	15	18	19
1969	100	16	7	5	3	0	84	30	20	33	17	18
1970	100	15	7	5	3	0	85	24	16	27	12	16
1971	100	13	6	3	3	0	87	22	18	47	10	18

Source: Computed from Europäische Gemeinschaften, *Analytische Übersichten*, Import.

TABLE 5 EEC imports of peanut oil from selected areas in tons and in percentage of total imports, 1960–71

Year	*EEC countries*	*Inter-EEC*	*EEC*	*AASM*		*Third countries*	
1960	170,611	5,073	165,538	111,386	67·2	54,152	32·8
1961	136,734	2,861	133,873	105,727	79·0	28,146	21·0
1962	147,289	6,791	140,498	104,991	74·7	35,507	25·3
1963	92,890	6,352	86,538	21,755	25·1	64,783	74·9
1964	81,093	13,138	67,955	25,305	37·2	42,650	62·8
1965	190,655	8,936	181,719	117,628	64·7	64,091	35·3
1966	246,400	9,983	236,417	150,513	63·7	85,904	36·3
1967	245,829	16,032	229,797	162,170	70·6	67,627	29·4
1968	242,219	32,327	209,892	160,839	76·6	49,053	23·4
1969	211,109	27,798	183,311	118,253	64·5	65,058	35·5
1970	233,730	20,816	212,914	148,329	69·6	64,585	30·4
1971	226,447	22,770	203,677	92,119	45·2	111,558	54·8

Source: Computed from Europäische Gemeinschaften, *Analytische Übersichten*, Import.

TABLE 6 Percentage distribution of EEC imports of peanut oil by selected countries/areas, 1960–71

	AASM				*Third countries*				
Year	*Total*	*Niger*	*Senegal*	*Others*	*Total*	*Nigeria*	*USA*	*Argentina*	*Others*
1960	65·3	3·3	57·2	4·8	34·7	0·2	–	18·2	16·3
1961	77·3	3·8	73·0	0·5	22·7	3·8	1·4	15·1	2·4
1962	71·3	1·8	69·1	0·4	28·7	1·1	–	18·0	9·6
1963	23·4	0·4	23·0	–	76·6	8·3	2·3	39·3	26·7
1964	31·2	–	31·2	–	68·8	9·7	12·7	3·2	43·2
1965	61·7	3·2	58·5	–	38·3	6·8	6·8	16·8	7·9
1966	61·1	3·0	58·1	–	38·9	1·8	0·5	24·6	12·0
1967	66·0	3·1	62·5	0·4	34·0	0·2	–	20·4	13·4
1968	66·4	3·1	63·3	–	33·6	–	–	15·0	18·6
1969	56·0	3·7	51·0	1·3	44·0	5·8	6·5	14·6	17·1
1970	63·5	4·5	57·4	1·6	36·5	5·4	1·1	12·0	18·0
1971	40·7	5·5	33·6	1·5	59·3	0·8	7·5	17·7	33·2

Source: Computed from Europäische Gemeinschaften, *Analytische Übersichten*, Import.

TABLE 7 Percentage distribution of EEC imports of raw tobacco by selected countries, 1960–71

Year	*Greece*	*Turkey*	*Bulgaria*	*USA*	*Brazil*
1960	12·6	4·9	3·0	28·8	5·3
1961	10·7	6·3	3·2	26·4	6·7
1962	11·3	9·1	4·4	24·4	7·4
1963	8·1	3·8	6·1	26·4	7·5
1964	9·7	3·3	4·9	24·6	7·9
1965	10·8	3·0	5·3	26·1	7·8
1966	11·4	4·9	6·0	26·5	7·9
1967	10·4	4·5	4·4	28·6	7·1
1968	12·7	5·3	5·6	26·9	5·5
1969	11·5	4·3	4·5	27·2	5·1
1970	10·8	5·4	3·3	22·2	7·2

Source: Computed from Europäische Gemeinschaften, *Analytische Übersichten*, Import.

2

SPECIAL ASPECTS

5

The Common Agricultural Policy and the Mediterranean Countries

J. S. MARSH

1. Introduction

The Common Agricultural Policy (CAP) affects both members and non-member countries in the Mediterranean area. By devices that influence the price of key products and regulate access to the Community's market, preference is given to the produce of member countries. Non-members cannot compete simply by offering goods at lower price. If they are to share in the largest food importing market in the world, they must do so on terms set by the Community.

For Mediterranean countries, the agricultural sector is of crucial importance. Table 1 provides some key economic data relating to selected countries in this regard. In contrast with more northerly countries, agriculture here accounts for a much larger share both of employment and of GNP. In all these countries agricultural production has tended to rise at rates in excess of the growth in population. Although improvements in diet may absorb some of the extra food, adjustments are also likely to be needed in the balance of trade – imports falling and exports of farm goods rising. If such increased outlets are denied, then the goal of sustained economic growth is likely to prove more elusive.

The countries concerned are, by contrast with the more northerly members of the Community, relatively poor. Table 2 gives some indication of this disparity in living standards. Had comparable statistics for some of the countries on the southern shore of the Mediterranean been available, the size of the gap would appear even larger. Such inequalities make for difficulties. Within the Community, the relative poverty of the Italian South influences a whole range of policies from economic and monetary union to the price paid for durum wheat. Outside the Community, the gap in wealth is one of the factors shaping the pattern of relationships with Mediterranean countries. If this gap were allowed to grow as a result of farm policies, other points of agreement between such countries and the Community might appear of little worth.

The Mediterranean countries have in common a specific interest in a

TABLE 1 Key economic indicators for selected countries (shown as percentage)

	Greece	*Portugal*	*Spain*	*Italy*	*France*	*Germany*	*UK*
Share of Agriculture in GNP 1969–70	19	18	14	10·3	6·8	3·8	3·0
Share of Agriculture[a] in total active employment 1970–1	40	31	29	20	14	8	3
Growth of Agricultural[b] Output, 1968/69–1960/61, Average Annual Rate	3·5	1·8	3·1	1·8	2·9	4·2	2·6

[a]Data relate to agriculture, forestry and fishing.
[b]Rates of Growth for Italy, France, Germany and U.K. 1965–71.

Sources: OECD Economic Survey of Greece, 1972.
MAFF Agricultural and Food Statistics for the Enlarged EEC. No. 2, November 1972.

TABLE 2 Comparative living standards in European countries, 1969–70

	Greece	*Portugal*	*Spain*	*Italy*	*France*	*Germany*	*UK*
GNP per head 1970 $	1,060	640	960	1,700	2,920	3,040	2,170
Private consumption per head $	640	480	650	1,090	1,720	1,650	1,340
Passenger cars per 1000 pop. 1970	22	47	71	187	245	237	213
Television sets per 1000 pop. 1960	10	37	167	170	201	262	284

Source: OECD – Economic Survey, Italy 1972.

range of agricultural products. The Italian Minister of Agriculture, Signor Natali, described these to a Council meeting as 'tomatoes, citrus fruit, wine and tinned fruits'. Other members also have interests in wine, tomatoes and so on, but in proportion to their total agricultural output these products are less important. This creates a clear conflict of interest between members of the Community that are Mediterranean countries and non-members that produce these crops. Any concessions to non-members may weaken Community preference and in this way damage the interests of established member states, notably Italy.

This paper attempts to explore the way in which the CAP impinges on these complex issues. It falls into three parts:

(*i*) How the CAP affects agriculture within the Community.
(*ii*) How the trade of non-members in the Mediterranean area may be affected by this policy.
(*iii*) The problems posed by the CAP for the Community's relations with Mediterranean countries.

2. How the CAP Affects Agriculture Within the Community

(*a*) *General*

The CAP is not a policy for agriculture; rather, it is a policy for the Community. That is to say, its central concern is not the level of farm output, farmers' incomes or food prices but the creation and continuance of the European Community. Agricultural problems matter, but ultimately they are secondary to the goal of full economic union.

Such a starting point is essential if the immense importance of political as distinct from economic forces in shaping the CAP is to be understood. The character of the policy, the level and pattern of agricultural activity which results and the distribution of gains and losses among members all owe more to the pressure of political forces than to inescapable economic necessities. Two types of political pressure may be distinguished. That from farmers upon their own member governments and that from governments which believe that some national interest is at stake. Inevitably, the policy bears the scars of conflicts of interest of both types.

As a minimal requirement, if agriculture were to be induced within the Common Market, goods had to move freely between countries, and producers had to enjoy a common level of protection vis-à-vis the outside world. Free movement of farm products between countries would have established a common price level as goods moved towards the places where prices were highest. Because in agriculture the range of production conditions varied greatly, it might, *a priori*, be expected that such a common price level would tend to be below the average of prices previously prevailing.

Such an outcome, although it demonstrates one of the main economic benefits expected from creating freer trade between countries, was unacceptable. In every member country, agriculture was going through a period of secular decline. Rising *per capita* incomes tended to widen the gap between earnings in agriculture and in other sectors. New labour-saving technology raised output despite a considerable flow of manpower to other sectors. Because demand for farm products grew more slowly, there was a continued pressure on the price of farm goods. Especially in those areas in which little alternative employment existed and for those people whose age and skills made the discovery of new jobs more difficult, the prospect of cuts in price resulting from the creation of a Common Market in agriculture was alarming. Before the Community existed, the various member countries had taken steps to ensure that farmers' prices were maintained. To have abandoned such safeguards was politically impossible. However, some modification was inescapable because each member operated at different price levels and employed different policy mechanisms. The founders of the Community decided not to have free trade in farm goods throughout the Community but to have a jointly managed market in which a common set of policy instruments would be used to regulate price levels.

The level at which prices were set depended on the use made of these policy instruments. For most manufactured goods the internal price level might be expected to reflect the prices at which imported supplies were available, plus some modest element of Community preference. For agricultural products, however, the world market was affected by the strongly protectionist policies adopted by most wealthy countries. These policies both limited the amount bought from the world market and resulted in extra production being sold on it. As a result, prices were often below the levels of production costs, even in exporting countries. The price-inelastic character of this market meant too that sudden shortages due to crop failures could result in sharp price increases. To expose farmers to so volatile a market was unacceptable. It was therefore agreed to insulate the internal market and to fix a minimum price level at which imports should be permitted. The level determined for Community prices would thus not only reflect the political pressures generated by the secular decline of agriculture, but also the degree of preference over third countries accorded to Community producers. Within the Community, high prices resulted in a strong element of preference for the agricultural exporters of France and Holland and at the same time enabled German farmers, whose costs were high, to survive. This relieved political pressures both between members and between farmers and governments.

A common price level and a common degree of Community preference have become two of the fundamental principles of the CAP. The third, common financial responsibility, was also a matter in which political decisions assumed central importance. In abstract terms, a policy of common minimum import prices and internal prices maintained at some common level could by achieved by co-ordinated action of member governments, each pocketing any revenues received and meeting any expenses incurred. Such an approach was ruled out for three reasons. First, it denied the spirit of creating a Community. Second, it would have lodged import revenues on products destined for countries within the Community in the exchequers of the states through whose ports they entered. Third, it would have placed the financial burden of supporting production that could not be sold within the Community at the desired price level upon those countries in which it was produced. In effect, it would have reduced the cost of the policy for Germany, a major importer of food, and required that the French and Dutch governments bear the cost of disposing of output produced by their farmers for which no market existed in the Community at the level of price fixed. Whether viewed from the angle of the 'European', who believed that the Community must have its own resources to finance its own policies, or from that of the national governments looking for a balance of advantage among members, joint financial responsibility, including the pooling of taxes on imports, was a political necessity.

(b) The Apparatus of the CAP

The CAP has two aspects, price policy and structural policy. Although it is true that any policy which influences the level of output is relevant to trade, Community structural policy has so far been on a very modest scale. Up to now it has been a secondary feature of the CAP both for members and non-members. This might not be true in future if the more ambitious proposals for structural reform which have been evolved since 1968 prove effective. At present, however, the main matter for concern is the CAP's price policy. In this section, a description of the general system is provided. This is followed by a more detailed account of the methods used to regulate markets of especial importance to the Mediterranean countries.

For key products the Council determines each year a 'target price'. This relates to a specific Community Market and is the price that the Council desires to prevail there. To protect it from being undermined by imports, a 'threshold price' is calculated at the port, which is equivalent to the target price minus the costs of moving the commodity from the port to the market to which the target price relates. The difference between the lowest world price offer, at the port, and the threshold price is then charged as a levy on all imports of the commodity. In principle, this means that no goods from third countries can be sold within the Community below the target price.

Price falls associated with excessive domestic production are countered by intervention purchase. At prices which are generally some 5–7 per cent below the target price, the market authorities of the Community buy products offered to them. This puts a floor in the market, but it also creates the problem of coping with any accumulated stock of produce bought at intervention. If the price drop is due to unfortunate timing in deliveries to market, later recoveries in price should enable the authorities to dispose of their purchases within the Community. If, however, there is no prospect of prices recovering because, at the fixed price, the market is oversupplied, then more radical steps are needed. These consist either of changing the nature of the product so that it can be sold in some other Community market than that which is under pressure (adding fish oil to wheat, for example, so that it can be used in animal but not human food), or of selling the produce abroad with the aid of an export subsidy.

Figs. 1 and 2 summarise the main features of a system of this character and draw attention to some crucial elements in its operation. As a convenient simplification imports are assumed to be available at a constant price

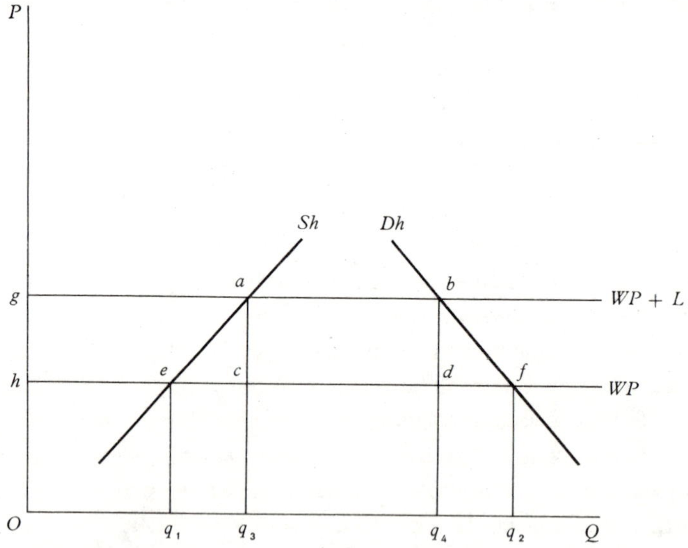

Fig. 1. *Sh* = Home supply. *WP* = World supply. *WP* + *L* = World supply plus levy. *Dh* = Home demand

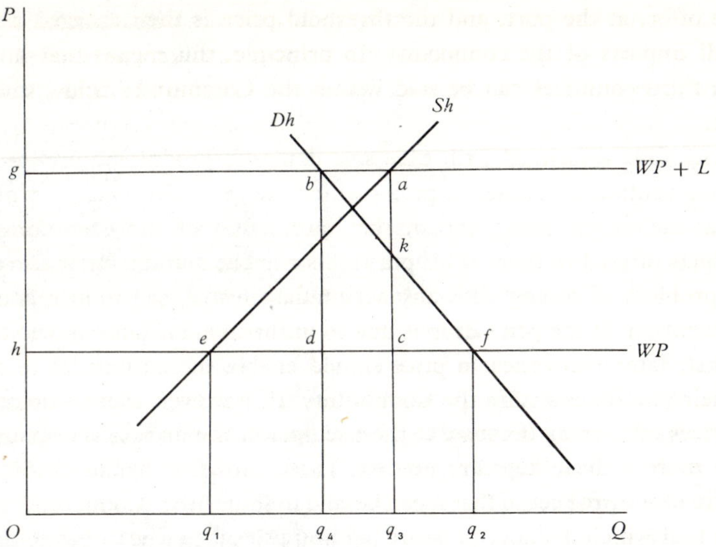

Fig. 2. Key as Fig. 1

regardless of the amount bought. The effect of imposing a levy (*hg*) is to reduce consumption from q_2 to q_4 and increase home output from q_1 to q_3. Imports fall from q_1q_2 to q_3q_4 in fig. 1. In fig. 2, imports are eliminated and an excess of home production over home consumption, equivalent to q_4q_3, appears. Given the elasticities of home supply and demand, the effect on trade will then depend upon the amount by which the price level fixed exceeds the world price. The consequences for the financing of the policy are equally interesting. In fig. 1, the area *a b d c* is captured as revenue. In fig. 2, *b a c d* must be given as a subsidy to reduce the price of surplus over home requirements to world levels. This corresponds to the cost of subsidies needed to sell the surplus production, $b\ a\ q_3\ q_4$, at world prices. In fig. 1, the imposition of the levy results in a reduction of consumer surplus, *g b f h*. Part of this is accounted for by a rise in producer surplus, *g a e h*, part by the cost of the extra resources employed at home, *a e c*, part in an addition to government revenues, *a b d c* and part is a loss to the community as a whole, *b f d*. In fig. 2, the element of government revenue disappears. In addition to transfers to producers from consumers equal to *g b d h*, further transfers of *b a c d* are needed from tax revenue. These transfers are in part an element of the resource cost of extra home production, *a e c*, and in part producer surplus, *g a e h*. The dead loss element is *k c f*.

Within the Community, producers and consumers are not distributed in the same proportion among member countries, and the implication is that a system of this type will not only redistribute consumer surplus in favour of producers and the common fund of the Community, but that its benefits and costs will be unevenly distributed among member countries.

The effect on any one member country will thus depend upon its net trading position; net importers will contribute to the maintenance of prices for net exporters. In practice, the operation of the system is greatly complicated by the fact that there is not one but a multiplicity of agricultural products. Thus, to appreciate the effect on any one member country it is necessary to assess the amount by which the internal price of each of the products it produces and consumes exceeds the world price level. In practice, this is an extremely difficult quantity to estimate. Prices vary substantially in the world market. The assumption that imports and domestic production are homogeneous and interchangeable in consumption is not wholly true. If the Community were to import larger amounts, the prices in the world market would be raised almost certainly by differing proportions for different commodities.

Table 3 gives some indications of the order of difference between internal and external prices around 1967, the period in which most prices were fixed. Despite the substantial methodological problems involved, it seems certain that the degree of protection accorded to various products varied considerably. There is no reason to believe that these gaps have disappeared.

Table 4 shows the composition of agricultural output by main commodities for the Six as a whole, for France and for Italy. Although the composition of French farm output is of a similar pattern to that of the Community as a whole, Italian agriculture is much more heavily orientated towards crop production. The crops of greatest importance are, in terms of the categories used, vegetables, fruit and 'other crops'. It has been a central contention of Italian arguments about the CAP that products of especial importance to Italy have received less protection than other goods subject to Community market organisation. Although the evidence available in Tables 3 and 4 does not prove this, it is consistent with such an argument.

For agricultural goods as a whole, Italy is a net importer. Table 5 provides a summary of the situation in 1972. So far as intra-Community trade is concerned, it is only in fruit, vegetables and wine that exports exceed imports. For meat, dairy products, cereals and sugar there is a substantial net import. To understand the impact of the CAP on Italy it is necessary to compare the extra revenue that Italy receives for fruit, vegetables and

TABLE 3 Estimate of difference between world price and community prices circa 1966/7. E.C. price as % world price

	USDA 1966/7	*Atlantic Institute 1967/8*
Soft Wheat	182	168
Durum Wheat	157	
Barley	142	165
Rye	163	181
Rice	117	–
Sugar	286	127[a]
Eggs	132	171
Poultry	131	154
Pork	146	152
Beef and Veal	175	
Butter	265	
Non fat dry milk	250	Milk 135[b]
Whole dry milk	195	
Cheese	137	
Olive Oil	115	
Oats	–	140
Potatoes	–	105

[a]Sugar beet.
[b]Milk at farm gate.
Source: Based on Kruen and Bernston, 'Cost of Common Agricultural Policy to the European Economic Community', USDA 1969, 'A Future for European Agriculture', Atlantic Institute, report of panel of experts, 1970, Paris.

wine, as a result of its membership of the Community with the extra costs that are incurred on these other items.

Table 6 shows that, in terms of the movement of funds through the Community budget in support of farm prices, Italy was a net loser between 1967/8 and 1970. In addition to this loss, the Italian economy must have incurred further substantial losses as a result of the CAP because the balance of agricultural trade within the Community was in favour of other members.

(c) The Regulations for Fruit and Vegetables, Olive Oil, Wine and Tobacco

Although the Mediterranean countries produce virtually all the goods covered by the CAP, they have an especial interest in citrus fruit and

TABLE 4 Percentage contribution to gross output by various farm enterprises, 1969

	EEC (Six)	*Italy*	*France*
Wheat	6·71	9·93	7·87
Barley	0·17	0·04	2·86
Oats	0·25	0·07	0·23
Maize	1·34	1·64	2·59
Rice	0·35	1·22	0·09
Cereals	10·69	12·95	13·73
Potatoes	2·40	2·23	1·99
Sugar beet	2·40	1·91	2·18
Vegetables	7·85	13·32	6·25
Fruit	4·75	7·88	3·74
Other crops	13·59	23·46	11·51
Total crops	41·74	61·74	39·42
Cattle	15·24	10·75	17·53
Sheep and goats	0·73	0·51	1·52
Pigs	12·98	8·56	5·41
Poultry	3·87	5·47	5·22
Other	2·24	1·59	4·75
Total livestock	35·07	23·9	37·44
Milk	17·61	9·87	17·67
Eggs	4·46	3·93	3·36
Other	0·71	0·19	0·36
Livestock product	22·78	13·9	21·39

Source: Based on MAFF Agricultural and Food Statistics for the Enlarged EEC, No. 2, November 1972.

tomatoes, covered by the fruit and vegetable regulations, olive oil, wine and tobacco. It is helpful, therefore, to summarise the main features of these rules as they are applied under the CAP.

(i) Fruit and Vegetables: In late 1972, the Council of Ministers revised the regulations for fruit and vegetables in order to take account of discontent in France and Italy with the working of the system.

TABLE 5 Italian trade in agricultural products, 1972 (million US $)

	Imports		*Exports*	
	World	*EEC*	*World*	*EEC*
Total (including non-agric.)	19,272	8,650	18,537	8,367
Food and live animals	3,767	1,723	1,246	690
Meat and meat products	749	358	47	19
Dairy products and eggs	430	369	60	16
Fish	188	43	27	14
Cereals and cereal preparations	560	100	140	49
Fruit and vegetables	252	57	871	541
Sugar	157	145	18	10
Coffee, tea, cocoa, spices	213	15	33	21
Feeding stuffs not unmilled cereals	190	88	24	5
Miscellaneous foods	18	14	22	18
Beverages	94	60	359	240
Tobacco	85	39	23	19

Source: OECD.

TABLE 6 FEOGA net debit (−) or credit (+) received by Italy – guarantee sector only

	1967/8	*1968/9*	*1969 (July–Dec.)*	*1970*
Million units of account	−97·8	−161·8	+0·5	−22·4
Reimbursements (%)	19·0	16·2	26·7	20·6
Contribution (%)	28·4	26·1	26·7	21·5

Source: MAFF Agricultural and Food Statistics for the Enlarged EEC, No. 2, November 1972.

A basic price which formerly was based on the average of three years' prices in representative Community markets is now determined by the Council of Ministers in what is described as a 'politically orientated' package. In relation to the basic price, a purchase price is fixed; 40–45 per cent for tomatoes, 50–55 per cent for apples and pears, and 60–70 per cent for other products.

Intervention purchase may take place by producer groups at a 'withdrawal price' somewhat above the purchase price, or by the market authorities in member countries when prices fall below the purchase price for more than three consecutive days. Elaborate rules exist to prevent goods purchased at intervention re-entering the market.

The Community applies quality standards to trade in fruit and vegetables, including tomatoes, and citrus fruit. Produce which fails to qualify at the lowest level is excluded from the market. Similar quality standards are imposed on imported produce, but imports of goods of the lowest category are prohibited.

Imports from third countries are subject to the common customs tariff. This is applied at a certain minimum import price known as the 'reference price'. If prices of goods offered fall below the reference price for two successive days, a levy is imposed. The reference price takes into account the average of producer prices in the last three years, the transport costs between producer and consumer regions of the Community and, since 1972, the development of the basic price and purchase price. For every market day an import price is calculated for each country of origin on the basis of importer/wholesaler prices. In addition, the Community has power to suspend totally or in part imports of a commodity that is threatened by sudden large-scale arrivals.

Exports of fruit and vegetables of Community origin may be subsidised by refunds which it has been possible to pre-fix since the modification of the policy in 1972. In effect, this permits Community exporters to compete in lower-priced world markets.

The Community also aids its own orange producers, first by subsidising contracts for the purchase of oranges of Community origin and of suitable quality in Community import markets, and second by means of grants to assist structural reform and the improvement of marketing.

(*ii*) *Olive oil*: Two target prices are fixed for olive oil. One, the producer target price, is designed to give a 'fair' return to the producer; the other, the market target price, represents the price the Community considers to 'permit the normal market flow of home production' having regard to the prices of competing products. In relation to the market target price, a threshold price is designated. An import levy, calculated on the basis of the difference between this price and prices reported to the Commission from the main producing and importing countries, is placed on olive oils from third countries. In addition to this variable levy on virgin oil, a fixed amount is added to imports of refined products, to protect the Community's refiners. Export restitutions may be given but they are not automatic.

The gap between the market target price and the producer target price is made up by a subsidy equivalent to the difference between the two. In effect, this resembles the UK deficiency payment system which allowed higher prices to be paid to farmers although consumers continued to buy at much lower world prices.

In 1972/3, the producer target price was fixed at 1247·00 u.a. (units of account) per ton, the market target price at 796·00 u.a. per ton and the intervention price at 723·50 u.a. per ton. These figures give some indication of the amount by which the 'user' price and the 'producer' price may deviate within the Community.

(iii) Wine: Regulations for the organisation of the wine market involved protracted argument among the six founder members of the Community. Ultimately, and just in time for the Common Market to be completed by the end of 1970, a highly complex set of regulations was evolved.

So far as internal trade and production is concerned, there are rules covering:

the planting of vines,
alcoholic strength,
enriching wine,
acidifying or de-acidifying,
blending of wines of Community origin,
appellation,
description of diluted or blended wines,
labelling,
control of production and movement, and
distillation.

For each representative type of wine produced in the Community and for each year there is a guide price. Intervention may take place by providing aids for the laying down of private stocks and for the distillation of wine.

The apparatus relating to imported wines is of similar complexity. In addition to a very important prohibition on the blending of imported with Community-produced wine there is:

a common external tariff,
a reference price and associated levy on imports offered below it,
an import licensing system,
a safeguard clause enabling further steps to be taken should prices fall despite the other devices, and
an arrangement for subsidising exports.

An interesting feature is the requirement that the Commission prepare each year an estimate of wine supplies. If a surplus is threatened, it may then authorise distillation. The effect is to prevent an excessive stock being carried forward to depress prices in succeeding years.

(iv) Tobacco: The Community of Six produced less than one-third of its tobacco requirements. For the Nine, almost four-fifths of supplies come from non-member countries. This dependence upon bought-in supplies is apparent in the character of the regulation of the market.

This establishes target prices for a representative reference quality of each of the nineteen types of tobacco grown in the Community. Intervention prices are set at 90 per cent of the target price. A premium is paid to tobacco buyers in respect of tobacco of Community origin. In effect, this is similar to a deficiency payment received by processors to encourage them to buy EEC produced tobacco.

Because the duties on tobacco are bound in GATT, there are no threshold prices or variable levies. The Common External Tariff (CET) is fixed in two parts. For tobacco at less than 1·36 u.a. per lb the duty is 23 per cent; at 1·36 u.a. and above the duty is 15 per cent. However, for the 23 per cent duty there is a minimum duty of 0·136 u.a. per lb and a maximum of 0·16 u.a. per lb. For the 15 per cent duty the maximum is 0·24 cents per lb.

3. How the Trade of Non-members in the Mediterranean Area is Affected

Table 7 indicates total imports by the Community in 1971 of various SIIC categories of food and agricultural products. It also indicates how much of this trade was internal to the Community and how much came from Greece, Spain, Turkey and Italy. Two important points can be resolved.

First, agricultural trade with the EEC is much more important to other Mediterranean countries than it is to Italy or to the Community as a whole. Imports of food and live animals, beverages and tobacco account for some

TABLE 7 Imports by the European Community 1971 from the world, from itself and from selected countries
(millions of $ US)

	World	*EEC*	*Italy*	*Greece*	*Spain*	*Turkey*
Total	99,071	49,425	6,914	381	1,170	314
0 Food and live animals	13,312	5,933	634	93	372	98
00 Live animals	892·4	493·3	0·3	2·1	3·3	0·3
01 Meat and meat products	1,910·6	1,124·8	19·3	–	3·6	0·3
02 Dairy products and eggs	1,079·7	936·2	18·8	0·1	0·8	–
03 Fish and fish preparations	677·7	180·3	8·3	3·2	38·4	7·6
04 Cereals and cereal preparations	2,269·7	969·4	35·0	2·3	0·4	0·6
09 Fruit and vegetables	3,124·2	1,325·1	507·5	80·6	308·1	79·2
06 Sugar, sugar preparations and honey	401·0	242·7	8·0	2·0	4·9	2·5
07 Coffee, tea, cocoa, spices and manufactures thereof	1,550·8	256·6	20·2	0·6	5·7	5·0
08 Feedingstuffs for animals	1,238	290·2	7·2	1·7	5·8	2·3
09 Miscellaneous food preparations	146·8	114·3	9·4	0·6	0·9	0·5
11 Beverages	690·2	474·7	174·6	13·8	24·8	0·1
12 Tobacco	563·9	156·9	13·7	45·0	0·1	27·5

Source: Statistics of Foreign Trade, Series B, January–December 1971, OECD.

13 per cent of total Community imports and 12 per cent of Italian sales to the Community. In contrast, 34 per cent of Spanish, 40 per cent of Greek and 44 per cent of Turkish exports to the Community are agricultural in origin. Similar importance attaches to the trade of other Mediterranean countries except where oil provides a substantial alternative source of revenue.

Second, there is a close similarity in the pattern of exports from Italy and from the non-member Mediterranean countries. Fruit and vegetables are important for all four countries listed. Tobacco matters much more to Greece and Turkey than to Italy. Wine exports are very important for Spain and Greece, whereas for Italy they are second in importance only to fruit and vegetables. The enlargement of the Community means that a much larger volume of Spanish wine exports will now have to surmount the barriers to trade exported by the CAP.

Table 8 reinforces the information given in the previous tables by extending the range of Mediterranean countries covered and by revealing the extent to which their agricultural exports are made up of a rather narrow group of products. It also emphasises the importance of the EEC (of Six) as a trading partner and the large share of agricultural exports in the total exports of these countries. Two of the countries listed, Algeria and Tunisia, sent more than 60 per cent of their exports to the EEC in this period.

It is then of significance to explore the extent to which the CAP has affected the sales of agricultural products by these countries to the EEC. The information that is available from Community sources shows no clear trend towards greater self-sufficiency in either wine or fruit and vegetables.

This impression is confirmed by statistics of Community production which show that no dramatic changes in output of these commodities has taken place.

It is tempting to conclude from such data, inadequate as they are, that despite the formidable apparatus of the CAP, no serious damage has resulted for third-country suppliers of the commodities listed. Such a conclusion is not permissible. The question is not only what has happened but also what would have happened in the absence of the CAP. Perhaps the least realistic assumption is that, if the CAP had not existed, trade would have been free. A much more likely hypothesis is that there would have been differing levels of protection, some of which might have been more restrictive than the CAP. Again, in the period covered by these figures, the policy for fruit and vegetables was operated on the relatively liberal basis of an arithmetical average of prices in representative Community markets. Now it is to operate on politically determined and presumably higher prices. Again, the wine regulation did not come into force until 1970, and so the figures given reflect hardly any CAP influence. It is also impossible to examine these figures on the basis that if the CAP had not evolved, all other relevant variables would have remained unchanged. The changed relationship between Algeria and France is clearly a matter of major importance in influencing the pattern of trade in wine.

TABLE 8 Exports of selected agricultural products from Mediterranean countries circa 1971 (000 US $)

Country	*Total exports*	*Total exports to EEC*	*Food, beverages*	*Fruit and vegetables*	*Citrus*	*Tomatoes*	*Olive oil*	*Alcoholic beverages*	*Tobacco*
Algeria, 1969	933,893	713,519	359,351	–	24,462	2,127	3,797	133,859	–
Greece, 1971	662,475	319,470	273,937	136,901	21,555	–	3,105	19,361	86,651
Israel, 1971	959,914	258,045	204,549	182,322	114,350	–	–	–	–
Morocco, 1970	488,020	–	246,870	182,971	–	–	–	9,849	–
Portugal, 1971	1,032,604	199,808	182,304	51,260	–	–	8,859	75,783	–
Spain, 1971	2,937,782	1,091,156	728,095	460,636	154,096	36,607	142,938	89,481	–
Tunisia, 1970	182,469	115,783	37,990	15,385	3,812	–	16,508	9,093	–
Italy	13,110,628	6,749,146	1,287,553	722,480	59,715	–	–	224,707	–
France	20,420,028	10,096,168	3,452,590	338,830	–	–	–	598,136	–

Source: UN Yearbook of International Trade Statistics 1970–1, New York, 1973.

TABLE 9 Degree of self-sufficiency in the EEC of Six (percentage)

	1958/9	*1966/7*	*1971/2*
Fruit			87
Fresh fruit (including preserves and fruit juice)	86	81	
Citrus fruit			52
Vegetables	104	103	100
Wine	95	92	95

Sources: 1958/9 and 1966/7, *The Community Ten Years On*; and 1971/2, Statistical Office of the European Communities (SOEC), European Agriculture in Figures; *Newsletter of the CAP*, January 1974.

TABLE 10 Production of wine, fruit and vegetables in the Community of Six, 1968–72

	1968	*1969*	*1970*	*1971*	*1972 (provisional)*
Wine (000 hectolitres)		128,270	154,194	132,954	128,567
Fruit (000 tonnes)	15,407	15,588	15,954	15,617	14,149
Vegetables (000 tonnes)	19,569	20,429	20,919	20,421	19,590

Sources: Statistical Office of the European Communities; *Newsletter of the CAP*, January 1974.

The same data tend to suggest that the benefits to Italy from the CAP, in terms of preference against imports from non-members, have been small. Again, it is important to recognise that the policy has in the last year been strengthened and that, in its absence, Italy might have found even greater difficulty in selling its produce to fellow members.

In fact, the proportion of trade in fruit and vegetables accounted for by intra-Community trade was higher in 1960 than for agricultural trade as a whole, 32 per cent of imports and 34 per cent of exports, compared with 18 per cent and 46 per cent for agricultural trade as a whole. Intra-Community trade has grown for both categories of goods (see Table 11),

TABLE 11 EEC imports and exports of agricultural goods, 1960–71
(million u.a.)

	Imports				Exports			
	1960	*1965*	*1970*	*1971*	*1960*	*1965*	*1970*	*1971*
All agricultural products	10,046	13,911	14,051	20,818	3,873	6,144	10,215	11,918
Of which intra EEC	1,785	3,344	6,516	7,791	1,775	3,337	6,531	7,794
% Intra	17.8	24·1	34·2	37·4	45·7	54·4	64·0	65·4
Fruit and vegetables	1,282	2,136	2,786	3,113	747	1,186	1,627	1,812
Of which intra EEC	414	779	1149	1329	404	750	1109	1269
% Intra	32·3	36·5	41·0	42·0	54·3	63·3	68·1	70·0

Source: OECD, *Agricultural Policy Reports, 1974*; the European Economic Community.

but the rate of increase has been rather less for fruit and vegetables than for agricultural goods as a whole.

4. The Problems Posed by the CAP for the Community's Relations with Mediterranean Countries

The Community's relationships with its southern neighbours have been typified by a growing number of specific arrangements. Each country has, until recently, come to some arrangement peculiar to itself. One common feature has been that agricultural trade has been subjected to a different approach from industrial trade.

In 1973, a new global approach was initiated. Apart from moves towards liberating industrial trade and providing economic and technical co-operation, tariff concessions were offered on agricultural goods, provided that steps were taken to ensure the smooth running of these markets. In effect, this means that cuts in the CET are offered provided that goods are offered only at the reference price. The cuts in tariff differed among countries – for example, 80 per cent for citrus from Maghreb countries and only 60 per cent from Israel and Spain. Again the time table for tariff reductions differs; for tomatoes, for example, Spain is offered a 60 per cent cut from 1 December to 31 March, while the same cut is offered to Maghreb countries from 1 November to 14 May. So far as wine is concerned, no concessions have been offered on blending imported wine with wines of Community origin, a major issue for producers of Algerian wine. Wines from Algeria, Morocco and Tunisia can enter without quota at a 75 per cent reduction in the CET, but wine from Spain is subjected to a quota to qualify for the reduction in tariff.

These proposals raise some specific problems, of which four may be mentioned briefly:

(*i*) The ban on blending wine imported into the Community with Community-produced wine is a major limitation on the value of the offer to Algeria. The Commission had suggested that the requirement to sell only at the reference price be suspended for five years to give the Algerian economy time to adjust. This proposal was rejected by the Council of Ministers.

(*ii*) The situation so far as olive oil is concerned has been much affected by the imposition of an export tax on sales from Spain. This came about in a situation of high prices associated with a partial failure of the Community crop. Spain provides about half the EEC requirements, some 60,000 out of 130,000 tons. The export tax is so arranged as to bear more heavily on bulk unrefined oil than oil in bottles. In effect, this damages the firms processing oil in the Community, especially in Italy. In these circumstances, the Italian government is unwilling to make any concessions in favour of Spain until this system has been changed.

(*iii*) The differing rates of concession offered to various Mediterranean countries are likely to prove a continuing source of disagreement. Israel and Spain feel that they should be accorded parity of treatment with North African countries. The value of concessions on tariff rate offered to any one country is substantially reduced if more generous concessions are offered to its competitors.

(*iv*) The offer of concessions on tariff rates to countries in the Mediterranean area is a matter of concern to all other countries producing similar types of goods. In effect, the Community appears to be creating a preferential trade area around itself. Several objections may be made to this. Third-country exporters – say, of citrus fruit – will find that their terms of access to the Community market, which absorbed 61 per cent of world imports in 1970, are less favourable. A system that allows Mediterranean countries to export to the Community, provided that they charge the reference price, allows them, in effect, to keep the levy. Other countries find that the levy on their imports goes to the Community's coffers. The whole concept of preferential trading groups is alien to the concept of GATT; it might be conceived as a step in the direction of the regionalisation of trade.

At a more fundamental level, the difficulties associated with agricultural trade stem from the underlying assumptions of the CAP. Four points must be made.

First, the general tenor of the Community's offers is to suggest that free trade should exist between the Mediterranean countries and itself. This is unattainable for agriculture. Internally, the CAP manipulates price levels according to politically determined criteria. The internal pattern of trade is thus not one in which the least-cost product replaces high-cost production, but one in which it first replaces lower-cost imports and then adds to Community stocks as it is purchased at intervention. If any other country were granted free access to the Community's market for products regulated in this way, the price level there would have to rise to Community levels, minus the cost of transport, and any excess of production over consumption would have to be purchased by the Community's market authorities. If this were not done, the prices deemed to be right by the Council of Ministers could not be maintained. The lesson is clear that if the Community really wishes to allow market forces to operate in the manner implicit in free trade, whether internally or with a small or large group of outside countries, it must be prepared to allow the price at which transactions occur to vary.

Second, the CAP as it stands represents a complicated and delicately balanced economic and political deal among members. Because it is a policy about prices, it is a policy that relates to commodities. Concessions about particular commodities must then affect this balance. Because Italy is a Mediterranean country, arrangements that increase the flow of competing fruit, vegetables, wine and so on reduce Italy's gains from membership of the Market. If this is offset by paying premiums for Italian production, then the true benefit of any concessions offered to the Mediterranean countries will be diminished. If it is not offset, the Italian negotiators might reasonably argue that the concessions given represent a loss to Italy on its main agricultural exports. Such a loss to Italy through pursuit of a policy determined by Community interests could be compensated by concessions on other products which Italy imports. In other words, if the preference accorded to fruit and vegetables falls, then so too should that given to cereals, meat and milk. Any other solution would destroy the basis of the deal with other members of the Community represented by the CAP.

Third, a major reason for the existence of the CAP is the social and political discomfort implicit in the adjustment problem of agriculture within the Community. A greater readiness to allow imports, entailed by any realistic concessions to the Mediterranean countries, would increase this need for adjustment. The Community's approach to adjustment difficulties has been first to maintain prices and second to give modest support to assist structural reform. From the viewpoint of present or potential exporters of farm products to the Community, this is a discouraging combination. It means that resources are being organised in farming within the Community on a basis that provides an acceptable living standard for the farmer only so long as these prices are maintained. In the short term, such a policy means that structural reform adds to output. In the long term, it makes any reduction in price more difficult. So long as third countries, with or without concessions on tariffs, are treated as residual suppliers, their prospects under the CAP must be poor.

Fourth, the offer of concessions on the CET element may be of little real significance. The CAP works in such a way that if the Community is over-supplied from its own production, the internal price level will fall below the reference price before intervention purchase occurs. Those outside who have to sell at reference price will be unable to penetrate the market. In conditions of under-supply, prices are likely to rise quite sharply where the demand for the agricultural products concerned is inelastic. They may well in such circumstances exceed not only reference level but also reference level plus the CET duty. At such prices, countries without concessions will also be able to sell to the Community. The range of prices over which an abatement of the CET would prove valuable may thus be traversed relatively quickly.

This analysis of problems posed by the CAP for relations with countries in the Mediterranean area reveals that much more than minor technical adjustments would be needed to make satisfactory arrangements possible. In essence, so long as prices are fixed to secure political and social goals and without real regard for the cost at which goods might be available from non-Community sources, the prospects for agreements which offer substantial benefits to agricultural exporters are poor.

It is, clearly, unlikely that a Community that has given such low priority to the misfortunes which its agricultural policies might cause to third-country agricultural exporters will suddenly mend its ways. Reform of the CAP is not likely to emerge as a result of a desire to improve trade alone, even with countries in the Mediterranean area. However, the CAP does not meet adequately the internal needs of the Community, and changes will take place. It would be reasonable to argue that when such changes are discussed, the claims other countries, and especially those with which the Community hopes to build closer relationships, should be more sympathetically considered.

6

Migrant Labour and Economic Growth: the Post-war Experience of the EEC Countries

GEORGE N. YANNOPOULOS

1. Introduction

For the past two decades all the countries of the enlarged European Communities with the exception of Italy and Ireland have relied either constantly or for most of the time on immigrant workers to reduce an almost continuous imbalance between domestic demand for and supply of labour. With the exception of the United Kingdom, the overwhelming majority of migrant workers in the EEC countries with a persistent labour shortage originated from Italy and the non-EEC countries of the Mediterranean basin. Indeed, from the early sixties the non-member countries of the Mediterranean area have become the major suppliers of migrant labour to the five European Economic Community countries (Germany, France and the three Benelux countries) with chronic labour shortages. Thus, although in 1957 52·3 per cent of all work permits granted for the first time to foreign workers in the original six EEC countries were to migrants from other EEC countries, in 1962 57·6 per cent of these work permits were granted to foreign workers from third countries essentially of the Mediterranean area. Since that year, immigration into the EEC from these countries has been growing in importance (Yannopoulos, 1969). This paper examines how far employment of foreign labour from the Mediterranean area has produced on balance economic benefits or costs for the host country.[1] As such, therefore, the paper approaches the problem of evaluating these costs and benefits from the standpoint of a 'nationalist' model rather than adopting an 'internationalist' model and the 'cosmopolitan' view on migration that goes with it. From the 'cosmopolitan' viewpoint, the welfare effects of international labour movements should be judged by comparing gains (or losses) to the nationals of the host country plus the private gains of the immigrant workers to the losses (or gains) to the remaining population of the country of emigration. In the framework of the 'nationalist' model, one concentrates

1 Host countries examined include: Germany, France, the Netherlands, Belgium and Luxembourg.

exclusively either on the country of emigration or on the country of immigration without having to postulate (as it should be necessary in case a 'world' or 'cosmopolitan' approach is adopted) a 'world social welfare function' (Johnson, 1968; Patinkin, 1968).

The paper starts by developing a theoretical framework for the analysis of the economic effects of immigration. This section is built upon the findings of previous studies and in its general approach is very much akin to the analytical framework introduced by G. M. A. MacDougall (1960) in his study of the benefits and costs of foreign direct investment. A question examined in this section is the possible complementarity between migrant labour and foreign direct investment. This possibility has not been investigated carefully in the migration literature so far. The following two sections examine the immigration policies of the EEC countries (excluding the three new members) in order to ascertain how far the post-war immigration into Europe was of the 'organised' and 'selective' variety as opposed to the 'spontaneous' type. The fourth section sets out to examine the most important characteristics (skills composition, family status and so on) of the migrant labour force from the Mediterranean area. Finally, the fifth section reviews available evidence relating to some of the points raised in the theoretical framework.

2. The Cost and Benefits of Immigration from the Point of View of the Host Country: an Analytical Framework

As a hypothesis, a simple framework is used; it is of the traditional variety, of perfect competition, constant returns to scale, single output similar to that developed by Berry and Saligo (1969) in their analysis of the effects of migration on the sending country. We further assume initially that there are no external effects, that the size of the capital stock is unaffected by changes in the size of the labour force and that immigration does not affect either the balance of payments directly or the terms of trade. The criterion that can then be adopted to evaluate the extent to which labour migration will be beneficial, from the point of view of the native population of the host country, is that real national produce plus the flow of services derived from additions to the public consumption goods, which increased revenues from taxation make possible, should increase by more than the share of immigrants in both the real national income and their use of public consumption goods. Disregarding the government sector for the moment, it is evident by inspecting fig. 1 that on the basis of the above criterion immigration will be beneficial to the native population of the host country. The line *MN*

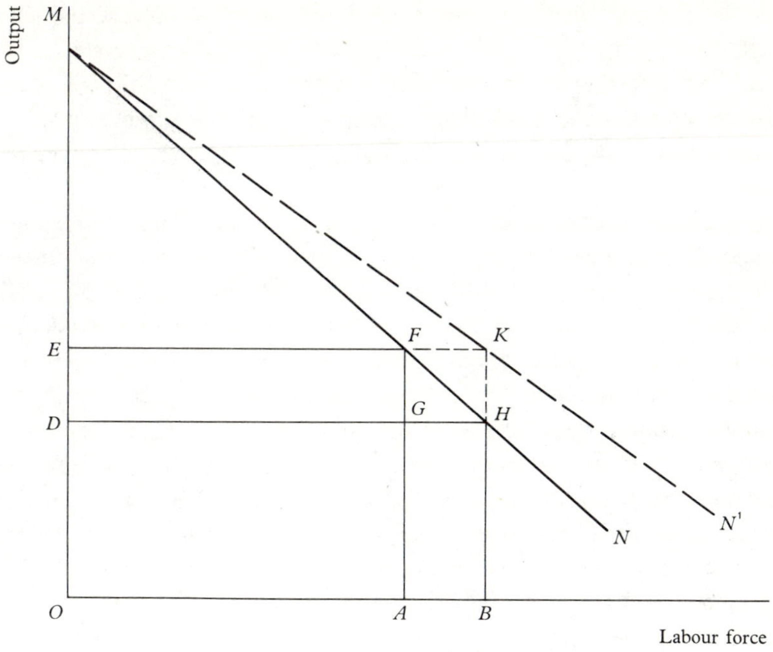

Fig. 1

indicates the marginal physical produce of labour line. The labour force before immigration was *OA*, and it was employed at a wage rate *OE* (assuming that *MN* is the marginal physical produce line corresponding to full employment). Immigration adds *AB* to the labour force and *FHBA* to the real national product. The immigrant population, however, receives only *GHBA*, whereas the rest of the real output *FHG* is appropriated by native capitalists. Thus the total real income of the native population increases by the area *FHG*. This area may further increase if foreign workers are subject to wage discrimination in the labour market. In that case, immigrant workers will be paid a wage rate below the value of labour's marginal physical produce, and thus the income accruing to the native population from the expansion of output will increase. It is obvious that immigration brings about a redistribution of income in favour of the host country's capitalists. The government, if it so wishes, can use its taxation policy to redistribute the total benefits area *FHG* between the host country's workers and capitalists. It is worth emphasising that it is here assumed that immigrant workers come to the country without any capital stock and consequently, because the whole of the capital stock is owned by the native population of the host country, the immigrant community will not be in a position to share the real product represented by the area *FHG*.

By introducing the government sector now, the results may have to be modified to the extent to which the immigrants' consumption of collective goods provided by the government exceed the additional revenues that the government collects following the increase in the host country's real income. It is conceivable that the government's tax revenues may increase by a faster rate than the expansion of the real national income, especially if the capitalists' income increases at a faster rate than the overall rate of increase of the national product. However, the appropriate comparison should be between the extra tax revenues derived from the income of the immigrant community, *GHBA*, to the extra resources needed to provide the additional public consumption goods (hospitals, schools, roads and so on) demanded by the immigrant labourers (*AB*) and their dependents. This will depend on the migrants' age structure, family situation, quality of the public services they demand, state of economies of scale in the use of road services and similar public facilities and so on. Many public facilities can be used equally efficiently in serving either small or large populations. However, if migrant workers tend to concentrate in already congested areas, the pressure on public services and investment will be higher. Another factor relevant here is to examine the need for public housing that the influx of migrant workers may generate. In view of the family situation of these migrants and given the demographic characteristics and the temporary nature of the stay of most of them, it is unlikely that the needs of the immigrant community in social overhead capital will be higher than the corresponding needs of the native households. Moreover, migrants are known to be prepared to tolerate housing standards lower than the average for the native population. The comparison here should be between the immigrants' demand for public services and social overhead capital provided through the government (either directly or indirectly through subsidisation) and the tax revenues raised from the migrant workers' incomes and consumption, with appropriate adjustments both for the demand for services and the extra revenue as a result of migration-induced increases in the income of the native population. Government revenue for taxation will change through both direct and indirect taxes. As to direct taxes, the changes resulting from the expansion induced through the additional migrant labour force will be equal to the taxable wages or salaries of foreign workers multiplied by the average tax rate plus the immigration-induced changes in the wages or salaries and the non-wage income of the native population multiplied at the appropriate marginal tax rates for these two income categories.

If the balance between changes in public revenues as specified above and the additional public expenditure for the provision of collective services specifically affected by the presence of immigrants is positive, then the resulting benefit will be shown either as an improvement in the level of public services available to the native population or as a reduction in the level of taxation.

Up to this point the effects of immigration on the total real income received by the native population have been examined. What will be the effect on real incomes *per capita*? It is obvious from fig. 1 that, because an extra amount of *FHG* is added to the total real income of the native population although the size of this population remains constant, the income per head of the native population will rise. The extent to which this rise in income *per capita* will be accompanied by increasing inequalities in the size distribution of income depends, of course, on how the ownership of the host country's capital stock is spread throughout the native population. Even if native workers own no capital, it does not follow that the real incomes *per capita* of the non-capitalist group of the native population will necessarily decline. Redistribution through the government taxation and public expenditure system may result in the transfer of most of the post-migration increase in the income of the native capitalists to the native workers. Redistribution in the same direction may also occur through trade-union action; increases in profits may make employers less reluctant to withstand pressures for wage increases by unionised labour. If through all these redistribution mechanisms the income represented by the area *DEFG* is transferred to the native workers, their incomes can be restored to the pre-immigration position.

If now employment income per native worker is considered in terms of average annual income expected over the period of the trade cycle, then native workers in countries pursuing migration policies involving the use of non-permanent migrant labour can obtain a higher average income over the cycle by shifting the burden of cyclical unemployment on to the migrant workers. There is some evidence (reviewed in section 5) that migrant labour was performing this 'buffer function' in a number of European countries. Foreign workers tend to concentrate in industries with above-average cyclical sensitivity. Furthermore, they can be 'removed' from the national unemployment total by being refused renewal of expired labour permits (with the loss of residence permit that it often entails) or by reducing the tempo of recruitment and thus deliberately failing to replace returnees.

It is sometimes argued that, apart from the effects of immigration on the material income *per capita* of the native population, there may also be an increase in what is referred to as 'psychic income' enjoyed by the native population. The source of this increase in 'psychic income' comes from the performing by migrant labourers of jobs that the native population is not prepared to take up. However, this additional 'psychic income' will be enjoyed by a small section of the native population only – namely, those who would have been forced to take up these jobs in the absence of migrant workers. This increment may not be enough to compensate the negative 'psychic' income of another section of the population, that derives displeasure from the semi-permanent presence in the community of clannish foreigners who insist on preserving their own habits, customs and language.

It is noteworthy that, irrespective of what happens to the income per head of the native population, the income per head of the combined native plus immigrant population – that is, the real national income *per capita* – will fall, because the average income per migrant will be less than the *per capita* income of the native population before migration. But the extent of this fall will depend on the activity rates of the two populations (native and migrants). The higher labour force to population ratio of the migrant community will ensure that this fall will not be proportional to the decline in the wage rate.

The above conclusions regarding the effects on immigration on real incomes *per capita* depend crucially on the nature of the model so far employed. By dropping the assumption of an one-commodity output and introducing instead a general equilibrium framework of analysis, it can easily be shown (Johnson, 1967) that, as long as products differ in their factor intensities, any increase in the labour resources available does not necessarily lead to a fall in the capital–labour ratio and hence in the wage rate. Given the terms of trade with which the country is faced, movements in factor prices can be avoided through the absorption of the increased labour resources by means of changes in the proportions in which products of different factor intensities are produced, provided that such changes do not bring the overall ratio of capital to labour in the host country outside the range consistent with the maintenance of the pre-immigration factor–price ratio.

If, further, the assumption of constant returns to scale is dropped, it is evident that a possibility emerges of price effects which affect real incomes even if money incomes *per capita* are kept constant. These price effects of immigration will stem from the differential rates of increase in the demand for the products of the various industries following the increase in aggregate income that the additional labour resources bring about (Corden, 1955). If this extra demand is directed towards products produced under increasing returns to scale, then their prices will tend to fall and thereby raise real incomes. The opposite will be true if the products of the industries which absorb the increase in aggregate expenditure are produced under diminishing returns. The results of the analysis may be further affected if the assumption is removed that migrant labour is homogeneous to the native labour. Supposing that the native labour force is subdivided into two separate compartments one consisting of low-wage labour (L_1) and the other of high wage labour (L_2), a further assumption may be made that migrant labour is primarily of the L_1 variety. Then, under these circumstances, the influx of migrant labour of the L_1 type will tend in fact to increase the ratio of aggregate capital to labour as if 'by diluting the quality of labour relative to the capital stock' (Epstein, 1973). This will then encourage a substitution of capital for both L_1 and L_2. So, although there will be a tendency for the wage rate of the sector where the immigrants enter (L_1) to fall, the substitution of capital for both L_1 and L_2 will produce an opposite effect – namely, a tendency for the wage ratio of both sectors to rise. The result will be that the wage rate in the labour market sector L_2 will definitely rise, whereas the wages of the sector with migrant labour will be subject to two opposing tendencies with the result indeterminate. Only if the two types of labour are more highly substitutable than are capital and labour of the L_2 sector will the wage rate of the sector where migrants are predominantly found rise definitely (Epstein, 1973). If this materialises, then it is clear that immigration may in fact bring about a redistribution of income in the opposite direction from the one shown in the original model where homogeneity was assumed between migrant and native labour.

However, perhaps the most restrictive assumption of the simple model so far employed is that maintaining that the size of the capital stock will not be affected by changes in the size of the labour force. This assumption is particularly restrictive especially in analysing the European experience, because immigration there has been taking place in a climate of rising business expectations and its initial function was to provide for the labour needs of an expanding economy. The economic climate into which the immigration is injected is a crucial factor in determining whether immigration acts as an expansionary force in the economy (Karmel, 1963). Increases in the labour endowments in the European countries of immigration were accompanying increases in the capital endowment; it was not simply a question of additional labour resources used in combination with a given capital stock. After all, politically one cannot expect a country to accept large numbers of immigrants in periods of low investment activity and unemployment. But, as it will be argued below, immigration has stimulated further growth in Europe through a variety of mechanisms, some of which are general and others specific to the post-war European environment.

The relationship between immigration and investment was first pointed out by B. Thomas (1973, chapter 10) in his celebrated work on North American immigration in the nineteenth century. He found that what he called the strategic component of investment in the US (that is, investment in construction, railways and so on) lagged regularly behind immigration during each of the periods of major European population movements into the US and that there was a switch in the order of lag each time a particular immigration wave was over, lasting until the next big emigration wave from Europe. However, as it is argued below, the impact of the post-war European immigration on investment has worked out through a different mechanism than by merely stimulating population-sensitive investment, as was the case in the USA in the nineteenth century. The main impact on capital stock formation in Europe has come through the effects of immigration on foreign direct investment. This point is further discussed below after explaining in detail all possible ways through which immigration may stimulate investment.

Let us now remove the assumption of a fixed capital stock from our earlier simple model. Indeed, in a dynamic analysis, the influx of migrant workers will affect the overall level of investment in three ways. First of all, immigration is likely to react favourably on business expectations, particularly if the expanding population implies also an expanding domestic market. Secondly, because the capitalists' propensity to save will be higher than the workers' propensity to save, a shift in the distribution of income is bound to increase the host country's savings ratio and therefore its rate of growth. A further increase in the national savings ratio (that is, the savings ratio of the combined native and immigrant population) may also be produced if the propensity to save of the migrant population is higher than the marginal propensities to save of native wage earners (with proper allowance for the remittances to their home country). Such a possibility should not be excluded given the attitudes of migrant workers and their often-noted strong desire to hold wealth. This will be one way through which immigration may influence the rate of domestic investment. But equally one can establish that the level of foreign direct investment in the host country may increase. This will happen if immigration into a given country tends to reduce the labour shortage in the non-traded goods sector to the extent that it slows down any increases of (or induces decreases in) the host country's prices of non-traded goods at a rate lower (higher) than the trends in the prices of non-traded goods in other countries.

Assuming that there are two countries with identical ratios of the prices of non-traded to traded goods and which experience the same labour shortage in the market for jobs for their non-traded goods sector; it is further supposed that immigrant workers enter and take up jobs in industries producing non-traded goods in the first country. The excess demand in the market for jobs in non-traded goods industries will thus be sufficiently reduced in the first country to allow for constant or very slowly rising prices for its non-traded goods. This, of course, presupposes that the presence of foreign workers will exert a downwards pressure on money wage levels. The empirical validity of this hypothesis will be examined later. The second country, where no immigrant labour takes up jobs, will experience a faster rate of increase in its prices of non-traded goods. Thus its ratio of the prices of non-traded goods to the prices of traded goods will exceed that of the first country. International factor mobility is often influenced by existing world differences in the ratios of the prices of traded to non-traded goods, because the price of the latter cannot possibly be equalised through commodity trade. As Hufbauer (1974, page 274) points out, 'multinational enterprises bid up cheap electricity, office buildings and labour wherever they are available'.

If in the initial position the ratios of the prices of non-traded to traded goods in the two countries were identical, the country that experiences a large influx of migrant labour into its non-traded goods sector will now have a higher ratio of traded goods prices to non-traded goods prices. Such a situation will encourage international firms to service the market of the host country from within, because such firms are particularly suited to take advantage in the existing inter-country differences in the price ratios of traded to non-traded goods. Assuming that multinational firms are in a position to exploit such differences, the initial flow of migrant labour will then be accompanied by subsequent foreign direct investment flows.

Whatever the cause of investment expansion, its ultimate impact will be to increase the capital labour ratio and hence to shift in fig. 1 the marginal physical product of labour line to MN^1. If this shift approximately coincides with the influx of migrant labour represented by the distance *AB*, then the whole increment in the host country's labour supply can be absorbed at the pre-migration wage rate *OE*. Real national income increases by *MKBAF*, but this increment is distributed between the native capitalists (*MKF*) and the immigrant community (*FKBA*). Because the area *MKF* is an addition to the pre-migration income of the native population, it follows that the native population is now better off after the immigration and the investment accompanying it.

Again, it is likely that the native labour force may gain as a result of a redistribution from native capitalists, through the progressive income tax system.

However, some adjustments to the above results must be made if the shift in the labour's marginal physical product curve is caused partly by foreign direct investment. In that case, if it is assumed that the proportion of foreign to domestic investment is p and the tax rate on foreign profits t, then the foreign capitalists will receive an income of $p(1-t)$ *MKF*, and consequently the income of domestic capitalists and of the total domestic population will be less than what it would have been if the expansion of the capital stock was undertaken by domestic capitalists. The increase in the income of the domestic population will be in that case $(1-p+t)$*MKF*. It can be concluded, therefore, that the benefits to the native population of the host country are likely to increase further if one relaxes the assumption that the size of the capital stock is independent of the size of the labour force and that there will still be net benefits to the domestic population even if one assumes that the increase in the capital stock takes place through foreign direct investment.

The relationship between labour migration and foreign direct investment established in the preceding paragraphs has further implications to those already elucidated by references to fig. 1. For foreign direct investment consists of a package of income generating assets of which technology and managerial know-how are important components. Thus the transplantation of superior technical and managerial knowledge which takes place through direct international investment has important implications in the further promotion of the economic growth of the host country. This point is particularly important, as one of the alleged adverse effects of immigration on growth is the slowing down of the pace of technical progress that would have taken place otherwise in conditions of acute labour shortages. The view that technical progress advances rapidly in periods of labour shortages gives thus a rather one-sided view of the relationship between technical progress and immigration. Other authors (Peston, 1969) emphasised additional favourable aspects of this relationship. The structure of immigration and, in particular, its skill composition is very important in this context. Immigration may add not only to the labour supply but also to the stock of human capital available in the country through the entry of skilled and professional manpower trained abroad (B. Thomas, 1973, Chapter 17). Migrant labour may be conceived in many cases as a factor complementary (rather than substitutable) to a host of sophisticated machinery embodying the latest technology. Often the case is that these machines must be operated in continuous shifts or generally in unpleasant surroundings. The drive for higher productivity may also require frequent shuffling about from one task to another. In all these cases there will be strong complementarity between migrant labour and technologically advanced machinery and thus immigration, far from being a hindrance to technological progress, may actually positively encourage the absorption of some of the more advanced techniques. Writing about the experience of Boston with Irish migrants, Handlin (1941) observed that 'no matter what degree of standardisation the technical process of manufacturing reached, the absence of a cheap labour supply precluded conversion to factory methods' (page 81). As an instance he cites the introduction of Howe's sewing machine (mid-nineteenth century), which was adopted on a large scale in the Boston area only after the influx of Irish immigrants.

The tempo of introducing labour-saving innovations is often slowed down not because of the existence of surplus labour but as a result of management efforts to buy up peace in industrial relations (Mishan and Needleman, 1968). Immigrant labour is highly unlikely to show resistance to the introduction of new machinery as is the case with organised, indigenous labour. Management may also find that the increase of automation in a given process may lead to the creation of more routine jobs, more repetitive, mechanical, low-status tasks (Power, 1973) which native workers, particularly in Europe, do not wish to undertake. In such cases, immigration and automation are complementary, not mutually exclusive.

However, there may be cases where such complementarity can not be established. In such cases, continuous recruitment of foreign labour may delay needed structural changes in the economy or prolong the life of existing capital goods. The case of textiles, where a substantial proportion of migrant unskilled labour is used, is often mentioned in this context. In terms of the international division of labour, migration by changing the ratios of unskilled labour to skilled labour and unskilled labour to capital among countries will tend to improve the locational advantages of countries where the ratios of indigenous unskilled labour to skilled labour and indigenous unskilled labour to capital are relatively small as places for establishing unskilled labour-intensive processes. The need for structural adaptation must then be judged on the basis of the new skill composition of the post-migration labour force. Earlier in this paper it was pointed out that certain types of migratory flows (for example, workers accompanied by their families) may result in a demand for social services in excess of the corresponding tax revenues of the government. With the quality of the public services maintained at its pre-migration level, a budgetary deficit will develop. In this case immigration will be associated with an expenditure multiplier larger than the corresponding output multiplier. This inflationary effect (which will be produced if there is no under-utilised capacity in the economy) may in fact counterbalance the initial effect of immigration in reducing the pressure of the demand in the labour market, and in certain instances it can produce an increase in the overall shortage in the labour market. This will further lead to an increase in money wages and consumer prices and to a reduction in the real disposable wage income per head of the native population. Disposable non-wage income will also be adversely affected, with a further repercussion on the volume of domestic industrial investment. These potential inflationary effects should not be considered in isolation from some other developments that will produce opposite effects. Migrant labour through its concentration in jobs in the public services sector will contribute to a slowdown in the rate of the costs of such services (Peston, 1971). Transfer to the host country of the migrant worker's family may coincide with the needs of the labour market for female workers (Nikolinakos, 1972, page 82). International migration acts as a substitute to interregional migration; it thus tends to reduce interregional differences in labour market shortages. Under these conditions, the national unemployment–wage relationship will tend to change, reducing, in effect, the national demand pressure (Archibald, 1969). The flexibility of migrant workers with regard to working conditions makes it possible to raise the number of hours worked and thus take off part of any developing labour market shortage. Immigrant workers tend also to be more mobile, as a larger proportion of them consists of young males. However, Mishan and Needleman (1968) argued that immigration does not necessarily remove bottlenecks from certain sectors, because a preponderance of migrant workers in such sectors transforms their occupations in the eyes of the native workers into inferior ones, thereby reducing the supply of native labourers to these sectors.

The impact of immigration on the average level of prices cannot be discussed without reference to an important type of dualism that characterises labour markets in advanced industrial countries. The important distinction here is between industries with a below-average rate of technical progress and productivity growth containing the majority of poorly paid jobs (B sector) and industries with an above-average rate of technical progress and productivity growth containing the majority of the better-paid jobs (A sector) (Lutz, 1963). The attractiveness of A-sector employment will induce workers to move from B-sector jobs to A-sector jobs. But the resulting shortage of labour in B sector may not necessarily eliminate the wage-rate differentials. Without changes in the relative wages, it will not be possible to bring about a balance between the demand for and supply of labour in the two sectors. The required change in the relative wage rates does not come about, either because negotiated wage rates may be regulated in practice on the basis of the sector's rate of productivity growth or because trades unions in sector A may explicitly pursue a policy of maintaining wage-rate differentials. In this last case, any attempt to raise the level of B-sector wages in such a way as to make its relative wage more favourable will simply be thwarted through the reaction of A-sector trade unions. Such a reaction will, furthermore, have the effect of raising money wages and the absolute level of prices all around with the unavoidable inflationary effects. Now, under such circumstances sector B will suffer from a serious chronic labour shortage, and any effort to remove this shortage through relative wage adjustment will prove in many cases unsuccessful and additionally a source of inflationary pressure in the economy. An analysis of the industrial distribution of the Swiss immigration (Lutz, 1963) had shown that most immigrants tended to occupy B-sector jobs: jobs in the textile and clothing industries, the hotel and catering trades and domestic services. Immigration acts, then, as a mechanism that corrects labour market distortions and particularly the persisting structural maladjustments between native labour supplies and the needs of the economy for unskilled, B-type labourers (Sauvy, 1948). By postponing the need for relative wage adjustments, the immigration process described above tends to reduce the risk of the inflationary effects that such adjustments may generate.

Before examining the empirical evidence bearing on these issues it will be convenient to remove some of the remaining restrictive assumptions placed earlier on the present analysis. One of these restrictive assumptions that has already been shown to be unrealistic is the assumption that immigration does not affect the balance of payments. The possibility already mentioned of foreign direct investment flows induced by the presence of migrant labour is one way through which the balance of payments will be affected. Immigrant remittances will also exert an influence, albeit in the opposite direction. Presumably, remittances tend to be larger in the cases of migrants unaccompanied by their families. The longer the period of stay of migrant workers, the lower will be the proportion of income remitted (Kindleberger, 1965).

The final impact of the capital flows induced by the favourable ratio of the prices of non-traded to traded goods will depend on the extent to which the investment undertaken is not of the 'export-discouraging' or 'import-creating' variety. The ultimate effect of the remittances on the balance of payments must be judged in conjunction to the contribution that such remittances make to reducing the foreign exchange constraint of the countries of emigration. By alleviating such constraints, remittances contribute to the growth in the international purchasing power of the sending countries, and thus may ultimately produce a beneficial feedback effect on the country of immigration through increased demand for the latter's exports.

The effects of immigration on the trade balance can be studied by means of the 'income' and 'price' effects generated by the inflow of migrant labour (Corden, 1955). The income effects stem from the increase in the aggregate expenditure which a larger labour force makes possible. The effect of higher level of aggregate expenditure on imports will depend on how the increment is divided between investment and consumption and on the import content of (*a*) marginal consumption and (*b*) marginal investment.

The 'price' effects of immigration can stem either from the impact on the general level of prices which the increased population may have or from a biased change in the production of importables and exportables, given the relative factor proportions in these two sectors.

To the extent to which immigration may increase rather than reduce demand pressure (that is, when the expenditure multiplier is larger than the output multiplier associated with immigration), inflationary price rises will adversely affect the overall position of the balance of trade of the country, assuming reasonable values for the elasticities of the demand for exports. If, however, the pre-immigration pressure of home demand is effectively reduced, then the relative competitiveness of the receiving country's exports will be improved and the possibilities for import substitution will be increased. There is some evidence (Centraal Planbureau, The Netherlands,

1972) which suggests that the main factor that differentiates between an intensification of the demand pressure or a reduction of this pressure is the extent to which immigration involves or not transfer of the migrants' families as well.

Changes in the production of exportables in response to changes in the demand generated by the increased expenditure from the employment of the migrant labour will influence the prices of exports, depending on the laws of return governing their production. If exportables are produced under increasing returns, their prices will tend to fall and, assuming an elasticity of demand for exports exceeding one, the value of exports will rise as well. If part of the increased expenditure is directed to importables and the industries producing these goods are also falling-cost industries, their prices will fall, encouraging a process of import substitution. Such primary price effects will be followed by secondary ones (Corden, 1955). For example, if domestic demand for exportables produced under increasing returns is elastic, then the fall in their prices will lead to a decrease in the expenditure on other goods, including imports. Also, when the prices of importables produced under increasing returns fall, there may be secondary repercussions on the expenditure on exportables if the latter are substitutable with the former.

All the price effects mentioned above will further exert an influence on the country's terms of trade, with the inevitable effects on real incomes (Dutta, 1973). Migration-induced terms-of-trade effects may move in either direction, depending on the laws of returns; the relative factor proportions and the income elasticities of demand for exportables and importables (Johnson, 1955).

The last assumption that it is now desirable to remove is that relating to the absence of external effects. A variety of external effects may be generated from immigration. They range from congestion and slum growth down to neighbours' annoyance at noisy gatherings. The most important of these external effects arise from the overall pressure in population densities created by the arrival of immigrants in already densely populated areas. The most striking example of this is found in the Netherlands, where about two-thirds of the labour permits granted in 1970 were to be found in the Western Holland Conurbation. In France, too, the heaviest concentration of migrant workers is to be found in the congested areas of the Paris region and of the Provence–Côte d'Azur Département.

Similar concentrations of migrant workers are also observed in Germany, where, in an effort to stop the further growth of slums in German cities, the government introduced in 1973 an outright bar on further migration to cities with an immigrant population of more than a quarter of the total.

3. The Immigration Policies of the EEC Countries

An important aspect of the immigration policies of the EEC countries that depend on foreign labour supplies has been their selectivity. Selectivity was secured primarily through a system of 'organised' immigration as opposed to a 'spontaneous' one. The basis of this organised immigration has been a series of treaties concerned with bilateral labour recruitment and employment of foreign workers between the labour-surplus countries of the Mediterranean basin and a network of recruitment agencies operating in the countries of emigration. These recruitment agencies are both governmental and private ones operated by major firms in Europe: for example, the Ford Company in Germany has its own agency in Turkey for the recruitment of migrant workers to be employed in its plants in Cologne and elsewhere. The extent to which official recruitment agencies are involved in the selection of migrants varies from country to country. Belgium, for example, does not have a system of official recruitment centres abroad, but Germany runs an extensive network of German commissions abroad which act as catalysts in matching jobs to the potential immigrants. In another respect, resort by industry to official recruiting centres abroad varies from country to country, depending on the efficiency with which these centres can meet the employers' need for labour rapidly, on the extent to which workers in the countries of emigration prefer to use parallel information channels through relatives or friends already working in the host country and also on the degree of co-operation between the authorities in the country of emigration and the recruitment centre. An Organisation for Economic Co-operation and Development (OECD) paper (OECD, 1972) estimates that the contribution of the German commissions abroad to recruitment was 26 per cent for Greeks in 1967 (65 per cent in 1968), 42 per cent for the Spaniards (73 per cent in 1968), 49 per cent for Turks (66 per cent in 1968) and 46 per cent for Portuguese (70 per cent in 1968). In France, organised migration accounted for about 22 per cent of the total in 1967, 18 per cent in 1968 and 33 per cent in 1969 (total excludes EEC workers, Algerians and nationals of French-speaking Africa and the Malagasy Republic). Another OECD report (OECD, *Review of Manpower and Social Policies*, 1967) estimates that in 1967 immigrant workers arriving in the Netherlands on their own initiative outnumbered those officially recruited by about 4 to 1. However, in subsequent years the Dutch government introduced a number of restrictions to encourage officially controlled recruitment. The desired degree of selectivity is often achieved directly through the bilateral labour recruitment agreements that most EEC countries have with the Mediterranean labour-surplus countries. The 1963 convention between Germany and Morocco on the temporary employment of Moroccan workers restricted recruitment and placement of Moroccan workers to the coal-mining sector.[2] The same was true of the earlier labour-recruitment agreements between Belgium and Spain (1956) on the one hand and Belgium and Greece (1957) on the other.

The treaties concerning migration, recruitment and placement of workers between France and several Mediterranean countries (Spain, Portugal, Morocco, Tunisia) specify upper age-limits for recruited migrant workers in agriculture, mining and other activities. In general, the foreign workers' access to employment is usually linked with the economic situation, although demographic considerations (those influencing the population structure) is sometimes – at least in the case of France – another factor shaping government policies on immigration (Bideberry, 1967). In all cases, a residence permit and an employment permit have to be obtained. In the case of Belgium, the application must always come from the employee, whereas in the case of Luxembourg the permit is issued only to the employer and not to the worker. A policy designed to meet immediate needs is usually inclined to be liberal as to entry but restrictive as to ultimate settlement. A policy the purpose of which is to influence the population structure through the integration of the foreign workers is restrictive at the time of entry. Conditions of prolongation of employment as specified in these treaties make it possible to regulate systematically the supply of foreign manpower according to the volume of unemployment. In Germany, prolongation of employment is from year to year, in Belgium for six months at a time up to two years, whereas in France renewal of employment permits is related to labour market conditions.

Another set of provisions of the various bilateral treaties on recruiting foreign labour concerns family immigration. France and Belgium adopt a liberal stand on the question of the admission of families, and they provide positive encouragements to that effect. In Germany, admission of families is not as a rule encouraged, although in three out of the seven treaties with Mediterranean countries in existence (those of Spain, Portugal and Greece), special undertakings are given to facilitate admission of the

2 This had been modified in a subsequent agreement.

migrants' families. On the other hand, in the Netherlands the existing treaties with the Mediterranean countries do not make any provisions for the admission of the families of the migrant workers; on the contrary, they specify in detail financial aids available for the return of the migrant worker at the termination of his labour contract.

4. The Dependence of the European Economies on Migrant Labour from the Mediterranean Area

The dependence of the five most northerly countries of the European Communities on migrant labour has been steadily rising since the early sixties. Between 1960 and 1971 Luxembourg's proportion of foreign workers out of its employed labour force increased from one-fifth to about one-third, Germany's from 1·4 per cent to about 10 per cent, Belgium's from about 6 per cent to 7 per cent and that of the Netherlands from slightly below 1 per cent to 2 per cent. In France, where information is available for census years only, the proportion increased from 6·9 per cent in 1962 to 7·6 per cent in 1968 (see Table 1). Thus, with the exception of Holland, the presence of a migrant labour force is by no means a marginal factor in the labour markets of a number of countries of the EEC. Indeed, for many years the inflow of migrant labour has been satisfying a high proportion of the increase in the demand for labour (see Table 2); in some years in

TABLE 1 Proportion of foreign workers in employed labour force (%)

Year	*Germany*	*Belgium*	*France*[a]	*The Netherlands*	*Luxembourg*
1960	1·4	–	–	0·8	–
1961	2·3	5·8	–	0·9	21·6
1962	2·0	5·8	6·9	1·0	22·7
1963	3·6	6·0	–	1·1	23·0
1964	4·2	6·6	–	1·5	24·9
1965	5·1	6·9	–	1·8	26·9
1966	5·7	7·0	–	2·0	27·7
1967	4·8	6·9	–	1·9	26·5
1968	4·8	6·7	7·6	2·1	26·9
1969	6·2	2·7	–	1·8	29·4
1971	9·4	7·0	–	2·0	32·1

[a]Available for census years only.
Source: EEC Commission; *La Libre circulation de la main d'œuvre et les marches du travail dans la CEE*, annual reports.

TABLE 2 Contribution of foreign labour to the annual increase in employment (%)

Year	*Germany*	*Belgium*	*France*[b]	*The Netherlands*	*Luxembourg*
1960	48·6	–	–	5·5	–
1961	48·3	4·9	–	4·3	88·2
1962	57·6	19·3	–	8·1	66·6
1963	52·9	30·2	–	16·6	100·0
1964	73·8	34·1	–	16·0	93·6
1965	431·0	11·1	13·7	23·6	72·2
1966	*a*	*a*	–	*a*	*a*
1967	3·8	*a*	–	16·1	78·0
1968	59·0	9·3	–	*a*	68·0
1969	86·0	10·1	–	19·3	70·0
1970	214·0	28·1	–	23·9	100·0

[a]Decline.
[b]Only for intercensus years (1962–8).
Source: EEC Commission, *La Libre circulation de la main d'œuvre et les marches du travail dans la CEE*, annual reports.

Germany (1965 and 1970), migrant labour far exceeded the increment in the nation's demand for labour, suggesting that migrant labour helped not only to provide for the higher labour demand but also to compensate for withdrawals from the domestic labour supply. It is also interesting to note that in periods of recession, with the number of returnees exceeding the number of new entrants the migrant labour force tends to decline.

What is now the importance of immigration from the Mediterranean non-member countries in the total migratory flows recorded in the five countries under consideration? Lack of consistent data makes it very difficult to provide comparable figures on the distribution of the stock of migrant workers by country of origin. Estimates of the World Bank (Hume, 1973) are reproduced here in Table 3. Table 4 provides information for the total number of migrant workers by major nationalities in the five countries of the original European Communities. The data do not refer to the same year, in view of the fact that for France and Belgium the latest available information refers to the year 1968. Thus, taking separately the Southern European countries of the Mediterranean basin, it can be seen that 56·5 per cent of Germany's immigrant labour, 43 per cent of France's

TABLE 3 Percentage distribution of migrant workers by country of origin[a]

Country of origin	Host country: Germany	France	Benelux	Switzerland	Total
1. Greece	12·7	1·0	2·7	0·8	5·1
2. Italy	24·8	17·9	31·2	60·7	28·1
3. Portugal	1·9	17·8	5·7	–	8·6
4. Spain	09·9	20·7	13·6	14·1	15·4
5. Turkey	15·5	0·5	8·4	1·0	6·3
6. Yugoslavia	16·5	3·0	1·5	2·7	7·5
7. Others	18·7	39·1[b]	36·9	20·7	29·1
Sum of 1 plus 3–6	56·5	43·0	31·9	18·6	42·9

[a]Based on 1969 figures.
[b]Over 25% of the workers in this group come from the Maghreb countries.
Source: Based on estimates of the World Bank *Finance and Development*, X, 1973.

TABLE 4 Foreign workers by country of origin (in thousands)

Country of emigration	Countries of immigration: Germany (1971)	France (1968)	Belgium (1968)	The Netherlands (1971)	Luxembourg (1971)
Yugoslavia	469	31	–	9	0·4
Spain	18	253	27	21	1·2[a]
Portugal	55	170	–	–	6·3
Greece	262	–	6	2	–
Turkey	424	3	8	26	–
Morocco	10	55	13	21	–
Algiers	2	242	2[b]	–	–
Tunisia	10	26	0·5[b]	–	–
Italy	405	219	70	–	11
Total EEC	524	262	99	–	27·1
Others	114	114	27	20	2·5
Total	2,169	1·254	182	100	37·5

[a]1970. [b]Estimates. [c]Excluding Surinamers and Antilleans.
Source: Germany: Amtliche Nachrichten der Bundesanstalt für Arbeit, Arbeitsstatistik, 1971; France: Census, 1968; Belgium, the Netherlands, Luxembourg: EEC Commission, *La Libre circulation de la main d'œuvre et les marches du travail dans la CEE.*

immigrant labour and 32 per cent of that in Benelux originated in 1968 from these countries. If workers from the three Maghreb countries are added, the proportions increase considerably, especially for France (raising them to 62 per cent) and the Netherlands (to 79 per cent). Similarly, the proportion of Mediterranean migrant workers including those of North African origin in Germany's total foreign labour force increases to 65 per cent. Thus, with the exception of Belgium and Luxembourg, where the major part of their migrant labour force is of intra-EEC origin, the other three countries (Germany, France and the Netherlands) draw their bulk of migrant labour from the Mediterranean countries. When migratory flows (rather than stocks of foreign labour) are examined, the increasing dependence of all five countries on Mediterranean labour is shown even more dramatically (Table 5). With Italian surplus labour rapidly drying up and with intra-EEC labour mobility failing to advance any further, the importance of migrant labour from the Mediterranean basin is constantly increasing. Thus, in 1970, 74 per cent of the total new migrant workers who moved into the EEC countries came from Mediterranean non-member countries, with Yugoslavia supplying 25 per cent of the total, Turkey 16 per cent, Portugal 13 per cent and Greece and Spain another 15 per cent together. The migratory flows from North Africa are under-estimated because, due to the privileged status of Algerian migrants in France, the National Office of Immigration (ONI) cannot record their exact numbers.

Historical ties, distance and political exigencies tend together to influence

TABLE 5 Proportion of migrant workers from the Mediterranean area in the annual flow of migrant workers in the EEC (Six)

Country of emigration	*1968*	*1969*	*1970*
Greece	7	8	7
Portugal	7	11	13
Spain	11	9	8
Turkey	13	15	16
Yugoslavia	16	24	25
North Africa[a]	–	4	5
Total: non-member Mediterranean countries	54	71	74
(Italy)	27	17	13

[a]Excluding Algeria from the French total.

Source: EEC Commission, *La Libre circulation de la main d'œuvre et les marches du travail dans la CEE.*

the direction of migratory flows from the Mediterranean area to the above five countries. Up to 1965, Germany relied primarily on Spain and Greece to supply it with the migrant labour needed. Since 1965, immigration from Greece and Spain has been reduced in importance, with immigration from Turkey and Yugoslavia (especially since 1968) growing fast. Together with Algeria, Spain and Portugal are the major suppliers of migrant labour to France. Immigration from Spain had been more important in the early sixties, whereas Portuguese immigration increased in importance in the late sixties. Indeed, of the total arrivals of foreign workers in France in 1970–1, 49·3 per cent were Portuguese and 9·2 per cent Spaniards. In the course of the sixties the number of new migrants from Morocco fell. In France, Yugoslav immigration has not acquired the importance that is has in Germany; only 5·7 per cent of the new arrivals of foreign workers in France were Yugoslavs in 1970–1.

Immigration from Spain remained of considerable importance for Belgium throughout the sixties. Migrant labour from North Africa (mainly Morocco) has acquired particular importance since 1965, whilst that from Turkey, although still important, tended to fluctuate somehow in the course of the sixties. Greek immigrants were more important in the late fifties and early sixties than they are in the middle seventies. The three Mediterranean countries that provide the major part of the annual migratory flows to the Netherlands are Turkey, Morocco and Spain. Greeks and Portuguese are also found in small numbers, with the number of Yugoslav migrants showing an upward trend.

In the late fifties it was still believed that these migratory flows would basically be of a temporary character; the need for migrant labour would vanish once the unusual conditions of the prolonged boom that followed the post-war reconstruction in Europe no longer prevailed. Experience since 1960 has clearly shown that there is no visible sign of an end to the dependence on migrant labour. Indeed, this dependence has acquired an aspect of permanency, with new hirings constantly exceeding the number of migrant workers returning home, with the exception of recession years. This picture emerges clearly from Table 6, which gives the ratio of returnees to new entrants in Germany over the period 1962–9. Here again some interesting contrasts emerge. The ratio of returnees to new entrants tends to be larger on the average for the Italians than the other three nationalities mentioned there (Greeks, Spaniards, Turks). Differences in the growth of employment opportunities between Italy and the other countries are probably basic in explaining the variations in the ratios of returnees to new entrants in Table 6. On the whole, it seems that the reference to *Gastarbeiter* to describe the position of the post-war migrant worker from the Mediterranean countries in Western Europe is not describing any longer the real state of affairs. Table 7 gives the length of stay of foreign workers from recruiting lands in West Germany. The data are based on a sample survey

TABLE 6 Ratio of returnees to new entrants, by nationality, Germany, 1962–9

Year	*Greeks*	*Spaniards*	*Turks*	*Total*
1962	0·37	0·40	n.a.	0·56
1963	0·36	0·54	0·28	0·70
1964	0·43	0·51	0·16	0·60
1965	0·55	0·57	0·26	0·55
1966	0·86	1·09	0·50	0·86
1967	4·36	5·15	2·28	3·11
1968	0·85	1·09	0·53	0·72
1969	0·22	0·42	0·20	0·41

Source: *Ausländischer Arbeitnehmer*, 1969.

TABLE 7 Length of foreign workers' stay, Germany, 1968

Year of arrival	*Recruiting lands*[a]	
	Men	*Women*
	percentages	
1960	12	2
1961	10	5
1962	10	8
1963	11	10
1964	16	14
1965	15	18
1966	11	18
1967	3	7
1968	12	18

[a]Excluding Yugoslavia.
Source: *Ausländischer Arbeitnehmer*, 1969.

conducted in the winter of 1968–9 by the Bundesanstalt für Arbeit. As this survey shows, 12 per cent of all male foreign workers and 2 per cent of all female foreign workers in Germany in 1968 had been staying in that country since 1960; almost one-third of all male migrant workers have in fact been staying in Germany for a period exceeding five years. As it was shown in section 1, it is possible that once immigration loses its temporary nature it may produce different effects on the pre-migration population of the host country.

5. Some Important Characteristics of the Migrant Labour Force in the Countries of the EEC

As the analysis of the first section made apparent, the economic impact of immigration is usually related to a number of important characteristics of the immigrant labour force and, in particular, to its industrial distribution, its skill and levels of educational attainment as well as the extent to which immigration of workers tends to be followed by the arrival at a later date of the worker's family. The importance of the first two characteristics is obvious, and that of the latter relates to the impact that immigration will tend to exert on the social services and the demand for social overhead capital.

An examination will first be made of the industrial distribution of the migrant labour force, bearing in mind the distinctions stressed in the first section. The major part of the migrant labour force in the countries under study is concentrated in a rather limited number of industries, although in all countries concerned one can find migrant workers employed in all sectors of economic activity. In Germany (see Table 8), the sectors absorbing the major proportion of foreign workers are metal production and engineering (28 per cent in 1969), building (15·5 per cent), textiles and clothing (9·5 per cent), electrical goods (8·6 per cent), private services and public services and administration (5·2 per cent each).

In terms of importance of foreign labour to particular sectors, the industries most dependent on migrant workers are the wholesale trade (21 per cent), iron and metals (17 per cent), plastic, rubber and asbestos (16 per cent), construction and related building trades (16 per cent), mining (13 per cent), leather, textiles and clothing (11 per cent), and steel, machinery and transport vehicles (10 per cent) (all figures refer to 1969). There are some interesting contrasts among the patterns of distribution by industry of workers of different nationalities. Almost half of male Yugoslav workers are employed in building (44·5 per cent), whereas almost two-fifths of male

TABLE 8 Foreign workers in Germany by industry, June 1969

Industry	%
Agriculture, forestry, fisheries	1·0
Extractive industries, energy	3·3
Metal production and engineering	28·3
Electrical goods	8·6
Chemicals	2·8
Textiles and clothing	9·5
Other manufacturing industries	13·7
Building	15·5
Commerce, banking, insurance	4·9
Private services	5·2
Transport	2·0
Public services and administration	5·2

Source: *Ausländischer Arbeitnehmer*, 1969, table 6.

workers from Greece, Spain, Turkey and Portugal are found in metal production and engineering. About one-fifth of Turkish male migrant workers are employed in building, and 14 per cent of the Portuguese in textiles and clothing. The electrical goods industries absorb 10 per cent of the Greek male migrant workers. As to female migrant workers, those of Yugoslav origin are more or less evenly spread among sectors with a relatively high concentration in the private services. Textiles and clothing and electrical goods absorb a large proportion of Greek and Turkish female workers, whereas textiles and clothing, metal production and engineering absorb almost two-fifths of Spanish and Portuguese female migrant workers. A large proportion (27 per cent) of the Greek female migrant labour is employed in metal production and engineering (Castles and Kosack, 1973).

In general, of all the foreign workers employed in Germany in June 1969, 32·8 per cent were employed in the various industries of the non-traded goods sector.[3] The percentage is likely to be higher if migrant labour of the Mediterranean area alone is considered, especially in view of such a heavy concentration of Yugoslav male workers in the building trades.

3 This sector consists here of the various service-providing activities. Admittedly, some of them (e.g., hotels and catering for tourists) do not qualify for this sector. However, some of the manufacturing activities (e.g., the brick industry, where migrant labour is employed) excluded from the above calculation should have been taken into account.

French census data on employment of immigrants by industry provide a similar lop-sided distribution but with the emphasis on slightly different sectors (Table 9). The largest concentration of immigrant employment is found in building and public works (30 per cent in 1968). Electrical goods and engineering absorb 12·4 per cent, agriculture, forestry and fisheries 8·7 per cent, and commerce 8·6 per cent. In contrast to Germany, the manufacturing industries absorb a smaller proportion of the migrant labour in France. Indeed, 53 per cent of migrant workers in 1968 were employed in France in the various industries of the non-traded goods sector. The picture does not change if one takes more up-to-date information relating to additions to the migrant labour force. In 1970, for example (Statistiques de Travail, Supplément, 1972), 53 per cent of the non-EEC migrant workers arriving in France were absorbed by the non-traded goods sector.

As in Germany, patterns of distribution by industry differ according to nationality. About 60 per cent, for example, of the Portuguese male migrant workers were employed in the building and public works sector, whereas

TABLE 9 Foreign workers in France by industry, 1968

Industry	%
Agriculture, forestry, fisheries	8·7
Extractive industries	2·8
Building and public works	30·0
Metal production	3·3
Engineering and electrical goods	12·4
Mechanical and electrical repairs	0·9
Glass, ceramics, building materials	2·5
Chemicals, fuels, tobacco and matches	2·6
Food and kindred industries	2·0
Textiles and clothing	4·1
Other manufacturing	5·2
Transport	2·2
Commerce	8·6
Finance, banking, insurance	2·1
Domestic services	5·1
Personal services	4·7
Water, gas, electricity	0·2
Broadcasting and transmission	0·2
Public administration, defence	2·4

Source: Census, 1968.

only 26 per cent of Moroccan workers were employed by the same sector. A large share (between 12 and 19 per cent) of North African male workers was also found in the engineering and electrical-goods industries. Agriculture absorbs an above-average percentage of the Spanish male workers, whereas a fairly large concentration (18 per cent) of Tunisians is found in the commerce sector. More than a half of the Spanish female migrant workers and about a half of the Portuguese ones were employed in domestic and personal services, whereas only 20 per cent of the Tunisians found employment there. Tunisian female migrant workers are absorbed in relatively larger proportions by commerce, whilst clothing and textile industries absorb about 10 per cent of the Spanish and Portuguese migrant female workers in France (Castles and Kosack, 1973). With regard to migrant workers employed in Belgium, a relatively larger proportion of them is employed in mining (about 17 per cent), with about 40 per cent employed in the industries of the non-traded goods sector and the rest (about 43 per cent) in the manufacturing industries (Braeckman, 1973).

The industrial distribution of migrant labour in the Netherlands has progressively shifted towards manufacturing industries and away from the non-traded goods sector. An analysis of the permits to work currently valid (Marshall, 1973, and EEC Commission) shows that the percentage of foreign workers still requiring a labour permit and employed in the industries of the non-traded goods sector declined from 33 per cent in 1960 to 17 per cent in 1970. In that year, the largest concentration of foreign workers with labour permits was found in metal production (32 per cent) with considerable concentrations in the food processing and tobacco industries (14 per cent) and textiles and clothing (8 per cent). However, in view of the fact that workers in the Netherlands do not require a labour permit after a stay of five years, the picture emerging from an analysis of labour permits may be misleading.

With regard to skill levels, French and German data based on sample surveys in the late sixties tend to indicate that (*a*) the proportion of non-manual workers out of the total foreign labour employed in those countries is a small one in both France (6·3 per cent in 1967) and Germany (8 per cent for men, 14 per cent for women in 1968), and that (*b*) the group of semi-skilled manual workers was the largest socio-economic group, representing 36·6 per cent in France (all workers) and 36 per cent for Germany (male workers only). Unskilled manual workers accounted for 31·9 per cent of all foreign workers in France and 34 per cent of male foreign workers in Germany. The group with the largest proportion of its members in the non-manual category in France was the group of Tunisian workers. Moroccan workers in France had also the largest proportion in the semi-skilled manual category. Yugoslav workers in Germany are by far more skilled than any other group of male migrant workers from the Mediterranean area. In 1968, 55 per cent of Yugoslav male workers in Germany were in the semi-skilled manual category, compared to 16 per cent for Turks, 15 per cent for Spaniards, 12 per cent for Portuguese and 7 per cent for Greeks (Castles and Kosack, 1973). Thus, as the proportion of Yugoslav workers in the total migrant workers employed in Germany was increasing, the overall skill level of the migrant labour force would have been rising. Trends in France are, however, different. An analysis of the data on new arrivals of migrant workers (Statistiques de Travail, 1972) shows that the proportion of unskilled manual workers rose to 42 per cent in 1971 (compared to the 32 per cent given by the sample survey of 1967). The proportion of skilled manual workers was about the same (25 per cent) with a smaller share of the non-manual group (2 per cent only).

An analysis by skill level of the foreign labour force employed by various German industries shows that the largest proportion of male foreign workers employed in vehicles, electrical goods, chemicals and textiles (that is, 50 per cent and over) is in the semi-skilled manual category, whereas the largest proportion of male foreign workers employed in iron and steel production (55 per cent) is of the unskilled manual category. This category accounts also for 40 per cent of male foreign workers in building. In this last industry, however, a relatively large share of male foreign workers is found in the skilled manual group.

Another characteristic of the migrant labour that needs to be examined in view of the influence that it exerts on the demand for housing and other social overhead capital is the family situation of migrant workers. Here the experience varies according to nationality. However, this variation in the migrant's family situation will most likely be influenced by the terms of the various bilateral treaties on labour recruitment, as well as on the interpretation that the authorities give to the conditions specified for family transfers. In Germany, for example, migrant workers can bring their familes after a stay of three years provided that they intend to work there for a further length of time and that adequate dwellings are available (Nikolinakos, 1972 page 82). The interpretation of the workers' intentions with regards to further stay is a matter left to the authorities. Thus, although 82 per cent of all Turkish male migrant workers in Germany are married, 54 per cent are there without their wives, whilst 61 per cent of the Greeks (with a proportion of married male workers not much different, 78 per cent) are staying in Germany with their wives. A similar situation arises with regard to Yugoslav workers (Table 10), where, as in the Turkish case, no provisions with regard to admission of family are specified in the bilateral agreement between Germany and Yugoslavia. In France, where more liberal provisions with regard to family admission are adopted, the total family members reunited in 1970 (80,952) were slightly less than 50 per cent of the arrivals of new workers during that year.

6. A Review of Some Empirical Evidence on the Economic Effects of Migrant Labour in the EEC

In this part of the paper a brief look is taken at the available empirical evidence that has a bearing on the issues raised, particularly in the first section of the paper. An attempt is made to find out from such studies how far resort to migrant labour actually reduces the pressure of demand in the labour market and what effect if any, it has had on wage rates.

In France, in periods of highly strained labour markets (1966, 1969, 1970), new arrivals of migrant workers have risen steeply. Tension in the labour market is measured by the trend of the ratio of registered unemployment and unfilled vacancies and the so-called manpower bottlenecks series

TABLE 10 Male immigrant workers by family situation; Germany, 1969

Country of emigration	*Married*		*Single*
	With wife (%)	*Without wife (%)*	*(%)*
Greece	61	17	22
Spain	44	30	26
Turkey	28	54	18
Portugal	34	44	22
Yugoslavia	26	50	24
Italy	35	29	36
Recruiting lands	39	33	28
Other countries	60	6	34
Total	41	30	29

Source: *Ausländischer Arbeitnehmer*, 1969, p. 53.

of the French business surveys. In years of reduced strain in the labour markets (1965, 1967, 1971), a slowdown in the migratory flows is recorded (OECD, 1973).

In a study of the intra-industry wage structure in West Germany (Bain and Panga, 1972), the industry wage rate in 18 industries was regressed on the industry's unemployment rate, the number of foreign workers employed there and the level of prices. The coefficients for foreign workers were significant, suggesting that an increase in the employment of foreign workers retarded intra-industry wages. This will then suggest that native labour employed in industries which hire foreign workers suffers a decline in its wage rates relative to the wage rates of the native labour in all other industries.

Far more important in its impact on the average expected incomes of the native labour force over the course of the trade cycle is the evidence relating to the 'buffer function' of foreign labour in the German labour market. During the 1967 German recession, the number of foreign workers decreased considerably. According to one estimate (Kayser, 1972), between September 1966 and March 1967 the foreign labour force was reduced by 23 per cent, the reduction ranging from 17 per cent for the Greek and Turkish labourers to 30 per cent for Italian workers. Another estimate covering the period between September 1966 and September 1967 (Bundesanstalt für Arbeit, 1971, page 64) shows the reduction of the foreign work force to be 30 per cent. During the first six months of 1967, the average unemployment for all workers in Germany was 4·5 per cent. Using these two measures, Dirickx, Freiburghaus and Sertel (1974, pages 34–5) estimate a discrimination factor ranging between 5·1(23/4·5) to 6·7(30/4·5). This discrimination factor is, in other words, the ratio of percentage decline in the number of foreign workers in the host country to the percentage decline in the indigenous employment, and measures the elasticity of firing migrant labour in response to rising unemployment among native workers. The existence of such a factor is explained by Dirickx, Freiburghaus and Sertel (1974, page 34) by pressures from foremen and middle management personnel on a management that is sensitive to maintaining good industrial relations with the most active and most organised sector of their labour force (namely, native labour).

How far discrimination exists in terms of wage differentials between foreign and native workers of equivalent skills is difficult to substantiate, on the basis of available statistics. Such is the case, for example, of a report in *Der Spiegel* (7 June 1971, page 92), asserting that in France 50 per cent of the skilled Algerian workers employed there were paid at the wage rate of the unskilled workers. Some 'discrimination' is to be expected on account of migrants' language difficulties or ignorance of the local labour market practices. The Bundesanstalt für Arbeit (1969, pages 80–82) found from an inquiry carried out in 1968 that German-speaking foreign workers were receiving higher wage rates than those with no knowledge of the language. Foreign workers may also be unaware of any differences between the wage rate negotiated through national collective bargaining and the (more relevant) plant wage rate (Nikolinakos, 1972, pages 88–9).

Several studies of the effects of immigration on *per capita* income levels in Germany (reviewed in Völker, 1973) have generally failed to distinguish properly between native and migrant population. In one of these exercises involving the use of a simplified input–output model, it was found that by subtracting from the foreign worker's share of national output (this share being taken as equal to that of the German worker's), his consumption expenditure, his social security costs and his remittances back home, the residual amount (DM 7,000 in 1970) was far below the *per capita* needs in industrial and social overhead capital (estimated at DM 150,000 in 1970). This seems to suggest that consumption standards over a period of time will have to be restrained and that some of the rise in living standards will have to be forgone by the native population in order to provide for the investment needed in industrial and social overhead capital.

However, by far the most comprehensive examination of the economic effects of immigration on the host country was undertaken by the Dutch Centraal Planbureau (1972), focusing, obviously, on the Dutch experience. The analysis was undertaken in the framework of a 50 equation model the basis of which is schematically shown below.

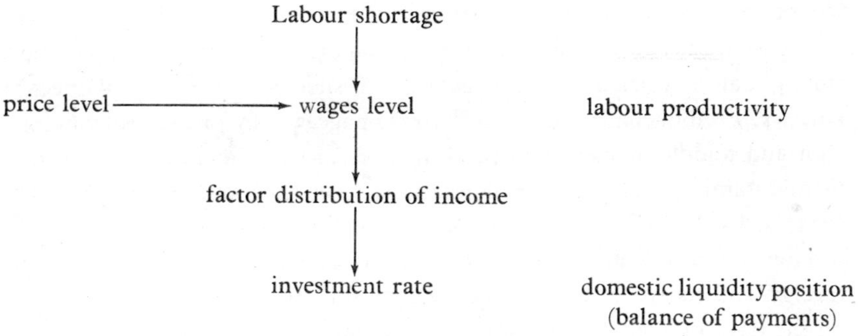

Integrated with it is also a government sector model for the estimation of the impact of immigration on public revenues and spending. The main results of the model are shown in Table 11. The effects of immigration were worked out by observing how an increase in the number of foreign workers employed equal to 1 per cent of the Dutch labour force in industry will affect the economy under three different assumptions: (*a*) that the workers enter Holland and stay there unaccompanied by their families; (*b*) that the families of the workers accompany them; and (*c*) that the increase in the number of foreign workers was accompanied by a complementary investment flow. The results do not produce great surprises and tend to confirm the main hypothesis advanced earlier in this paper. An inflow of immigrant workers not accompanied by their families will reduce the labour market tension (measured as the difference between the full capacity demand for labour and the labour supply available, both expressed as percentages of the industrial labour force) and the average wage rate and, furthermore, will make possible a reduction of the tax burden of the native population as

TABLE 11 Effects of an increase of the migrant labour force equal to 1% of the industrial labour force (shown in percentages)

	Unaccompanied foreign workers only	*Unaccompanied foreign workers with a complementary form of investment*	*Migrant workers with families*	*Increase of 1% in domestic labour supply*
Labour shortage	−0·63	0	+0·11	0·52
Wage level	−0·49	+0·68	+0·21	−0·15
Consumer prices	−0·16	+0·62	+0·17	+0·14
Real disposable wage per Dutch Employee	+0·03	+0·53	−0·11	+0·13
Nominal disposal non-wage income	+1·08	+2·40	−0·09	+1·67
Margin between public revenue and public expenditure (1% of industrial production)	+0·24	+0·60	−0·09	+0·38

Source: Centraal Planbureau, The Netherlands, The Hague, Occasional Papers, No. 2.

the expected revenues from taxation will exceed additional expenditures undertaken on behalf of the migrants. However, if the inflow of migrant labour takes place together with a complementary investment growth, the labour market situation, after the effects of both changes are worked out, will be left unaffected and the level of wages will now increase. But the shift in the distribution of income in favour of non-wage income will still persist. The fiscal advantage is higher than before. This picture changes radically when the effects are worked out on the assumption that migrant workers are accompanied by their families. This type of immigration is both inflationary and disadvantageous from the fiscal point of view. It turns against the native wage-earning population, whose average real disposable income is now reduced.

As the number of longer-staying migrants increases (see section 3 above) and more family transfers take place, the inflationary impact of migrant labour will tend to become more acute. This trend will be also aggravated by the efforts to integrate foreign workers with the local communities in an attempt to solve the increasing social problems from the emerging ghettos in the European cities. Such integration involves, among other things, the raising of the standard of housing, schooling and so on available to the migrant communities. In the Dutch exercise referred to above, it was calculated that public spending associated with an increase in the number of foreign workers by 40,000 persons (that is, 1 per cent of the Dutch industrial force in 1969) varies dramatically depending on the extent to which the worker's family is also admitted with him. The exercise assumed that in the case of family admission the size of the average family of a foreign worker is the same as that of the average Dutch family and that the infrastructure per migrant family will be the same as that of a native family. The results in millions of guilders at 1969 prices are shown in Table 12. Thus the public expenditure on housing for a single worker or a married foreigner working in the host country without his wife is only one-eighth of the corresponding expenditure for an average migrant family.

Given the restrictive assumptions of the Dutch exercise and in particular that the 'needs' for infrastructure per person and per family were taken to be the same irrespective of whether the single worker or the worker's family are native or foreign, the above estimates of the effects of a change in immigration policies on public expenditure are most likely on the conservative side. A German estimate (Sommer, 1973) shows that if foreign workers are fully integrated, and if their families as well as the workers themselves receive the same quantity and quality of infrastruc-

TABLE 12 Public spending and admittance of foreign workers' families, in the Netherlands, 1969 (millions of guilders)

	Foreign workers only	*Foreign workers' families*	*Foreign workers and their families*
Annual recurring expenditure for public services	55	125	180
Subsidies and loans for house building	95	650	740

tural facilities as the native population, then the cost of investment in infrastructure will rise from about DM 30,000 to DM 150,000–200,000 per worker.

The inflationary effects from increases in public spending were kept under control in the past through the policy of 'organised' immigration, which ensured that the immigrants' effective demands for housing and social infrastructure were maintained at a level below that of the native worker. In this respect it is interesting to note that, when the German Ministry of Labour and Social Order regulated in 1971 the conditions for the dwellings of foreign workers, it found it necessary to specify (presumably in order to abolish existing practices) that there must be one bed per person in the hostels for foreign workers, that no more than two beds can be put one on top of the other and that no more than four beds can be accommodated in one room (Nikolinakos, 1972). At about the time when this ministerial regulation was issued, Bucher (1972, page 158) was reporting that in a six-room house in Frankfurt's west end it was usual to find about forty workers living together. It is also interesting to note that in the EEC Commission annual Social Reports, the yearly French contribution to the construction of new centres for foreign workers living alone is recorded in terms of number of beds rather than in terms of dwelling units of a specified size. It is estimated (*Financial Times*, 3 May 1973) that at least 1 million out of $3\frac{1}{4}$ million immigrants in France live in Bidonvilles or shanty towns, the shacks being squalid and dangerous. To the extent that a change in immigration policy towards fuller 'integration' and increasing family transfers will produce the inflationary effects suggested above, one would expect a potential adverse effect on the balance of trade. For countries like Germany this may be one way to eliminate some of its sizeable trade surplus. Part of this surplus was in the past reduced through the rising amount of remittances sent to the immigrants' countries of origin. During 1967–71 (see Table 13), the overall size of immigrants' remittances from Germany increased about three times. During the same period, immigrants' remittances from the Netherlands increased by about 50 per cent, those from Belgium-Luxembourg by more than 50 per cent (and by 170 per cent if only the remittances of the Mediterranean migrants are considered) and those from France by 54 per cent.

Although all the EEC countries experienced large inflows of foreign (and particularly American) private direct investment, nevertheless it is not possible at this stage to ascertain how much of this inflow has been induced or assisted by the immigration policies of the European countries. Such policies not only raised labour availability there throughout the period but also helped to make available in Europe non-traded goods at relatively more advantageous terms. To ascertain the impact of these factors on

TABLE 13 Immigrant's remittances (millions US $)

	From				
To	*Germany*	*France*	*Holland*	*Belgium*	*Total (EEC Six)*
World					
1967	537	–	11	26	–
1968	537	556	10	26	1,129
1969	770	730	15	42	1,557
1970	1,175	768	22	40	2,005
1971	1,450	857	17	42	2,366
*Non-member countries**					
1967	325(251)	–	9(0)	11(9)	–(–)
1968	325(238)	432(146)	8(0)	11(10)	776(394)
1969	527(334)	575(170)	13(3)	19(16)	1,133(523)
1970	847(505)	681(158)	16(2)	25(18)	1,569(683)
1971	1,081(629)	778(–68)	12(1)	30(19)	1,901(817)

* Basically Mediterranean countries.

Figures in brackets refer to Greece, Spain and Turkey together.

Source: OECD.

foreign direct investment is not simply a matter of looking at the migrant workers directly employed by foreign subsidiaries in Europe but must be the subject of a comprehensive exercise that will include all relevant factors which influence the size and direction of private direct investment flows. However, apart from the indirect influence by the impact on the prices of non-traded goods, the possibility of using migrant workers in countries of relatively more stable business and investment climates and of plentiful external economies rather than in their countries of origin has not escaped the attention of some of the largest multinational enterprises. The case of Ford, maintaining its own recruitment agencies in Turkey, was already mentioned. Drewer (1974) refers to the case of Brown-Boveri (the electrical engineering multinational), which relocated to West Germany investment planned in Switzerland when Swiss immigration restrictions made impossible the resort to additional migrant labour.

7. Conclusion

The above review seems to suggest that, although the employment of 'guest workers' provides important benefits over a period of time to the native population of the country using this type of 'organised' immigration, its continuation over a longer period is extremely problematic. The use of migrant labour helps to maintain the momentum of export-led growth. With the process of export-led growth going on, the demand for additional migrant labour is kept at a fairly high level. As the dependence of the economy on migrant labour increases, the proportion of migrant workers with longer periods of stay will also be increasing and with it the demand for additional social overhead capital. The process of urban ghetto formation that accompanies the increase in the size of migrant labour will lead to pressing social problems with the dangers of violent eruptions such as those experienced in Rotterdam in 1972 and in Marseille in 1973. The need for 'integrating' the migrant communities with the indigenous population will then be stressed as a way of removing the dangers inherent in the process of creation of a depressed proletariat living in hopelessly outdated conditions. But assimilation and integration involve substantial expenditure on social infrastructure. At this point, the expenditure multiplier will surpass the size of the output multiplier. The growing shortages in the labour market will lead to an increase in the demand for foreign labour. The process of migration will then become 'self-feeding', more migrant workers needed to provide for the needs of the 'assimilated' migrant communities. The nineteenth-century 'melting-pot' experience of the United States can not be repeated in twentieth-century Europe with its severe resource constraints.[4]

The solution to Europe's manpower shortages cannot be supplied any longer either by increasing the turnover of the migrant labour (the so-called rotation system) or by humanising the process of immigration through 'assimilation' and 'integration'. Neither will increasing automation give the answer, as there will still be the shortage in the markets for menial, routine jobs created by the process of automation itself and which Western Europeans have become loath to accept.

A radical solution can be found only through a re-sourcing of investment, through a phased relocation of labour-intensive processes from Western and Northern Europe to the countries of the Mediterranean area. A first step towards this will be the enactment of a comprehensive regional 'foreign investment guarantee and taxation treaty' between the EEC and its Mediterranean associates and associables. Measures like the German one (1973) to raise the recruitment fee imposed on German firms from DM 300 to DM 1,000 per worker can only marginally help.

The approach outlined above must, then, be complemented by a more vigorous effort by the EEC to utilise the pockets of persistent unemployment.

Within Europe there exist considerable pools of unutilised labour, not only in the agricultural sector but also outside it, because of interregional differences in activity rates and persisting interregional differences in unemployment rates. Such sources of unutilised labour could well account for over 2 million people – a figure almost comparable to the size of migrant labour force from the Mediterranean area. A reference again to the Dutch exercise shows (see last column of Table 11, page 130) that this alternative to migrant labour from third countries is more beneficial to the native working population: the reduction in the wage level is less, and the fiscal advantage is greater.

Given the limited labour mobility that characterises the Common Market areas of labour surpluses, utilisation of these surpluses can be achieved through a more active regional policy at both the national and the Community level.

4 Even in Australia it has been recently suggested that the attempt to solve labour shortages by increasing the supply of immigrant labour adds more to aggregate demand than it does to aggregate supply of goods and services. (A. L. Hall of the Australian National University, quoted in the *Financial Times*, 28 August 1973.)

REFERENCES

Archibald, G. C. (1969). The Phillips curve and the distribution of unemployment. *American Economic Review*. May.

Bain, T., and Panga, A. (1972). Foreign workers and the intra-industry wage structure in West Germany. *Kyklos*, 820–4.

Berry, R. A., and Saligo, R. (1969). Some welfare aspects of international migration. *Journal of Political Economy*, 778–94.

Bideberry, P. (1967). Bilan de vingt années d'immigration. *Revue Française des Affaires Sociales*. April–June.

Bucher, H. (1972). The housing problems of migrant workers. In *Foreigners in our Community*, H. van Houte and W. Melgert (eds.). Amsterdam: Keesing.

Bundesanstalt für Arbeit, *Ausländischer Arbeitnehmer*, annual.

Castles, S., and Kosack, G. (1973). *Immigrant workers and class structure in Western Europe*. London: Oxford University Press.

Centraal Planbureau, The Netherlands. (1972). *The economic effect on the Netherlands of recruiting foreign labour*, Occasional Paper No. 2.

Corden, M. (1955). The economic limits to population increase. *Economic Record*. November, 242–60.

Dirickx, Y. M. I., Freiburghaus, D. and Sertel, H. R. (1974). *Incidence of the energy crisis on the employment of foreign workers in West Germany*. International Institute of Management. Berlin (mimeographed).

Drewer, S. (1974). The economic impact of immigrant workers in Western Europe. *European Studies* **18**.

Dutta, A. (1973). *International migration, trade and real income* – a case study of Ceylon, 1920–1938. Calcutta: The World Press Private Ltd.

EEC, Commission. *La Libre circulation de la Main d'œuvre et les marches des travail dans la CEE*. Annual

(1971). *Etude comparative des politiques migrataires des états membres de la CEE à l'égard des pays tiers*. Brussels.

Epstein, L. (1973). Some economic effects of immigration: a general equilibrium analysis. *Canadian Journal of Economics* 174–90.

Handlin, O. (1941). *Boston's immigrants*. Cambridge, Mass.: Harvard University Press.

Hufbauer, G. C. (1974). Multinational corporations and the international adjustment process. *American Economic Review*. May (Papers).

Hume, I. M. (1973). Migrant workers in Europe. *Finance and Development*, March, 2–6.

Johnson, H. (1955). Economic expansion and international trade. *The Manchester School*. May, 95–112.

(1967). Some economic aspects of brain drain. *The Pakistan Development Review* VII (3), 379–411.

(1968). An 'internationalist' model. In W. Adams, (ed.), *The Brain Drain*. London: Macmillan.

Karmel, P. H. (1963). The economic effects of immigration. In H. W. Arndt and M. Corden, eds. *The Australian economy*. Melbourne: F. W. Cheshire.

Kayser, B. (1972). *Cyclically-determined homeward flows of migrant workers*. Paris: OECD.

Kindleberger, C. P. (1965). Emigration and economic growth. *Banca Nazionale del Lavoro Quarterly Review* **74**, 235–54.

Livi Bacci, M. (1972). *The demographic and social patterns of emigration from the Southern European countries*. Florence.

Lutz, V. (1963). Foreign workers and domestic wage levels, with an illustration from the Swiss Case. *Banca Nazionale del Lavoro Quarterly Review*. March, 3–68.

MacDougall, G. M. A. (1960). The benefits and costs of private investment from abroad: a theoretical approach. *Economic Record*, 13–35. Reprinted in J. H. Dunning, ed. *International Investment*. Pengiun Modern Economics.

Marshall, A. (1973). *The import of labour: the case of the Netherlands*. Rotterdam University Press.

Mishan, E. J., and Needleman, L. (1968). Immigration, some long-term economic consequences. *Economia Internazionale*. Part A, 281–300; Part B, 515–25.

Nikolinakos, M. (1972). Economic foundations of discrimination in the Federal Republic of Germany. In *Foreigners in our Community*. H. van Houte and W. Melgert, ed. Amsterdam: Keesing.

OECD (1967). *Review of manpower and social policies: manpower and social policy in the Netherlands*.

(1972). General social and economic aspects of intra-European manpower movements: trends and policies. A note of the manpower division. In *Foreigners in Our Community*, H. van Houte and W. Melgert, eds. Amsterdam: Keesing.

(1973). *France: economic survey*.

Patinkin, D. (1968). A 'nationalist' model. In W. Adams, ed. *The Brain Drain*. London: Macmillan.

Peston, M. (1969). Effects on the economy. In E. J. B. Rose, ed. *Colour and citizenship*. London: Oxford University Press.

(1971). The economics of immigration. *Race Today*. March, 82–3.

Power, J. (1973). The new proletariat. *The New Internationalist*. October, 17–20.

Sauvy, A. (1948). Some aspects of the international migration problem. *International Labour Review*, LVII (2), 18–37.

Sommer, T. (1973). Der Gastarbeiter. *Encounter*. November, 61–2.

Statistiques de Travail (1972). Supplément No. 7 of '*Bulletin Mensuel*,' Ministère d'Etat, Chargés des Affaires Sociales, Paris.

Thomas, B. (1973). *Migration and Economic growth: a study of Great Britain and the Atlantic economy*. 2nd ed. Cambridge: Cambridge University Press.

Völker, G. E. (1973). Impact of Turkish labour migration on the economy of the Federal Republic of Germany. *German Economic Review.* XI (1), 61–77.

Yannopoulos, G. N. (1969). Economic integration and labour movements. In G. R. Denton, ed. *Economic integration in Europe.* London: Weidenfeld and Nicolson.

3

COUNTRY STUDIES

7

Greece's Association with the European Community: an Evaluation of the First Ten Years

G. J. KALAMOTOUSAKIS

Introduction

On 1 November, 1962 Greece became a 'privileged' associate member of the EEC on the basis of an agreement falling under the provisions of Article 238 of the Rome Treaty. The agreement of association went beyond the establishment of a customs union. It called not only for the complete abolition of all barriers to trade between Greece and the European 'conomic Community (EEC), over a transitional period of twenty-two years, but also for the harmonisation of Greece's agricultural, financial and transportation policies with those of the Community.

Significantly, until Greece decided to become an associate member of the EEC, little consideration had been given to the impact of the formation of a customs union between an under-developed country and a group of highly industrialised countries on the economic development of the LDCs. Accordingly, an attempt is being made in this chapter to fill the existing gap by examining the effects of Greece's association with the EEC on the economic development of Greece.

The questions therefore asked in this chapter are (*1*) why did the Six offer Greece a costly, 'privileged', preferential status in the Community over a period of twenty-two years; (*2*) has the effect of the association with the EEC been a strategic factor in the rapid expansion and the changing structure of Greece's exports; (*3*) has the association thus far been a contributory factor in Greece's economic growth and industrial development; and (*4*) will the association accelerate growth in the future?

The chapter concludes that the answer to the first question appears to be largely political, whereas the answers to the remaining three questions appear to be affirmative.

On balance, the agreement of association has led largely to *trade creation* effects which were favourable to Greece as well as to the EEC countries and the United States. Indeed, the association provided the opportunity for accelerated industrial development and a broadening of Greece's manufacturing base through a market expansion of exports, especially to the EEC.

From the point of view of the Community's interests in the trade negotiations with the US, the Greek experiment is also of significant importance. In fact, the results of the study suggest that the American fears that associate membership of the Mediterranean less developed countries with the EEC will divert trade from the US are exaggerated. Rather, the results of the study support the view than an enlarged Common Market that includes such countries as Spain, Israel, Morocco and Tunisia will most likely lead to more trade with America, not less.

1. The Role of Customs Unions in Economic Development

There are at least four ways in which trade can have a beneficial effect on economic development. First, trade can stimulate a slow-growing economy through a rise in the demand for its exports. This effect is important as a dynamic element if: (*1*) domestic idle resources are effectively mobilised to meet the demand, and the adjustment is not made at the expense of the domestic market; and (*2*) the increase in the utilisation of domestic resources would not have come about anyway as a result of autonomous developments in the domestic sector (Samuelson, 1954, 1962).

Second, increased exports may provide an incentive for capital movements into developing economies and a stimulant to domestic capital formation. This capital movement can occur in response to differential factor endowments between developed, capital-abundant economies and under-developed, capital-scarce ones; or in response to a rise in demand in the export sector of the under-developed economy which opens up opportunities for large profits.

Third, imports allowed by increased exports or capital inflows can provide the capital goods and raw materials that are indispensable for economic development.

Fourth, trade can be the vehicle for the dissemination of technology. This is the usual argument of those who point out that latecomers can ease their development problems by acquiring, at almost no cost, the latest techniques of production (Haberler, 1959; Nurkse, 1959).

In the following discussion an attempt will be made to show how a developing country can attain a higher economic growth rate by forming a customs union with a country, or group of countries, that is already highly industrialised. It will also be demonstrated in the model that follows that a customs union between dissimilar economies of disparate sizes is likely to lead to large gains for the smaller of the member countries. The analysis applies to the Greek case and to countries such as Turkey, Austria, Israel, Spain and Portugal.

Trade Creation and Trade Diversion

Static analysis of customs unions has attempted to predict whether the removal of barriers to trade between two countries will lead to more or less efficient allocation of the economic resources of the world. The general conclusion of this analysis has been well summarised by Meade in his statement that 'the formation of a customs union is more likely to lead to a net increase in world economic welfare if the economies of the partner countries are actually very competitive or similar but potentially very complementary or dissimilar' (Meade, 1955). The simple argument that a customs union will always, or nearly always, raise world welfare, because free trade maximises global welfare, has been shown by Meade to be incorrect. Viner has also pointed out that the formation of a customs union does not necessarily result in higher welfare. The reason for this is that a customs union may lead either to trade creation or trade diversion (Scitovsky, 1958; Pezmatzoglou, 1962). A customs union, Viner concluded, is more likely to bring gain the greater the degree of domestic competition before the union.[1] Makower and Morton showed that if trade creation was going to occur, the gain would be larger the more dissimilar were the cost ratios in the two countries (Makower and Morton, 1953).

Meade's conclusions and Makower's and Morton's findings are not at all contradictory. Meade showed that gains will result if both countries produce the same commodity, whereas the others showed that customs unions between two countries with complementary economies 'would, if they brought gain at all, bring large gains' (Makower and Morton, 1953).

Further, R. Lipsey showed that, given the volume of a country's international trade, joining a customs union is more likely to raise the country's welfare in proportion as (*1*) the volume of trade with non-member countries is high, and (2) the total volume of foreign trade in relation to domestic purchases is low (Lipsey, 1960; Lipsey and Lancaster, 1957).

1 Meade, however, was able to show that Viner's analysis was incomplete. Whether a customs union would lead to trade diversion or trade creation would generally depend upon the initial level of import duties of the partner countries. As a result, Meade concluded 'that the formation of a customs union is more likely to raise than lower economic welfare, the higher are the initial duties on each other's products which the partner countries remove'.

From the above discussion, it is clear that static customs-union theory has concerned itself mainly with the gains (or loss) from a more (or less) efficient allocation of resources after the customs union is formed. The principal usefulness of this traditional theory has been to delineate the conditions for a gain to occur through trade creation as opposed to a loss of welfare when trade diversion outweighs trade creation.

The dynamic effects set up by the reallocation of resources due to a union are, as in all dynamic theory, much more difficult to assess. The literature has not solidly formulated the conditions, or magnitudes of the dynamic effects set up by the reallocation. But in general terms, the reallocation of resources, as a result of tariff changes, has at least the following effects: (*1*) possible benefits from the economies of scale and external economies; (*2*) a change in the terms of trade; (*3*) forced changes in efficiency due to increased foreign competition; and (*4*) a change in the rate of economic growth, as a result of the reallocation of resources and the three dynamic factors. So far, the theory of customs unions has been almost completely confined to the investigation of product specialisation,[2] with some slight attention given to the economies of scale and the changes of the terms of trade. The case of forced changes in efficiency due to increased foreign competition has not been considered as important, because traditional theory makes the assumption that production is carried out by processes which are technically efficient. Similarly, the case of changing the economic growth rate through the formation of a customs union has generally been overlooked by customs-union theory.

A Model of a Customs Union between a Developed and an Under-developed Economy

To make explicit the static effects of a customs union on an under-developed economy, such as Greece, which joins a customs union of advanced countries, such as the EEC, the following model is helpful (Lipsey, 1960; Meade, 1955). It indicates the effect of the formation of the EEC on the access of many of Greece's competitive imports to that market. Greek tobacco exports to EEC, for example, have increased since the association as a result of the discriminatory common external tariff (CET) imposed by the EEC on competing oriental-type tobacco and the

2 For a critical evaluation of the argument that gains will be the result of specialisation, see Johnson, Feb. and Sept. 1958; Scitovsky, 1958; Pezmatzoglou, 1962.

minimum purchases of Greek tobacco by the French and Italian state monopolies.

The EEC–Greece association, in so far as the static effects are concerned, corresponds roughly with the model set up. The EEC will get little static gain due to a decline in P_w, (see fig. 1) whereas Greece will acquire considerable gain through (*a*) improvement in terms of trade, and (*b*) increase in exports.

In addition, the numerous effects ignored by static theory described earlier can be incorporated into this analysis. If the impact of the change in tariffs causes economies of scale and so on, then *E*'s supply curve will shift further, and this may be a greater gain for *E* (and the world) but at no cost, and indeed a gain through development for *G*.

The model is not a complete one, for it does not take into consideration the short-run effects of the customs union on global welfare. Neither does it take into account the so-called tertiary effects – namely, the changes in welfare resulting from whatever measures are needed to restore balance-of-payments equilibrium after the formation of the union (Meade, 1955).

Assume a four-country world in which two countries are under-developed, producing primary commodities, and the other two are advanced, producing manufactured goods. The former are termed countries *G* and *A*, and the latter *E* and *B*. The products of *G* and *A* are perfect substitutes for each other. Trade is multilateral, except that there is assumed to be no trade between *G* and *A*, the primary producing countries. Assume that a customs union is formed between *G* and *E*. Under these conditions, what will be the effects of establishing this union? The impact in the market for primary commodities *G* and *A*'s exports) is shown in figure 1.

D_E is the demand schedule of *E* for *G*'s and *A*'s exports (primary products) without tariff D'_E is its demand schedule with *E*'s non-discriminatory specific (pre-union) tariff. *B*'s demand for *G* and *A*'s goods in D_B. Adding horizontally, we get an aggregate demand schedule for the primary commodity export of *G* and *A*;

$$D_T + D_E = E_B.$$

The total supply of *G* and *A*'s goods is given by

$$S_G + S_A = S_T.$$

It is implicitly assumed here that *G*'s supply of exports to *E*, at world prices, is less than *E*'s aggregate demand for *G* and *A*'s goods.

Prior to any discrimination or preferential tariff reduction, the level of

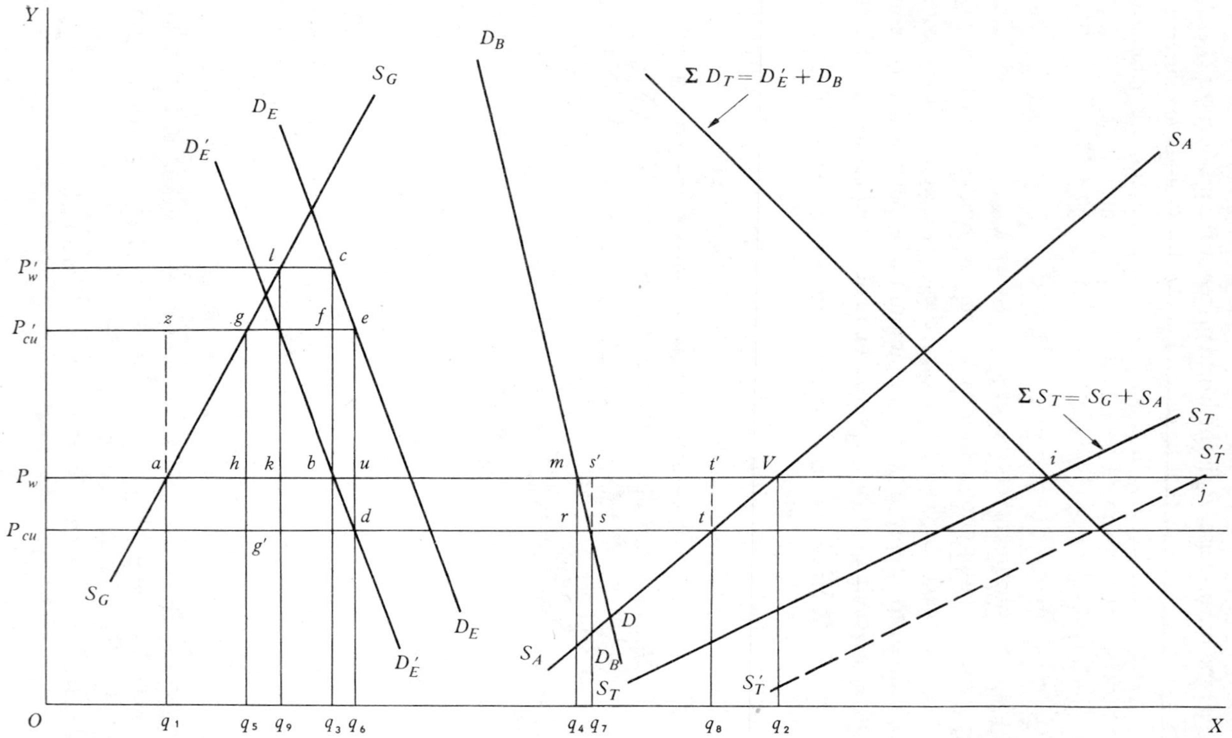

Fig. 1. Quantity of G' and A's exports

output and prices for G and A's products are assumed to be determined by the world market forces of aggregate demand and supply – namely, D_T and S_T. Thus, in this case, P_W is the world price for the products of G and A. The respective outputs at that price level is Oq_1 for G and Oq_2 for A. The effective price of GA exports in E is P'_W because of the non-discriminating specific tariff t_0. It is assumed here that G exports all its output to E and that E buys Oq_1 from G and $q_1\, q_3$ (= ab) from A. Similarly, A supplies B with Oq_4 of its exports. The rest of A's output $q_2 - q_4$ (= $q_1\, q_3$) goes to E.

After the establishment of the customs union between G and E, it is assumed that the latter eliminates its tariff on its imports from G. Because E's aggregate demand for G and A's goods exceeds G's supply of these goods, A will continue to supply E with that amount of exports which G cannot provide. As a result of this, the world demand schedule will remain unchanged after the tariff reduction. In fact, only quantities supplied by the the countries G and A change.

The initial effect of the tariff reduction will be as follows: G's producers will now receive a non-tariff price higher than the world price for their exports to E. This higher price is equal to the world price P_W plus the discriminatory tariff that A's producers must continue to pay for their exports to E. The new supply curve S'_T then relates world output to world prices under conditions where G's producers receive $P_W + t_0$ (where t_0 equals the specific tariff collected by E) for their outputs. S'_T will then be below S_T at any world price P_W. The distance between S_T and S'_T ($ij = ak$) will then be determined by the amount of specific non-discriminating tariff collected by E and by the slope of G's curve. With the establishment of a customs union, a new world price will become effective, P_{cu}. At this price level, G's producers will be receiving an effective price for their exports to E equal to the new world price plus the specific tariff, $P_{cu} + t_0$. Because of this higher price, G will expand its total output from Oq_1 to Oq_5, thereby altering the relative distribution of exports of G and A's exports to E. Thus, the new price P_{cu} is now lower than the previous world market P_W. As a result of this price change, the domestic price for GA's exports falls from P'_w to P'_{cu}, and the quantity demanded domestically in E rises from Oq_3 to Oq_6. Similarly, the quantity demanded in B also rises from Oq_4 to Oq_7. Whereas the total output of G increases, the total output of A decreases from Oq_2 to Oq_8. At this new equilibrium level, A still supplies E with $q_7\, q_8$ (= $q_5\, q_6$) of its exports, and domestic consumption in both E and B increases by $q_3\, q_6$ and $q_4\, q_7$ respectively.

The removal of the preferential tariff will lead to changes in welfare.

Firstly, E will gain a consumer's surplus equal to *cfe* ($= 1/2\ dp_w\ dM_E$) in fig. 1 as a result of the increased consumption of GA goods. This gain is termed a gain from trade creation. Secondly, E will enjoy a gain in its terms of trade with A. This results from the lower price that E now pays for A's exports and is equal to the change in the world price $P_w\ P_{cu}$ times E's imports from $A(q_5\ q_6)$, which is equal to the area *hudg*. At the same time, E will suffer a decline in its terms of trade with G. This loss will be equal to A's original production times the difference between the amount of the tariff and the change in world price. This loss is measured by the area P_w $az\ P'_{cu2}$ or $(t_0 - dp_w)$. X_G is G's total supply of exports at the original world price P_w. Similarly, E suffers another terms-of-trade loss on the volume of its former imports from A, which are now replaced by imports from G. This is obviously a loss due to trade diversion. This loss is measured by the difference of the area *azgh* and *bfeu*, which is equal to $(t_0 - dp_w)\ dX_G$.

To determine whether the relative position of E's welfare has improved or deteriorated after the elimination of the specific tariff, an aggregation must be made of the total gain that results from trade creation and the total loss that results from trade diversion. If the difference is a positive one, then E's welfare will be improved; if it is negative – that is, if the total gain is less than the total loss – E's welfare will deteriorate. Adding up the components of imports (M) and exports (X), we get:

$$W'_E = dp_w\ (M_E + 1/2\ dM_E) - t_0\ (X_G + dX_G - dM_E)$$

Since $M_E + 1/2\ dM_E$ is greater than $X_G + dX_G$ by assumption, then if dp_w is equal to t_0, E will gain from a tariff reduction. The usual case, however, is for dp_w to be less than t_0. In this case, the sign of E's welfare change becomes indeterminate. In short, as the impact of the tariff removal on the world diminishes, a decreasing value of X_G relative to M_E is necessary if the expression is to be positive.

We now turn to the change in welfare for country G. First, G will enjoy a producer's surplus and a terms-of-trade gain on the initial volume of its exports. This gain in fig. 1 is represented by the areas *agh* plus $azP_{cu}P_w$ and is equal to $(X_G + 1/2\ dX_G)\ (t_0 - dP_W)$, which will always be positive except in the limiting case where $(t_0 = dp_w)$. This positive change in G's welfare will be larger, the smaller the change in the world price relative to E's specific tariff and the more elastic the elasticity of supply of G's products.

It may be recalled from the earlier discussion that E's gain is maximised when the change in world price resulting from the tariff removal is as large as possible, whereas G's gain is maximised when the world price remains unchanged. In short, the magnitude of the world price change relative to E's tariff will play a determining role in the distribution of gains resulting from trade in GA goods between the customs-union partners.

In accordance with this analysis, it can be concluded that the net change in the welfare of the entire customs union is equal to the sum of the change in the two countries, $cfe + agz - (ahgz - bfeu) + gduh$, which will be equal to the expression:

$$W'_{cu} = dp_w (M_E + dM_E - X_G - dX_G) + 1/2\, dp_w (dX_G - dM_E) + t_0 (dM_E - 1/2\, dX_G)$$

Considering, however, that $M_E + dM_E$ is greater than $X_G + dX_G$, then the first parenthesis of the expression will always be positive. The second parenthesis will also be positive, provided that dX_G is greater than dM_E. Since dX_G is a function of $t_0 - dp_w$, while dM_E responds to dp_w, and since it is presumed that the change in world price will be a small fraction of t_0, dX_G will generally be larger than dM_E as long as the slopes of the relevant demand and supply curves are roughly of the same order of magnitude. The third parenthesis will be positive as long as dM_E is greater than X_G.

It then becomes apparent that the customs union will enjoy an increase in welfare as long as $dX_G > dM_E > 1/2\, dX_G$, in which case all terms of the expression will be positive. Thus, if the formation of the customs union has even a moderate impact on the price of GA goods, there will be a stronger supposition that the customs union as a whole will gain on its trade in those goods.

What has been attempted in this section is to construct an explanatory model that describes the effects of a customs union on an under-developed economy. The plan of the rest of the article is to assess the impact of these various forces – both static and dynamic – within the specific context of the Greek economy.

2. Greece's Negotiations with the OEEC, EFTA and the EEC

Although the economic growth rate in the pre-association period, 1953–62, was satisfactory, the deficit in the merchandise trade account continued to increase as a result of the rapid growth of imports and the relatively slow increase in agricultural exports. Particularly disconcerting for Greece was the development of its trade with the countries that subsequently made up the EEC, and which continued to provide over 40 per cent of its rising imports while taking in progressively a smaller share of Greece's exports. By 1961, for example, Greek exports to EEC fell to less than 32 per cent of total exports from an average of 48 per cent between 1953 and 1957. Moreover, a large expansion of Greece's exports was improbable even if foreign markets had been readily available. Greece has been faced with a shortage of arable land, so that agricultural output can be increased only by new techniques and land reclamation through irrigation. The maintenance of a satisfactory overall growth rate therefore hinges to a considerable extent on a vigorous expansion in industrial output and exports.

Hence, the various attempts on the part of the Western European countries in the late 1950s to promote economic growth and industrial development through the expansion of foreign trade, both regionally and globally, were of particular interest to Greece. In this context Greece, prior to considering any form of participation in the EEC, took part in the lengthy negotiations (1957–8) of the Organisation for European Economic Cooperation (OEEC), which at that time considered a British proposal for a European free-trade area embracing all Western European countries – an alternative to the Common Market. However, the wide divergence of views rendered these negotiations inconclusive.

With the breakdown of the OEEC negotiations, England, Austria, Iceland, Portugal, Sweden and Finland (associate member) formed the European Free Trade Association (EFTA). This group of countries also invited Greece to participate in the establishment of the proposed European free-trade area. Greece rejected this opportunity because the preferential treatment that it and other developing countries requested in the OEEC negotiations were, once again, turned down.

Hence, after more than two years of protracted negotiations, Greece was faced with a situation in which the EEC had entered its second successful year of operations, while a separate and rival economic association among the other industrially advanced countries, EFTA was imminent. Greece thus faced the danger of being excluded from regional economic and political grouping among those nations which provided it with traditional markets and constituted its closest political and defence associates.

From the Greek point of view, the economic advantages of integration with the EEC should derive from a stronger competitive position within a large and expanding market, a more efficient allocation of resources, economies of scale and an improvement in the level and composition of trade with the European countries. Another potential advantage was that by being a member of a powerful trade bloc, Greece would also enjoy a position of strength in negotiations with third countries. All these developments involve changes in factor proportions, technology, the size of the markets and the pattern of new investment. If realised, it was agreed, these developments should induce a higher rate of industrial growth and rising *per capita* income (Seitovsky, 1958; Pezmatzoglou, 1962).

However, as late as 1961 Greece was still characterised by economic dualism and a *per capita* income of only 36 per cent of that in the EEC. In Greece's view, therefore, participation in a regional grouping of developed countries that fostered trade expansion through the complete abolition of all barriers to trade had to be accomplished in stages. Indeed, participation in the Community, it was agreed, should ensure that changes in trading patterns would not only be gradual, but would also give time and opportunity to make any adjustments which might prove necessary. It was also agreed among the Greeks that the cost of joining the EEC – namely, the threat to domestic industry from foreign competition – would be the price that they should be prepared to pay for the anticipated economic and political advantages.

At the time of negotiations with the EEC, Greece had the choice to apply for either full or associate membership. The Greeks chose the latter. And their choice was the correct one: if Greece had opted for full membership, it would have been risking catastrophic consequences because (*a*) direct and unconditional membership would have meant acceptance of the accelerated time-table among the Six for the complete abolition of all tariffs and quantitative import controls and the elimination of all foreign exchange controls, and (*b*) the geographic orientation and composition of Greek exports, consisting largely of few agricultural products having a low price and income elasticity of demand and a high elasticity of substitution, were substantially tied to the EEC countries. Consequently, if trade with the EEC was to be fully liberalised while foreign exchange controls were eliminated, there was no doubt that the volume of imports in Greece would have risen sharply, at least in the short run, whereas exports would have remained, at best, stable. Additionally, part of Greece's limited supply of investible funds would have been attracted to the Community, precipitating thereby a serious balance-of-payments crisis.

3. The Choice of Not Applying for any Form of Association

A decision not to join, when at last Greece had the opportunity to do so, would have been a rejection of a historic opportunity to become a member of a regional grouping of countries that were Greece's traditional economic, political and defence associates. By staying out, Greece would have been unable to influence political events that would have seriously affected both its economic and political interests. Additionally, if Greece were to stay out of the Common Market altogether, the productivity gap that existed at that time would have probably continued to widen as a result of decreasing competition and the inevitable increase in protective tariffs. Such an increase in tariffs would have become necessary in order to protect domestic production, burdened continuously by rising costs. In the final analysis, Greece would probably have been able to export some agricultural products, but mostly under unfavourable conditions vis-à-vis the agricultural exports of its integrated competitors.

An alternative to joining the EEC would, of course, have been found if Greece had opted for completely centralised planning similar to that of Yugoslavia and the Soviet-type economies. Centralised planning, however, could not have been adopted and/or implemented in Greece for the following four very important reasons. First, the Greek economy in the decade of the 1950s had already achieved a very respectable GNP growth rate of 5·8 per cent per annum under relatively free economic and political institutions. Secondly, Greece's past political, cultural and economic ties with Western Europe were substantially enhanced in the early 1950s through Greece's participation in Western Europe's new political, economic and social institutions.

Thirdly, not only were the Eastern European markets unable to absorb all of Greece's agricultural exportables, but, more importantly, trade with these countries had always been based on bilateral clearing agreements. Hence, it did not provide any foreign exchange earnings necessary to cover Greece's traditionally large trade deficit.

Fourthly, even if the Soviet Union had agreed to absorb all of Greece's exports in order to gain political influence in the Mediterranean region in general and in Greece in particular, the prevailing East–West politico-military realities, such as they were in the 1950s, would not have allowed the Greeks to go through such a major realignment of their foreign policy orientation.

Another alternative to joining the EEC would have been to imitate Israel's experiment. For Greece, such an alternative simply did not exist in the 1950s or, for that matter, in the 1960s. In contrast to Israel's relatively broad industrial base, high level of technical skills of the labour force, high capital inflows in the form of direct investment and foreign credit availability, and substantial or even unprecedented unilateral transfers from the rest of the world, Greece, as late as 1961, had largely a dual economy with over 50 per cent of its population in agriculture, an inadequate supply of agricultural exportables, a negligible amount of manufacturing exports, a very low level of technical skills, an inadequate industrial base, a limited infrastructure, chronic and at times critical balance of payments deficits and a real scarcity of both domestic and foreign capital resources.

By staying out of the EEC, therefore, Greece would have been forced to adopt a policy of political isolation coupled with economic protection[3] that would have in turn led to a retardation in the level of economic activity in Greece even if other countries did not retaliate. Accordingly, the alternative to economic stagnation through isolation made it necessary for Greece to choose some form of association with the EEC. An associate membership, it was agreed, would tend to cushion the impact of economic transformation, and it would also contribute to the attainment of a higher growth rate.

4. An Evaluation of the Results: the First Ten Years

In view of the record of the negotiations and the predictions of the theory, it is generally asked why the Six offered Greece a costly 'privileged' preferential status in the Community over a period of twenty-two years. The answer to this question appears to be largely political.

The reasons for the favourable outlook of the Six towards Greece went beyond economic considerations, because the cost of the preferential treatment outweighed all possible economic benefits for the Community. Indeed, the reasons were largely political, reflecting the Community's broad politico-economic perspectives and considerations – to wit, the movement

3 This point of view is given by S. G. Triantis (1961). In his view, if a country has poor soil and subsoil resources, a small economy and an unfavourable geographical location, the proper policy is a high protectionist commercial policy that will secure whatever little industry already exists. In support of this reasoning, Triantis stresses the infant industry argument and argues that, because the existing industries in a country like Greece are small, they should be treated collectively as one infant industry requiring protection.

Notably absent from Triantis' argument is the requirement that if the infant industry argument is to be justifiably invoked, increasing returns to scale must be apparent. The implicit assumption of Triantis' thesis is that economies of scale due to economic development will be less than economies of scale resulting from infant industry protection (which in turn assumes decreasing costs). Hence, he concludes that, in the absence of strict and permanent protection, the efforts of under-developed countries at industrialisation and economic development are bound to fail.

towards an independent and economically and politically united Europe. By offering Greece a 'privileged' preferential status within the Community, the Six expected to accomplish three distinct policy goals: (*a*) to assist Greece prepare its economy for full membership; (*b*) to replace the overwhelming influence of the United Kingdom and the United States in Greece's political, economic and foreign affairs; and (*c*) to establish the Community's credibility regarding its intentions for implementing Article 238 of the Treaty of Rome.

The answer to the second question posed at the beginning of this chapter – has the effect of the association with the EEC been a strategic factor in the rapid expansion and the changing structure of Greece's exports? – is yes, it has. Greece's exports in the post-association period increased at a considerably faster rate (13·1 per cent annually) than the pre-association period (6·8 per cent annually). Significantly, the increased growth rate in Greece's exports between 1962 and 1972 is largely attributable to the phenomenal increase of Greek exports and especially industrial exports to the EEC countries. Over this period, for example, exports to the EEC increased 15·2 per cent annually against 4·2 per cent annually in the pre-association period. Hence, as a result of the rapid growth of exports to the EEC over the past decade, the Community's share in Greece's total exports increased progressively to over 42 per cent in 1971 and 1972 from less than 32 per cent in 1961.

Significantly, the rising production of manufacturing exportables, which has been directly related to the agreement of association, also resulted in an improvement in the growth rate of exports to the United States and a rather substantial drop in the growth rate of exports to the Soviet-type economies. Greek exports to the United States between 1961 and 1972, for example, advanced by 14·6 per cent annually compared with 9·8 per cent annual growth rate in the 1953–61 period. Conversely, as the EEC market became readily available to Greek exports and as the product mix of Greece's exportables improved in favour of manufacturing goods exports, the annual growth rate of the country's exports (largely citrus fruits, tobacco and cotton) to the Soviet-type economies fell to 8·3 per cent from 19·6 per cent in the pre-association period.

On the side of imports, the overall impact of the association was also favourable to Greece. Imports from the Common Market countries as well as total imports in the post-association period advanced at the annual rate of 13·7 per cent, compared with 19·3 per cent and 9·0 per cent annual growth rate respectively in the pre-association period. Compared to the pre-association period, imports from the EEC in the last ten years advanced at a slower pace, whereas the rate of increase of Greece's total imports increased. Indeed, the higher rate of increase in all imports reflects largely the considerable improvement in the growth rate of imports, especially capital goods imports, from the United States (10·6 per cent annually) in comparison to the pre-association period (7·8 per cent per year). Moreover, because of the barter character of Greece's trade with the Soviet-type economies, imports from these countries advanced at a considerably lower rate (10·6 per cent per year) in comparison with the pre-association period (17·0 per cent per year).

On balance, the agreement of association has led largely to trade creation effects which were favourable to Greece as well as to the EEC countries and the United States. As to the diversion effects, if any, they affected, largely, Greece's trade with the Soviet-type economies. And to the extent that trade diversion occurred, it was also favourable to Greece, because (*a*) it permitted Greece to reduce the degree of monopsony enjoyed by the Soviet-block countries, especially for Greece's agricultural exports, and (*b*) it enhanced Greece's ability to earn foreign exchange in Western European markets and in the United States, and thereby to narrow the gap in its merchandise trade and current account. Hence, the favourable shifts in Greece's merchandise trade with the Community are undoubtedly attributable to the special arrangements made with the Six to facilitate Greece's development. Of these arrangements, the three most important for Greece are, of course, the preferential treatment accorded to Greek tobacco, the favourable treatment and protection accorded to Greek manufactures in the EEC, and the Community's commitment to facilitate the harmonisation of Greece's agricultural policies with those of the Six through Greece's participation in the Community's institutional and financial machinery, the Fonds Européen d'Orientation et de Garantie Agricole (FEOGA), that has already been set up to implement common agricultural policy. This policy involves export rebates and intervention in the domestic market through price supports to help the Greek farmer align his prices with those of the Community. In fact, Greece could receive up to $200 million per year once harmonisation becomes effective.

As a result of the concessions that have already been realised, Greece has been able to increase its volume of tobacco exports to the Community by over 60 per cent between 1961 and 1972. In addition, the association facilitated the rapid expansion of such exports as citrus, fresh fruit and vegetables, processed fruits and juices and wine for industrial uses. On the side of manufactured exports, the results have, indeed been impressive. By 1972, Greece's industrial exports reached the $330 million mark. Of these, over $160 million, or 49 per cent, were taken in by the EEC countries against a nominal amount of less than $3 million in 1962.

Much of the improvement, of course, in the growth of Greece's industrial exports is accounted for by a relatively limited, albeit widening, number of industrial products. The importance, however, of these industrial exportables (already substantial) will in time become decisive as a result of the dynamic potential for growth that characterises these products. Coupled, therefore, with the large size of the EEC market and the preferential treatment that the Community accords to Greek industrial exports, the potential for growth of such exportables as textiles, chemicals, pharmaceuticals, petroleum products, anti-knock compounds, nickel, steel, rolled sheet metal, electrical machinery and furs is, indeed, very large. In fact, it may be said that the favourable effects of the association on the growth of Greek exports to the EEC and on Greece's growth and development in general have only begun to be realised.

The answer to the third question posed at the beginning of this chapter – has the association thus far been a contributing factor in Greece's economic growth and industrial development? – is also yes, it has. Why? For one, the effect of the association on foreign investment was clearly very advantageous to Greece. In spite of the strong incentives and guarantees offered to foreign investors prior to the association with the EEC, the inflow of private foreign business investment was negligible. By way of comparison, foreign capital inflow, both private and public, since 1962 has been substantial. Indeed, not only did the 1962–72 period account for over 80 per cent of the total long-term capital inflow and 75 per cent of all suppliers' credit since 1953, but it also accounts for a major change in the structure and composition of the annual increments of capital inflow in favour of productive private and public investment.

Of course, it has been said that part of the hefty $2·02 billion net capital inflow that entered Greece since 1962 would have gone there regardless of the agreement of association. Although this suggestion may be partly true as far as the non-business capital inflow is concerned, the same cannot be said for either the bulk of capital inflow that went into private business investment or for the investment that was directed into financial assets. First, in the absence of the agreement of association and the preferential treatment and protection accorded to Greek manufacturing exports in the Community, private business investment would not have been attracted either into export-oriented and/or import-substituting manufacturing industries or into financial assets. Moreover, a continuation of the pre-association lack-lustre performance of Greece's exports in general and manufacturing exports in particular would have induced the domestic commercial banks and other financial institutions to shy away from innovations that they have recently introduced and from issuing sizeable long-term claims to foreigners payable in convertible currencies.

Beyond the favourable impact of the association on the inflow of private and public business capital, the agreement of association enhanced Greece's supply of capital in another direct way. Thus far, the Community has made available to Greece a substantial amount of low-cost capital ($125 million) through the European Investment Bank (EIB) and is committed to negotiate additional low-cost, long-term loans (up to $250 million).

The answer to the fourth question – will the association accelerate growth in the future? – is again affirmative. Greece's economy in the post-association period not only grew at a higher annual steady rate of 7·5 per cent than the 5·8 per cent annual growth rate of the pre-association period, but, more importantly, it accomplished some of the fundamental structural changes that will help the country achieve full membership in the European Community before 1984. In addition to the rapid increase in exports over the 1962–72 period, investment and domestic savings increased materially, from an *average* of less than 16 per cent of GNP between 1953 and 1962 to an *average* of over 22 per cent between 1962 and 1972.

As a result of the rising investment to GNP ratio, the rapid increase in production, the phenomenal rise in total exports and, especially, the increase of industrial exports to the EEC, Greece's composition of GDP has undergone considerable change in favour of secondary and tertiary production. The relative importance of agriculture in GDP declined substantially, to less than 18 per cent of GDP in 1972 from more than 28 per cent in 1962. And as agriculture became progressively less important in the post-association period, the share of manufacturing in GDP increased materially, rising to over 21 per cent in 1972 from 15 per cent in 1962 and 12 per cent in 1953.

Not less important is also the fact that in the post-association period the growth rate of Greece's GNP, GNP *per capita* and output per worker rose, whereas that of the EEC countries actually fell. As a result, although the gap between *per capita* GNP in the EEC and Greece remained wide, it narrowed considerably over the last decade, from 36 per cent of that in the EEC in 1962 to over 48 per cent in 1972.

Hence, the accelerated growth rate of GNP and *per capita* income in Greece since 1962 suggests that: (*a*) the level of economic activity in Greece was relatively unaffected by the economic fluctuations in the EEC, and (*b*) the rapid growth in real output has been associated, to a large extent, with the rapid expansion of Greece's exports to the EEC and the rising remittances that followed the exodus of Greek largely unskilled labourers to Germany over the last decade.

In view of the evidence presented, it is therefore reasonable to suggest that the association has so far contributed to Greece's economic growth through: (*1*) the reversal of the downward trend in the share of Greek exports to the Common Market group and the subsequent marked expansion of exports, especially of industrial exports to the EEC; (*2*) the direct increase in the supply of traditionally scarce capital; (*3*) the marked rise in the volume of private foreign investment directed, to a considerable extent, into export-oriented and import-substituting industries; (*4*) the absorption by the EEC countries of large quantities of unemployed or disguisedly unemployed Greek labour; (*5*) the rising foreign exchange earnings remitted to Greece from workers in the Community; (*6*) the realisation of dynamic gains from the repatriation of emigrants who took their training abroad; and (*7*) the improvement in the quality of management and the free transfer of new technology through the location of foreign firms in Greece.

Greece's association with the EEC has thus provided the opportunity for accelerated industrial development and a broadening of the Greek manufacturing base, while a period of high protection against foreign competition is still enjoyed by domestic producers, and tariffs on the Community's Greek industrial imports have been completely eliminated. Meanwhile, Greece already exports to the Community a sizeable part of its industrial output, and the prospects of the future expansion of manufacturing exportables is indeed favourable. Similarly, the prospects for harmonisation of Greek agriculture with that of the Community and the economic benefits that will accompany it – to wit, export rebates and domestic price supports – are at the present time quite within reach.

Additionally, the political benefits that are related to the agreement of association are not less important than the economic benefits thus far realised. Although it is true that nationalism is still a very strong force in Western Europe, it is also true that the movement towards European unification is no longer considered unrealistic. Unification in Europe will undoubtedly go on. For even weak federal experiments like the early

American Confederacy of separate states have a way of drawing power to the centre, and this will happen in Europe. Perhaps this union will not be as close and unified as in the United States or the Soviet Union, but in the end a strong, centralised European federal union will prevail, nonetheless.

It is axiomatic that Greece must be in such a union – not because history has placed that country on a pedestal for being the place where the ideas of freedom and democracy were born; not because European geo-political considerations determined that Greece's geographic location is strategic to its needs; not because Greece is physically part of Europe; but rather because the Greeks consider themselves Europeans with a stake in the shaping of Europe's political, social and economic future. And if the economic miracle which associate membership of the EEC has brought continues to benefit Greece, the country will be in a position to assume its responsibilities of full membership in the EEC before 1984, for the Greeks cannot afford to miss the historic opportunity to participate, indeed for the first time, in the European councils that will shape economic, political and social developments in the region for many years to come.

Finally, the empirical evidence supporting the favourable outcome of the Greek experiment confirms the theoretical formulations. These suggest that a preferential status of an LDC in a customs union of a group of highly industrialised countries will have the following results. Firstly, static gains will accrue through favourable trade creation effects which benefit not only the LDC but also the industrial member countries of the union. Secondly, there will be dynamic gains for the LDC resulting from the reallocation of resources and tariff changes, which in turn lead to (*a*) economies of scale and external economies, (*b*) changes in the terms of trade, (*c*) forced changes in efficiency due to increased foreign competition, and (*d*) changes in the rate of economic growth, as a result of the resource reallocation and the three dynamic factors mentioned above.

REFERENCES

Haberler, G. (1959). *International trade and economic development.* Cairo: Bank of Egypt.

Johnson, H. G. (1958). The gains from free trade with Europe: an estimate. *Manchester School.* September.

(1958). The criteria of economic advantage. *Bulletin of the Oxford University Institute of Statistics.* February.

Lipsey, R. G. (1960). The theory of custom unions: a general survey. *The Economic Journal.* September.

Lipsey, R. G., and Lancaster, C. J. (1957). The general theory of second best. *Review of Economic Studies*, XXIV.

Mackower, H., and Morton, G. (1953). A contribution towards a theory of custom unions. *The Economic Journal.* March.

Meade, J. E. (1955). *The theory of customs unions.* Amsterdam: North-Holland.

Nurkse, R. (1959). *Patterns of trade and development.* Stockholm: Wicksell.

Samuelson, P. A. (1954). The gains from international trade. *Readings in The Theory of International Trade*, H. S. Ellis and L. A. Metzler, eds. Philadelphia.

(1962). The gains from international trade once again. *Economic Journal.* December.

Scitovsky, T. (1958). *Economic theory and Western European integration*, Stanford University Press; and also Pezmatzoglou, J. (1962). *Syndesis tes Hellados Meta tis E.O.K.* (The Association of Greece with the EEC.) Athens: Bank of Greece.

Triantis, S. G. (1961). *Common Market and economic development.* Athens: Center for Economic Research.

Viner, J. (1950). *The customs union issue.* New York: Carnegie Endowment.

8

The EEC and Turkey: an Analysis of the Association Agreement and its Impact on Turkish Economic Development

JOHN N. BRIDGE

Of the seventeen countries bordering the Mediterranean (excluding France and Italy), the European Economic Community (EEC) has agreements, ranging from associate to technical agreements, with fourteen countries. Of these Turkey was one of the first countries to apply for associate membership, almost two years after Greece's application.[1] After considerable discussion of this application, Turkey signed an agreement on 12 September 1963 with the EEC whereby Turkey was to achieve associate membership with the hope of full membership with the mutual consent of both parties. The 1963 agreement specified a number of stages through which Turkey would pass: a preparatory phase, a transitional phase and a final phase.[2] The preparatory phase was designed to last a minimum of five years and a maximum of ten, the transitional phase was designed to last a minimum of twelve years and a maximum of twenty-two. The final phase would become operative only as a means of moving to a position of full membership of Turkey in the EEC. The time-table set in 1963 meant that Turkey could enter this final phase as early as 1980 or as late as 1995.

The preparatory phase was characterised by unilateral aid from the EEC to Turkey in terms of preferential tariffs and quotas on specific agricultural products and a $175-million loan to assist with industrial development projects. The basic aim of this aid was to strengthen the Turkish economy in terms of its exports and its industrial structure preparatory to the transitional stage. During the transitional phase, it was envisaged that there would be a gradual shift to a customs union, with the principle of reciprocity being established. In particular, it was intended that the transitional phase should include the acceptance of the common external tariff

1 J. Lambert, 'The Cheshire cat and the pond: EEC and the Mediterranean area', *Journal of Common Market Studies* X (September 1971), no. 1, 37–46.

2 *Accord créant une association entre la Communauté Economique Européenne et la Turquie* (Ankara, 1963).

(CET) system; the gradual acceptance of the Common Agricultural Policy (CAP) (in fact, there were certain exceptions to this statement, which will be mentioned later) and the general relaxation of factor immobilities as outlined in the Treaty of Rome.

The 1963 agreement set up three bodies to co-ordinate economic and political relationships between the EEC and Turkey: (*a*) the Mixed Parliamentary Commission; (*b*) the Council of the Association; and (*c*) the Association Committee.[3] It is primarily through these latter two bodies that Turkey has negotiated the different stages of its relationships with the EEC. For instance, requests for increases in quotas for Turkish agricultural exports have normally been channelled through the Association Committee.[4]

In the preparatory phase, quotas were established for Turkey's main agricultural exports – namely, tobacco, raisins, dried figs and hazel-nuts. A review of these quotas by Can in 1966 revealed some interesting features, which are summarised in Table 1.[5]

Turkey has been able to exceed its hazel-nut quota quite significantly, simply because it has a virtual world monopoly in the production of hazel-nuts. It is interesting to compare this with tobacco, where Turkey is just one of many suppliers of oriental tobacco to the EEC. The degree of world competition can influence the effectiveness of the quotas. Looking at these quotas over a longer period, Seyda came to the conclusion that they had been instrumental in restraining trade between the EEC and Turkey.[6] For instance, between 1965 and 1968 tobacco exports from Turkey to all countries rose by 20·5 per cent, but exports to the EEC rose only by 4·4 per cent. Similarly, for raisins the figures were 32·1 per cent and 25·4 per cent. For hazel-nuts and figs, total export growth amounted to 34·5 per cent and 23·8 per cent respectively, but to the EEC it amounted to 53·4 per cent and 30·7 per cent. Between 1965 and 1968 the overall growth in agricultural exports to the EEC was less than that to the USA, European Free Trade Association (EFTA) and Eastern Europe. Seyda commented that 'with the exception of modest increases in hazel-nut and fig exports to the

3 Economic Development Foundation, 'Turkey–EEC relationships'. *Turkish Economic Review* VII (November–December 1966), nos. 8 & 9, 31–3.

4 Economic Development Foundation, *op. cit.* 32.

5 T. Can, 'Economic relations of Turkey with the Common Market: 1955–1965', *Turkish Economic Review* VII (May–June 1966), nos.2 & 3, 35–7.

6 M. Seyda, 'Effects of EEC membership on Turkey's exports', *Turkish Economic Review* X (May–June 1969), nos. 2 & 3, 30.

TABLE 1 Quotas and actual exports of agricultural produce 1965 (tonnes)

Commodity	*quota*	*actual*
Tobacco	12,450	8,774
Raisins	30,000	29,715
Hazel-nuts	17,000	41,263
Dried figs	13,000	12,203

Source: Adapted from T. Can, 'Economic relations of Turkey with the Common Market; 1955–1965', *Turkish Economic Review* VII (May–June 1966), nos. 2 and 3, 35–7.

EEC, there has been no significant development in Turkey's exports to the Community as a result of the partnership'.[7]

By 1967, of 430 Turkish export items, four had quotas imposed on them; 105 were not protected under the common tariff policy and 327 were protected by the Community's common tariff rates against third countries, of which Turkey, during the preparatory phase, was one. The four quota exports accounted for over 40 per cent of total exports at that time. Thus, where concessions were granted to Turkey, the overall effect on exports was negligible, and, in fact, as Table 2 shows, the share of the EEC in Turkish exports fell slightly from 1964–8 and even by 1973 the share was only slightly more than in 1963. Thus, on the evidence of the pattern of major exports to the EEC from Turkey, it is clear that the effects of unilateral trade concessions in the preparatory phase were barely felt.

The preparatory phase was also intended as a period when the EEC would provide financial assistance on a unilateral basis. The 1963 agreement provided for a $175-million loan over the preparatory phase period. By December 1968, only $53 million had been utilised, although agreements had been reached for the disbursement of a further $56 million. The problem here seems to have been that the Turkish economy has responded very slowly to this financial stimulus. This financial provision was intended, specifically, for private industrial investment projects which would strengthen the industrial structure and lead to growth in industrial output. Clearly, the absorption rate of this financial aid has been low; but why this has been so is very difficult to evaluate. One possible explanation is that the private sector as a whole seems to have been at a disadvantage to

7 Seyda, *op. cit.* 30.

TABLE 2 Percentage distribution of Turkey's imports and exports by major country groupings, 1961–73

Year	*EEC*		*EFTA*		*Others*	
	Exports	*Imports*	*Exports*	*Imports*	*Exports*	*Imports*
1961	37·1	32·5	18·0	18·0	44·1	49·5
1962	40·5	30·2	19·3	16·6	40·2	53·2
1963	38·0	28·5	24·5	16·3	37·5	55·2
1964	33·5	28·7	23·7	16·9	43·8	54·4
1965	33·8	28·5	18·0	16·6	48·2	54·9
1966	35·0	32·9	18·8	17·6	46·2	49·5
1967	33·8	34·7	16·8	19·8	49·4	45·5
1968	33·1	36·9	17·1	20·5	49·8	42·6
1969	40·0	36·1	15·0	20·5	45·0	43·4
1970	40·1	34·6	17·2	17·9	42·7	47·5
1971	40·0	39·4	19·0	18·4	41·0	42·2
1972	38·4	41·2	19·5	19·6	42·1	39·2
1973	38·8	43·3	19·8	20·0	41·4	36·7

Sources: *Türkiye Istatistik Yilligi*, 1964 and 1971, *Aylik Istatistik Bulteni*, Türkiye Is Bankası, *Review of Economic Conditions 1974*.

Notes: The percentages for column 3 are calculated on a residual basis.

the public sector as far as financial provision is concerned. As Fry has commented: 'By far the most significant cleavage in the credit market is that between the public and private sector borrowers. The public sector invariably obtains funds at considerably lower costs than the private sector. Furthermore, on most criteria, credit availability would appear to be far greater for the public sector'.[8]

Although this comment applies to domestic credit markets, it is easy to see how this disadvantage could affect private sector access to foreign aid. Equally, it could be argued that insufficient viable investment projects existed to absorb this financial provision. Unfortunately, evidence to substantiate either of these two points is not readily available. However, it is a fact that the $175 million made available by the EEC has not been fully

8 M. Fry, *Finance and development planning in Turkey* (Leiden: E. J. Brill, 1972), p. 147.

absorbed and this, in itself, may have implications for financial assistance in the transitional period.

The preparatory phase could have ended in 1968, and, in fact, there were indications on both sides that Turkey would move to the transitional phase in the minimum time required. However, the negotiations on the further step soon revealed fundamental disagreements. The disagreements were of two kinds: firstly, there was disagreement in the Council of the Association over the precise concessions to be allowed to Turkey in the transitional phase and the phasing in of reciprocity; secondly, there was disagreement within Turkey about the negotiations. In particular, by 1969 it was clear that the State Planning Organisation was urging the Ministry of Foreign Affairs to slow down, basically on the grounds that the effects of trade liberalisation on a bilateral basis would be damaging to the Turkish economy. This pessimism probably arose from the relatively low rates of GNP growth achieved in the first two years of the Second Development Plan. Between 1968 and 1972, a 7 per cent per annum growth in GNP was planned, with industrial output growing at approximately 11 per cent per annum. Over the planning period as a whole, GNP rose at an average rate of 5·7 per cent per annum, while agricultural output rose by 4·2 per cent per annum and industrial output by 7·8 per cent per annum.[9] However, the growth rates recorded in 1968 and 1969 were both below the average for the planning period as a whole, and there must have been some doubts as to whether the Turkish economy could achieve a growth rate consistent with its desires to move into the transitional phase. More specifically, the growth of industrial output was probably sufficiently low for there to be some concern about the effects of trade liberalisation on Turkish industrial output.

Thus between 1968 and 1970 there were protracted discussions between the EEC and Turkey on the precise terms of the transitional phase. These negotiations centred on three main issues: (*a*) the status of Turkish agricultural and industrial goods in EEC markets; (*b*) the conditions relating to Turkish workers in Europe; and (*c*) financial aid during the transitional phase. When E. Noel, Secretary-General of the EEC Commission, spoke in Turkey in 1969 on the transitional stage, he also stressed the need to unify agricultural policies and social rights.[10] The basic dispute between Turkey and the EEC during these negotiations was over the phasing of

9 Türkiye Is Bankası, *Economic indicators of Turkey 1968–1972* (Economic Research Department, Ankara, 1973), p. 1.

10 E. Noel, 'Turkey's relations with the EEC', *Turkish Economic Review* x, (November–December 1969), nos. 8 & 9, 56–9.

industrial tariffs. The EEC wanted only 40 per cent of EEC exports to Turkey to be subject to a maximum twenty-two-year waiting period, whereas Turkey wanted a higher percentage of exports to be restricted, to try and preserve protection for its domestically produced goods as long as possible.

Turkey's intention to move into the transitional phase was never in doubt, but the timing as far as Turkey was concerned was crucial. One of the main points that is developed in the Third Five-Year Plan (1973–7) is that if the common economic policies of the EEC are imposed on Turkey *before* Turkey has reached a stage of economic, social and political development consistent with benefiting from these policies, then the restrictions imposed by these common economic policies may severely inhibit Turkish development.[11] It was essential for Turkey to achieve an agreement which would provide sufficient protection for its industrial goods for sufficient time to allow the growth in industrial output that would make industrial goods ultimately competitive with the EEC.

On 23 November 1970, Turkey signed an additional protocol with the EEC, laying down the conditions, procedures and time-table for the transitional phase. The protocol became effective from the date of exchange of instruments of ratification. An interim agreement was established to cover the intervening period, and the additional protocol eventually became effective in 1973. Thus Turkey ends the transitional phase in 1995, assuming that the maximum period of twenty-two years is adhered to. Basically, the 1970 agreement called for the setting up of a customs union between Turkey and the EEC, established through the removal of customs duties and equivalent taxes; the adoption of CETs and the elimination of quantitative restrictions. The transitional phase will encompass the complete liberalisation of industrial products, except iron and steel, and will act as a preparatory phase for agricultural products.[12] To meet Turkish demands for a phasing of liberalisation with respect to industrial goods, the 1970 protocol specified that 45 per cent of all industrial goods would be liberalised after twenty two years and the remaining 55 per cent after twelve years. Thus Turkey gained some concession from the EEC on the liberalisation of industrial exports from the EEC, but by no means as much as had been hoped for. A full account of items on the twenty-two-year list appears in annex 3 of the protocol. Suffice it to say here that more than six

11 J. N. Bridge, 'Some political and social aspects of planning in Turkey 1963–1973', Mimeograph.

12 E. Olgun, *Turkey–EEC relations during the transitional period* (USAID/Ankara Economic Planning Division, 1971).

hundred industrial goods are included and, perhaps most significantly, among them are many items of machinery and chemical products – on both of which Turkey is heavily dependent in terms of imports.

Turkey will eliminate the differences between its tariffs on non-member countries and the CET over a twelve-year period in the case of industrial goods on the twelve-year list and twenty-two years in the case of the twenty-two-year list. On Turkish exports, the EEC rate of liberalisation is immediately applied and Turkey is required to liberalise its imports over an eighteen-year period, when 80 per cent liberalisation will become effective. This liberalisation applies specifically to industrial goods. Quotas are still in force on major agricultural exports.

One area where restrictions on Turkish exports was retained was textiles. All textiles except cotton yarn, raw fabric and machine-woven carpets will be fully liberalised immediately, but these three items are subject to quotas which will be reduced to nil over twelve years. As cotton yarn accounted for over 21 per cent of visible exports in 1972, this quota is a considerable restriction for Turkey.

In terms of agricultural products Turkey has been unable to gain free access to the EEC. It is hoped that all agricultural products can be phased into the CAP over a twenty-five-year period. Initially, the EEC maintains the right to impose customs duties up to 50 or 60 per cent of the CET on olives, grapes, fresh figs, some dried fruits and citrus fruits. Although raisins and tobacco are customs free, hazel-nuts are subject to a 2·5 per cent *ad valorem* duty on a quota of 18,700 tons. This quota is little different from the one agreed on in the preparatory phase and is significantly below existing exports to the EEC.

The financial protocol included a provision for a loan of $220 million over a five-year period consisting of $195 million with a thirty-year term and an eight-year grace period with the possibility of a further $25 million provided by the European Investment Bank (EIB), for private-sector projects only.

Finally, free movement of workers between the EEC and Turkey is scheduled to be phased in between the twelfth and twenty-second years. Turkish workers employed in the EEC achieve immediate equal status with other workers in terms of conditions of work and remuneration.

At the time of the 1970 agreement, the Turkish Foreign Minister, Mr Cağlayangil, said:

> We have to make much greater efforts now towards industrialization. Every assistance and support will be extended by the Government to

> achieve this... the commitments have been spread over a long period and are not an impossible task for the economy... Now a huge market of high purchasing power is opening with suitable conditions for all sorts of products and manufactured goods from Turkish exporters, industrialists and entrepreneurs. By entering the transitional period we have not completed our membership with the EEC. On the contrary, we are just beginning.[13]

We now turn to examine in more detail the possible effects that the annex protocol may have on Turkish development. This examination will concentrate on the potential changes in Turkey's trade relations with the EEC and will investigate some of the internal repercussions of these changes.

Goodman, writing in 1969 on Turkey's prospects in the EEC, came to the conclusion that 'until Turkey can find the way to generate the resources that would allow her to maintain a reasonably balanced trade with the Common Market union with it may remain a dream for more than a generation'.[14]

This view is based on the premise that viability in a customs union rests ultimately on the balance of payments, and in the absence of long-term capital inflows adjustments to long-term deficits must occur in the visible trade account.[15]

The gradual removal of tariff barriers between Turkey and the EEC and the establishment of a CET will expose Turkish exports and domestic production to direct competition, which will result in a continuing trade deficit. The ability to rectify this deficit is limited on a number of counts. Firstly, as over 40 per cent of all imports emanate from the EEC, unilateral tariffs on EEC member states on this proportion are ruled out. The CET will limit the extent to which Turkey can discriminate against third countries, and devaluation will probably be less acceptable in the transitional phase than in the preparatory phase. The only other solution is to compensate for the trade deficit with large capital inflows. It is true that overall balance of payments surpluses have been recorded over the last five years; but whether earnings on the capital account can be expected to cover an ever-increasing deficit on visible trade (as indicated in Table 3) is very difficult to say. For instance, during 1972 visible imports expanded 23·1 per cent whereas visible exports expanded 4·7 per cent. In 1973, imports

13 Quoted in the *Turkish Economic Review* XI, (July–August 1970), nos 4 & 5, 16.

14 S. S. Goodman, 'Turkey's trade prospects in the Common Market: an exploratory study', *Journal of Common Market Studies* VII (1968–9), 305–26.

15 Goodman, *op. cit.* 306–7.

TABLE 3 The value of Turkey's merchandise trade, 1961–73 (in TL million)

	Exports	*Imports*
1961	3,120	4,585
1962	3,430	5,599
1963	3,312	6,216
1964	3,696	4,878
1965	4,173	5,193
1966	4,414	6,521
1967	4,701	6,216
1968	4,467	6,934
1969	4,831	6,785
1970	3,613	9,597
1971	9,090	17,725
1972	11,875	21,564
1973	12,814	29,265

Note: Before August 1970 the basic exchange rate was 9 TL = $1. From August a three-tier system was introduced; (*a*) 15·15 TL = $1 – for imports; (*b*) 14·85 TL = $1 – for exports; (*c*) 12·00 TL = $1 – for selected exports. Rate (*c*) was changed to 13·00 TL = $1 from July 1971.

From December 1971 the following rates apply; (*d*) 14·00 TL = $1 – for exports. (*e*) 14·30 TL = $1 – for imports.

Sources: *Türkiye Istatistik Yilligi 1971* and *Aylik Istatistik Bulteni*, various issues.

expanded again by 35·7 per cent and exports rose only by 7·9 per cent. This increasing gap partly reflects the effects of devaluation, as more liras are paid out for a given volume of imports; but it also reflects the competitive state of Turkey vis-à-vis its main trading partners. Over a longer period, 1963 to 1973, export growth has been approximately at 6·5 per cent per annum (at 1963 prices), and import growth has been at approximately 9·0 per cent per annum. This means that an increasing capital surplus is required if this trade deficit is not to be a restraint on development. Data on capital flows are very incomplete, but the official balance of payments data indicate a decline in the capital account surplus in 1972, and the large surpluses generated in 1970 and 1971 are probably due to the considerable liberalisation of private capital flows into Turkey, which can be taken as a once-and-for-all event. Accepting this argument, then long-run balance-of-payments stability must rest on adjustments in the trade balance. The Organisation of Economic Co-operation and Development (OECD) suggested as early as 1966 that the only feasible remedy to the trade deficit, which they saw as being long-term in nature, was a policy of import substitution.[16] Thus rapid industrialisation becomes the key to the problem of the balance of payments. Industrialisation is important in two respects. In the first place it can ultimately affect total import demand, and in the second place it can stimulate the growth of exports. At the present time, over 70 per cent of visible exports are in agricultural products and, assuming that the income elasticity for such products is lower than for industrial products, there may be a long-run improvement in Turkey's terms of trade if industrialisation leads to a distribution in total exports away from agricultural products.

This question of industrialisation can, therefore, be looked at from two different but not exclusive angles: firstly, industrialisation leading to import substitution; and secondly, industrialisation leading to rapid export growth. These two aspects are obviously interconnected. An increase in industrially produced export goods could lead to an increase in imports, unless domestic production can provide the necessary inputs. Equally, a policy of import substitution in the short-run may stifle export growth in the long-run. In this situation there is obviously a need to strike some sort of balance between the two. How this balance is assessed will depend very much on how current trade data are interpreted. Tables 4 and 5 provide data on major Turkish imports and exports from 1965 to 1973.

The major feature of Table 4 is that almost a quarter of all imports consists of non-electrical machinery. This heavy reliance on imported machinery may be expected to continue in the near future if rapid industrialisation is not going to be constrained by supply shortages. Equally, any policies on import substitution would have to take account of the distribution of imports outlined in Table 4. Petroleum products, chemicals, textile fibres and possibly cereals probably cannot be substituted in the near future, and with a rapid rate of industrialisation, it can be expected that the volume of these items will increase rapidly. Similarly, it is difficult to see how the import of iron and steel can be reduced significantly. Already the iron and steel industry in Turkey, which is a State Economic Enterprise, is producing steel at subsidised prices, and there is the possibility that this subsidy system will have to be reviewed in the light of the associate agreements, although the rapid increases in world steel prices during 1973 and 1974 may have made domestic steel more competitive.

There was some optimism expressed in the late 1960s that Turkey would

16 OECD, *Country report: Turkey* (Paris, 1966), p. 30.

TABLE 4 Turkish imports by major commodity groupings: 1965–72 (as percentages of all imports)

	1965	*1966*	*1967*	*1968*	*1969*	*1970*	*1971*	*1972*	*1973*
Cereals	4·7	2·6	0·3	–	2·4	5·8	*	*	*
Textile fibres	3·6	3·2	3·1	2·7	2·7	2·3	*	*	*
Petroleum	10·0	7·6	7·8	8·2	7·7	7·4	11·0	9·9	10·5
Chemicals	5·3	4·8	5·9	6·3	7·2	7·3	*	*	9·1
Fertilisers	3·1	3·9	5·4	6·2	7·0	3·2	2·8	4·0	6·3
Iron and Steel	8·8	7·6	5·4	4·4	4·7	7·6	11·3	9·4	11·7
Textile yarn	3·0	2·6	3·0	2·8	2·3	2·0	3·5	3·5	2·5
Machinery	23·2	25·0	27·0	27·5	22·8	22·6	27·9	33·1	30·2

Notes: (1) The commodity classifications correspond to the SITC two-digit commodity categories. (2) Imports of cereals are influenced by PL480 shipments, which are not accounted for in this table. (3) Machinery does not include electrical machinery. (4) Some items for 1971–3, marked *, are classified differently and are thus not recorded for these years. The dash shown against cereals for 1968 signifies that the figure involved was insignificant.

Sources: As for Tables 2 and 3.

TABLE 5 Turkish exports by major commodity groupings: 1965–73 (as percentage of all exports)

	1965	*1966*	*1967*	*1968*	*1969*	*1970*	*1971*	*1972*	*1973*
Fruit and vegetables	24·1	21·5	26·4	26·8	31·2	25·3	21·4	22·3	19·6
Tobacco	19·5	21·9	22·6	19·1	15·2	11·8	12·7	14·7	10·0
Textile fibres	24·7	28·4	27·2	29·9	22·7	28·0	28·5	21·6	23·2

Note: The commodity classifications correspond to the SITC two-digit commodity categories.

Sources: As for Tables 2 and 3.

be able to expand domestic oil production sufficiently to reduce imports quite significantly. The data in Table 4 would suggest that this has not occurred or, perhaps more to the point, domestic production, whilst expanding, has not grown as fast as domestic demand. By 1974, Turkish domestic production of 3·5 million tons of oil per annum accounted for only one-third of domestic demand. Again, rapid industrialisation will probably increase the demand for oil in the short-run and almost certainly will put increasing pressure on the trade balance, through the higher oil prices that have operated since October 1973. The fact that many items of machinery will enjoy protection under the twenty-two-year list means that considerable encouragement has been given to Turkish industry to attempt to substitute domestic production for imports in this field. Perhaps a more significant argument as far as imports is concerned is that the EEC is already the major exporter of these major Turkish imports, and the gradual reduction of the existing tariff barriers during the transitional phase will probably have the effect of increasing the flow, and, even if import substitution occurred, there is no guarantee that this increased domestic output could compete in internal markets after years of tariff protection.[17]

As far as exports are concerned, the predominant feature of Table 5 is the heavy concentration of exports in agricultural products and also the variability of these exports. Between 65 and 70 per cent of all exports are accounted for by the three major categories itemised in Table 5 – namely, fruit and vegetables, tobacco and textile fibres. All these items are, to a certain extent, influenced by climatic conditions. The good harvest years of 1967 and 1968 illustrate this point. Given this natural variability, then any predictions about growth in total exports have to be extremely cautious. A historical look at this situation reveals that the slow growth of exports is probably due partly to adverse export prices and partly to the variability in the volume of exports. During the 1950s and early 1960s, the commodity terms of trade moved generally in favour of Turkey; but from 1966 onwards there has been a gradual decline. At the moment, insufficient evidence is available to predict with any accuracy how export prices can be expected to behave in the near future. One indicator, however, is the trend in some primary commodity prices. These are summarised in Table 6.

Clearly, even cotton prices have not been able to compensate for the increasing costs of imports, and the absolute value contribution of tobacco has declined, which is also illustrated in Table 5. Bearing in mind the natural variability in production caused by climate and the evidence available on export prices, the prospects for a rapid expansion in export earnings are very poor. Given this situation, some change in the structure of exports is called for. For instance, there is considerable support in Turkey for the idea that cotton yarn should be processed in Turkey. This argument has two advantages: firstly, it creates more industrial output and hence employ-

17 Goodman, *op. cit.* 326.

TABLE 6 Export prices for cotton and tobacco 1968–74 (based on $ prices per kilogram)

Year	Tobacco	Cotton
1968	1·26	0·55
1969	1·00	0·63
1970	1·03	0·66
1971	1·24	0·83
1972	1·32	0·85
1973	1·05	1·76
1974	1·40	1·85

Note: The tobacco prices are based on the average export price received by the State Monopoly for American and oriental tobacco. The cotton prices are based on the minimum export price for Aegean St. I cotton.
Source: Türkiye Iş Bankasi, *Review of Economic Conditions*.

ment; and secondly, clothing entering the EEC is totally exempt from tariffs, whereas cotton yarn benefits, initially, only from a reduced tariff.[18]

On a more general basis, Turkey may have to look to industrial development which corresponds more closely with its factor endowments. Broadly speaking, this would imply concentration on labour-intensive industries processing agricultural products, assuming that the appropriate technologies for such a strategy were available. However, any process of industrialisation is faced with some fairly formidable structural problems.

One of the interesting features of the Third Five-Year Plan was that it included a long-term perspective on Turkish development which, presumably, was intended to coincide with the transitional phase. Within this perspective a number of fundamental problems were highlighted, the solution to which would determine the prosperity of Turkey in the future. The problems highlighted are: (*a*) high levels of unemployment (12 per cent recognised as unemployed, with the marginal unemployment rate – that is, new entrants – of 64 per cent, (*b*) a low *per capita* income in relation to the rest of Europe, coupled with a maldistribution of income: (*c*) very high rates of population growth, accompanied by high dependency rates (an estimated

18 E. Olgun, *Public and private sector views on Turkey's entry into the transitional stage of its association with the European Economic Community* (USAID/Ankara, Economic Planning Division, March 1971), p. 10.

net population growth rate of 2·6 per cent); (*d*) an inadequate education system (inadequate in that it cannot provide the education levels consistent with high rates of growth); (*e*) poor health services; (*f*) a low level of provision of essential services in urban areas; (*g*) insufficient domestic savings; (*h*) low levels of capital utilization and technology in industry and agriculture; (*i*) the dominance of exports by agricultural products; and (*j*) an archaic public administration system.[19] These problems are not all directly related to a policy of industrialisation; but it is certain that if they are not solved, industrial progress will be much slower than is envisaged, and given the time-table in the transitional phase, very rapid structural adjustments are necessary. The question is, can this sort of structural change be accomplished during the transitional phase? Obviously, views on this question differ quite considerably. The optimism expressed by many Turkish officials in 1970 was on the basis that the additional protocol provided a considerable challenge to Turkish development which could be met successfully. Taking a more pessimistic point of view, it is only fair to point out that many of the structural problems mentioned here were also highlighted in the First Five-Year Plan in 1963, and the fact that little progress had been made towards their solution by 1972 does not augur well for the future.

Rapid industrialisation is almost certainly the major factor which will determine how successfully Turkey emerges from the transitional phase. Internally a considerable number of structural problems exist, and externally Turkish goods are fairly rapidly going to be exposed to direct competition with EEC goods. During 1973, the prospects for manufacturing output improved. Overall GNP rose in real terms by 6·4 per cent, giving an average growth rate of 7·1 per cent for the 1969–73 period. Significantly, an 8·2 per cent fall in agricultural output was compensated for by a 15·2 per cent increase in manufacturing output. If this type of progress in the manufacturing sector were to continue, then Turkey could face the rest of the transitional period with more confidence.

Two further issues need to be explored to complete this discussion on industrialisation: firstly, the possible effects of private foreign capital; and secondly, the attitudes of indigenous groups in Turkey to the transitional phase.

Of the totalled planned investments in the Third Development Plan, over 50 per cent are expected to be financed through direct foreign aid sources. In fact, the Plan envisages an average annual inflow of $186 mil-

19 USAID/Turkey Mission, *Unofficial translation and summaries of selected sections and tables of the Third Five-Year Development Plan, 1973–1977*, pp. 11–13.

lion. In addition to this it is estimated that there will be a need for $56 million of private foreign capital per year. Thus the total investment programme hinges crucially on private and public foreign capital. As far as private foreign capital is concerned, the annual flow from 1968 to 1973 averaged $37 million.[20] In addition, there seem to be indications that more restrictions are being put on foreign capital, in terms of conditions associated with profit remittances and the need to guarantee specific export targets (for instance), which have had the effect of reducing the flow of foreign capital.[21] Taking these two factors into consideration, it is very difficult to see how the Third plan investment programme can be realised. If there is a shortfall in investments, this will retard the industrialisation programme and will make it just so much more difficult for Turkey to become competitive with the EEC in industrial products.

The attitudes of indigenous groups can be split into two categories. One category is concerned with the general economic feasibility of the transitional phase as far as Turkey is concerned, and the second category includes a wide range of political and economic opinions that tend to question the whole basis of the associate agreement.

Essentially, economic arguments centre on the issues of the customs union, agricultural policy, factor movements and, perhaps less important, financial provisions.[22] As far as the customs union issue is concerned there seems to be a clear disagreement between the State Planning Organisation and other ministries concerned with the association agreement. For instance, the Ministry of Foreign Affairs and the Ministry of Commerce see the transitional phase as a perfect opportunity to expand the industrial potential in Turkey. On the other hand, the State Planning Organisation sees the entry into a customs union as an occasion for the rapid exposure of Turkish industry to competition for which it will not be prepared. In particular, the State Planning Organisation points to the restrictions placed on textile exports to the EEC – the one area where it is claimed that Turkey is competitive. Factor movements seem to be seen in a more favourable light, with stress being placed on the potential reductions in unemployment and the foreign exchange earnings generated by remittances from abroad, although the general cut-back in economic activity in Europe in 1974 now

20 Economic Intelligence Unit, *Quarterly economic review: Turkey*, 1973, no. 3, p. 25.

21 The Law for the Encouragement of Foreign Capital Investment (No. 6224) enacted in 1954 adopted a very flexible attitude to foreign investment. It seems as if the interpretation of this law has changed in recent years.

22 Olgun, *op. cit.* p. 8.

makes this a rather volatile source of foreign exchange. In addition, it could be argued that Turkish migrants are trained at zero cost in Europe and are, therefore, in the long run, a costless source of trained labour. Of course, the biggest problem is the methods of absorbing migrant workers back into local communities. There is a general belief, as noted earlier, that Turkey has not gained much from the agricultural aspects of the protocol and that this will continue to be the case, although it is conceded that general tariff reductions could be an impetus to agricultural production in general and may lead to more diversification in output. The total financial provision in the transitional phase is not sufficiently large for it to be a centre of controversy. Thus economic arguments about Turkey–EEC relations hinge around the customs union and its associated conditions and factor movements. The attitudes that have been discussed briefly here are highly subjective and probably capture only a small element of the discussions going on in Turkey on the transitional phase. However, it is clear that the timings scheduled in the transitional phase are crucial, and the ways in which the Turkish economy responds to these changes will determine how successful the transitional phase is from Turkey's point of view.

From a political point of view, the elections in October 1973, which resulted in January 1974 in a coalition government being formed between the People's Republican Party and the National Salvation Party may have some bearing on relationships with the EEC in the future. The National Salvation Party (led by Necmettin Erbakan) prior to the elections spoke out against the EEC on principle, but it is significant that in government these fundamental criticisms have become muted. However, the Republican People's Party had some misgivings about the association agreement also. Mr Ecevit, the Turkish Prime Minister, expressed his dissatisfaction with the concessions granted to Turkey in the transitional phase, and also criticised domestic efforts in industry and agriculture immediately after the elections.[23] The policy document issued by the coalition government in January 1974 did call for some revision of the associate terms with the EEC. In particular, revision is being sought with respect to the further protection of Turkish industry and further concession for Turkish exports into the EEC. Even if these concessions are granted, the time normally taken to deal with such requests will mean that no visible benefits will accrue to Turkey over the next two years – that is, up to 1976.

Taking a longer-term perspective, any further concessions granted to Turkey may well rest on the overall commitment that Turkey has to

23 In an interview with *Le Monde*, quoted in *Milliyet*, 2 November 1973.

ultimate membership. If there is any doubt about the overall intention, then concessions will probably be more difficult to achieve. Equally, developments in the relationships that the EEC has with other Mediterranean countries will influence the position in future. For instance, the question of the accession of Spain and the way in which this opens out the market may be important.

There are two further factors relating to Turkey–EEC relations, that can be introduced briefly. Firstly, domestic inflation in Turkey does not seem to have been checked by the numerous measures in 1970. Since the 67 per cent devaluation in August 1970, the wholesale price index has risen by over 100 per cent and the predicted annual rate for 1974 is 30 per cent.[24] This inflation is considered to be largely demand-induced from migrant worker remittances and increasing agricultural incomes, caused by rapidly rising world commodity prices. Whatever the causes of the inflation, the effects may soon be felt in industrial production. This may necessitate a formal devaluation or more severe domestic deflationary policies. Either way, the industrialisation programme will probably be affected.

Secondly, Turkey already has trade links with Pakistan and Iran, through Regional Co-operation and Development (RCD). It is very difficult to see how this link and the one with the EEC will affect Turkey. It is conceivable that, if Turkey became a full member of the EEC, the RCD countries would then establish more formal links with the EEC.[25] Equally, there are some political elements in Turkey which would favour a stronger RCD agreement in preference to anything negotiated with the EEC.

This survey of Turkey–EEC relations has concentrated on the effects on Turkey. The basic point that seems to come out of the discussion is that the benefits of the transitional phase can accrue to Turkey only if industrialisation proceeds at a rapid pace. It has been argued that there are a number of factors which might inhibit this industrial growth, and the Turkish economy may find itself deriving little or no benefit from the present arrangements.

24 Economic Intelligence Unit, *op. cit.* p. 6.

25 N. Islam, 'Regional co-operation for development', *Journal of Common Market Studies* V (1966–7), 283–301.

9

Development of the Maghreb and Its Relations with the EEC

ROBERTO ALIBONI

1. Political–Institutional Aspects

The documents instituting the European Economic Community (EEC) contain provisions concerning Tunisia, Morocco and Algeria. These provisions constitute the historical and institutional foundation for relations between the EEC and these countries.[1] In a statement of intent that was annexed to the Rome Treaty, the Community members affirmed their willingness to reach association agreements with Tunisia and Morocco and to contribute to economic and social development of these countries. On Algeria, which then constituted three French *départements*, was conferred member status, and Algeria thus received financial aid from the Community. After independence in 1962, Algeria requested and obtained *de facto* continuation of its preferential status, with the exception of new grants of aid. Since then, the position of Algeria has not been defined, and at the present time constitutes a true juridical anomaly within the Community's system of external relations. Member nations, in fact, apply different systems with regard to Algeria.

In 1969, after long and difficult negotiations, the EEC, Tunisia and Morocco concluded association agreements based on Article 238 of the Rome Treaty. The contents of the two association agreements are nearly identical. With the exception of products already covered by the European Coal and Steel Community (ECSC) Treaty – refined petroleum products and cork products – full exemption is foreseen for importation of Moroccan and Tunisian industrial products into the EEC. In fact, for agricultural products the EEC has granted concessions for a group of products of wide

1 For the political–institutional background of EEC–Maghreb relations see: B. Etienne, 'Maghreb et CEE', in CRESM, *Les économies maghrébines* (Paris: CNRS, 1971), pp. 165–97; Henig, S..'The Mediterranean policy of the European Community, *Government and Opposition*', VI, 1972, no. 4; Zartman, *The politics of trade negotiations between Africa and the European Economic Community* (Princeton, N.J.: Princeton University Press, 1971).

interest to its members (oranges, olive oil, fish products and so on). When the agreements were reached it was estimated that in the agricultural field the concessions covered approximately 50 per cent of Moroccan agricultural exports to the EEC and approximately 70 per cent of those of Tunisia. Overall, these concessions total around 60 per cent of Moroccan exports to the EEC and approximately 70 per cent of those of Tunisian origin.

These agreements were presented as a means of establishing free-trade areas under the terms of Article 24 of the General Agreement on Tariffs and Trade (GATT), even though the total of the exchanges covered thereby appears insufficient to meet the normal GATT criteria. The latter, in fact, requires an exchange coverage of approximately 90 per cent. Nevertheless, it is upon this basis that the Community, in spite of considerable resistance on the part of Morocco, has requested and obtained agreements based on reciprocal concessions. Thus Tunisia has granted preferences for a list of products amounting to 40 per cent of its imports from the EEC; Morocco has made concessions for a total equal to 10 per cent of its imports from the EEC. From a formal standpoint, the Moroccan concessions are not preferential, because, as a result of the Algeciras Act of 1906, they are extended *erga omnes*. But, from a practical point of view, they concern products of which the Community is the primary exporter. On the other hand, both on the part of Tunisia and Morocco, the opening of quotas in favour of the EEC was preferential. Some of these quotas will gradually be decreased as local industry proves itself capable of production to replace imports from the EEC.

Other noteworthy points to be considered are: exceptions to the Most Favoured Nation clause with respect to the EEC, provided that Maghreb regional integration develops; rules of origin which permit a non-local value added equal to 50–60 per cent; the institutional structure constituted by a Council composed of member parties to supervise the agreement.

At the end of 1972, in an attempt to organise the numerous relationships undertaken with respect to Maghreb nations and with nearly all other Mediterranean countries, the Commission proposed global policy for the entire Mediterranean region.[2] The Commission's proposals envisaged that the EEC would progressively establish a free-trade area for agricultural and industrial products of the region, and at the same time institute a programme for technical and financial assistance. It should also develop an acceptable plan for labour emigration and for co-operation for environ-

2 G. P. Papa, 'An overall Mediterranean policy', *European Community*, 11, November 1972, 16–17.

mental protection. Exchange of industrial products would be liberalised at varying speeds, depending upon the degree of development of the individual countries. The most delicate question would be that of ensuring, in spite of restrictions imposed by the Common Agricultural Policy (CAP), liberalisation of agricultural exchanges sufficient to reach the coverage required by the GATT so that a free-trade area can legitimately be spoken of. In view of the importance of agricultural exchanges in the Mediterranean, the Commission has calculated that at least 80 per cent of the Community's agricultural imports from countries of this area must be liberalised.

This overall policy has generated criticisms and discussions. The accession of the three new member nations has had the effect of braking its application and reducing its more abstract aspects. In any case, this policy, conceived with a view to a multilateral approach, is shifting towards a set of bilateral agreements, even though similarly conceived.

In this connection, at the end of June 1973, the Council gave to the Commission a first mandate for negotiation of the association of Algeria and renewal of associations with Tunisia and Morocco, as well as agreements with Spain and Israel. By the end of 1974, negotiations are still continuing with the aim of reaching agreements to improve the agricultural provisions and include financial and technical co-operation besides that in trade. However, the difficulties encountered in concluding negotiations after so many years are due more to crisis in the EEC than to real difficulties in engineering agreements. Briefly, then, this is the political-institutional background of economic relations between the EEC and the Maghreb. In this study we shall attempt to examine the relationships between the Community and the Maghreb nations from the point of view of the latter countries and their requirements for development. The primary question we shall try to answer is: what role has the relationship with the EEC played in the economic development of the three Maghreb countries?

To reply to this question, we shall first of all briefly examine the primary aspects which characterise the economic evolution of the Maghreb nations. We shall subsequently consider their foreign relations and, finally, we shall attempt to define the role of relations between the Community and the Maghreb.

2. Development of the Maghreb

After independence (1956), with the 'Préplan' (1962–4), the primary aims of Tunisian planners began to be delineated: modernisation of agriculture and industrialisation extending to various sectors, in line with linkages allowed by the Tunisian market. In quantitative terms, the aim was to increase the total product by 75 per cent by 1971.

To reach these objectives, Tunisian planners proposed ambitious investment efforts. Gross investments foreseen for the three-year period 1962–4 alone amounted to 330 million dinars (in 1962 the GDP was 323 million dinars). Foreign aid was relied upon to provide 155 million of this total. Nevertheless, the 1965–8 plan began before acquisition of the means necessary for this investment, and the Treasury had to finance a not inconsiderable portion of the programme. What developments in production were realised in the period which we are considering?

Between 1962 and 1968, the GDP at factor cost increased at an average rate of 4·4 per cent. During the same period, commerce – a sector fully invested by the co-operative experience – increased by 3·2 per cent and industry and agriculture increased by 7·4 per cent. For the latter, the loss of dynamism is evident, nevertheless: the rate calculated for the period 1963–8 scarcely reached 3 per cent. The economy did not respond to the investment-indebtedness endeavours planned by the state. This failure was occasioned to a considerable extent by the failure of the co-operatives, particularly the agricultural ones. In addition to reduction of agricultural production, failure in this field signified the perpetuation of a restricted internal market and the resultant impossibility of increasing industrial production. In 1969, in fact, the attempt to advance the reform of agrarian structures by incorporating the modern agricultural sector with the co-operatives met with a reaction on the part of land holders and brought about the downfall of Ahmed Ben Salah and his economic policy.[3] This crisis provoked a vacuum in which past failures and the lack of orientation for the future piled up. Between 1963 and 1971, the GDP development rate decreased to 3·7 per cent. That of agriculture fell to 0·7 per cent.

The economic policy of Ben Salah, which was interrupted just at the moment when its potential for success could have been evaluated, can be judged only with difficulty. In any case, the gravity of his failures rests in the fact that he left Tunisia without other real alternatives. Subsequent political-economic trends, consolidated in the 1973–6 plan, do not appear to remedy the situation. Violently severed from the only attempt which, although poorly conducted, aimed at the social integration necessary for its development, the Tunisian economy has once again been firmly taken

3 J. Chérel, 'Tunisie, histoire d'un échec', *Les Temps Modernes* (March 1972), 1482–502; R. Stone, 'Tunisian cooperatives: failure of a bold experiment', *Africa Report* **6** (1971), 19–22.

into the hands of the middle class, whose interests are recognised by the neo-Destourian party. This bourgeoisie has consolidated its control over the commercial facilities that formerly it nearly lost and has tightened its grip on landed property as the co-operatives were closed down. Unable to invest in the industrial sector, which continues to be state-controlled, the middle class is investing in the tourist industry. In that it neglects the problem of agriculture and of social integration, the return to 'capitalism' has no meaning other than that of a return to the situation which preceded independence.[4] The priority given to tourism, the tax haven for foreign investments, the emphasis on the export industry, the renewed recourse to foreign aid, all of the primary options of recent Tunisian economic policy are the result of renouncing the decision to constitute an internal market by means of the modernisation of agriculture. These trends accentuate and consolidate Tunisia's dependency without guaranteeing development. Under the cloak of economic policy they represent nothing but escapism.

Algeria, since independence in 1962, has concluded a first phase of structural development in which was formulated a complex, ambitious plan for further advancement. It is now entering the phase which will be decisive for the success of its aspirations.

The primary aim of Algerian planners is economic independence by means of a rapid introversion. In other words, their objective is to create a 'coherent structure',[5] (intersecting chains of sectors). In this way, developments in each sector are communicated to the others without being dispersed outside the Algerian economy. With this in mind, the objectives having priority are those instituting a basic industrial sector (steel and chemicals) and a metal-working sector (mechanical and electrical industries) capable of providing producer goods. The fundamental objectives, however, are those of providing an internal market for both basic commodities and producer goods. This, in fact, is the condition for realising introversion of the economy, laying the foundations for self-sustained development. Naturally, this is the most delicate point in the project for Algerian development, because it first of all involves the problem of the modernisation of agricul-

4 J. Poncet, 'L'économie Tunisienne depuis l'indépendance', in CRESM, *op. cit.* pp. 89–110; see p. 109.

5 The works of G. Destanne de Bernis are the best illustration of Algerian planning and development: 'Le plan quadriennal de l'Algérie (1970–1973)', in CRESM, *Annuaire de l'Afrique du Nord 1970* (Paris; CNRS, 1971), pp. 195–230, 'Les industries industrialisantes et les options algériennes', *Tiers Monde* (July-September 1971), 545–63; 'L'economie algérienne depuis l'indépendance', in CRESM, *op. cit.*, pp. 9–37.

ture, making the latter the core of its internal market. If agricultural modernisation should fail, 'industrialization is being challenged with regard to its current trend and the only logic within the sphere of which it can be conceived. Recourse to exports, provided that this is possible, which is far from certain, may perhaps in part safeguard functioning of the plants, but the overall construction of independence would be shaken to its core'.[6] Having at first neglected agriculture, in order to lay the foundations of the industrial sector, Algerians are now confronting the problem. Thus, the Algerian economy has entered a phase which is decisive to the course of the nation's development. What were the achievements realised up to the present?

Certain indications can be drawn from an examination of data concerning the 1960s. Industrial and artisan output increased by 16 per cent per annum between 1963 and 1969, and this sector grew more rapidly than any other. This increase is a measure of the Algerian achievement in carrying through their industrialisation plans. The most recent data – although not comparable with those mentioned above – indicate continuation of a satisfactory evolution in the industrial field, production in the various branches of which grew by a minimum of 10 per cent in 1971.[7]

The overall development rate of the GDP, on the contrary, does not appear satisfactory when measured against expectations. In 1963–70 it was equal to 5·9 per cent, whereas the plan envisaged 9 per cent. To a great extent this was due to slow movement in the agricultural sector, which, during this period, grew by a scant 1·5 per cent per year, a rate insufficient to provide food for the Algerians or to prevent migration of the population to the cities.

The industrial development established in Algeria is too recent to be capable of absorbing the agricultural workers who have been driven out from their sector. Not only is it recent, but it has also selected highly capital-intensive sectors and techniques; it cannot even absorb urban unemployment. This delay is really expected: Algerian planners, in fact, foresee that only by 1980 will industry, through expansion beyond its fundamental sectors, be able to begin to assimilate unemployed labour forces. However, the rural exodus is not included in these forecasts and constitutes a very dangerous factor of tension.

Agrarian reform – called the 'agrarian revolution', although it is less radical than that contemplated by the Tunisians – is the means upon which

6 G. Destanne de Bernis, 'Le plan quadriennal', *op. cit.* 209.

7 A. Benachenou, 'Chronique économique. Algérie', in CRESM, *Annuaire de l'Afrique du Nord 1971* (Paris, CNRS, 1972), pp. 445–74; see pp. 448–9.

Algerian planners are relying to meet this fundamental difficulty in the development of their country.[8] At the same time they foresee a certain increase in agricultural investments, even if the efficacy of these investments depends less on their volume than on the success of the reform itself.

Nevertheless, many difficulties remain. Because appropriation will be on a limited scale, it is estimated that the land available for redistribution will amount to 1 million hectares. However, the grantees should number about 600,000. This means that each of them will receive 2 hectares. Moreover, if – as appears likely – the plots to be granted amount to 10 hectares each, so as to obtain an agricultural sector suited to the mechanical implements which Algerian industry has begun to produce, only 100,000 peasants would receive land.[9] This would result in further unemployment or a new agricultural sub-proletariat (*khammes*) and not in a market for the growing industrial sectors. Two-hectare farms, on the other hand, are equally incapable of creating a wide market.

In reality, the middle class, which guides development of capitalism in the Algerian state, although constrained by the vital need for the modernisation of agriculture, does not appear to be willing to embark on the necessary confrontation with the land owners, having resolved to expropriate them. This is why failure is risked in the incipient industrialisation in the agricultural sector. In addition, as in Tunisia, these policies risk the creation of a rift between tradition and reform, thus preparing the way for failure of the latter. In this regard, it is remarkable that no plans have been made for the expansion of a self-management sector, although the latter is efficient despite subjection to bureaucracy and administrative prices. The Algerian middle class, uncertain in its alliances with the peasant and land-owning population and incapable of defeating them by integrating the peasants into the capitalist system and, moreover, trapped by its choice of high-capital industrial sectors and techniques, without any signs of the creation of a flourishing agricultural sector and the establishment of medium or small business enterprises, is faced with a great challenge: outright success or else semi-integration between the centre and the periphery, a position that would indeed be difficult.

In contrast to the profound changes that shook the Tunisian and Algerian economies, continuity is the hallmark of that of Morocco. After a brief experience with a nationalistic government which attempted to lay the

8 P. Santacroce, 'La riforma agraria in Algeria', *Monthly Review* (Italian ed.) (July–August 1973), 35–40; R. Weexsteen, 'La "Revolution agraire" de l'Algérie', *Le Monde Diplomatique* (September 1973), 16–17.

9 Benachenou, *op. cit.* p. 466.

foundations for independent development, Morocco's monarchy renounced development of the industrial sector envisaged in the 1960–4 plan, and excluded the local middle class from political power. So it has initiated growth without development of the Moroccan economy.

From Table 2 it can easily be seen that agriculture, mining, industry and construction have, with the passage of time, maintained their relative proportions. A Moroccan economist has written, 'au Maroc les années se ressemblent'.[10] Within this stationary structure, however, the position occupied by agriculture is much more important than that in Tunisia and Algeria. In effect, the principal cause of stagnation in the Moroccan economy appears to be connected with the fact that, although the development of agriculture is the primary objective of Moroccan economic policy, governmental efforts in this regard have been of limited efficacy, due to the absence of structural reforms. The undistinguished record of Moroccan agricultural policy is reflected in the rate of agricultural development, which in the years between 1963 and 1971 barely reached 3·4 per cent per annum on average. This datum becomes more significant when it is realised that 61 per cent of the active population is engaged in agriculture.

The sector given second priority by Morocco – that is, tourism – has also turned out to be relatively disappointing. In recent Moroccan planning, industry is not given a high priority. For this reason, public investments are directed to it only to a very limited extent. Although according to the doctrine of the *chérifien* government private investments hold an important, indeed pre-eminent role, in reality they are few, and speculative activities are preferred over those of production. Private Moroccan capital has been expended above all for redemption of holdings of French emigrants, trade and for real estate and foreign speculation.

Resulting from governmental failures in the field of agriculture, lack of interest in industrial development and the limited inclination towards capitalistic development on the part of the wealthy classes, is stagnation – growth without development – of the Moroccan economy, which now appears to be nearing the same extroversion and dependence as that of the Tunisian economy, even though for Morocco the crisis appears less dramatic.

3. Maghreb Foreign Relations

Integration into the international market is, at the same time, demanded of the three Maghreb nations, and it is one of their objectives. However,

10 F. Oualalou, 'Chronique économique. Maroc', in CRESM, *Annuaire de l'Afrique du Nord 1971*, *op. cit.*, pp. 481–503; see p. 503.

whereas Algeria appears to aim at an independent integration, Morocco and Tunisia do not seem to have the same desire.

To avoid being led astray by the similarity of indications which evidence an analogous degree of integration or external dependency, emphasis must be laid upon this different approach. Thus, among these indications, the ratio between exports and the GDP or that between imports and the GDP appears sufficiently high for all three of the Maghreb nations: in the case of Algeria, the former was 24 per cent in 1970 and the latter 30 per cent. With regard to Tunisia these ratios were 13 per cent and 22 per cent, respectively, and for Morocco, 13 per cent and 19 per cent. These three countries, however, have recourse in an equally high measure to external resources, either in the form of grants or credits, and face a foreign indebtedness which is generally considerable. According to data supplied by the World Bank, in 1971 the ratio between debts and exports was 18 per cent in Tunisia and 9 per cent in Morocco. As far as Algeria is concerned, foreign estimates set this ratio at 15–17 per cent, although according to the Algerians it is 10–13 per cent.[11] Then, the importance borne by a single product or by a few products in the export structure of the three countries may be considered. To name only agricultural products, Algerian wine, Tunisian oil and Moroccan citrus fruits constitute from 14 to 16 per cent of the total exports of each country. In addition, from a geographical point of view, trade on the part of these three countries appears to be concentrated equally. In 1971, Morocco exported to the EEC 57 per cent of its total exports. It purchased 49 per cent of its overall imports from the EEC. Tunisia sends to the EEC (1969–71 average) 55 per cent of its exports and imports the same percentage from the EEC. For Algeria as well, in 1970 the EEC was the principal customer (73 per cent) in addition to being the principal supplier (65 per cent). To all this, finally, must be added the importance to Algeria and, to a lesser extent, to Morocco of remittances by emigrants and the importance of revenue resulting from tourism accruing to Tunisia and, to a lesser degree also, to Morocco.

Beyond the similarity of the picture of dependency and integration projected by these figures, the importance and dynamism of these images appear to differ from country to country. This point is worth developing. In more explicit terms the question to be answered is: what relationship exists between the different development programmes and foreign relations of the Maghreb countries?

11 N. Grimaud, 'Les finances publiques de l'Algérie', *Maghreb-Machrek* **56** (1973), 30–7.

The case of Algeria is without doubt the most interesting. Algerian economic policy is progressing along two primary lines. On the one hand, Algeria is attempting to attain its independence by placing at the service of its objectives of introversion a prudent, strict financial policy, both internal and foreign. Sources of energy play a fundamental role in this, provided, above all, that they are appropriately managed. On the other hand, Algeria is trying to become integrated into the international market through the institution of a strong basic industrial sector and of highly capitalistic and competitive techniques. In other words, Algeria is explicitly attempting to overthrow the type of integration which links it to the international market: from an integration typical of under-developed, colonial countries to that of an industrialised nation; from a dependent integration to an independent integration. This, of course, is the other, functional and necessary side of the picture of internal development, traced previously.

The primary financial objective of Algerian economic policy towards foreign countries is that of maintaining an autonomous equilibrium in its long-term balance of payments. Various elements render this task arduous. First of all, there is the fact that the agricultural–food balance bears a deficit arising out of the deficiencies in the development of agriculture which we have previously pointed out. Secondly, there is an important lag between effective integrated functioning of industrialisation projects and their gradual start. During this time lag – that is, during the current phase – the importation of producer goods weighs very heavily on the commercial balance. Furthermore, importation of producer goods is achieved by means of credits. Algeria's high level of foreign indebtedness, previously noted, is due in fact to contraction of commercial credits for the importation of equipment and other basic capital commodities. For example, between 1970 and 1971, foreign indebtedness increased from 8–9 billion dinars to 12·7–13·7 – that is, by 50 per cent – because of the 1·5 billion dinar loan from the Eximbank destined for the Arzew-Ouest gas liquefaction plant and the 1·7 billion Soviet loan for enlargement of the El Hadjar steel complex.[12]

The factors that counterbalance these difficulties, which reflect both structural problems and intense industrial transitional efforts, and that permit equilibrium in the balance of payments consist, on one hand, of remittances from emigrants and, on the other, on natural gas and petroleum resources. Nevertheless, as has previously been emphasised, it is above

12 Grimaud *op. cit.* 34.

all Algerian management of these resources that gives them a function in the economy tending towards equilibrium and autonomy. Algerian strategy regarding long-term equilibrium and autonomy in the balance of payments, in fact, far from weighing upon financial contributions resulting from energy resources, has made of these resources a platform for development and diversification of the country's own financial possibilities, a sort of multiplier of Algerian financial capability and credibility. The *stock en terre* functions as a guarantee for acquisition of resources on the international market, while its financial countervalue is neither directly nor entirely engaged. This permits the Algerians on the one hand to maintain a high level of reserves (which, in turn, constitutes a further guarantee on the international market) and, on the other, to draw from diverse and numerous sources of financing.

However, the keystone of equilibrium envisaged with regard to Algerian payments consists of recovery of national sources of energy and of revaluation of prices. These provisions should not be viewed so much as a supplementary source of income, either fiscal or from exports, but primarily as performing the essential function of stabilising the heavy Algerian imports of producer goods which have been attracted by a high level of inflation. Secondly, they should be considered as a means for placing energy at the disposal of the Algerian economy at a cost lower than the international rate, with consequent effects upon the commercial balance. Finally, revaluation of the *stock en terre*, although traumatic with respect to the canons of international capitalism, nonetheless has the effect of increasing the value of the pledge which the Algerians are making use of for their policy of international financing. That is, it represents a means of penetrating the international financial market. Algerians are running a race against time: difficulties greater than those foreseen in the agricultural sector and delays or inefficiency in the industrial sector could subject this financial project to severe strain, together with the entire plan for development. If the mechanism for development is not set into motion in time, certain current tensions – unemployment, inflation, low agricultural productivity – could reach breaking point and subsequently be transformed into vehicles for a new dependency. This is all the more true since the highly capitalistic type of development chosen by the Algerians integrates them to a greater extent and for this reason exposes them even further. Thus Algeria needs international assistance and co-operation to sell its wine (although this is merely a transitory problem), to maintain present emigration rates, to export items that should be only temporarily industrial surpluses, but, above all, to obtain financial resources and technical co-operation, turning to maximum advantage its available supplies of energy.

The situation in Morocco and Tunisia differs in two fundamental respects from that prevailing in Algeria: firstly, these two countries do not have surplus energy (as in Morocco), or have it in only a limited quantity (Tunisia), although they possess an agricultural surplus; secondly, the resources provided by this surplus come within a structure which, as we have seen, appears inadequate to transform them into development of the economy. In other terms, whereas Algerian foreign relations are functional with respect to a plan for introversion that in the not too distant future should reintegrate Algeria into the international market at a level quite different from that at which it started on independence, Moroccan and Tunisian foreign relations, on the contrary, fix their respective economies upon the level of international integration in which they now find themselves. Therefore, integration and dependency have differing meanings depending on whether one is speaking of Algeria or of Tunisia and Morocco. For the latter two nations, integration takes the form of actual dependency; for Algeria, provided that its plans succeed, it should take the form of inter-dependency with the industrial sector of the capitalistic world.

The Moroccan and Tunisian agricultural surplus is above all one of agricultural products for export. Especially in the case of Morocco, the food deficit is noteworthy and constitutes a negative factor in that country's relations with foreign countries. The exportable agricultural surplus, which for Tunisia consists primarily of olive oil and for Morocco of fruit and vegetables, is generally produced by the most modern sector and constitutes an enclave in the economy of the two countries because it exists only as a result of the existence of foreign nations. On the other hand, imports of producer goods are considerable because an industrial sector exists, but they are not compensated by an equivalent productivity increase in the sector itself. This imbalance, which by now is structural, is, with regard to Morocco, partially countered by remittances from emigrants and, to a lesser extent, by tourism, whereas for Tunisia the tourism–emigrant ratio functions in inverse proportions. Nevertheless, it is the recourse to foreign resources, under the form of grants and investment, that plays a fundamental role in Tunisian and Moroccan foreign relations. This represents another important point of divergence from the Algerians, especially as concerns direct investments. This recourse takes the form of an indebtedness (higher in the case of Tunisia) for which only scarce possibilities for rescue can be foreseen.

On the other hand, in economies such as those of Tunisia and Morocco, direct foreign investment is concentrated in sectors geared to export, tourism included, where it attracts local capital and establishes an activity which has limited multiplicational effects upon the economy in which it is installed. Recent Tunisian prescriptions for foreign investment, which practically constitute regulations for the establishment of free ports, may favour all types of investment, but with equal invalid or negative effects. Actually, direct foreign investments in an economic and political context such as that of Morocco and Tunisia are placed beside enclaves of agricultural production and exportation, and together with these, risk increasing the dualism of the economy.

From this review, the foreign relations of Tunisia and Morocco do not appear encouraging. The governments of these two nations require co-operation and aid, on the one hand, to augment or maintain their agricultural export shares and, on the other hand, to obtain financial assistance and direct investments. Even if they are obtained, the problem is to know whether and to whom they will be useful. In the case of Algeria it might be possible to reply in terms of national development and growth. In the case of Tunisia and Morocco, this appears more difficult.

4. The Role of the EEC in the Development and Foreign Relations of the Maghreb

As we have seen, the EEC is by far the most important partner of the Maghreb nations. Moreover, it must be considered that these relations have an institutional basis through association agreements or could acquire it within a short time, as is the case with Algeria. It is natural, therefore, that a relationship of such importance, both from an economic and a political–institutional standpoint, has a note-worthy influence upon the development of the Maghreb nations. We now propose, after examination of the internal and external evolution of the Maghreb countries, to evaluate this influence.

An examination of agreements – both those in effect and those which have been prosposed – can be conducted in different ways. Community rhetoric takes it for granted that these represent an advantage for Maghreb nations, and Community spokesmen concentrate their attention upon the improvements in agricultural aspects of the agreements. Because the CAP basically continues to represent protection for European farmers, many of whom produce the same items as Maghreb farmers, this Community agricultural contribution continues to be unsatisfactory, in spite of the ingenuity of officials in Brussels in inventing complicated exceptions to the already complicated Community rules for agricultural policy. Another approach to the problem, however, is to ask if the agricultural aspect is really so important, or to demand further clarification of its importance. For an examination of EEC–Maghreb relations more closely connected with development problems, the latter approach appears to be more useful.

In reality, the agricultural approach is less important than is generally believed, as a result of observation of the prominence it is given on the negotiating stage. This becomes apparent if account is taken of the requirement for development of the Maghreb nations rather than of their export structure. In fact, the efforts exerted to maintain a place on the European orange market, that of olive oil or fresh tomatoes, tend to maintain and consolidate the present export structure of the Maghreb countries. Does this represent an advantage for the development of the Maghreb nations? The Algerians have already decided that it is not advantageous. Their defence of outlets for their wine – currently assisted by purchase commitments on the part of the Soviet Union – is acknowledged to be transitory. Algerian attention is directed towards an agricultural production destined above all to feed its population and towards an export structure of a predominantly industrial nature. A structure of exports in which wine would be as important as it is today would correspond to *de facto* continuance of colonial conditions. The unexpected closure of the French market to Algerian wine bears witness to this situation even to those who might have forgotten it. In reality, the Algerian government seems to be oriented towards utilising possible relationships of association with the EEC to diversify its own exports, rather than to crystallise the present structure. This, after all, is very reasonable, because the true advantage offered by association agreements lies in the almost total liberalisation of industrial trade and not in tortuous agricultural concessions.

For Tunisia and Morocco, by contrast, the agricultural aspect of association agreements continues to be predominant. In this they demonstrate little propensity to modify their own structures. Thus, for Morocco, a goodly share of the importance of the association agreement rests in arrangements that ensure commercialisation of oranges to the European market. Is this really important, however, for Moroccan development? From a general point of view, maintenance of an export structure in which oranges play such an important part has the same meaning for the Algerians as conservation of a structure in which wine holds an important position.

Oualalou[13] argues that the loss of DH 72 million foreseen by the government for 1973 if Morocco were not associated with the EEC constitutes an important factor at the foreign trade level, but 'at the national level and that of economic development it must be considered differently, and the lack of earnings should serve as an incitement to changes in the economic policy'. The currency brought in by the sale of oranges should not, in fact, be over-estimated. Moreover, it should be considered that the type of access to the EEC market allowed by the association agreement emphasises the characteristics of an enclave, which are manifested at present by the export sector, and the effects of such a characterisation. In fact, the agreement, to keep income levels assured by protection to the European farmers, does not permit free access to Moroccan oranges but fixes high minimum prices for them. The difference between the high minimum prices fixed by the EEC and the lower prices at which Moroccan exporters are able to sell constitutes an extra profit which has only negative effects on Morocco's development. The most important reason for this is that this profit does not stimulate the producers to expand production because the share on the European market is limited (they can sell oranges at higher prices, but are not allowed to sell more oranges); secondly, this profit goes to an already rich enclave and leaves other sectors of agriculture unaffected. Thus, the lack of balance in the agricultural sector which is largely responsible for backwardness in the Moroccan economy is accentuated. Although this might come within the social views of the *chérifien* monarchy, it does not take a proper place in a plan for development.

The case of Moroccan oranges appears symbolic, and it leads us to pose a fundamental question, namely, is it the Community that is conducting a neo-colonialist policy, or is it the countries concerned that are making a conservative use of the Community? The reply to this question is not simple. There is no doubt that the countries concerned attribute importance to their old agricultural export structure, either failing in their attempts to overcome it or avoiding attempts of this nature. But does the association agreement permit diversification? Only with difficulty does the agreement allow diversification in agricultural exports by Maghreb partners, but it permits diversification with regard to exportation of industrial products as well as the possibility of protection for rising industries. In this sense, as we have already observed, a more advantageous use may be made within

13 F. Oualalou, *L'assistance étrangère face au développement économique du Maroc* (Casablanca: Les editions maghrébines, 1969), p. 220.

the framework of association, provided that, as in the case of Algeria, there exists a policy of development and modernisation. Nevertheless, because the policy of association is intended to be a better framework of co-operation for development than others, two observations may be made. The first is that the protection extended to processed agricultural products and safeguards for textiles of the EEC do not constitute an advantage. After all, an industrialisation programme can be valid even if, without being ambitious and capitalistic like that of Algeria, it has a notable effect upon the development of certain light industries such as textiles or upon the development of the foodstuffs industry. This last observation appears to be of particular importance in view of the advantage that Morocco and Tunisia in particular would find in specialising in these products. There remains, then, the question of petroleum production. The attitude of the EEC is reserved, while awaiting the establishment of a common energy policy. The second observation is that a pure and simple commercial liberalisation must be accompanied by a programme that favours the industrial development of these countries; liberalisation is otherwise nothing but an empty gesture.

Now, co-operation can certainly not be limited as it currently is, *de facto*, to food aid. In this connection it should be emphasised that this aid is not only marginal within the sphere of co-operation, but it is even harmful, to the extent that it competes with those crops – cereals, sugar – by means of which the Maghreb nations might reach a balanced production of food. Assistance in the area of foodstuffs combined with the type of access reserved for agricultural products might end in a dangerous spiral. As Hager wrote, 'for the countries of the region a combination of a high price policy for fluctuating exports with artificially cheap imports would mean a perpetuation of dependence'.[14] The sphere of co-operation should evidently be extended to that of finance, technology and industry. It is upon this basis that the framework furnished by association can be seen to be dynamic and efficacious.

It is reasonably certain that financial co-operation will be directed towards loans and private investments and, to a lesser degree, towards grants. Here again the point of departure for any evaluation is constituted by the capability of the Maghreb nations to utilise these resources. For a country such as Algeria, that, to a certain extent, has ensured a self-regulating equilibrium on a long-term basis for its balance of payments, the

14 W. Hager, 'The Community and the Mediterranean', in M. Kohnstamm and W. Hager, eds., *A nation writ large?* (London: Macmillan, 1973), pp. 195–221; see p. 211.

intervention of financial resources constitutes a factor of acceleration in the development under way. The Algerians, having chosen a highly capitalistic development based upon advanced techniques, must not lose contact with the industrial 'centre'. At the same time they look with mistrust upon direct investments and are jealous of the autonomy and manœuvrability of their own economy. They are therefore searching for forms of co-operation which, while placing at their disposal financial means and know-how, are less intrusive than direct foreign investments. This does not mean that they do not accept them, but that they do this only to a limited extent and under certain conditions.

For Tunisia and Morocco, the financial resources that the EEC might make available could be less advantageous for the independent development of the two countries. Direct investments meet no obstacle. The problem is to know if and where capital will be drawn into these two countries. In spite of the ample facilities granted to investors, the amount of foreign capital in Morocco has not grown very markedly. As previously mentioned, Tunisia has promulgated legislation which is extremely favourable to direct investments. Nevertheless, no advantages have been derived from these facilities, because foreign investments directed towards markets restricted as are those of Morocco and Tunisia constitute enclaves within the few dynamic sectors, such as tourism or other export sectors. Their effect, as already noted, is that of accentuating the dualism of the economy and its under-development. Considerations concerning financial loans cannot be very different.

The addition of aid to agreements of association, therefore, appears to be a factor of development, as in the case of commercial exchanges, especially if the countries which benefit therefrom are capable of utilising them. If not, financial co-operation does nothing but temporarily plug the deficit in the balance of payments, and its negative side is represented by an increasing indebtedness towards foreign countries. The problem is not so much one of choosing among various forms of financial intervention – for example, private investments or grants – as it is of deciding on structures capable of channelling this investment towards the objective of national development. In this sense, the Algerians have greater possibilities, not only because of their possession of energy resources but also because the local middle classes aspire to national integration and independence. In Algeria there does not exist a bourgeois sector of a cosmopolitan nature, marginal to the industrial 'centre'. The Algerian programme – upon the success of which many uncertainties depend – is that of a successive

TABLE 1 Algeria: structure of the GDP at current prices (%)

	1963	*1966*	*1970*
1. Agriculture	17·6	11·9	11·6
2. Petroleum, gas, mining and power	16·1	22·5	20·6
3. Industry and construction	13·7	15·1	24·5
4. Transport, trade and services	30·8	37·3	31·4
5. Administration	21·8	13·2	11·9
Total	100·0	100·0	100·0

Source: N. Boudoukha, '*L'accumulation financière et la politique des investissements en Algérie*', '*France–Algérie*', special issue, 1972 55–9.

TABLE 2 Morocco: structure of the GDP (1960 prices) (%)

	1963	*1966*	*1970*
1. Agriculture, fisheries	32·5	29·3	31·1
2. Mining, power	8·0	9·0	8·1
3. Manufacturing, construction	18·5	19·7	19·7
4. Transport, services	17·6	19·2	18·3
5. Trade	23·3	22·5	22·7
Total	100·0	100·0	100·0

Source: A. A. Belal and A. Agourram, 'L'économie marocaine dupuis l'indépendence', in CRESM, *Les économies maghrébines* (Paris, CNRS, 1971); F. Oualalou, 'Chronique économique. Maroc, in CRESM, *Annuaire de l'Afrique du Nord, 1971* (Paris, CNRS, 1972).

TABLE 3 Tunisia: structure of the GDP at factor cost (1966 prices) (%)

	1963	*1966*	*1970*
1. Agriculture, fisheries	29·2	24·1	17·8
2. Power, oil and mining	3·6	5·9	10·1
3. Industry, construction	18·7	20·9	21·0
4. Transport, trade, services	48·3	48·9	51·0
Total	100·0	100·0	100·0

Source: Ministère du Plan, *Tableaux de synthèse* (Tunis, 1972).

TABLE 4 Gross domestic product: selected rates of growth

	1964	1965	1966	1967	1968	1969	1970	1971	1963–71
Morocco									
GDP[a]	0·6	2·3	−2·2	7·0	12·2	1·3	4·6	5·1	3·4
Agriculture	−2·2	5·3	−11·7	10·4	29·6	−8·3	1·9	5·9	3·4
Mining	11·3	0	−1·6	0	68·9	−36·7	0	1·6	5·4
Industry	3·1	−0·7	3·7	5·1	3·4	6·0	5·6	5·9	3·5
Tunisia									
GDP[b]	2·5	6·0	1·4	−2·5	9·0	1·8	4·4	11·5[c]	3·7
Agriculture	−10·0	17·0	13·5	−21·7	19·4	−12·4	2·2	25·3[c]	0·7
Oil, power	80·8	1·1	53·4	80·3	27·7	11·5	12·9	−1·5[c]	29·5
Industry	22·6	4·2	10·2	3·1	5·4	3·8	3·4	11·0[c]	8·4
Algeria									
GDP[d]	5·3	2·1	7·0	7·2	11·7	9·3	5·0[c]	n.a.	5·9[f]
Agriculture	−8·6	14·2	−25·0	27·7	4·3	4·1	−4·0[c]	n.a.	1·5[g]
Oil, power	10·2	4·6	48·8	5·6	6·2	6·6	2·7	n.a.	11·7[f]
Industry	18·1	7·6	0	7·1	53·3	26·0	13·6[e]	n.a.	16·0[f]

[a]At factor cost; 1960 prices. [b]At factor cost; 1966 prices.
[c]Provisional. [d]Current prices.
[e]Provisional; including construction and public works.
[f]1963–9.
[g]1963–70.
Sources: As for tables 2 and 3; and N. Grimaud, '*Les finances publiques de l'Algérie*', *Maghreb-Machrek* **56** (1973), 30–7.

integration at the international level, but in the role of an actor rather than as a supernumerary.

If one must give an evaluation of the association agreements, both in their present form and in the more complete one that they should assume, it can be said that taken alone they do not appear to be instruments of subordination to European capitalism. In other words, the presentation of Moroccan and Tunisian structures is neither favoured nor imposed by these agreements. It is rather the lack of a progressive will that has induced Morocco and Tunisia to choose association with the EEC, but, above all, to utilise it as if it were an instrument for the preservation of their agricultural structures. Beyond this is the lack of the political decisions required to set in motion the development process. In the case of Algeria, which has made these political decisions, the possibility of an alternative use of relations with the EEC is significant.

10

Trade Agreements Between the EEC and Arab Countries of the Eastern Mediterranean and Cyprus

GEORGE V.VASSILIOU

Introduction

This paper deals with the relations between the European Economic Community (EEC) and Cyprus, Lebanon and Egypt, the only countries in the Eastern Mediterranean area with which the EEC until 1972 had not entered into any formal trade or association agreement.

As all negotiations were carried out in the course of 1972 and the agreements had come into operation at some date in the early part of 1973, it is impossible to deal in this paper with the impact of the agreements on the economies of these countries and their trade and commercial relations with the EEC. Accordingly, the chapter is limited to an examination of the current trade relations between the EEC and the three countries and a critical assessment of the trade and association agreements offered by the EEC. The chapter covers all three countries but concentrates mostly on Cyprus.

1. Trade Relations Between the EEC and Cyprus, Egypt and Lebanon

The enlarged EEC is by far the greatest trading partner for Cyprus and Lebanon and the second most important for Egypt, the economy of which, as it is known, is very closely related to the economy of the COMECON (Council for Mutual Economic Aid) countries. Overall, Cyprus in 1971 imported nearly 60 per cent of its requirements from the enlarged EEC, compared to a share of 5·6 per cent from the USA and 7·7 per cent from COMECON, whereas for Lebanon this amounted to 36·2 per cent compared to 9·2 per cent from the USA and 8·4 per cent from COMECON (see Table 1). Looking at the export side, however, it is apparent that it is only for Cyprus that the enlarged EEC is a very important outlet and particularly the UK, which absorbs 41·6 per cent of all Cyprus exports, compared to 25·4 per cent to the eight countries in EEC and only 10 per cent to the

Table 1 EEC: share in foreign trade of Cyprus, Lebanon and Egypt

	Imports				*Exports*		
Countries	*Cyprus* US *$267.172*	*Lebanon* *$1,129.920*	*Egypt* *$1,015.633*	*Countries*	*Cyprus* *$118.197*	*Lebanon* *$257.231*	*Egypt* *$841.935*
UK	28·7	14·6	2·5	England	41·6	3·7	2·0
EEC (8)	30·5	21·6	26·8[a]	EEC (8)	25·4	6·5	7·9[b]
Greece	6·0	*	*	Greece	3·8	*	*
USA	5·6	9·2	9·5	USA	*	3·0	0·8
Japan	4·4	3·6	1·3	Japan	*	*	3·7
COMECON	7·7	8·4	32·0	COMECON	10·5	4·5	56·1
Arab countries	1·7	8·5	6·0	Arab countries	6·8	64·3	8·1
Others	15·4	34·1	20·9	Others	11·9	18·0	21·4
Total	100·0	100·0	100·0	Total	100·0	100·0	100·0

[a] Including W. European countries.

[b] Including Denmark and Ireland.

* Insignificant.

Source: Republic of Cyprus, Statistics of Imports & Exports, 1971; République Libanaise, Statistiques du Commerce Extérieur, 1971.

COMECON countries. For Lebanon and Egypt, however, 10 per cent of total exports were absorbed by the EEC. Lebanon's biggest partners are the other Arab countries and Egypt's COMECON.

A more detailed analysis of trade between Cyprus and Lebanon on the one hand and the EEC on the other (see Tables 2 and 3) proves very clearly that for practically all industrial products, like chemicals, manufactured articles, transport equipment and so on, the enlarged EEC completely controls the markets, supplying anything between 50 and 70 per cent of their total requirements. For example, Cyprus imports 70 per cent of its chemicals from the enlarged EEC, and Lebanon 54·2 per cent; 76 per cent of all machinery and transport equipment in Cyprus are imported from the EEC, and 61 per cent of all transport equipment and transport and telecommunication equipment in Lebanon are imported from the EEC. The only other major source of supply for these countries is Japan, COMECON and the United States, but in none of the fields involved do they really represent a considerable share of the market compared to the predominance of the industrial goods of EEC origin.

In Egypt the situation is somewhat different. Where, because of the close connections of Egypt with the Soviet Union and other COMECON countries and because of the importance of barter agreements, a considerable proportion of Egypt's mechanical equipment is supplied by the Eastern bloc. The EEC, however, still provides quite a considerable quantity of machinery, equipment and other industrial goods and altogether follows very closely the share held by the COMECON countries.

On the export side, a complete dependence on the EEC markets on the part of Cyprus is quite evident (see Table 4) and only a marginal importance for Lebanon and Egypt. Two-thirds of all Cyprus's exports go to the EEC, but within this the predominance of the UK market is evident, for this alone absorbs more than 40 per cent of all Cyprus's exports. The importance of the UK market becomes even more apparent taking into consideration the fact that 60 per cent of all goods exports and 43 per cent of all beverage exports were absorbed by the UK market, whereas the old EEC was a very small market for Cyprus's agricultural produce but a very considerable one for its minerals, which were in fact exported to West Germany. Looking, however, at the export of industrial products, the situation becomes completely different, as the EEC accounts for only a small share in Cyprus's exports, the majority of which goes to other countries. Thus nearly two-thirds of the output of Cyprus's industry which comes under ITC classifications 6 and 8 is exported to neighbouring and other countries, and only one-third to the enlarged EEC.

TABLE 2 Cyprus: imports by countries of origin and product categories, 1971

	Food and live animals	*Beverages and tobacco*	*Inedible raw materials (not fuels)*	*Mineral fuels, lubricating and related materials*	*Animal and vegetable oils and fats*	*Chemicals*	*Manufactured goods, classified chiefly by material*	*Machinery and transport equipment*	*Miscellaneous manufactured articles*	*Commodities and transport, unclassified*	*Total merchandise*
Total	(13,492) %	(1,233) %	(2,740) %	(8,534) %	(1,981) %	(8,935) %	(30,866) %	(28,704) %	(7,926) %	(2,457) %	(106,868) %
Countries											
UK	16·4	27·7	5·4	7·5	5·6	30·3	26·5	43·1	33·0	54·4	28·7
Denmark	5·6	1·7	0·2	0·1	2·2	2·1	0·5	0·6	0·8	*	1·3
Ireland	3·5	0·1	0·1	–	*	0·4	*	*	0·1	–	0·5
EEC (3)	25·5	29·5	5·7	7·6	7·8	32·8	27·0	43·7	33·9	54·4	30·5
W. Germany	1·3	0·7	0·7	0·4	3·7	12·0	7·0	12·0	8·8	0·5	7·2
Italy	1·0	0·5	2·7	40·5	*	9·0	6·7	12·8	8·8	0·3	10·2
Luxembourg	–	–	–	–	–	–	0·5	*	–	–	0·2
Holland	6·6	6·2	1·6	17·9	27·2	4·1	1·4	2·0	1·7	0·5	4·3
Belgium	2·0	*	0·1	0·1	–	1·3	3·0	0·4	0·8	*	1·4
France	4·0	4·1	1·3	5·5	5·2	7·7	7·2	5·2	2·4	0·4	5·4
EEC (6)	14·9	11·5	6·4	64·4	36·1	34·1	25·8	32·4	22·5	1·7	28·7
EEC (9)	40·4	41·0	12·1	72·0	43·9	66·9	52·8	76·1	56·4	56·1	59·2
All others	59·6	59·0	87·9	28·0	56·1	33·1	42·7	23·9	43·6	43·9	40·8
Total	100·0	100·0	100·0	100·0	100·0	100·0	100·0	100·0	100·0	100·0	100·0

*Insignificant.

–No trade at all.

Source: Republic of Cyprus, Statistics of Imports & Exports 1971.

TABLE 3 Lebanon: imports by section and country origin

		EEC %	USA %	Japan %	COMECON including China %	Arab countries %	Others %	Total
1.	Food and live animals	24·3	0·8	3·2	16·1	12·9	42·7	100 (122,913)
2.	Fruits, vegetables, legumes, etc.	11·4	12·6	–	13·7	14·2	48·1	100 (237,959)
3.	Animal and vegetable oils and fats	71·4	8·9	–	–	1·6	18·1	100 (29,080)
4.	Beverages and tobacco	27·9	30·5	2·3	12·6	3·1	23·6	100 (142,273)
5.	Raw materials	14·2	0·3	–	2·1	75·9	7·5	100 (139,487)
6.	Chemical materials and products	54·2	11·1	0·6	3·1	2·1	28·9	100 (182,041)
7.	Plastic materials	51·1	9·0	16·4	2·2	–	21·3	100 (69,258)
8.	Manufactured goods, Leather and Dressed skins	11·1	0·7	–	–	63·0	25·2	100 (38,654)
9.	Wood and carbons	2·8	1·5	–	48·2	–	47·5	100 (45,148)
10.	Paper, etc.	17·9	17·1	1·1	11·0	2·0	50·9	100 (86,757)
11.	Textiles, etc.	51·2	2·5	5·6	5·1	4·7	30·9	100 (284,802)
12.	Made-up articles	23·7	–	3·6	10·5	–	62·2	100 (4,837)
13.	Non-metallic mineral manufactures not elsewhere specified	48·9	2·9	3·8	13·4	0·8	30·2	100 (38,552)
14.	Pearls, diamonds, etc.	31·6	–	1·5	0·4	0·4	66·1	100 (304,584)
15.	Iron and steel	38·5	3·4	3·1	30·7	1·5	22·8	100 (202,642)
16.	Machinery and Electrical machines	46·5	16·1	7·5	2·2	–	27·7	100 (282,274)
17.	Transport equipment, telecommunications	61·3	22·9	6·2	0·7	–	8·9	100 (170,396)
18.	Scientific and control instruments, photo equipment	23·0	11·3	14·6	0·4	–	50·7	100 (37,478)
19.	Firearms and Ammunitions	35·1	–	–	36·4	–	28·5	100 (4,542)
20.	Commodities not classified according to kind	32·9	11·4	11·0	3·7	–	41·0	100 (26,851)
21.	Art articles for collection	27·5	–	–	–	–	72·5	100 (1,361)
	Total	36·2	9·2	3·6	8·4	8·5	34·1	100 (2451,919)

– No trade at all.

Source: République Libanaise, Statistiques du Commerce Extérieur, 1971.

TABLE 4 Cyprus: exports by countries of destination and product categories, 1971

	Food and live animals	*Beverages and tobacco*	*Inedible raw materials (except fuels)*	*Mineral fuels, lubricating and related materials*	*Animal and vegetable oils and fats*	*Chemicals*	*Manufactured goods classified chiefly by material*	*Machinery and transport equipment*	*Miscellaneous manufactured articles*	*Commodities and transport unclassified*	*Total merchandise*
Total	24·114 %	4·786 %	10·388 %	14·000 %	89·000 %	517·000 %	1·326 %	3·226 %	2·207 %	612·000 %	47·276 %
Countries											
UK	58·4	43·1	6·7	–	57·3	3·9	36·5	48·0	21·5	44·6	41·6
Denmark	0·1	*	2·3	–	–	*	*	*	*	0·5	0·6
Ireland	0·9	0·3	0·8	–	–	–	–	–	*	0·2	0·7
EEC (3)	59·4	43·4	9·8	–	57·3	3·9	36·5	48·0	21·5	45·3	42·9
W. Germany	1·8	0·7	48·8	–	–	–	1·2	0·8	0·9	2·5	11·8
Italy	3·0	0·4	7·9	–	*	*	2·1	2·1	0·2	1·5	3·5
Luxembourg	–	–	–	–	–	–	–	*	–	–	*
Holland	6·1	0·5	3·7	–	–	*	0·5	0·1	0·3	1·0	4·1
Belgium	0·1	*	0·6	–	–	0·1	*	0·1	0·1	1·5	0·2
France	6·6	0·1	4·5	–	–	1·2	0·2	0·7	0·1	1·5	4·5
EEC (6)	17·6	1·7	65·5	–	–	1·3	4·0	3·8	1·6	8·0	24·1
EEC (9)	77·0	45·1	75·3	–	57·3	5·2	40·5	51·8	23·1	53·3	67·0
All others	23·0	54·9	24·7	100·0	42·7	94·8	59·5	48·2	76·9	46·7	33·0
Total	100·0	100·0	100·0	100·0	100·0	100·0	100·0	100·0	100·0	100·0	100·0

*Insignificant.

–No trade at all.

Source: Republic of Cyprus, Statistics of Imports & Exports, 1971.

For both Lebanon and Egypt, exports to the EEC are at present of marginal importance compared to the total exports. Nearly two-thirds of all Lebanon's exports go to the neighbouring Arab countries, whereas Egypt's largest trading partners are the COMECON countries, which in 1971 absorbed 56 per cent of all exports. Compared to that, only 7·9 per cent went to the EEC countries (before its enlargement), but even including the share of Denmark and the UK this total is still below 10 per cent.

The EEC is thus by far the biggest supplier of Lebanon with both industrial and consumer goods, but is only a very minute marginal importer, creating thus a huge trade imbalance between the two countries.

For Egypt the situation is slightly different, as imports, partly because of the known shortage of foreign exchange, were strictly controlled. Even so, however, the lack of balance is evident with imports from the EEC worth well over £E100 million and total exports of less than £E40 million. Further, although imports cover all types of industrial and certain types of consumer goods, exports consist mainly of onions and garlic and a negligible quantity of industrial goods.

2. The Association Agreement Between Cyprus and the EEC

In examining the association agreement between Cyprus and the EEC, one has to bear in mind that it consists of two parts: one part refers to the relations between Cyprus and the old EEC of the Six, and the other refers to the relationship between Cyprus and the UK. From the Cyprus Government's point of view, the main achievement of this association agreement was that it secured for a transitional period of four years more or less the same conditions for the export of Cyprus wines and agricultural produce to the UK market as those prevailing until the association of the UK with the EEC.[1] As far as the long-term development of the Cyprus economy is concerned, that part of the agreement which refers to the relations between the EEC of the Six and Cyprus is of more vital importance because, after

1 The new conditions imposed as from 1 January 1973 with the entrance of the UK into the EEC are not as favourable as they were before the entrance of the UK. The two most important groups of products that are affected by these are sherry and potatoes. Thus, for sherry, an export quota was imposed that is equal to the average exports of the last 3 years, excluding therefore the possibility of increase in exports at the old preferential system; what is more important, reference prices that are substantially higher than the price at which Cyprus sherry was exported to the UK would be introduced after 3 years. Furthermore, for potatoes, an export quota was imposed which froze the volume of Cyprus exports to the size of exports in 1972.

the transitional period of the first five years, it is the concessions secured through that agreement that would be valid for the enlarged Community as well.

It is, of course, true that the present agreement specifies that negotiations for the new phase will start eighteen months earlier but, as far as Cyprus is concerned, these negotiations will not be on an equal footing from the beginning because it is vital for Cyprus to retain its traditional export markets for its agricultural produce and wine, which absorb more than two-thirds of all its exports. It is therefore evident that Cyprus would have to agree to whatever conditions the EEC will be prepared to offer, as otherwise a complete readjustment of the economy will be necessary, the political repercussions of which would be unacceptable to the present Cyprus Government. Such a realignment would mean complete dependence on the COMECON countries, although even that would not necessarily secure the absorption of some of Cyprus's produce and, particularly, sherry.

The agreement between Cyprus and the EEC covers both industrial and agricultural projects. The following sections present an analysis of the concessions granted by the EEC, firstly for agriculture and secondly for industry.

Agriculture

The negotiations between the Cyprus Government and the EEC regarding a preferential treatment of Cyprus's agricultural produce proved very frustrating and of a limited scope, as finally they covered only citrus fruit and carobs. In neither of the two cases, however, were the concessions granted by the EEC of any particular benefit to Cyprus. For carobs, duties were negligible, amounting only to 8 per cent, and insignificant from the Cyprus point of view because Cyprus is practically the only source of supply together with Crete and Spain and the whole production of carobs is easily absorbed by European industry. Therefore, the abolition of the duty did not in any way create any changes for the improvement of exports by Cyprus to the EEC, and in that sense it can only be seen as a special favour to the processing industries within the EEC.

Regarding citrus, however, which is one of the most vital products for the Cyprus economy, the concessions were extremely small and did not solve the problem of the discrimination that already existed in the EEC markets against Cyprus produce. It is known that Greece enjoys a 100 per cent reduction of duties and the Maghreb countries, one of the largest producers, an 80 per cent reduction. Therefore, the 40 per cent reduction, although placing Cyprus on the same footing as Israel and Spain, did not offer a serious advantage. Furthermore, the reference price system was still imposed and no quota whatsoever was offered to Cyprus for the export of processed citrus products like juices, segments and so on. No other product was covered at that stage, and the justification given by the EEC was that new negotiations would take place at a later stage when the EEC had formulated its common Mediterranean policy. The Commission promised that, when the common Mediterranean policy was formulated, Cyprus would be offered the same special preferential rates as the other countries of the area within the framework of the policy.

Although it has not been officially announced, it is now understood that the EEC has completed its first round of negotiations regarding a joint Mediterranean policy, and accordingly some new concessions are about to be granted to Cyprus covering some categories of agricultural produce.

At first sight these concessions (see Table 5) seem to be considerable, but in actual practice they offer practically nothing to Cyprus because of the limited time period for which the reductions in custom duties are valid and these concessions do not take account of seasonal exigencies. For example, it is very well known that the bulk of the Cyprus carobs and potatoes are exported later than the periods referred to in the agreements, that Cyprus cannot export any quantities of fresh grapes by plane and has no possibility whatsoever of exporting bulk quantities by sea before the 17 July.

For citrus produce, the increase in the tariff reduction from 40 to 60 per cent is of course welcome, although the Maghreb countries are still more favourably treated and for lemons the tariff is retained at the 40 per cent level. Furthermore, the reference prices are maintained for both oranges and mandarins. The only new addition welcome to Cyprus is the inclusion of manufactured citrus produce like segments and juices, but here again there are limiting factors. With the exception of grapefruit, for which the Community has no reason to impose any limitations as there is practically no production, orange segments can be exported only in large packs thus excluding the possibility of retail packs and marketing under a Cyprus brand, while for orange juice the reference prices are maintained.

Overall, therefore, the much-publicised and long-awaited Mediterranean policy has very little to offer to Cyprus if the concessions described above are to be the only ones offered. There is no doubt that it does not in any way help to assure future progress for Cyprus's agriculture.

TABLE 5 List of concessions granted

Description	*Reduction* (%)	*Period and other conditions*
New concession		
New potatoes	40	1 Jan.–15 May
Carrots	40	1 Jan.–31 March
Aubergines	60	1 Dec.–30 April
Fresh grapes	50	2 Nov.–30 April 18 June–17 July
Melons	50	1 Nov.–30 April
Locust bean seeds	50	
Grapefruit segments	60	
Orange segments	40	Large packs
Orange juice	60	Maintenance of reference price
Grapefruit juice	50	
Wines	75	
Tobacco	100	
Olive oil		Economic advantages 5 u.a./100 kg Trade concessions 0·5 u.a./100 kg
Increase in preference		
Oranges	60	Maintenance of reference price
Mandarins	60	Maintenance of reference price
Grapefruit	60	

Industry

In the field of industry, the Community appeared to be more generous by offering an overall 70 per cent reduction in duties in return for a gradual reduction of duties by Cyprus of 35 per cent. The advantages offered to Cyprus, however, are greatly limited by the Community's rules of origin, which are standard, not only for Cyprus but for all countries with which the Community has negotiated an association or trade agreement. The essence of these rules of origin is that it makes it practically impossible for light industry in Cyprus or other developing countries to export products to the EEC which are not made out of raw materials imported from the EEC. As the only industries in Cyprus capable of exporting were the textile and clothing industry, during the negotiations the Cyprus Government asked for exemptions from these rules for a great range of products like knitted goods, towels, ladies' clothing and underwear, men's and children's wear. Unfortunately, the Community insisted on retaining all these regulations with the exception of children's and men's wear (SITC 6101) where, however, a quantity limitation was immediately imposed specifying that exports should not exceed 100 tons per annum.

3. Agreements with the Arab Republic of Egypt and Lebanon

In December 1972 the Community signed agreements of basically similar content with the Arab Republic of Egypt and with Lebanon. The essence of these agreements is that they provided for an immediate reduction for industrial goods of the customs tariffs of 45 per cent, rising to 55 per cent on 1 January 1974, and for some special concessions for agricultural produce, the most important of which are a 40 per cent reduction on citrus fruit (which probably will be increased to 60 per cent in line with the new policy), a 25 per cent reduction on onions and rice and reductions varying from 25 to 50 per cent for cotton, potatoes, fruits and vegetables. However, for all these agricultural products there are seasonal limitations which, with the notable exception of cotton, limit greatly the capacity of the agriculture of both countries to export to the EEC. On their part, Egypt and Lebanon undertake to reduce duties for EEC goods originally by 30 per cent with the undertaking to increase the reductions gradually to 50 per cent. It is, of course, understood that the Community's regulations concerning rules of origin are valid for both countries and, moreover, certain restrictive quotas are imposed, the overall effect of which is to limit greatly the benefit that Egyptian and Lebanese industry might have from the association.

4. Overall Assessment of the Treaties

As the treaties have been in operation only for a very short period, it is impossible to provide data or to predict safely the effect that they will have on the development of relations between the countries concerned and on their economies. An assessment of these treaties has to be limited to an examination of the value of the concessions granted by the EEC and the importance of these concessions compared to the requirements of the countries. The following sections thus analyse first the concessions granted on the agricultural and second on the industrial sector.

Agriculture

It is a well-known fact that, because of the stipulations of the Common Agricultural Policy (CAP) it was extremely difficult to obtain special concessions for the export of agricultural produce to the Community unless

TABLE 6 EEC Trade with Lebanon and Egypt

Items	Imports by EEC		Exports by EEC	
	Lebanon	Egypt	Lebanon	Egypt
Total imports and exports	$35 million (%)	$158 million (%)	$244 million (%)	$279 million (%)
Animals and animal products	–	–	6	2
Cereals	–	4	3	25
Vegetables and fruits	8	14	–	–
Provisions	6	3	–	–
Cotton, etc.	3	33	–	–
Other agricultural products	43	4	3	–
Sub-total agricultural products	60	58	12	28
Raw materials	9	1	3	1
Petroleum and fuel minerals	3	28	2	8
Chemical materials	–	–	13	16
Manufactured goods	20	12	27	15
Machinery and transport equipment	8	1	31	29
Other manufactured materials	–	–	12	3
Sub-total, other products	40	42	88	72
	100	100	100	100

of course it referred to items that were not produced by any of the Community countries, as, for example, carobs and cotton.

For many years the Community was not prepared even to discuss reductions on other products – with the exception of citrus, which was the corner-stone of the so-called Mediterranean policy until 1972, and for which the Community has agreed to grant tariff concessions and at the same time has introduced reference prices in order to satisfy the Italians.

Overall, the shortcomings of the agricultural policy and concessions granted by the EEC can be summarised as follows:

TABLE 7 Cyprus: exports by main countries of destination

Items	*UK*	*EEC (6)*	*Denmark and Ireland*	*All other countries*	*Total domestic exports ($ US)*
Oranges	35·7	23·7	2·8	37·8	100 (7,120,858)
Lemons	32·0	53·0	0·1	14·9	100 (2,115,126)
Grapefruit	68·9	20·7	0·4	10·0	100 (3,372,918)
Other citrus fruit	74·3	9·2	–	16·5	100 (70,130)
Grapes, fresh	88·2	2·4	–	9·4	100 (1,760,800)
Fruit juices	41·3	3·9	–	54·8	100 (359,403)
Grapefruit segments	97·6	–	0·2	2·2	100 (540,131)
Potatoes	87·1	–	–	12·9	100 (4,486,214)
Carrots	100·0	–	–	–	100 (534,627)
Locust beans (whole, kibbled, etc.)	46·6	37·6	–	15·8	100 (1,072,781)
Tobacco, manufactured	10·6	5·0	–	84·4	100 (642,368)
Agricultural products either fresh or processed, excluding wines and spirits	37·9	12·6	0·4	49·1	100 (3,338,543)
Total exports of agricultural products, excluding wines and spirits	55·5	17·4	0·9	26·2	100 (25,413,899)
Wines and spirits	52·7	0·8	0·3	46·2	100 (3,783,058)
Total agricultural exports	55·1	15·2	0·8	28·9	100 (29,196,957)
Minerals	6·5	69·4	3·3	20·8	100 (9,416,596)
Manufactured articles and other commodities	33·8	2·2	0·7	63·3	100 (3,447,447)
Total domestic exports	42·5	26·3	1·4	29·8	100 (42,061,000)

Source: Republic of Cyprus, Statistics of Imports and Exports, 1971.

(*i*) The size of the concessions varies among the Mediterranean countries even for products of exactly the same nature (like citrus), and this places some of these countries in a disadvantageous position. This is particularly important for Cyprus which, although it has entered

TABLE 8 Share of Cyprus and Egypt exports of selected agricultural products in EEC imports.

	European market (tons)	*Egypt, exports (tons)*	*%*	*Cyprus exports*	*%*
Potatoes	649,653	3,000	0·5	125,056	19·2
Onions	608,413	45,284	7·4	7,000	*
Fruits					
Apples	1,114,788	–	–	–	–
Mandarins, etc.	454,035	66,000	0·01	490,000	1·1
Oranges	1,974,759	15,454	0·8	42,143	2·1
Grapefruit	301,358	222,000	0·1	38,672	12·8
Lemons	323,814	45,000	0·01	13,534	4·2

*Including W. Germany, France, Switzerland, Sweden, Denmark, Norway, Austria.

into an association agreement, still does not receive treatment as favourable as the Maghreb countries and Greece.

(*ii*) The size of the concessions is extremely limited and covers only a very small range of products, excluding a wide variety of products that these countries can produce and export to the EEC under more favourable conditions than the EEC countries can produce and trade them.

(*iii*) All concessions, particularly for so-called sensitive products, have a quota limitation, thus limiting the possibilities of growth in the countries concerned – as, for example, in the case of the quota imposed on Cyprus's exports of potatoes to the UK.

(*iv*) The agreements do not offer any potentiality of diversification to Cyprus or to the other countries. On the contrary, they tend to oblige these countries to develop only those fields for which the Community is prepared to offer tariff concessions irrespective of the potentialities and requirements of the countries involved.

Industry

At first the concessions granted by the Community in the industrial sector seem to be considerably larger, and generally the Community tends to give the impression that although it is obliged to be protective in agriculture, it is more generous in industry. In fact, however, the policy of the Community is not at all more liberal in industry than it is in agriculture. The overall reductions in custom duties are of only academic interest to these countries, but where they are likely to be advantageous – as in the case of the textile or knitting industry for Cyprus, Egypt and Lebanon – then, immediately, other regulations are imposed, the aim of which is to limit the danger of competition with the industries of the EEC and to turn the industries of these countries to satellites of EEC industrial enterprises. This is the essence of the very elaborate rules of origin that have been worked out by the Commission and of the quota control imposed where even the rules of origin are not considered to provide satisfactory protection.

Overall, therefore, it can be stated that the Community, instead of trying to help the Mediterranean countries to develop by following a generous and open policy, in actual practice place a number of limitations on the growth of these countries, and thus the Community gains more advantages than it offers. This can be seen clearly from an analysis of the benefits offered to Cyprus and those obtained by Cyprus (Table 9), and this is even more true for Lebanon and Egypt, which, in general, gained fewer benefits than Cyprus.

In relating the size of the concession granted by the Community to Cyprus to those concessions granted by Cyprus to the Community, consideration has been taken both of the absolute size of the concessions and of the total trade of Cyprus and the Community. The results show very clearly that, although Cyprus receives on average a marginal preference of 1·6 per cent on all its exports to the Community, the Community receives immediately a margin of 2 per cent, which will grow to 5 per cent when the full concessions offered by Cyprus have come into effect.

This margin in favour of the Community is expected to increase rather than decrease in the future because of the tendency of Cyprus's imports to increase at a faster rate than exports.

In addition to these very clear-cut advantages that the Community gains with these agreements, one should also point out the fact that customs preferences do not really have the same effect on the exporting industries of two countries, and they certainly have a very different effect on the exporting industries of small developing countries compared to those of the European countries. As it has already been seen in the analysis of trade relations between Cyprus, Egypt and Lebanon on the one hand and the EEC on the other, in practically all sectors of industrial products the EEC has a controlling share of the market, dictating therefore terms of supply, prices and so on. It is accordingly evident that whatever the rate of import duty imposed by the governments of Cyprus, Lebanon or Egypt, this does

TABLE 9 Comparison of preferences between Cyprus and the EEC

(a) Preferences given by enlarged EEC on exports from Cyprus

% of trade		
29%	Fresh citrus (8% oranges; 3·2% lemons; 2·4% grapefruit)	4·6%
2	Locust beans, kibbled	8%
11	Clothing and shoes (70% of 13·9% average EEC tariff)	9·7%
100% = C£31·7 million		1·6%
		Average margin of preference on Cyprus exports to enlarged Community

(b) Preferences given by Cyprus to enlarged EEC

Sample items	*% of trade*		*1973*	*1978*
52	9	Foodstuffs	1·45%	3·11%
6	1	Beverages and tobacco	negl.	negl.
32	2	Crude materials, fats and oils	0·43	0·99
40	8	Petroleum, etc.	negl.	negl.
270	80	Manufactures and semi-manufactures	2·55	6·21
400	100	Total	1·9–2·2	4·7–5·3
C£61·9 million or approximately			2%	5%

Note: Commonwealth preferences in each direction are disregarded in this comparison.

not really affect in any way the pricing policy of the exporting industries from the EEC, because for these three countries there is no alternative source of local supply and therefore the local price to consumers within the country will finally be arrived at after adding on the c.i.f. prices of the exporting industries, duties and all other local expenses. However, a Cypriot industrial firm producing clothes or any other product is clearly aware that total Community imports from Cyprus cover only a minute fraction of total requirements of the local markets, and that price levels are fixed not by the requirements of the exporter but by the price structures and costs of the European industry. Accordingly, any duty protection has a direct effect on the pricing policy of the exporting industry from Cyprus, because the level of retail prices cannot be ignored when exporting. Thus the price asked by an exporter from Cyprus, Lebanon or Egypt is always reduced to make up the difference in import duties. We thus have a situation in which, whereas the industries exporting from the EEC impose their own prices and whereas protective duties by the Mediterranean countries are paid by the consumer, the exporting industries of the Mediterranean countries have themselves to absorb the duties imposed by the EEC. Therefore the Mediterranean countries have to shoulder the weight of duties both when they are importing and when they are exporting. This is why it is vitally important for these countries to be able to secure free entrance for their products, which is probably the only way to achieve considerable growth of their industries without being obliged to reciprocate in every possible way.

One therefore is obliged to draw the conclusion that the policy of the Community towards Cyprus, Lebanon and Egypt until now has been anything but generous and, in many cases, particularly as far as agriculture and certain industrial sectors are concerned, inward-looking, protective and neglecting the interests of the countries that the Community alleges it wants to help. In this respect there is no doubt that the creation of the Community has a very negative effect on the countries involved, because it created a unified front which these countries have no way of breaking. If the Community did not exist, then Cyprus, Lebanon and Egypt would have been free to export practically all they wanted to countries like the UK, Germany and Benelux in return for some preferential treatment for the exports of those countries. However, the creation of a common front on behalf of the Community and the adopted policy of unanimity and veto rights enabling each member of the Community to impose its interests in the formulation of external agreements leads to a situation where, as a result of certain interests of one country – as, for example, for citrus in Italy or wines in France – the whole Western European market is practically closed for the Mediterranean countries. This undoubtedly is not a healthy situation and, despite the difficulties involved in finding new markets for their produce, there is no doubt that the countries of the area will try to create alternative outlets in order to escape from this strait jacket imposed by the Community. If in order to secure such outlets they were to offer preferential treatment to other industrial countries, then no doubt the Community would lose one of its most profitable and more rapidly growing export markets. It is therefore in the long-term interest of both the Community and the Mediterranean countries to be able to find a solution, and no doubt the main effort has to be made by the Community.

11

The Economic Integration of Spain with the EEC: Problems and Prospects

JUERGEN B. DONGES

Introduction

In 1959/60, there was a radical shift in Spain's economic development strategy from a strongly autarchic to a cautiously outward orientation. A group of neo-liberal technocrats who for the first time since the Civil War entered governmental administration obviously understood that the establishment of the European Common Market (EEC) (1957) and the introduction of external convertibility by the highly industrialised countries (1958) would enlarge the pattern of economic growth in Western Europe and thereby open new possibilities of rapid economic development for Spain. After all, the government recognised that economic integration was an important device for promoting economic development. This is particularly true if industrialisation is considered as a corner-stone of rapid economic and social progress (as was, and is, the case in Spain). The arguments in favour of more integration are too well known to need a detailed elaboration here. Essentially, they refer to the economies of scale that can be achieved in a wider market than the relatively small national one, to the increase of overall efficiency that will result from the more competitive environment, and to the improvement in the allocation of resources that can take place by arriving at a product-mix according to the country's comparative advantage. Whatever the degree to which Spain was able to reap the benefits of integration, the economic boom, which the country has been experiencing since 1960, and which deserves to be regarded as an outstanding success story in terms of income expansion as well as of growth and structural changes of production and foreign trade,[1] proves that the opening of the economy was rewarding thus far.

1 For details see J. B. Donges, 'From an autarchic towards a cautiously outward-looking industrialization policy: the case of Spain', *Weltwirtschaftliches Archiv* **107**, No. 1 (1971), 48 ff.

Because the government had great faith in the positive effects of future trade expansion between Spain and the Western European countries, it tried to attain some kind of economic association with the EEC – in spite of the resistance of vested interests (also politically motivated). In March 1970, eight years after the first official application was made, Spain signed a bilateral preferential trade agreement (PTA) with the EEC. By this agreement, which became effective in October 1970 and covers an initial period of six years, the EEC is committed to grant concessions on Spain's agricultural exports and to provide tariff reductions on Spanish manufactured exports; in return, Spain must liberalise global quotas formerly applied to agricultural imports from the Common Market as well as gradually to reduce customs tariffs on manufactured imports from the Community. Iron and steel products have been expressly excluded from the agreement, because they are covered by the former European Coal and Steel Community (ECSC). For all those who had wanted Spain to become an associate member of the EEC, the PTA is far from being a satisfactory arrangement. Whether or not the PTA paves the way for arriving at some sort of formal Spanish membership in the EEC after 1977 is, however, still a matter of conjecture. Although most of Spain's leading policy makers and academic economists think that such an integration is desirable, in EEC member countries, there are strong objections, which are governed by well-known political considerations. Whatever the outcome, it seems to be certain that for economic reasons both Spain and the EEC ought to be prepared to consolidate and extend their mutual trade relations.

Taking a closer economic relationship as desirable, it appears worth while to analyse the PTA with a view to detecting implications and promises for the Common Market for the Spanish economy. The major questions to be discussed in this context refer to the relative importance of the Common Market for the Spanish economy, to the pros and cons of this agreement in the light of both the recent accession of Denmark, Ireland and the United Kingdom to the EEC and the Community's trade policy towards developing countries, and to the kind of adaptation of Spain's manufacturing sector that is necessary to meet the increasing competition from abroad. This chapter aims to examine these questions critically and as succinctly as possible. To begin with, some background data on the trade relationship between Spain and the Community are presented.

Survey of Spain's Trade with the EEC

The EEC is one of the most important markets for Spain's exports and one of the main sources of supply of importable products (Table 1).

TABLE 1 Relative importance of the Common Market for Spain's foreign trade

Commodity group[a]	*Total value in US $ million*		*Percentage share of EEC*				*Compound annual rates of increase (%) 1962–71*		
			Six		*Enlarged*		*World*	*EEC (6)*	*EEC (enlarged)*
	1962	*1971*	*1962*	*1971*	*1962*	*1971*			
Imports									
Food and live animals	193·16	556·92	10·5	17·1	19·0	22·9	12·5	18·8	14·8
Beverages and tobacco	32·92	100·63	2·1	3·3	7·1	21·5	13·2	18·7	28·0
Crude materials except fuels	272·99	861·78	8·5	10·6	15·9	17·2	13·6	16·3	14·5
Mineral fuels and related materials	246·33	811·69	8·7	4·8	12·2	5·4	14·2	6·8	4·2
Animal and vegetable oils and fats	69·93	26·44	7·5	17·0	8·2	20·1	−10·2	−1·7	−0·8
Chemicals	135·46	525·82	63·3	53·5	75·1	63·9	16·3	14·1	14·2
Basic manufactures	176·63	598·74	51·6	50·6	64·1	64·3	14·5	14·3	14·5
Machinery and transport equipment	404·09	1,201·43	50·5	57·7	70·1	69·8	12·9	14·6	12·8
Miscellaneous manufactured articles	37·88	251·94	42·5	44·3	54·6	57·4	23·4	24·0	24·1
Total	1,569·43	4,935·65	29·8	32·9	40·6	41·6	13·6	14·8	13·9
Exports									
Food and live animals	328·89	634·94	48·7	45·9	70·8	60·9	7·6	6·9	5·8
Beverages and tobacco	34·46	93·15	21·0	24·2	67·3	55·4	11·7	13·4	9·3
Crude materials except fuels	61·28	100·59	55·2	50·3	67·2	65·6	5·7	4·6	5·4
Mineral fuels and related materials	44·65	125·74	11·8	47·0	25·5	57·8	12·2	30·9	22·9
Animal and vegetable oils and fats	44·90	177·66	55·8	64·4	58·9	68·8	16·5	18·4	18·5
Chemicals	36·31	141·57	22·8	29·5	39·8	39·6	16·3	19·7	16·2
Basic manufactures	82·89	590·72	25·7	36·2	42·8	43·6	24·4	29·2	24·6
Machinery and transport equipment	53·52	621·54	13·4	33·1	14·3	39·4	31·3	45·2	42·5
Miscellaneous manufactured articles	48·08	448·72	15·2	20·4	24·3	25·1	28·2	32·4	28·6
Total	736·01	2,937·78	37·4	37·1	55·2	46·7	16·6	16·5	14·5

[a] According to 1-digit SITC. Sub-totals do not necessarily add to the totals because of non-specified trade in commodities.

Source: Calculated from United Nations, *Commodity Trade Statistics*, various issues.

(*a*) In 1971, the original Six bought 37·1 per cent, and the present Nine 46·7 per cent, of Spain's exports, and their share in Spain's total imports amounted to 32·9 and 41·6 per cent respectively. For some commodity groups these shares are significantly higher, particularly when the enlarged EEC is considered. Examples on the side of Spain's exports are animal and vegetable oils, non-oil-related crude materials and foodstuffs. As to imports from the EEC, the significance of these is particularly evident in the case of machinery, transport equipment, basic manufactures and chemicals.

(*b*) The expansion of total trade between Spain and the EEC during the last decade has been remarkable in absolute and percentage terms (when compared with the experience of other semi-industrialised countries), but not more rapid than the growth of Spain's total trade. This phenomenon reflects the fact that the country, in its attempt to diversify the foreign trade structure, did not rely exclusively on the potentialities of the Common Market but also enlarged trade with other areas of the world, particularly the US and Latin America.

(*c*) Among the EEC member countries, West Germany was the most important purchasing market for Spain's export products. In 1971, it bought goods worth about $358 million, which represents 32·8 (26·1) per cent[2] of Spain's total exports to the Community. West Germany is followed, in decreasing order of importance, by France, with 29·2 (23·2) per cent, the United Kingdom 18·1 (18·1), Italy 18·3 (14·6), the Netherlands 13·3 (10·6), Belgium–Luxembourg 6·4 (5·1), Denmark 1·6 (1·6), and Ireland 0·6 (0·6). From the perspective of the EEC countries, Spain appears, however, as only a marginal supplier in the Common Market: it contributed 1·2 (1·5) per cent to that Market's total imports. As far as Spain's imports from the EEC are concerned, 37·1 (29·4) per cent came from West Germany in 1971; the other countries followed in the same order as above as sources of supply. Again, Spain's importance as a market for the EEC countries' exports is modest; only 1·7 per cent went to Spain in 1971.

An analysis of the composition of Spain's exports to and imports from the EEC reveal the following features:

(*a*) The import structure shows a significant dependence on capital goods. About 43 (41) per cent of Spain's total imports from the Community was accounted for by this major product category in 1971; important items were industrial machines, engines, electrical power machinery, office machines and road motor vehicle parts. Basic manufactures (such as textile

2 Figures in parentheses refer to the enlarged EEC.

yarn and thread, glassware, and non-ferrous metals, apart from iron and steel) and chemicals (such as organic elements, plastic materials, and pharmaceutical products), amounting to approximately 19 (19) and 17 (16) per cent respectively, constituted the next largest commodity groups. This is predictable, given the difference between Spain and the EEC with respect to stage of development, capital–labour proportions and natural resource endowments.

(*b*) The same holds for Spain's export structure. Almost one-third of the total value of Spanish exports to the Common Market consisted of foodstuffs (particularly of fish products, oranges and fresh vegetables) in the reference year. Basic manufactures and capital goods also play a noticeable role in Spain's export trade with the EEC: they accounted for about 20 (19) per cent and 19 (18) per cent of total export value respectively. The similarities between export and import structure illustrate the importance of intra-industry (rather than inter-industry) specialisation in the trade with the EEC. Moreover, it should be noted that the broad groups of capital goods include mainly metal-working machinery, passenger cars, and ships– that is, product-cycle goods in the Vernon-Hirsch sense, where Spain could become comparatively efficient after catching up with the (foreign) production technique embodied.

When trying to assess whether or not the expansion of trade with the EEC is beneficial to Spain, one can hear arguments in some Spanish quarters that it is not. Those who adhere to this view can cite the evidence that the value of Spain's exports to the Common Market in 1971 was higher than the imports from the EEC in only 18 (19) out of 45 items. Outstanding instances are fruit and vegetables with an export surplus of \$223·5 million (\$307·8 million) and olive oil with \$107·2 million (\$108·9 million). However, it lies in the nature of a semi-industrialised country, such as Spain still is, that there are trade deficits with the far more developed EEC. Provided that Spain does not pay higher prices for goods imported from the Common Market than for those available elsewhere, trade deficits can be considered to be a good indicator of benefits (rather than disadvantages) accruing to the country from its trade relations with the EEC; they reflect certainly the extent to which the Community transfers resources to Spain at world prices and to which a rational division of labour is enhanced – that is to say, all the talks about sign and even size of bilateral trade balances is rather misplaced.

TABLE 2 The profile of concessions

Spain

Product coverage for tariff reductions[a]

Total imports from EEC	$1,200m.
Imports of ECSC products	$88m.
Duty-free under MFN tariffs and free-port regulations	$185m.
Products excluded	52m.
Product coverage (73% of total imports)	$875m.

Tariff reductions (%)

		1970	*1973*	*1974*	*1975*	*1976*	*1977*	*Total*
List A		10	10	10	10	10	10	60
($48m.)	or:	(10)	(10)	(12·5)	(12·5)	(12·5)	(12·5)	(70)
List B		5	5	0	5	5	5	25
($271m.)	or:	(5)	(5)	(5)	(5)	(5)	(5)	(30)
List C ($414m.)		5	5	0	5	5	5	25
List D ($142m.)		0	0	0	0	0	0	0

Average tariff cut by January 1977: 22·9% (25·5%)

Liberalisation of import quotas[b]

(*a*) Applicable only to manufactured products

(*b*) Consolidation of quota abolitions: 80% of manufactured imports from EEC = $857m.
If new import quotas on the remaining 20% are established, at least 75% of the quota has to be allocated to the EEC.

(*c*) Opening of 84 global import quotas:

Basic value	$96m.
+ 13% cumulative increase in six years	$104m.
	$200m.
− Maximum limit of 5% of total imports from EEC for global import quotas	$64m.
Liberalisation of import quotas by January 1967	$136m.

[a]Reference year: 1968.

[b]Reference period: 1966–8 (average)

Table 2 *(continued)*

EEC

Product coverage for tariff reductions[a]

Total exports to EEC	$454m.
Exports of ECSC products	$5m.
Duty-free exports under MFN tariffs	$69m.
Products excluded	$121m.
Product coverage (57% of total exports)	$259m.

Tariff reductions (%)

		1970	*1972*	*1973*	*1974*	*1975*	*1977*	*Total*
General list		30	20	10	0	0	0	60
($70m.)	or:	(30)	(20)	(10)	(10)	(0)	(0)	(70)
Special list		10	0	10	0	10	10	40
($9m.)								

For agricultural and fishery products there will be tariff reductions in the order of 25 to 100% (in some cases subject to maximum amount limitations) affecting $180m.

Average tariff cut by January 1977: 47·8% (51·1%)

Liberalisation of import quotas

Total abolition for manufactured products (in some cases there are maximum amount limitations for preferential treatment)

Source: Compiled according to the regulations of the Agreement.

Nature of the agreement

The extent to which the agreement will intensify trade relations between Spain and the Community depends clearly on the degree of effective reductions in tariff and non-tariff protection. In principle, all tradable goods (with the exception of iron and steel products) were regarded as being eligible for liberalisation through the agreement. An examination of the scheme shows, however, that there are important differences in the concessions agreed upon, presumably because of conflicts of interest between the parties.

As can be seen from Table 2, Spain's concessions consist of gradual reductions in import protection affecting 71 per cent of the country's imports from the EEC in the base year, 1968. The coverage of the EEC concessions is less extensive. In addition, the Community has excluded many products of export interest to Spain because of that country's supply potential. This is particularly true of agricultural and fishery commodities, of which only 46·5 per cent will enjoy tariff reductions, in some cases (such as oranges, lemons, wine) subject to ceiling limitations and in some others (such as tomatoes, grapes) to seasonal limitations. But even for a number of manufactured products, some of which are relatively labour-intensive, the EEC was interested in not giving too much; for instance, Spain's exports of cotton and some petroleum products will enjoy only a quantitatively limited preferential treatment, and its exports of cork manufactures, of cotton yarn and thread, and of pile and chenille fabrics have been excluded from the Agreement. This sort of restrictiveness on the part of the EEC is, of course, not surprising at all; it is perfectly consistent both with the Common Agricultural Policy (CAP) typically aimed at achieving specific social objectives (Article 39 of the Treaty of Rome) at the expense of foreign producers (and domestic consumers) and with the spreading of nationalistic and neo-mercantilistic philosophies within the Community which justify the preservation of actually or potentially 'sick' industries at the expense of the well-being of the general public. One may argue that Spain has also tried to protect industries, workers and farmers against the impact of imports from the Common Market. To the extent that this is true, it will lead to a less efficient domestic economy. The point here, however, is that there is simply an asymmetry in the impact of freer trade: assuming equal liberalisation policies, it will be much greater in Spain than in the Common Market, because Spain is a marginal supplier in the EEC market for most products (particularly the manufactured ones), whereas the Community's producers, being far more efficient, might be able to invade the market of the less advanced Spanish economy and to hurt Spanish labourers seriously by putting them out of work. Moreover, the different degrees of development in Spain and the EEC leads one to believe that both affected firms and workers in the EEC are better able to adjust to the impact of imports than firms and workers in Spain.

Notwithstanding the restrictive elements in the PTA, the import tariff cuts staged over six years could be advantageous for Spain. On a superficial view, at least, the agreement represents an improvement, compared with the previously existing conditions, for its trade with the

Common Market. The average reduction of EEC tariffs is, from a relatively low level, 47·8 per cent; that of Spain's tariffs is, from a relatively high level, 22·9 per cent (Table 1).[3] Other things being equal, these tariff cuts are bound to increase the magnitude of trade flows between both partners – to what extent, is an empirical question. As the time elapsed since the agreement is very short, it is too early to quantify the mutual trade expansion which has resulted from the PTA. *Ex ante* estimates may be of some use, but one has to know the price elasticities of demand for imports and supply of exports in both Spain and the EEC, and the elasticity of substitution between preferred and non-preferred products in both markets. In view of the well-known conceptual problems involved in the estimation of price elasticities, combined with some shortcomings in the available data, no elasticities (neither in the short- nor in the long-run) have been measured. In order to obtain an idea of the possible trade expansion, let us assume infinite demand and unitary supply elasticities for Spain's exports to the Community and infinite elasticity of supply and −0·5 elasticity of demand for the EEC's exports to Spain. These assumptions imply a growth of Spain's export of the same magnitude as the tariff reductions offered by the EEC, while the EEC exports to Spain would increase by roughly 11 per cent on average.

The trade pattern which is to emerge from the reciprocal tariff concession is closely related with the allocative effects which the PTA may bring about.

(*a*) The impact on the allocation of resources is properly judged not from nominal tariffs on products but from tariffs in terms of the value added at which the commodity in question is produced ('effective tariffs'). This is so because the combination of PTA output and input tariffs determine the extent to which a domestic producer will have to operate with a value added lower than that which existed before the agreement.[4] Ideally, one should therefore try accurately to quantify the new effective rates of tariff protection and then to estimate the subsequent effects of effective tariff changes on trade flows. This approach might be more relevant for

3 If the EEC reduces the tariffs on products included in the General List by 70 per cent, Spain will reduce tariffs for List A by 70 and for List B by 30 per cent. As a result, the depth of the tariff cuts will increase somewhat.

4 The rate of effective tariff protection is usually defined as

$$e_j = (t_j - \sum_{i=1}^{n} a_{ij}t_i)/(1 - \sum_{i=1}^{n} a_{ij}),$$

where t_j and t_i are the nominal tariffs on the output and the inputs and the a_{ij} are the intermediate inputs per unit of output.

Spain than for the EEC. As one can reasonably assume that the small share of Spain in EEC trade renders the position of its exporters with respect to EEC producers more or less analogous to that of perfect competitors, they might not be able to influence the output and input prices prevailing in the Common Market; hence the PTA is not likely to reduce the effective protection accorded to EEC producers through the Common external tariff (CET) below what it would otherwise be.[5] The protection of Spain's producers, however, is likely to change. The practical and conceptual problems involved in an attempt to quantify those changes are, again, so great that one may want to avoid going too far. For the purpose at hand it was regarded as sufficient to provide some indication of the reduction in effective tariffs; this can be accomplished by means of applying simple rules of thumb. The rough estimates presented in Table 3 are based on the, admittedly somewhat arbitrary, assumption that the nominal tariffs on final products and on the major inputs used in their manufacture have been reduced in a like manner. This means that effective tariffs in Spain will move, more or less, in step with the nominal tariffs. Taking, for the sake of simplicity, the average tariff cuts as indicators of the tariff reductions accorded to all products traded between Spain and the EEC, one can then easily obtain the new rates of effective tariff protection.

(*b*) Treating the evidence available with due caution, it points towards the conclusion that despite the PTA a tariff structure persists on both sides which is escalated according to the stage of manufacturing undergone by a particular product.[6] It is evident from the post-PTA effective rates of protection in Spain as well as in the Community that these rates remain, on

5 For a detailed discussion of this point and an illustration with some exemplary cases, see L. Gámir, *Las preferencias efectivas del Mercado Común a España*. Madrid, Editorial Moneda y Crédito, 1972, pp. 177 ff.

6 This type of tariff structure for the EEC as a whole has been found by B. Balassa, 'Tariff protection in industrial countries: an evaluation', *Journal of Political Economy*, **73** (December 1965), 573–94. Although Balassa's estimates refer to 1962 and the Community has since then reduced its external tariffs, particularly as a result of the Kennedy Round, it did so in a way that prevented the cascading phenomenon from disappearing. Some fresh evidence (for 1972) on two Common Market countries – Germany and the United Kingdom – which was presented recently, corroborates this statement. See J. B. Donges, G. Fels, A. D. Neu *et al.*, *Protektion und Branchenstruktur der westdeutschen Wirtschaft* (Tübingen: J. C. B. Mohr, 1973), pp. 16–35; N. Oulton, 'Tariffs, taxes and trade in the UK: the effective protection approach', *Government economic Service Occasional Papers*, no. 6 (1973).

TABLE 3 Effective rates of tariff protection in Spain's industry and estimated effective rates of preferences for the EEC exports, 1968 (percentages)

	Effective rates of protection [a]			*Effective rates of preferences* [a]	
	pre-PTA	*post-PTA (22·9%)*	*post-PTA (25%)*	*Col. (1)-Col. (2)*	*Col. (1)-Col. (3)*
Industrial branch	*(1)*	*(2)*	*(3)*	*(4)*	*(5)*
Consumer goods					
Knitting mills	47·4	36·5	35·6	10·9	11·8
Clothing	2·6	2·0	1·95	0·6	0·65
Other finished textiles	40·0	30·8	30·0	9·2	10·0
Footwear	102·9	79·3	77·2	23·6	25·7
Leather products	45·5	35·1	34·1	10·4	11·4
Furniture	44·2	34·1	33·2	10·1	11·0
Printed matter	11·0	8·5	8·3	2·5	2·7
Soaps, detergents, perfumes	22·6	17·4	17·0	5·2	5·6
Motor and bicycles	180·0	138·8	135·0	41·2	45·0
Automobiles	21·9	16·9	16·4	5·0	5·5
Precision instruments	30·8	23·7	23·1	7·1	7·7
Intermediate goods					
Yarn	10·0	7·7	7·5	2·3	2·5
Cloth	169·7	130·8	127·3	38·9	42·4
Cork	78·9	60·8	59·2	18·1	19·7
Lumber	−0·9	−0·69	−0·68	−0·21	−0·22
Tanning industry	47·8	36·9	35·9	10·9	11·9
Paper and pulp	51·3	39·6	38·5	11·7	12·8
Manufactures of paper and cardboard	182·9	141·0	137·2	41·9	45·7
Rubber and asbestos products	17·6	13·6	13·2	4·0	4·4
Basic chemicals	31·0	23·9	23·3	7·1	7·7
Synthetic materials	112·5	86·7	84·4	25·8	28·1
Plastic materials	29·0	22·4	21·8	6·6	7·2
Other non-basic chemicals	53·0	40·9	39·8	12·1	13·2
Glass industry	47·3	36·5	35·5	10·8	11·8
Cement	23·1	17·8	17·3	5·3	5·8
Other non-metallic minerals	46·3	35·7	34·7	10·6	11·6
Iron and steel	69·9	53·9	52·4	16·0	17·5
Non-ferrous metals	62·4	48·1	46·8	14·3	15·6

Table 3 (*continued*)

	Effective rates of protection[a]			*Effective rates of preferences*[a]	
	pre-PTA	*post-PTA (22·9%)*	*post-PTA (25%)*	*Col. (1)- Col. (2)*	*Col. (1)- Col. (3)*
Industrial branch	*(1)*	*(2)*	*(3)*	*(4)*	*(5)*
Metal castings	108·6	83·7	81·5	24·9	27·1
Finished metal products	37·8	29·1	28·4	8·7	9·4
Capital goods					
Metal industry for construction	93·4	72·0	70·1	21·4	23·3
Agricultural machinery	22·3	17·2	16·7	5·1	5·6
Other non-electrical machinery	26·6	20·5	20·0	6·1	6·6
Electrical machinery	30·0	23·1	22·5	6·9	7·5
Shipbuilding	71·6	55·2	53·7	16·4	17·9
Aircraft industry	−5·6	−4·3	−4·2	−1·3	−1·4
Railroad equipment	4·1	3·2	3·1	0·9	1·0

[a]For method used see text. Non-traded inputs were treated as goods with no tariffs. The figures have not been adjusted for the extent to which the system of protection defends an over-valuation of the peseta.

Source: Calculated from Organization Sindical Española: Tables input-output de la economía española, year 1968 (mimeographed). Banco de Bilbao: *Arancel de 1960 y disposiciones complementarias*, June 1968.

average, highest for consumer goods, lower for intermediate products and lowest for capital goods. This cascading structure of tariffs entails a discrimination against export products based on raw domestic materials and/or those that are labour-intensive export products (mainly processed food and consumer goods) in the manufacture of which Spain may have a comparative advantage and the EEC as a whole a comparative disadvantage. It follows that, whatever the real impact of the PTA on Spain's exports to the Common Market, a good deal more exports could be achieved if the agreement had produced more rational tariff structures. It is a matter of conjecture whether the PTA reflects the weak position of Spain in the

EEC trade and, consequently, also in the negotiations, or whether the Spanish government was not aware of the need to formulate its bargaining strategy in terms of effective rates of protection.

(*c*) The likelihood that the effective rates of tariff protection in the EEC will not be affected by the PTA and the fact that most of the initial CETs are already relatively low might seem to be an argument against the significance of the EEC preferences for Spain's exports. This would be wrong for at least three reasons. First, the tariff preference enables Spanish exporters, owing to their assumed price-taker position, to raise their price (net of CETs) for products they want to sell in the Common Market up to the level at which the preferential tariff-inclusive sale price equals the price in the Community.[7] Second, the margin of preference enjoyed by Spanish exporters compensates them partially or totally, for the negative effective protection imposed by Spain's tariff structure and which they were facing to the extent that they had to pay tariff-inclusive prices for material inputs,[8] while they obtained (only) the Common Market prices on their export sales. In other words, the subsidy component of Spain's effective tariffs on exportables into the EEC will become positive, while the tariff preferences granted by Spain to EEC exporters will reduce the degree of implicit taxation of value added obtainable in exporting to the Common Market; in extreme cases, the effective tariff protection of Spain's exports can become – so far as trade with the Community is concerned – positive. Third, all this reduces the bias against exporting inherent in Spain's tariff structure and might encourage firms to increase their production for export at the expense of third (non-preference-receiving) countries with whom Spain is competing.

To sum up the picture obtained so far: the PTA could be regarded, at the

7 The margin for price increase related to value added at international prices reflects the rate of subsidy that is accorded to Spain's exporters. The magnitude of this subsidy appears important, as is shown by L. Gámir, *The Common Market, the U.K. and the effective preferences to Spain* (mimeographed, February 1973). The subsidies, which have been calculated on the basis of 1970 tariffs and value added for 26 manufacturing branches and assuming a 70 percentage tariff cut in the EEC, varies between 1·5 per cent (shipbuilding) and 42·9 per cent (fabrication of cellulose, paper and cardboard), the unweighted average being 24·2 per cent.

8 There is a kind of drawback scheme in Sapin, but it does not reimburse export firms for tariffs paid (directly or indirectly) on all inputs used in the production of exportables.

time it was concluded, as an important step in the direction of intensifying the economic relations between Spain and the EEC, as well as of encouraging Spain's exports and promoting the country's economic development (although it has accomplished less than had been intended). Politically, it had the immense value of 'forcing' the Spanish government to do what was good for the country from a social point of view (that is, to liberalise its trade), but what had been much more difficult to undertake without the agreement because of the resistance offered by powerful inward-lookers. Indicative of this is the fact that the trade liberalisation process which began so vigorously in 1959/60 was losing momentum during the late 1960s.

Now, however, there is the question of whether or not the value of the PTA to Spain's export sector is likely to be reduced by both the unilateral Generalised System of Preferences for developing countries (GSP), implemented by the EEC in July 1971, and the accession of Denmark, Ireland and the United Kingdom to the Community, which became effective in January 1973.[9]

(*a*) The GSP, despite being subject to a number of shortcomings, is doubtless far more generous than the PTA, particularly as far as manufactures are concerned.[10] Because industrial exports of 91 developing countries and 47 so-called dependent territories are admitted in principle free of customs duties by the EEC member countries, Spanish exporters, who have to pay tariffs, are in a disadvantageous position in comparison with their competitors in the GSP-receiving countries (particularly Argentina, Mexico, Hong Kong, Singapore and Yugoslavia). This is especially true of consumer goods, which are still relatively highly protected in the EEC; and it holds true even if one recognises that the geographical proximity of Spain to the Common Market may offset part of the competitive disadvantage resulting from the GSP. The discrimination against Spain would become more serious if the GSP, which the United States is planning to enact, also excludes Spain.[11]

9 It should be noted in addition that the concessions offered to Spain by the original Six seem to be inferior to those granted through bilateral agreements to Greece (1962), Morocco (1970), Tunisia (1970) and Turkey (1964, 1970). By contrast, the PTA appears superior to the agreements concluded by the EEC with other countries of the Mediterranean basin, such as Cyprus (1972), Egypt (1972), Malta (1971), Israel (1970) and Lebanon (1972).

10 For a comparative analysis see R. Tamames, *Acuerdo preferencial CEE/España y preferencias generalizadas* (Barcelona: Dopesa, 1972).

11 This is quite likely to happen because the US Trade Reform Act of 1973,

(*b*) The enlargement of the EEC is likely to add to the erosion of the value of the PTA. This is particularly true of agricultural products. The main cause lies in the fact that tariffs on agricultural imports in the Three, before their accession to the EEC, were considerably lower than the tariffs of the original Six (weighted average nominal tariffs were 12 and 21 per cent respectively); besides, the Three previously granted direct subsidies to aid their agriculture, whereas the Six have implemented a system of variable import levies that soaks up any attempt of third-country suppliers to expand exports by selling at prices below the internal target price in the EEC. The enlargement of the EEC, therefore, implies a substantial increase of protection in an area that is very important for Spain (more than 50 per cent of Spain's agricultural exports go to the United Kingdom). In addition, the envisaged equalisation of the Three's agricultural prices with those of the original Community is likely to encourage farmers to expand their output and in turn to raise the level of self-sufficiency and reduce import needs to be satisfied by third countries. On the other hand, the high trade barriers prevailing against agricultural imports from Spain prevent EEC consumers from changing their consumption habits in favour of items which Spain could offer at lower prices. As far as manufactured products are concerned, the new situation does not look as bad. But even here the Three granted in many cases (particularly in the consumer-goods industry) lower effective protection to domestic producers than did the original Community[12] and they will have to change this now in the course of the progressive introduction of a customs union between the Six and the new entrants. To the deterioration of the conditions of market access for Spain's exporters, one has to add trade diversion effects which are likely to result from the fact that the dismantling of intra-EEC tariffs (as the Three become integrated into the Community) will place producers inside the enlarged Community (even the less efficient ones) in a better competitive setting than Spain's suppliers. Finally, it should be mentioned in passing that the trade structure between Spain and the Three differs greatly from

according to current plans, provides for the denial of preferences to those countries which extend preferential treatment to the export products of another developed country or group of countries.

12 It is interesting to see in this context that – in 1972 and taking into account the Kennedy Round effects – the average effective rate of tariff protection for the manufacturing industry as a whole (excluding food, beverages and tobacco) was 6·4 per cent in the United Kingdom as compared to 10·1 per cent in Germany. The nominal tariffs were, on average, 3·8 and 7·8 per cent respectively.

that between Spain and the Six. If the acceding countries adopted the PTA in its original form, they would therefore reach an even lower coverage than that of the PTA, especially as far as agricultural products are concerned. It follows from all the above that, although the Three would get easier access to the Spanish market, Spain's exports have to overcome new trade barriers.[13] The phasing-out of the Commonwealth preferences can be expected only partially to offset the negative impact to Spain's exports of the EEC enlargement. On the one hand, Commonwealth countries have been given the option to apply either for an association or a preferential trade agreement with the enlarged EEC; on the other hand, the United Kingdom, as well as Denmark and Ireland, will adapt their preferential schemes for developing countries to the Community's GSP.

Although the answers to the questions raised are bound to be speculative, the author is strongly inclined to expect that the GSP plus the widening of the EEC will have a certain diversionary impact on Spain's export trade. Needless to say, the loss of exports to the preferred developing countries as well as to the enlarged Community is not likely to occur in the form of a decline in absolute values. What one has to expect is that Spain's exports to the Common Market will be less than they would have been otherwise.

The Challenge to Spain's Industry[14]

Notwithstanding the above arguments, the preferential treatment of trade between Spain and the EEC is certainly of value to both sides, provided that

13 In the meantime, the EEC has recognised the urgent need to revise the Agreement with Spain. But no concrete solutions to the problem have so far been found, with the exception of an enlargement protocol concluded in December 1972, according to which the original PTA will not be applied to the trade relations between Spain and the three new members until new negotiations have taken place. It was not until July 1974 that the EEC submitted to Spain the draft of a new agreement. This offer rests on the idea of establishing – for manufactured products – a free-trade zone between the enlarged Community and Spain. The EEC would abolish tariffs on industrial imports from Spain by mid-1977, while Spain would have to remove its tariffs on manufactured imports from the Common Market by mid-1980. Again, the EEC is taking care to protect its domestic markets. The result is that the practical value of this offer for Spain is not as great as it may appear, because 42 per cent of Spain's manufactured exports to the EEC will qualify for preferential tariff treatment only up to a more or less restrictive ceiling. Most of Spain's agricultural exports will be kept excluded from the new agreement.

14 Agriculture is left out in the following remarks because agricultural trade

the export supply potential of the beneficiaries is high.[15] Producers of the Community ought to have no difficulties in expanding their exports to Spain in response to the tariff reductions. For Spain's manufacturers, however, the integration with the Common Market represents a greater Challenge. Will they be able to compete effectively with the many highly efficient EEC industries in the markets of Spain and the Nine? What kind of policies is the Spanish government to follow in order to bring about the indispensable structural improvements and to strengthen the international competitiveness of the country's industry?

Judging from Spain's economic performance after 1959, which has been analysed elsewhere,[16] one may be inclined to face the future with reasonable confidence. Reaction of entrepreneurs to the intensification of foreign competition during the process of import liberalisation proved the ability of many Spanish firms to improve organisational and technological efficiency in production rather quickly. And the spectacular increase in Spain's manufactured exports during the 1960s can be ascribed in not too small a proportion to an improvement of international competitiveness within Spanish manufacturing industry. It is, therefore, not unreasonable to expect Spanish industry to be capable of exploiting the opportunities of increasing integration in the future, too. The availability of excess capacity, combined with the relatively low export-to-output ratio, indicate that output for exporting into the Common Market may be expanded in many cases at constant costs; where that is not possible, exporters might still be able to compete by selling their products marginally priced.

However, one can hardly overlook the fact that Spain is still in the process of becoming an industrialised economy and that, subsequently, it is still beset with a number of basic structural problems, which might make

presents a number of special problems that deserve more attention than can be devoted in the limited space available for this chapter. An interesting analysis of the issues involved is provided by Gámir, *Las preferencias efectivas, op. cit.* ch. 2.

15 Of course, it is not only preferential treatment that matters when assessing the effects of the integration process. The outcome will depend on a great variety of factors (such as selling price, quality, terms of payment and of delivery, and marketing), which determine the degree of competitiveness with respect to foreign suppliers.

16 See the author's articles: 'From an autarchic towards a cautiously outward-looking industrialization policy', *op. cit.* pp. 55 ff., 'Spain's industrial exports: an analysis of demand and supply factors, *Weltwirtschaftliches Archiv*, **108**, (1972), no. 2, 198 ff.; 'Shaping Spain's Export Industry', *World Development*, **1** (September 1973), 19 ff.

it difficult for domestic producers to compete successfully for market shares at home and abroad as well as to consolidate achieved export positions.

(*a*) One serious structural weakness is due to the proliferation of firms and to the small scale of production in many enterprises. This is true even of those sectors like the chemical industry, iron and steel industry and transport equipment, in which the minimum efficient size requirements are, for technical reasons, quite high. Of all manufacturing firms in Spain, about 90 per cent employ fewer than fifty persons; the Gini-index of concentration in total manufacturing is not higher than 0·5 (the theoretical upper limit being unity); the value added per employee in Spain's industry reaches only 40 per cent of the Community's productivity level; a similar gap exists as to the volume of sales per employee; and Spain has only sixty-five manufacturing firms with an annual turn-over of more than US $25 million, whereas the corresponding number in, say, Germany is 390 and in France 360. All this results in cost disadvantages vis-à-vis EEC manufacturers.

(*b*) Additional structural problems have shown up in the form of a lack of specialisation among firms, a partial obsolescence of installed equipment, the use of manual rather than industrial production techniques in some branches, a fragmentation of distribution lines, a lack of standardisation of products, an unbalance of quality standards within branches, a lack of integration of production lines within individual firms, an inadequate provision with finance (particularly working capital) the protection of employees against lay-off, an overstaffing and a more-than-one-occupation attitude of employees in a number of enterprises controlled by the public Instituto Nacional de Industria, a reluctance among many entrepreneurs to adapt imported technologies to market size and resource endowments, and a poor performance of management in many firms. Under such circumstances the competitive position of Spanish industry in the markets cannot but remain weak.

(*c*) What are the implications of these structural weaknesses for industrial prices in Spain? If Spanish manufacturing firms tend to suffer, on average, from structural backwardness compared with enterprises in the EEC, their costs and prices would be higher than in the Common Market. If one looks around in Spain, one will find much evidence that lends support to this conclusion. More formally, this view has been tested by computing ratios of Spanish to EEC prices for 275 industrial items. The results are summarised in Table 4. No precise meaning should be read into these figures, which can only indicate in a rough manner the order of magnitude involved. Bearing all qualifications in mind, it can be seen that in nine out of

TABLE 4 Ratios of Spanish to EEC prices[a], 1967–9

Commodity group	*Number of items*	*Mean ratio (unweighted)*	*Standard deviation of single ratios*
Processed food	20	0·721	0·16
Beverages	6	1·032	0·65
Textile products and Clothing	24	0·886	0·27
Footwear	12	0·813	0·19
Paper products	6	1·190	0·22
Printed matter	7	0·641	0·12
Basic industrial chemicals, Pharmaceutical products and toilet preparations	49	0·974	0·36
Glass products and Ceramics	6	1·040	0·14
Iron and Steel	19	1·117	0·21
Non-ferrous metal products	5	1·140	0·09
Finished manufactures of metal	9	0·866	0·14
Non-electrical machinery	7	1·054	0·07
Electrical apparatus	37	1·086	0·32
Ships	6	1·065	0·11
Automotive industry	36	1·008	0·13
Jewellery, Toys, Musical instruments	26	0·893	0·35

[a]Prices charged to final purchasers of commodities.
Sources: Calculated from Comisaría del Plan de Desarrollo Económico y Social: *Industria básica del hierro y del acero* (Madrid, 1968); Instituto Nacional de Estadística: *Precios al consumidor en los paises del Mercado Común y en España* (Madrid, 1970), data provided by Spanish firms.

sixteen branches, Spanish domestic prices are higher than the corresponding EEC prices; most out of line are paper products, iron and steel, and non-ferrous metal products. The iron and steel industry illustrates particularly well the scope of the problem in question. Although material input prices and labour costs do not put Spanish steel-makers in an unfavourable position, actual prices of, for instance, flat products are up to 20 per cent higher in Spain than in the Community. This fact is bound to inhibit many other industries, for which steel is a major material input, from being efficient producers (at least as long as Spain's industrial legislation requires domestic industries to use Spanish steel even if it could be purchased more cheaply abroad).

TABLE 5 Actual domestic resource costs by major manufacturing sectors in Spain, 1968[a] (Pesetas required to produce US $1.00 of output)

Sector	*Number of branches*	*Mean (unweighted)*	*Standard deviation*	*Coefficient of variation*
Consumer goods industries	30	76·09	11·77	15·46
Intermediate goods industries	20	84·80	10·14	11·95
Capital goods industries	6	121·44	85·82	70·67
Total manufacturing	56	84·06	32·92	39·16
Total economy	86	79·97	27·74	35·56

[a]For method, see text.
Source: Computed from the 1968 Spanish input–output table.

(*d*) The costs of actual resource misallocation to Spanish society as a whole appears to be considerable, as can be seen from Table 5. In 1968, the domestic resource costs per unit of foreign exchange were, on the average, higher than the official exchange rate of 70 Ptas to the dollar.[17] This implies that the same output, when produced abroad, had required less real resources (value added). The fact that the domestic resource costs are higher for the manufacturing sector than for the economy as a whole may be a result of the great variety of policy instruments which affect just this sector. The dispersion in social profitability as between the major manu-

17 The method by which domestic resource costs per unit of output have been calculated is the standard one. The following formula was used:

$$d_j = \frac{\sum_i a_{ij}^h s_{ij}}{\left(\frac{1}{1 + t_j} - \sum_i \frac{q_{ij}}{1 + t_i} s_{ij}\right) \cdot \frac{1}{r}}$$

where a_{ij} stands for the costs of domestically-owned primary factors used in the jth activity; s_{ij} for the column vector of the inverted Leontief-matrix of domestic material inputs $(I\text{-}D)^{-1}$ required by j; t_j and t_i for the nominal tariffs on the finished product and the inputs, respectively; q_{ij} for the value of imported inputs per unit of output; and r for the exchange rate.

facturing sectors as well as within each of these sectors brings out quite clearly the degree of resource misallocation incurrred by the country in sustaining its existing industrial structure, optimal allocation would require the domestic resource costs of different activities to be, at the margin, equal. In manufacturing industry, some branches regarded as particularly successful exporters have relatively high domestic resource costs; this is especially true of shoes (92·79 Ptas/$), furniture (84·90 Ptas/$), finished metal manufactures (89·59 Ptas/$), non-electrical equipment (84·95 Ptas/$) and ships (92·48 Ptas/$). Evidently, the price paid for the tremendous export effort during the 1960s was substantial, for the production of those (and other) commodities involved a cost much higher than was worth while to the economy (at the given exchange rate). All this emphasises the importance of devoting serious thought to the improvement of resource allocation in Spain.

The Spanish government is aware that the solution of all these problems, which largely date back to the pre-1959 period, cannot be left entirely to the market-place. What is required, at least temporarily, is the comprehensive formulation of policies providing the right signals for reorganising and modernising the industrial sector so that private firms can undertake the appropriate actions themselves.[18] The policy guidelines of the Third Four-Year Plan (1972–5) are directed to that end. A well-conceived structural policy must include, among other things, the establishment of minimum plant sizes for new investments, the promotion of mergers among Spanish firms and between Spanish firms and foreign partners, the concen-

18 The way in which Spain's industry will perform might also be intimately related to policies of the foreign firms that in many cases control Spanish companies. As long as those foreign firms impose, for example, export restrictions on their Spanish partners, they might discourage local investment in new production capacities, thus maintaining production at sub-optimal levels and making unit costs higher than they would otherwise be. It is, perhaps, not widely known that export restrictions have been extensively applied until very recently in Spain by private foreign investors, particularly in the automobile industry and in both electrical and non-electrical machinery. But now it seems that the Spanish government is determined to refuse approval to all foreign investments which stipulate such limitations. An actual case in point is the application of the Ford Motor Company to build a plant for passenger car production near Valencia (its biggest in Europe). The approval was given only after Ford agreed, among other things, to create from 1977 on an annual export potential equivalent to at least US $ 230 million. (In 1973, Spain's total exports of passenger cars amounted to US $ 154 million.)

tration of sales through the creation of producer associations, a relaxation of the severe restrictions on the dismissal of unneeded workers and devices to carry out quality controls. In addition, the restructuring of industries, which was started in the First Four-Year Plan period (1964–7) by means of establishing 'industrial growth centres' and 'concerted actions' of firms and the government, is to continue.[19] And so is the expansion of the infrastructural network on a proper scale (particularly in the field of education and manpower training).

The government should not contemplate the possibility of granting special protection to industries that are, and will remain, unable to withstand competition from abroad; otherwise substantial inefficiencies in resource allocation would arise which would entail (static and dynamic) costs for the economy as a whole. It should envisage, on the other hand, the promotion of export activities so that they are given the same chances to develop as import-substituting industries. Such a structural policy is likely to impose severe strains on the weaker firms and workers, although the stronger parts of the industries will gain in form of higher productivity and real income. Some provisions are then indispensable to compensate for the losses of all those affected by the integration process and the concomitant shifts of production; such assistance would also neutralise resistance against structural readjustment which may not be felt any longer as being an unjust hardship but as a temporary sacrifice involved in a promising long-term venture.[20]

The Outlook

The prospects for intensifying economic relations between Spain and the EEC in the future appear somewhat ambiguous.

(*a*) Spain has a vital stake in expanding trade with a highly developed economic area such as the Common Market, that has at the present time a population of 253 million and a *per capita* income of US $2,500 and, therefore, one of the highest purchasing powers in the world. On

19 For an evaluation of some of the results obtained so far, see L. Gámir *et al.*, *Política económica de España*. Madrid: Guadiana de publicaciones, 1972), ch. 13.

20 The apparent cost to the Spanish government of adjustment assistance could be partly matched by simplifying and rationalising the present complex system of industrial incentives, which provides in many cases excessive benefits to firms, which contains a great deal of overlapping and which cause the government a substantial loss of revenue (estimated in the order of US $500 million annually).

the other hand, Spain can become an increasingly important market for EEC exports and direct investments because of the undisputed high development potentialities of the country.

(*b*) This means that the Spanish government should carry on the process of gradually opening up the national economy; the political leaders, as well as public opinion and the individual sectors of economic life, are, in the majority, ready to continue this venture.[21] Larger balance-of-trade deficits, which are likely to arise in this context, might not cause foreign-exchange problems of any kind; they can be offset by earnings stemming from foreign tourism (which are expected to remain very high), by long-term capital inflows from the EEC on which the PTA might have a favourable influence, and by export expansion itself, which might accelerate once Spanish entrepreneurs become more outward-minded.[22] If, despite all this, a balance-of-payments problem arises there is always the possibility of exchange-rate adjustment to ensure equilibrium.

(*c*) No doubt, the motivation for economic integration with the EEC will rapidly disappear if the Community's attitude towards Spain shows no awareness of that country's economic and commercial interests. The EEC should, therefore, accept more rapidly than hitherto the pressure of competition from Spain. This pressure is most unlikely to cause what EEC countries euphemistically call 'market disruption'.[23] Where individual firms

21 A case for a stronger economic integration of Spain with Latin America, instead of with the EEC, has been made by a few respectable Spanish economists. See, for instance, R. Tamames, *Estructura económica de España*, 6th ed. (Madrid: Guadiana de Publicaciones, 1971), pp. 771 ff. Although it has to be recognised that Spain may find some marketing advantages in the Latin American countries, the author really believes that from Spain's national point of view there are no alternatives between integration with the EEC and integration with Latin America. Spain can afford to have both, and it would probably be contrary to its interest to neglect the value of an economic approximation to the Community.

22 As a matter of fact, an increasing number of Spanish entrepreneurs are beginning to understand that the key to future industrial growth is the foreign market. One can already observe that firms are paying more attention than in the past to studying foreign markets, to participating in international fairs and to differentiating their products by trade marks and customer service. For an interesting study on Spain's export entrepreneurs, see J. Viúdez, 'The export behaviour of Spanish manufacturers: an evaluation of interviews', *Kiel Discussion Papers*, No. 25 (November 1972).

23 If this argument is applied to any other Mediterranean countries with which the EEC has concluded a PTA one may run into a 'fallacy of composition'.

are exposed to serious dangers, this would be a reliable indication that they have ceased to be internationally competitive. This is likely to happen, especially with labour-intensive activities due to labour-scarcity in the Community. The firms concerned must be made to understand that they should not try to embark upon defensive investment but respond to changing conditions by retreating from their traditional locations and by shifting, instead, the compromised segments of their production, as well as their know-how, to the lower-wage country, Spain. This would be in the interest of the Community itself: the emigration of workers from Spain (at present about 1·6 million) would become less urgent and would reduce, subsequently, both the environmental costs on the EEC and the drain on economic activity and the social problems in Spain; consumers in the EEC countries would benefit from a greater supply of less expensive goods; and the reallocation of resources would have a positive effect on the Community's productivity growth and, hence, widen the scope for increases in real income.

Some people may doubt that the EEC will really behave in a liberal spirit. They may question whether the neo-mercantilists among the Nine will be ready to desist from preserving comparatively inefficient industries, and whether long-sighted economic arguments can prevail over the power of political prejudice. Moreover, critics may argue that the Community has, after the enlargement, an even more diversified production structure, so that the member countries may consider the gains from more trade with Spain (and other third countries) as too low to risk political unrest resulting from increasing import competition. The author admits that he has doubts of this type too, particularly because Spain does not have a countervailing

Although the impact of increasing imports from Spain upon the Common Market will be small, the total impact of imports from all Mediterranean countries can nevertheless be large. Whether or not this view is right is an empirical question. If it is, it does not weaken the present argument but points to the need for a far-reaching adjustment assistance policy in the Community to encourage 'declining' domestic industries to transfer their factors of production to activities of greater comparative advantage. As is well known, the EEC has already accepted the rationale of adjustment assistance – when it established the European Social Fund to help those affected by increased intra-European industrial competition. Contrary to common belief, the author is convinced that in-depth research would reveal that even rapidly increasing imports from Spain and the other Mediterranean countries do not significantly aggravate existing problems arising from changes in demand structure, from technological progress and from competition by other developed countries.

power at all. But he is not (yet) so sceptical as to throw up his hands in despair. It should be reasonable to expect that, sooner or later, politicians in the Community will learn how to think and act in terms of economic and social welfare. The one-sided preoccupation of the governments with the interests of producers is less readily tolerated today, particularly by the younger generation, than it once was. One can already perceive incipient signs of an emerging consumer lobby which may be able to counter protectionism. In addition, there seems to be a growing concern about accelerating inflation in a number of major industrialised countries, including Germany, France and the United Kingdom. If the control of inflation is going to obtain, in the medium run, higher priority than the fight against unemployment, the gradual cutting of import trade barriers may be regarded as a means of reducing inflation to rates that are socially and politically more acceptable. Nevertheless, it may well be the case that all these considerations are a matter of wishful thinking. Then, the prospects for Spain's economic integration with the EEC, are of course, not as rosy as they could be. The natural reaction in Spain would be one of disappointment, frustration and hesitancy about Europeanisation, with obvious implications for the country's economic order and political system.

12

The EEC and Israel

SERGIO MINERBI

Israel's deep interest in the European Economic Community (EEC) can easily be understood when it is realised that the Community today is the major partner in Israeli trade. In 1973, Israel's imports from the Nine members of the Community amounted to $1,602 million, out of a total import of $2,989 million (53 per cent), while it exported $560 million worth of goods out of a total of $1,446 million (39 per cent).[1] In absolute figures the Israeli market shows a dimension much bigger than its population of 3 million people would suggest, and compares favourably with other Mediterranean countries with a bigger population. Exports from the Community to Israel in 1973 were bigger than to Lebanon or Morocco, thanks also to the fact that Israel has already applied a wide liberalisation and there are almost no quantitative restrictions in force today. It is the purpose of this chapter to examine briefly, after a short résumé of the historical background, the main lines on which the impact of the EEC on the Israeli economy may be felt.

The Historical Background

The government of Israel did not wait very long before trying to establish contacts with the EEC. As a matter of fact, the ink of the signatures on the Treaty of Rome was not yet dry when Israel tried to establish contact with the Community. The reasons that prompted this immediate approach were of various kinds. First of all, there was the economic reason, as Europe was already a major partner in Israel's foreign trade. Another evident reason was a political one, as Israel, being isolated in its own area, was looking for friends elsewhere and first of all in Western Europe. It was, one may recall, the time of the intense love affair with France, immediately after the Suez Campaign in 1956. Furthermore, the future of the European Community was still very unclear, and no-one knew exactly what could eventually come out of the projects of customs union, political unity and so on. As often

1 *Monthly Foreign Trade Statistics* XXIV, No. 12 (Jerusalem: December 1973).

TABLE 1 Israel's trade with the countries of the EEC in the years 1971–4 (in millions of US dollars)

	Imports				*Exports*			
	1971	*1972*	*1973*	*I–VI 1974*	*1971*	*1972*	*1973*	*I–VI 1974*
Italy	85·17	166·66	151·65	108·9	22·74	28·49	35·32	31·1
Belgium	74·70	121·61	143·51	74·8	44·38	46·24	75·63	61·0
W. Germany	237·89	229·85	511·87	344·2	88·61	103·66	137·65	71·4
Holland	79·60	83·11	166·13	96·8	55·85	67·44	97·95	69·1
Luxembourg	0·57	0·91	1·45	0·2	0·01	0·01	0·031	0·2
France	85·97	95·23	129·71	76·1	45·82	55·38	63·54	45·6
UK	277·14	362·56	478·81	296·5	99·60	111·25	140·80	83·4
Denmark	9·79	8·83	12·29	8·2	4·78	5·73	7·60	4·0
Ireland	7·01	1·41	13·31	4·4	0·85	0·65	0·94	0·4
Total enlarged EEC	857·84	1,070·17	1,607·73	1,010·1	361·84	418·85	561·46	366·2
Total all countries	1,883·28	1,983·16	2,987·22	1,957·7	958·59	1,146·97	1,448·66	1,047·0

Source: Israel Central Bureau of Statistics, *Foreign Trade Statistics Quarterly* No. 4 (January–December 1973); for the year 1974: The Ministry for Industry and Commerce.

happens, the Israelis, being outside the Community, did believe in its future development, perhaps even more than the Europeans themselves.

The first Israeli memorandum was submitted to the Commission of the EEC on 30 October 1958, and in 1959 Israel was, among third countries, one of the first to nominate an ambassador to the EEC.[2]

Israel requested the conclusion of a global agreement on 27 September 1960, in its reply to a questionnaire by the Commission. However, negotiations led only to a trade agreement, which was signed on 4 June 1964 and which became operative on 1 July of that year. Under it, Israel was granted an average 20 per cent reduction on some twenty export items of minor importance as well as a 40 per cent reduction on grapefruit.[3] However, because of its non-preferential nature, the value of the trade agreement was limited, and the Israeli government continued to press for full association and presented a formal demand on 4 October 1966.

In the middle of the Six Day War, on 7 June 1967, the Commission proposed to the Council of Ministers to negotiate a preferential agreement with Israel. For two years negotiations went on behind the scenes; the Commission was convinced that complete liberalisation of trade with Israel would not raise any special difficulty, but suggested only a preferential trade agreement because of the political situation.[4] Holland and Germany were in favour of an agreement with Israel, although France opposed it for reasons connected with the political situation prevailing in the Middle East. A major change in the French stands was announced in the meeting of the Council of Ministers of 22 July 1969, when Foreign Minister Schumann stated that whoever was in favour of a preferential agreement with Israel must at the same time accept the same principle for any Arab country asking it. Once this idea was accepted by the other members of the Community, the way was open for a decision, and on 17 October 1969 the Council issued the necessary mandate for the negotiations 'within the general framework of its Mediterranean policy and in expectation of a balanced development in its relations with the countries of the region'.[5] Finally, a preferential agreement was signed on 29 June 1970 in Luxembourg, and on the same day a similar agreement was signed between the EEC and Spain.

2 S. I. Minerbi, 'Les relations d'Israël avec la Communauté Economique Européenne', *La Communauté et les pays méditerranéens* (Brussels: Université Libre de Bruxelles, 1970).

3 S. I. Minerbi, 'Israël et le Marché Commun', *L'Europe en formation* (November 1964).

4 Bulletin *Europe* (Brussels, 24 June 1969).

5 Commission, *Bulletin of the European Communities* (August 1970).

The Trade Preferential Agreement

Because an association was refused to Israel, mainly on political grounds, the agreement enforced on 1 October 1970 does not fall within Article 238 of the Treaty of Rome. Nevertheless, a new interpretation was given to Article 113, on which the agreement is based, in order to give it a preferential nature.[6]

Under its clauses, more than 850 dutiable Israeli goods exported to Common Market countries benefit from a reduction in the Community's customs tariffs. Progressively this reduction has reached 50 per cent, in accordance with the following time-table: 30 per cent at the date when the agreement became operative – namely, on 1 October 1970 – and a further 5 per cent each on 1 January 1971, 1972, 1973 and 1974. There are, however, certain exceptions. Thus 'sensitive' products are on a special list: for instance, on aluminium products there is a maximum tariff reduction of 34 per cent, and on automobiles one of 28 per cent, while a fixed reduction of 50 per cent applies to cotton fabrics up to an annual quota ceiling of 300 metric tons. Totally excluded from any reduction are bromine and bromides, superphosphates, phosphoric acid, plywood, cotton yarns, stockings, knitted outerwear, plate glass, and iron and steel pipes.

In exchange, Israel undertook to grant tariff reductions on part of the dutiable products of the Community imported to Israel, both industrial and agricultural. These export goods were divided into four categories, and the last customs reduction on 1 January 1974 reached the cumulative value of respectively 30, 25, 15, and 10 per cent for each category.

As for agricultural products, the EEC granted a 40 per cent reduction on the following fruits grown in Israel: oranges, mandarins, lemons, grapefruit, bananas and avocado. Other reductions include 30 per cent on fresh vegetables and 40 per cent on fruit preserves. Sugar, chocolate, pasta products and biscuits are subject to specific regulations within the framework of the Common Agricultural Policy (CAP), and consequently have not been granted any reductions. The principle was accepted during the negotiations that the value of the customs reduction given by Israel should be equal to 40 per cent of that granted by the EEC to Israel.[7]

6 The full text of the agreement was published in the *Journal officiel des Communautés européennes*, L. 183 (17 August 1970).

7 Y. Friedmann, 'The agreement between Israel and the Common Market' (in Hebrew), *Rivaon le Kalkala* (September 1970).

The Enlargement of the EEC

The accession of Great Britain, Denmark and Ireland to the Community on 1 January 1973 created a completely new situation that could deeply affect the Israeli economy. Israel was worried mainly by the changes that would occur in Great Britain, although for many manufactured commodities the adjustment of the British tariff to the Common external tariff (CET) is actually bringing down the British duties as they were originally higher than the CET. The first adjustment was made on 1 January 1974, and the whole process will be completed in four annual steps ending on 1 July 1977.

However, for food items the Community's tariffs are much higher than the original British ones and 'manufactured' food products fall under the same rule. The British market has for years been traditionally the most important outlet for Israeli fresh oranges and citrus juices. In 1973 Israel sent to Britain 25 per cent of its exports of fresh oranges, 22 per cent of its grapefruit, as well as 67 per cent of its natural orange juice and 78 per cent of its grapefruit juice.[8] The share of the British market supplied by Israeli oranges was between 50 and 60 per cent in recent years.

The citrus market is of major importance to Israel but the following disadvantages are likely to be set it in the period ahead. First of all, duties for third countries had to go up: from 5 to 20 per cent for fresh oranges; from nil to 19 per cent for orange juice; from nil to 15 per cent for grapefruit juice; from nil to 12 per cent for tinned grapefruit. In the same transition period ending on 1 July 1977, tariffs will go down to nil for member states of the EEC, while Morocco and Tunisia, enjoying a reduced duty of 4 per cent on oranges, will be very much favoured in a market where Israel traditionally held a strong position. As a result, there could be a serious danger of diversion of trade in favour of Greek, Moroccan and Tunisian oranges against Israeli fruit. Moreover, it would become impossible to switch oranges from the Six to Great Britain, as was done in the past, to avoid the danger of paying a countervailing duty when the selling price fell below the reference price.

8 The figures for the year 1973 were: fresh oranges exported to Great Britain, \$17 million out of \$70 million; grapefruit, \$8 million out of \$36 million, orange juice, \$8 million out of \$12 million; grapefruit juice, \$7 million out of \$9 million. See *Foreign Trade Statistical Quarterly*, No. 4 (Jerusalem, 1974). For the year 1970 see the interesting brochure Anglo-Israel Chamber of Commerce, *Israel and the enlargement of the the EEC* (London, June 1972).

In the field of industrial products, there could also be some new hurdles. Plywood produced in Israel from African timber is exported mainly to Great Britain (83 per cent of the total in 1973, valued at $7·9 million). Here the tariff had to go up from 5 per cent to a full 13 per cent. In contrast, Gabon, an associate member, would enjoy duty-free access to the British market.

The same problem arises for some chemicals, such as bromine. From a nil tariff at present, duty under the CET should go up to 12 per cent, leading to a possible dislocation of sources of supply. The same principle applies to phosphoric acid produced by the Arad complex (with a programmed export of about $16 million), and to bromides and superphosphate fertilisers.

The Mediterranean Policy

At the meeting of the EEC Council of Ministers on 26/27 June 1972, Maurice Schumann, French Foreign Minister, presented a completely new idea: that a 'global solution for manufactured products' be found to solve most of the problems of Spain, Israel and other Mediterranean countries.[9]

The official Israeli reaction to the French proposal was clearly stated by Foreign Minister Eban in a press conference on 7 August 1972:

> I was asked about an idea proposed by Mr Schumann, of a Mediterranean free-trade area including Israel. I think it is a positive idea. It responds to Israel's desire to be associated with a large market and a large community into which its exports would have free entry. We must understand, and our industrialists, too, that reciprocity is involved. We would have to open our market, which is a large one for Europe, much more widely . . .

On 6 and 7 November 1972 the Community Council set out the guidelines of the global approach which was to include all the countries of the Mediterranean plus Jordan, with the aim of creating free-trade areas progressively covering also the main agricultural products, and for some countries (Maghreb and Malta) organising financial co-operation as well.

On 30 January 1973 a protocol was signed by the Community with Israel[10] and a formal promise was given that a new agreement should be negotiated and should enter into force before 1 January 1974, when the

9 G. P. Papa, 'The Mediterranean policy of the EEC', *European Yearbook* 1973.

10 Commission, *Sixth General Report on the activity of the Communities, 1972* (Brussels, February 1973).

first adjustment to the CET was due to take place in Great Britain.

The Council gave a first mandate to the Commission on 25/26 June 1973, but nevertheless it was not possible to respect the time-table and to complete the package deal with the Mediterranean countries of the 'first round' (Israel, Spain, Morocco, Tunisia, Algeria and Malta) before the end of the year. Thus at the very last moment the British Government decided unilaterally to apply a 'standstill' – that is, not to raise British duties on imports from the six Mediterranean countries, and not to implement in their regard the rules of adjustment to the CET established in the adhesion Treaty. The dangerous repercussions on the Israeli economy deriving from the British adhesion were therefore temporarily avoided.

During the long internal discussions on this subject, a wide difference of opinions appeared among the member states of the Community.[11] France gave all its support to Spain and to the Maghreb countries and stressed its friendship for the Arab countries. Italy was torn between the necessity of paying for most of the concessions to be made on agricultural products of the Mediterranean countries, generally in competition with its own, and the desire to play fully its role of a Mediterranean power. Germany, the main commercial partner of the Mediterranean countries, was in a delicate position created by its obligations to Israel and its desire to reach an understanding with the Arab countries, but generally gave a very positive contribution in removing the obstacles in the way of the agreement with Israel. In the Benelux countries there were conflicting pressures: the businessmen were eager to establish stronger links with Spain, whereas Parliament and public opinion were, for political reasons, against Spain and in favour of closer links with Israel. A compromise was found, according to which an agreement with Spain, without any political character, would be a counterpart to a parallel agreement with Israel, with the widest possible political meaning. The global approach was based on this compromise, which enabled each member state to foster the political and economic goals desired in accordance with its sympathies and interests.

Great Britain was worried about the financial implications of the global approach and wanted to define first the general policy of the Community on aid. In order to avoid the opposition of the United States to the Mediterranean policy, Great Britain asked and received assurances that no reverse preference should be given by the southern Mediterranean countries, with the exception of Israel, to the Community.

11 Informations Méditerranéennes, *Les relations entre la CEE et les Pays du Bassin Méditerranéen* 1 (Brussels, June 1974).

The Proposed Agreement for a Free-Trade Area

After a first round of negotiations, the Commission sent back its proposals to the Council, accepting most of the Israeli requests, in order to obtain a 'supplementary mandate'. The Council met again, and in its session of 22/23 July 1974 gave the general guide-lines for a new mandate which should be elaborated in its final form by the Permanent Representatives in Brussels.

The broad lines of the Council's proposals establishing a free-trade area for industrial products are as follows. The Community will progressively reduce its duties on Israeli industrial products, reaching a full franchise by 1 July 1977, when the adjustment of new member states and the reduction for ex-EFTA (European Free Trade Association) countries will also be completed. Some Israeli industrial exports, like textiles, aluminium products, bromine, oil-refinery products, should be subjected to quantitative ceilings or a surveillance regime until 1979. Israel, for its part, should lower its duties at a slower pace. For 60 per cent of the volume of its industrial imports from the Community, the first reduction will take place on the day when the new agreement comes into force and will reach a full franchise by 1980. On more sensitive products, or 40 per cent of Israeli imports, on which local industry should not be exposed too rapidly to European competition, the transition period will be extended until 1985. Israel asked that the transition period for the first list (60 per cent) should be extended until 1985, and, for the second list (40 per cent) that it should begin only on 1 January 1978 and be accomplished by 1989. Moreover in order to allow the future development of new 'infant industries', Israel should be permitted to re-establish duties, on a level not exceeding 20 per cent of the volume of its industrial imports from the Community.

No free-trade area is envisaged for agricultural products, but the reduction of the tariff on fresh oranges will rise to 60 per cent, and the reduction of that on natural juice will be 70 per cent, as a result of a special effort made by the British delegation for lowering the duty on all foodstuffs as much as possible. A special meeting should take place after 1977 in order to ensure that some progress is made on the Community's concessions in favour of Israeli agricultural products.

A chapter on co-operation is included in the agreement, but it is of rather limited scope and all actions are referred to future meetings of the Mixed Commission.[12]

12 *Telex Méditerranéen*, no. 20 (Brussels, 25 July 1974).

The proposed agreement has built-in imbalance in favour of the Community, for several reasons: (*a*) the free-trade area applies to industrial products only, although 35 per cent of Israeli exports to the EEC are agricultural products; (*b*) the value of the preferences given is larger for the Community, because the volume of their exports to Israel is almost three times as big as their imports, and because the average rate of duties is much higher in Israel (25 per cent) than in the EEC (7·8 per cent).

Because of this built-in imbalance, pure commercial measures cannot alone achieve the closing of the gap at present existing in the form of the huge deficit in the balance of trade, and it is absolutely necessary to expand economic co-operation in all its forms: industrial, technological and financial co-operation.

Probable Impact on Agriculture

The export of fresh and processed agricultural produces included in the CAP of the Community is very important to Israel. In the year 1972 agricultural exports represented 40·61 per cent of total Israeli exports to the enlarged Community ($170 million out of $418 million). If added value only is taken into consideration, then this percentage is even higher, while only 5 per cent of total European exports to Israel is agricultural produce.

The main problem arises from the export of fresh oranges to the Community, where Israel has an important part of the market. Citrus represents about 32·6 per cent of the value of Israel's crop production (697 million Israeli Lire in 1972/3 out of 2·138 million IL), and export is the main outlet as 81 per cent of total production was exported as fresh fruit and a large part of the processed citrus was exported as well.[13] Sixty-seven per cent of oranges was sent to the enlarged Community in the season 1971/2.[14]

It is therefore of paramount importance to avoid any discrimination against Israeli citrus compared with that from other Mediterranean countries. Several times in the past the Commission has recognised the principle of giving a fair chance to all producing countries of the Mediterranean area. When Morocco and Tunisia were allowed a duty reduction of 80 per cent on their exports of oranges to the Six in the year 1969, this was done taking into account their previous franchise in the French market. The same idea should be kept in mind now after the accession of Great Britain to the Community.

The accession of Great Britain to the EEC will have the double effect of extending the system of reference prices to Israel and of opening this

13 Bank of Israel, *Annual Report for the year 1973* (Jerusalem, May 1974) p. 229.

14 Informations Méditerranéennes, *op. cit.* II, p. 343.

market to the imports from the Maghreb countries, which will enjoy a bigger customs reduction than Israel: 80 per cent instead of 60 per cent. Israel has repeatedly asked for full equality of treatment with all Mediterranean producers from outside the EEC, and its seems that the Commission is willing to propose that in three years the customs reduction on Israeli oranges should reach 80 per cent.

The system of reference prices suffers from serious disadvantages. The producers, in Israel or in Morocco, are not in a position to foretell at the time of shipping what prices their produce may fetch in the EEC sometime later, as prices may well be influenced by exports from other Mediterranean countries. The EEC Commission hoped to put a brake on exports to a market which had become over-supplied, but during the season 1972/3 it became evident that some Spanish producers preferred to continue exports even below the reference prices, being confident that at least their first shipments would probably not be affected by a countervailing duty.

Considering the fact that the only producers of oranges inside the EEC are the Italians, providing about 3 per cent of total imports of EEC countries, one could think of much better ways of protecting their legitimate interests than such a complicated system. The EEC Commission could encourage a stricter co-operation and a measure of co-ordination among all exporting countries from the Mediterranean region. Efforts in this direction by CLAM, the Liaison Office of Mediterranean Citrus producers, have produced only the beginnings of collaboration.

In the year 1972 Israel exported a total of 473,000 tons of 'Shamouti' oranges (of which 315,000 tons went to the EEC) and 202,000 tons of grapefruit (from which 173,000 tons went to the EEC). But citrus is not the only Israeli agricultural product exported to the EEC. Flowers, fresh vegetables, fruits like avocado, melons and others are regularly exported to Europe in growing quantities. The proportion of agricultural produce being exported is steadily rising notwithstanding the many organisational difficulties in collecting perishable products from many producers, shipping it in the proper way and finding the right channels for marketing abroad. In the high season, special cargo planes leave Lod Airport every day for Europe, and more than ten refrigerated ships ply three times a week between Haifa and Europe. New means of transport can be used successfully and the price of shipping can be lowered only if great quantities are exported. On the other hand, the export of fresh vegetables and fruit can be directed almost exclusively to the Western European market, which is relatively near and is sufficiently sophisticated to demand such expensive items as out-of-season fruits.

In addition to US $109 million worth of citrus of different kinds, US $37 million of other agricultural products were exported in 1972 to the nine countries of the EEC.

Probable Impact on Industry

Because water and cultivatable land are already used almost to their limit, any hope of raising exports and gradually closing the gap in the balance of trade must rely upon industry. Its place in the Israeli economy is steadily growing, and its share in the GNP rose from 21 per cent in the year 1950 to 26 per cent in 1973. During the years 1969–72, industrial production rose at a yearly average of 13 per cent in real terms, and according to recent planning it should continue to rise in the next four years at a rate of 11 per cent yearly.

Industrial exports increased during the first nine months of 1973 (before the October War) by 14 per cent in real terms, but if diamonds are excluded, their added value being very low (19 per cent), then we find an increase of 3 per cent only. Israel must make a great effort to achieve the objective, stated in government planning, of a yearly increase of 15–18 per cent in the years 1974–8, which should raise industrial exports, without diamonds, to $1,250–1,400 million in 1978 from $633 million in 1973.[15]

This may explain why the Israeli authorities consider it so important to guarantee the unhampered growth of local industry. It is still difficult to assess the impact of the existing preferential agreement, enforced in 1970, as the period of implementation was not long enough. But in the years 1971 and 1972 the rate of increase of the total imports from the Community of Six to Israel was considerably higher than the rate of increase of Israeli exports to the Six, thus raising the trade deficit.[16] The boom of the Israeli economy in the years preceding the Yom Kippur War greatly increased demand for imported goods as well as for local goods, thus preventing perhaps a more rapid increase of exports. Moreover, the floating of some European currencies, and the consequent changes in the rate of exchange of the Israeli pound in comparison with European currencies, greatly influenced Israeli exporters.

The free-trade area agreement now envisaged has been received with mixed feelings by Israeli industrialists inspiring at one and the same

15 Ministry for Commerce and Industry, *Development Plan for Industry in Israel, 1974–1978* (in Hebrew), (Jerusalem, May 1974).

16 Imports from the Six increased by 25·5% in 1971 and 23·7% in 1972, while exports to the Six increased respectively by 25·2% and 15·5%. See Informations Méditerranéennes, *op. cit.* 1, pp. 134–5.

time great hopes of a large market and anxieties concerning the exposure of local factories to the competition of European firms. Here are some of the arguments against the new agreement:

(*i*) Israel has almost no local raw materials and practically all production input for local industry must be imported; moreover, shipment raises their cost. In addition, Israeli industry lacks the long tradition of the Europeans and it dates mostly from the 1950s, as at the beginning of Jewish resettlement priority was given to agriculture. Zionist ideology stressed the importance of a physical return to the land.

(*ii*) If the existing level of tariffs is compared, one may see that while the average CET today on industrial products is about 7 per cent, the average Israeli tariff is much higher, reaching about 25 per cent. It is thus probable that the inter-commodities substitution with local Israeli goods for which price elasticity of demand is rather high would probably be important. In other words, the well-known effect of 'trade creation', when additional imports may displace part of local production, could be considerable. It is probable that re-allocation of production among different branches of Israeli industry would become necessary.

(*iii*) The rate of reduction granted to Israeli manufactured goods entering the EEC will be very low: an average of 3·5 per cent, as the average of 7 per cent has already been cut from many items by 50 per cent according to the present preferential agreement. Such a low real reduction could have some bearing on such homogenous items as chemicals or fertilisers, but not on very sophisticated Israeli products for which the producers' reputation and the existence of proper marketing channels may prove more important than a small cut in custom duties. In other words, much depends on the elasticity of European demand for Israeli goods.

(*iv*) An important problem will be the protection of infant industries to be established in the foreseeable future, most probably in peripheral areas where external dis-economies will be great, and where sharp local social problems exist.

(*v*) A major handicap of Israeli industry is its extreme fractioning; in the year 1971/2, about 83 per cent of industrial establishments employed ten people or fewer. This is due to historical reasons as well as to the deep desire of the average Israeli to be independent and to the widespread entrepreneurial drive. These small plants are seldom capable of dealing efficiently with exports, and perhaps one solution could be to create a roof organisation dealing with all the necessary paperwork as well as organising common buying of raw materials and joint selling abroad. This organisation would have a task similar to that carried out by the Ministry of Defence since the Six Day War in 1967, when more and more orders were passed on to local industry, substituting for imports. The Ministry's people would prepare all the necessary technical specifications, the costing, and would enforce a strict quality control and demand the respect of deadlines, assuring on the other hand long-term contracts with no possible surprise about the rate of profits.

(*vi*) Israeli economy may be slow in seizing the new opportunities offered by the free-trade area because of some bottlenecks. As before the war of October 1973, the main problem remains the overheating of the economy and the lack of manpower with very few possibilities of rapidly expanding production in any branch. Immigration is continuing, and in the year 1972 the number of new immigrants reached 42,112, but time is needed before new immigrants can become a part of the productive process while they learn the language, find a suitable job and sometimes undergo retraining. Notwithstanding the inevitable inflationary effects, immigration is still considered in Israel as an important asset for local economy. It remains to be seen if mobility of labour can be increased and people switched from services to industry and from one industrial branch to another.

Let us now examine some of the beneficial effects that a free-trade area could have on Israeli industry.

(*i*) First of all there is the clear prospect of economies of scale. The Israeli market being very limited, the entrepreneur who wants to use the most efficient methods of production – like, for instance, modern automatic equipment – may install sub-optimal equipment, or exploit only partially optimal equipment during the first years of its existence.[17] The free-trade area should speed up the process of modernisation and the necessary technological changes, as the opening of a new, wider market would encourage investment in new advanced industries in which the optimal size of the plant is much above the demand of the Israeli market. It will also permit full utilisation of the equipment already existing in some plants but not yet fully exploited as under-capacity was decided upon as a lesser evil in the short run.

(*ii*) The agreement with the EEC will accelerate the process of industrial concentration which has already begun. The war of October 1973, with its prolonged period of emergency for the Israeli economy,

17 T. Scitovsky, *Economic theory and Western European integration* (London: Unwin University Books, 1958), pp. 113–15.

may prove that the big concerns could cope more easily with the difficulties of manpower shortage and the drastic shortage of vehicles, switching their limited resources from one plant to another inside the same concern. Yet, for evident social reasons the government may feel compelled to save as many small plants as possible from the big European industries and their strong competition.

(*iii*) Less competitive plants should not be protected and new investments in less efficient branches should not be encouraged. As most new investment plans will be submitted to the Ministry of Trade and Industry in order to obtain the advantages of the incentive scheme allowed under the investment law, this danger can be avoided because the Ministry will take into account the fact that in the free-trade area that will operate in the future only efficient branches and plants can survive.

(*iv*) The main hope is that the much bigger size of the market to which Israeli manufacturers would have access may favourably influence the volume of foreign investments in Israeli industry. It remains to be seen if, in the general context of the world economy today, the expectation of a greater influx of capital investment from Europe and the United States will materialise.

In the last few years there has been a steady increase in private investment from abroad in the Israeli economy: from $12 million net in 1970 to $62 million in 1971, and $124 million in 1972. But only a small part of these investments were directed to the creation of new industrial plants, so that the rapid increase had only little bearing on industry. Financing for industrial development still comes mainly from governmental sources, but technical know-how and proper channels of commercialisation are badly needed.

Some efforts have been made recently to try to check which Israeli industrial products would suffer most from European competition and which would profit most from the new market. This involves measuring, in an indirect war, the elasticity of demand for European imports into Israel, and cross-elasticity of demand in Israel between imports from the EEC and local products.

Beni Toren, of the World Institute in Jerusalem, has developed a series of indicators which, properly weighted, should give a rather good idea of the vulnerability of each product.[18] For each indicator a scale of five possible

18 World Institute, *The impact of the agreement on a free trade area with the Common Market on industrial products* (in Hebrew), (Jerusalem, August 1973).

answers is given, and for each of the three hundred products examined a questionnaire was prepared. These are the main indicators:

How much more of the particular product will be exported to the EEC, due to the tariff reductions?

How much more efficient will production be as a result of tariff reduction in Israel?

Is it possible to switch to export bigger quantities than today?

Is the industrial equipment suitable for producing a different product if the present one must be stopped because of competition?

Is manpower capable of a switch?

Is the plant situated in a development area with local social problems?

What percentage of local production may the competitive import be?

But if it is still rather difficult to find out the future results of complete franchise on local industry, one may safely suppose that a positive result could be a better allocation of resources, with a beneficial effect also against inflation. A different question is that of deciding in which direction Israeli industry should develop in order to realise the plans for the future and to make the best use for the new opportunities offered by the free-trade area. In other words, it should now be determined in which branches Israel has a comparative advantage over other countries.

In a very general way it may be said that the comparative advantage of Israel is in industries using advanced technology or at least a high percentage of technical and professional people out of total manpower employed for the production of any single product. An empirical way of finding out which branches enjoy a relative advantage is to check which products are exported today, but the objection to this method is that because of subsidies or other distorting factors, the fact that a certain item is exported today does not necessarily prove that it really enjoys a relative advantage.

A rather better picture can be obtained by introducing the rate of growth of the export of different branches over a certain period of time. In the period 1969–72 the rate of growth was as shown in Table 2.

A slightly different approach has been followed by Professor Hirsch in a recent article.[19] Professor Hirsch takes into consideration the fact that according to the Israeli government forecast for the years 1972–6, the exports would rise by 13 per cent each year or about twice as much as the yearly rate of growth of GNP (7·3 per cent). At the end of the period, total

19 Z. Hirsch, 'Israel's policy for industrial export' (in Hebrew), *Rivaon le Kalkala*, No. 77 (April 1973).

TABLE 2 Rate of growth, 1969–72

Food industries	74%
Textiles	58
Leather	106
Chemicals	22
Machinery	49
Electrical and Electronic equipment	218[20]

export should reach 44 per cent of total GNP – a very high percentage, which has until now been matched only by Holland, Belgium, Hong Kong and similar export-minded countries. Considering that citrus and its products cannot be greatly expanded because of natural limitations and that in diamonds Israeli exports have already reached a considerable quantity (in 1972 US $389 million were exported, or about 32 per cent of total Israeli industrial exports, and in 1973 US $557 million, or 46·8 per cent of total exports), Professor Hirsch reaches the conclusion that new branches should be developed. In the branch of textiles, only ready-made clothes and fashion may have a future. But the main branches that should be developed are chemicals, machinery and electronics, as they employ a high percentage of engineers, technicians and professional people in which Israel definitely has a relative advantage, their products generally meet a high income elasticity of demand and, finally, there is already a rather important local demand. This thesis is supported by the observation of the exports of several countries grouped according to their GNP *per capita*. It may generally be said that in countries with lower GNP *per capita*, textiles represent a higher percentage of total exports than in richer countries. On the contrary, countries with a higher GNP *per capita* show a higher percentage of chemicals, electronics and machinery out of their total exports.

Another difference concerns the country of destination of exports, and here one may say that the more developed a country, the higher is the percentage of its exports sent to industrialised countries. According to Professor Hirsch, Israel should continue the process that has already begun, in which a higher percentage of total exports is sent to markets in industrialised countries.

Again, it may safely be assumed that these ideas, which are anyway necessary to implement the planning for export increases, are also in line with the prospect of a free-trade area with the EEC.

20 Bank of Israel, *Annual report for the year 1972*, pp. 56–7.

Pressure Groups

Inside Israel there is practically no pressure group against an eventual free-trade area with the EEC, while the citrus growers are very much in favour of the closest possible link with the EEC, the main customer of their product. In so far as the industrialists are concerned, they naturally demand that the customs protection that they have enjoyed until now will not be lifted suddenly in order to allow the necessary time for a gradual and painless adjustment to new conditions, but their attitude has not been characterised by frontal opposition to the whole project.

No political party has expressed any opposition to a free-trade area; Israel is an open society, and from the extreme left to the extreme right all political forces appear to realise that it is in the country's interest to develop all kinds of international links.

In the countries of the Community many powerful pressure groups have been at work, generally behind the scenes, to hamper serious progress in the negotiations with Israel. This probably derived more from narrow-mindedness than from the necessity to defend real economic interests, with the exception perhaps of the citrus growers of southern Italy who succeeded in the end in preserving their rights without blocking the access of the Mediterranean producers. In some industrial branches there are producers inside the Community who fear the consequences of an expansion of imports, although for most items Israel is no more than a marginal supplier and cannot endanger anyone. Oil companies, some of them national companies owned by member states of the Community, have never concealed their sympathies for the Arab oil-producing countries. But the situation radically changed in the wake of the onset of the oil crisis following the Arab–Israeli war of October 1973. Most of the European governments were panic-stricken by the threat of an oil embargo on the eve of the winter that could not only stop domestic heating but completely paralyse industry heavily dependent on oil imports from Arab countries. Most probably the oil crisis would have come anyway, with or without the Arab–Israeli war, because oil-producing countries were trying to raise oil prices that in real terms did go down during the period 1950–70. Restriction in production was a logical consequence of purely economic facts, as big producers like Saudi Arabia were no longer willing to expand production in exchange of devalued foreign currency.

But no matter what was the rationale behind the crisis, and notwithstanding the practically non-existent impact of the embargo which was not felt even in Rotterdam, the reaction of the Community members was one of internal disarray and great external weakness. Not only did France and

Great Britain prevent any help to Holland, but they also led the Nine to a political decision of a clearly anti-Israeli nature, with the hope of pandering to the Arab countries and thus assuring the steady flow of oil which was still coming anyway. Many observers think that the surrender to the oil blackmail manifested in the declaration of 6 November 1973 was even more complete and far-reaching than the Arab states themselves could have hoped.[21]

The declaration was widely criticised by the European press, but this did not prevent the governments of the Nine from pursuing the same policy. During the European summit in Copenhagen on 14/15 December 1973, there was a visit by four Arab ministers, and the idea of a concerted co-operation between the Community states and the oil-producing countries, especially Arab ones, was adopted. Subsequently, the idea developed into that of an Euro–Arab dialogue which had to overcome some obstacles like the bilateral initiative taken by some members of the Community, and the opposition of the United States to any independent initiative on the oil question or on the political problems of the Middle East conflict.

The ministers for Foreign Affairs of the Nine, in the framework of their political co-operation, decided in Bonn on 10 June 1974 to discuss with Arab representatives the procedures of the dialogue. The chairman, Herr Genscher of Germany, declared that in keeping with the Nine's policy of balance in the Middle East the President Ortoli would also meet Israel representatives.[22]

A preliminary meeting was held in Paris on 31 July 1974 with the participation of Mr Sauvagnargues, Foreign Minister of France, in his capacity as Chairman of Council of Ministers, Mr Ortoli, President of the Commission, Mr Riad, Secretary General of the Arab League and Mr Jaber, Foreign Minister of Kuwait.

Many Israelis have no hard feelings against the projects of regional co-operation that the Community intends to offer to some Arab states whether under the heading of the Mediterranean global approach or under that of the Euro–Arab dialogue. The two frameworks are definitely separated, but it was felt in the Community that serious steps forward in the Mediterranean policy towards the Maghreb countries, and later towards Egypt, Syria, Lebanon and Jordan, could greatly improve the chances of success of the Euro-Arab dialogue.

21 Bulletin *Europe* (7 November 1973).

22 Press and Information Office of the Government of the Federal Republic of Germany, *The Bulletin* (19 June 1974).

Israel may thus remain one of the few countries in the Mediterranean whose links with the Community will be loosely based on Article 113 of the Treaty of Rome, and one of the few that must offer reverse preferences to the Community. The case of Spain is very different, as it is clear that one day Spain will become a full member of the Community. It is therefore very important that the Community should keep its promises of fair-mindedness and that Israel should not be discriminated against in any way.

One could also imagine a constructive role for the Community in the Mediterranean, according to which the people of this area, coming closer to the Community, would eventually also come closer to one another. But it is the prevailing opinion in Israel that to play such a role the Community should have the political courage to implement in this area a truly even-handed policy instead of leaning to the side of the oil-producing Arab countries.

4

THE GLOBAL CONTEXT

13

Commercial Relations Between the EEC and the Mediterranean Countries: an Analysis of Recent Trends in Trade Flows

GIAN-PAOLO PAPA AND
JEAN PETIT-LAURENT

1. The Enlarged Community and Its Trade Relations with the Mediterranean Area

As experience from the first talks with the Mediterranean countries shows, the member states themselves are unaware of the ultimate 'global' outcome of their separate commitments and at the same time are well aware of the importance of the Mediterranean area for their security and for the stability of their energy supplies. Although not spelt out at the Community level, these very general considerations on the part of each member state have dictated the Community's attitude towards the Mediterranean countries. On their side, by expressing their willingness to co-operate with a Europe that is relatively nearby, economically powerful and politically undefined (and for that very reason uncompromised), and by asserting their choice against American or Soviet influence, these countries have certainly taken out an option that goes well beyond the framework of commitments undertaken on the spot.

These initial commitments cannot, however, be understood unless account is taken of the whole economic relationship between the Community and the Mediterranean countries, whose interest lies not only in the movements of capital, the exchange of ideas, knowledge and culture but also in population movements (tourism, migrant workers) and in trade.

It can therefore be assumed that, in their first phase, the agreements concluded between a Community which was still only a Common Market and the majority of Mediterranean countries were the expression in the only language available to the Community (namely, the language of trade) of political and economic intentions of a much wider scope.

Trade, the Basic Element of an Overall Strategy

The foundations of the relationship with the Mediterranean countries were laid at a time when divergences among the member states took away any initiative from the Community. Its attitude was definitely passive in response to applications from the Mediterranean countries, who received long-delayed answers mostly confined to the area of trade, which was within the Community's jurisdiction.

It is no exaggeration to say, then, that each Mediterranean country, considered separately, had a European policy well before the Community realised that it had a *de facto* Mediterranean policy. Indeed, each Mediterranean country had already worked out for itself exactly what the Community could mean for it in the various sectors of its development, well before the Community realised that it was building up bit by bit a mosaic which soon came to represent a Mediterranean totality of a far wider scope than the merely commercial context.

By a strange twist of events, as the Community gradually became aware of the regional character of its commitments, most of the Mediterranean countries began to feel frustrated at the idea of being grouped together within the same overall strategy, and each of them, with increasing vigour, began asserting its own individuality and the unique character of its bilateral relationship with the Community.

It could be said that too pragmatic an approach (an à la carte Mediterranean) created the rather theoretical risk of concealing the problems that were common to the whole area, whereas an overall approach, if too systematised (a table d'hôte Mediterranean) would fail to take account of the considerable differences between Mediterranean countries and to adapt to them.

Furthermore, it is to be feared that, as long as relationships between the Community and the Mediterranean countries remain multilateral and no intra-Mediterranean co-operation is feasible, the other matters of common interest (conservation of the environment, transport, energy, tourism, manpower co-ordination, even the financing of development plans and so on) connected with the organisation of the Mediterranean area will not find any satisfactory solutions.

In other words, the more non-commercial arrangements are contained in the planned bilateral agreements, the less likely these agreements are to be typically Mediterranean, and the more like variations on other forms of development aid. As the Mediterranean has become a geographic entity, it would in these conditions be concerned mainly with the agricultural products thought of as Mediterranean (wine, olive oil, various citrus fruits and early vegetables), products for which Mediterranean–Europe trading complementarity is considerable.

At a time when an overall approach tends to transform certain trade agreements into more ambitious agreements, it must be stated that the most global and the most specifically Mediterranean part of the agreements is still to be found in the field of trade.

First of all, it must be pointed out that any references to the Mediterranean is absent from the Treaty of Rome, which contains only provisions (protocols) connected with the maintenance of the customs arrangements between certain countries (incidentally, Mediterranean ones) and their former parent-states, as well as certain declarations aimed at their possible association.

Articles 238 and 113 form the legal basis of the relationships between non-member states. Article 238 allows for the possibility of the Community's setting up associations, but with no defined characteristics or objectives. Article 113 concerns more especially the commercial policy of the Community.

Two remarks may be made about these articles: (*a*) The interpretations made of Articles 238 and 113 have changed somewhat. It is relatively recently that the Community decided to give a political meaning to the concept of association, particularly by refusing to conclude agreements of association with European countries whose institutions seem incompatible with the proper working of democracy; in like fashion, it has been agreed that Article 113, used till then in the context of measures *erga omnes*, could be used as a basis for the granting of preferential arrangements; (*b*) Whether one turns to Article 238 or to Article 113, the Community's powers to conclude agreements are limited by the delegations of power granted by the member states by virtue of the Treaty of Rome. As a result, the Community properly so-called has the power, in essentials, to act only in the commercial context (excluding the products covered by the European Coal and Steel Community (ECSC) Treaty, for which the member states have retained their sovereignty in the area of negotiations with non-member states).

The result of all this is that the Community as such is a valid negotiator with the Mediterranean countries only in the field of trade, all other matters having to be discussed at a conference of the member states within the Council.

It is almost impossible to appreciate the Mediterranean agreements if account is not taken of the way in which Community institutions operate. First of all, the Council of Ministers had considerably impaired its own efficiency by making only unanimous decisions, contrary to the Treaty, which even in trade matters requires only a qualified majority. Secondly, a recent limiting factor is met with in the supporting structures created by the Council. As it can physically cope only with simplified options and arbitrations, the Council delegates the dossiers to a permanent Committee of Ambassadors. Heavily overworked, this committee in turn passes on the dossiers to troupes of experts for studying. In practice, the middle echelon (the Committee of Permanent Representatives) functions as a decanting chamber, sends to the upper level (the Council) only very simply formulated questions, if possible in the shape of alternatives, and passes down to the lower level (the group of experts) the questions on which a compromise has not yet been reached. The dossier of a negotiation mandate can thus 'go up and down in the lift', question after question, for several months before it is fully elaborated, as the points of agreement are officially published without any debate, at first provisionally then definitively when the whole body of questions hanging fire have been settled one after the other.

With this kind of mechanism, the contents of a negotiation mandate are for the most part put together on the level of the group of experts – that is, a process in which the technical ministers of the member states are effectively represented and in which the influence of pressure groups is wielded more easily than in matters of general policy.

One result of the organisations being constituted in this way is that on the political level of the Council of Ministers the dossier is to all intents and purposes lost from sight from the time when it is first decided to study a mandate to the time when it is formally ratified. The outcome of this situation is that a first mandate is inevitably aligned on the highest common denominator of the member states as regards the demands of the Community and on the lowest common denominator as regards supplies. A negotiation can therefore succeed only after the initial mandate has been altered, which entails horizontal to-ing and fro-ing of dossiers or parts of dossiers, by means of an imaginary 'endless belt' connecting the conference chamber with the vertical 'lift' of Community decision-making. The practice of unanimity, the influence of pressure groups, political abstention and the slowness and unwieldiness of the procedure make the Community an inefficient and unsympathetic negotiator.

These factors, then, have a negative influence on the commercial contents of the agreements, at least the first generation ones which, apart from the one with Greece, must all be considered as only a first step.

From this point of view it can be stated that the fewer real concessions contained in a trade agreement, the more important were political or at least tactical ulterior motives from the point of view of the Mediterranean countries.

Commercial Priority

As pointed out earlier, a number of constraints and limitations characterised the first Mediterranean agreements and essentially confined them to trade.

Quite apart from the feeling, which is deeply felt but vague and undefined on the theoretical level, of the role of the Mediterranean in the security of Europe and the importance for oil supplies of the area's stability, the member states, during the period 1967–72 which was so crucial for the increase in links between the Community and the Mediterranean countries, were not in agreement about any of the main issues of foreign policy: the Middle East, the Spanish political regime, the Atlantic policy, currency or even the working of Community institutions. Any real decisions about foreign policy towards the Mediterranean were quite out of the question.

Furthermore, the member states were much divided on the question of the priority to be given to the Community's worldwide responsibilities on the one hand and its regional commitments on the other. The pursuit (and the financing) of relationships with the Yaoundé countries was conducted with only moderate enthusiasm: certain states were reluctant to get involved in new obligations in the field of development until results had been achieved in other areas, such as generalised preferences or the enlargement of the Community.

It also needs to be said that during that period the Community was more concerned with completing the unification of its internal markets than with external relationships. In this connection it should be noted that particularly in the agricultural sector, the unification of agricultural markets was not accompanied by a simultaneous setting up of a common system for imports, as is the case for certain fruits, vegetables and their processed versions, all of these products involving the Mediterranean countries. So, not only did internal concerns take precedence over the Community's external affairs, but even in the field of trade, the absence of a common policy handicapped the Community's negotiating powers. For these reasons, the strongest element of persuasion in the applications made by the Mediterranean countries lies in the joint awareness that on the one hand the setting up of a common policy was a serious threat to the interests of the Mediterranean countries, and that on the other it seemed to be impossible to find solutions to the real difficulties invoked by these countries in a non-preferential context.

It is no exaggeration to say that the whole Mediterranean policy began with the realisation that there was a Mediterranean agriculture and that it could be safeguarded only within a framework of solutions that would prove stable and lasting, and that would maintain an acceptable balance among the different suppliers of the Community.

It was then that the putting together of aggregates concerning the Mediterranean area revealed its importance when considered as a totality, something that had not happened for thousands of years.

Global Estimates of the Importance of Trade Links

The Mediterranean's Share in the Foreign Trade of the Enlarged Community

No national or international organisation considers the Mediterranean as a totality or publishes aggregates for the area. The figures at our disposal (Table 5) concern all the bordering countries (except France and Italy), plus Portugal (which is included so as not to break up the homogeneity of the Iberian peninsula, and also by reason of its preferential links with the Community as a former European Free Trade Association (EFTA) country), and Jordan (taking into account the historical links between that country and its coastal neighbours). This totality, besides, is the one in which the Community took an interest in the framework of the overall strategy selected by the Council of the Community.

Its importance is considerable: the area defined in this way represents for the Community an outlet more or less equal to the US market. The exchange flow for imports is almost twice as great as trade with Latin America and two-and-a-half times bigger for exports. On a scale of magnitude, it can be stated that the commercial importance of this area is that of Latin America, plus the USSR, plus Japan according to figures for 1971, published by the Organisation for Economic Co-operation and Development (OECD).

Despite the importance of oil imports from the area, the trade balance of the Community has remained constantly slightly positive.

However disparate it may be, the aggregate thus constituted forms a market of considerable size and rapid expansion.

The Community's Share in the Foreign Trade of the Countries Belonging to the Mediterranean Area

It might appear rather artificial to add together the foreign trade figures of countries which differ very widely from one another in degree of industrialisation, oil resources or revenue. However, the Mediterranean as a whole, although made up of very dissimilar countries, is not in the long run, thanks to basic similarities due to geographical factors, any more disparate than a European partner whose economic unity is brought about by taking into account geographical differences and political divergences which make it a very inadequate negotiator.

Ecological unity on the one hand, market unity on the other: these define two easily identifiable totalities, on the basis of different criteria which nevertheless grant each of them its own personality and its own credibility.

The result of the aggregation of foreign trade statistics for the Mediterranean countries is, however, very impressive, for it can be seen that the Community takes more than a half share of the World trade of these countries (whereas they represent only about 12 per cent for the Community).

This estimate explains, firstly, the value of the Community for the Mediterranean countries and, secondly, the fact that they took an interest in the Community before it realised, at first separately and later collectively, their importance for it.

Already greater than half their average total trade, the enlarged Community's share should also be raised to include the fact that about 40 per cent of exports are imported duty-free or pay trivial duties in international trade. It can therefore be estimated at more than two-thirds of the Mediterranean area's exports, the value of the products for which it might pay to negotiate trade concessions with the Community.

2. Analysis of the Exchange Flows from the Community's Standpoint

Comparative Interests of the Community in Its Original Composition and of the New Members

Although the Six form an economically coherent whole and the Three are not a homogeneous entity, it is of some interest to estimate the overall importance of trade flows between these two groups of countries and the Mediterranean.

The first remark concerns the balance between producer and consumer interests within the enlarged Community. It is an undeniable fact that, as regards Mediterranean farm produce, the entry of Nordic countries reinforces the position of countries like Germany and Benelux, which are very concerned about combating inflation and avoiding price increases, and which are politically sensitive to the pressures of importers and the criticisms of trade unions.

The second major observation has to do with the fact that the Mediterranean means less to the Three than to the Six (9 per cent as against 16 per cent), and that trade interests are much more localised; consequently, the 'totality' of the Mediterranean does not strike them as at all self-evident.

On the one hand, however, it can be stated that the development of exchanges between the Three and the Mediterranean countries is conducted in as favourable conditions as with the Six, and, on the other, that the total balance-sheet for the Nine is not noticeably different from that for the Six – that is to say that the share of the Mediterranean in the trade of the Nine remains considerable (of the order of 13 per cent), and still represents twice that of Latin America.

The Mediterranean for the Member States

Germany: There is a considerable amount of harmony between the political concerns and the commercial interests of Germany in the Mediterranean. The traditional relationships with Turkey, Spain and Portugal, the care taken to maintain the image of 'the German people's friendship for the Arab people', the obligations towards Israel, naturally lead the German government to pursue balanced relationships, within an overall policy, with the whole of the area. The role of the Mediterranean in the security of Europe and the incidences connected with the instability of the oil situation in the Near East are not underestimated at Bonn, which would like to see the Community contribute to the peace and prosperity of the area.

Although this political 'globality' is not followed up by commercial action, not conceived on the Mediterranean scale but directed towards each individual market of the countries bordering on the Mediterranean, German interests there are both considerable and diversified. Germany has, in fact, become the major client and the chief supplier of the Mediterranean countries taken as a whole, not only amongst the countries of the Community but in the whole world. Moreover, even if its main interests centre on the Iberian peninsula, very substantial exchange flows exist with

Yugoslavia, Greece, Turkey, Malta, Cyprus, Israel, the Maghreb countries and Libya.

Germany, then, is a very dynamic element in the development of relations between the Community and the Mediterranean.

Italy: Of all the member states, Italy is the one that has most developed its exports to the whole of the Mediterranean. This situation is explained by the favourable geographical position of Italy, by its great number of links with the different Mediterranean countries and by its fast industrial development. As the most Mediterranean of the Community countries, Italy is torn between its deeply felt need for the Community to have a Mediterranean policy and the fear that it might suffer if one is drawn up. If the political importance of a Mediterranean policy is felt strongly throughout Italy, the plan for trade with the Mediterranean (exports of industrial products, imports of farm produce) – a simplified plan that is anyway only partially accurate – causes satisfaction in northern Italy and discontent in southern Italy. This already out-of-date concept of exchanges based on complementarity is unable to take into account the future development of intra-Mediterranean relations, a development which will be linked to an overall drive to modernisation throughout the whole area.

Despite these difficulties, which are in the main psychological and political, Italy in the last ten years has more than quadrupled its sales to the Mediterranean area. Its percentage share of the total exports from Europe has risen from less than 10 per cent to nearly 30 per cent. It is now ahead of France as a supplier to the area and comes second after Germany.

Lastly, as it does not itself buy Mediterranean farm produce, Italy has the best trade surplus with respect to the whole of the area, in which its exchange networks are very diversified, with a predominant interest in Yugoslavia, for obvious geographical reasons.

France: For geographical and historical reasons, France's trade with the Mediterranean has been mostly drawn towards the Iberian peninsula and the Maghreb. France has compensated for the very slight progress of its exchanges with the countries of the Maghreb to a very large extent with exchanges with Spain. All the same, it must be accepted as understandable that the Maghreb countries should have wanted to loosen trade links which sometimes bordered on excessive monopoly (in some years France provided more than two-thirds of these countries' imports).

Nevertheless, although the Maghreb countries have managed to diversify their suppliers, France does not seem to have succeeded in diversifying its sales to the rest of the area, and it looks as though only the western Mediterranean is of any real concern to French businessmen and politicians. Markets expanding strongly like those in Yugoslavia, Greece and Turkey, seem to have been relatively neglected.

As for the only really buoyant market in the southern Mediterranean (except for Libya) – Israel – there has been a psychological reaction against French products; meanwhile, although France was taking a relatively larger share in Egyptian imports, these were a long way from experiencing an increase comparable with Israeli imports.

France was indeed the member state which advocated most strongly an overall strategy, but above all for tactical reasons, and with a view to the advantage to be gained by extending to Spain an agreement similar to the one concluded with Portugal. It cannot be said that France has succeeded in translating into trade the possibilities offered by its geographical position and the quality of its products with the whole of the area.

Benelux: The exchanges between the Benelux countries and the Mediterranean countries confirm the efficiency of these countries' traders. Although their geographical proximity to the area is less, they have made spectacular inroads there and, relatively speaking, have made the biggest progress of all the member states.

A priori the Benelux countries were not affected by an overall strategy which might lead to co-operative ventures, firstly because they were not at all disposed to get involved in a regional policy, as their perspective was worldwide, and secondly because their governments experience certain difficulties in obtaining from their respective Parliaments the necessary funds for financial aid. The emphasis was put first on trade, and non-preferential trade, if possible.

It is undoubtedly the desire not to single out Israel from either the Maghreb countries or Spain that has included Benelux to accept the preferential policy undertaken by the Community towards the countries bordering on the Mediterranean, and next to involve itself in a global approach to these relationships.

Besides, the trade balance of Benelux penetration of the market is satisfactory, especially when the accelerated development of the Spanish, Yugoslav, Greek and Israeli markets, the place to be filled on the Maghreb markets after the French withdrawal, the increased buying power derived from oil, mainly in Libya, are taken into account.

United Kingdom: Although the Mediterranean countries taken together represent quite a considerable part of the United Kingdom's exports, it is characteristic firstly, that the export interests of the United Kingdom should be very circumscribed in scope (Spain, Portugal, Libya and Israel, in particular) and secondly, that countries offering important outlets for the Community (for example, the Maghreb countries and Turkey) are only very secondary markets for it. On the other hand, by virtue of previous special relationships, Malta and Cyprus are of a relatively significant importance to the United Kingdom, by comparison with the exchanges between these countries and the other member states.

This situation explains why an overall Mediterranean strategy does not seem at all necessary to the United Kingdom, firstly for commercial reasons, considering the very fragmentary nature of its exchanges with the various countries of the Mediterranean basin. Secondly, in so far as this globalisation involves a regional policy of co-operation, undoubtedly the United Kingdom would not have spontaneously placed the Mediterranean in the forefront of its regional concerns.

Another element, more psychological than political in character, contributes to the initial half-heartedness of the United Kingdom: indeed, an almost total withdrawal of the British presence out of the Mediterranean had been taking place, and now it is a question of sharing in the setting up of a Community influence in the area.

The Community, then, is asking the United Kingdom to swing about rather suddenly, something that British realism can adapt to very easily but in a way that for the time being could hardly go beyond the stage of passive consent.

Denmark and Ireland: For Denmark and Ireland, the fulfilling of the Community's contractual obligations in accordance with the acts of entry does not tally with any well-defined present commercial interest. The trade between the countries bordering on the Mediterranean and these two new member states is in point of fact very slight. No Mediterranean country, even Spain, represents 1 per cent of the foreign trade of either state, and the Mediterranean as a whole does not exceed 3 to 4 per cent of their total world exports.

Nevertheless, such a situation does not imply indifference, for the Mediterranean countries are a tempting outlet, especially for certain farm produce (dairy produce, for instance), and it would not be surprising if a few years hence Denmark and Ireland began to imitate the Benelux countries and to take their turn at a Mediterranean apprenticeship which on the whole would be profitable.

Analysis of Trade Flows from the Viewpoint of the Countries Bordering on the Mediterranean

Eastern Mediterranean: There seems to be sufficient justification for examining separately the trade flows of Mediterranean countries which, for obvious geographical reasons, feel most drawn to the markets of Central and Eastern Europe.

It seems to the authors that this should embrace all the countries bordering on the Mediterranean from Yugoslavia to Egypt, in a clockwise direction, and including Cyprus. For political reasons, Israel, which has access only to Central European markets, in Austria and Switzerland, is omitted.

The Eastern Mediterranean, as defined above, represents about 50 per cent of exports from the Mediterranean. It is a dynamic unit, with countries whose foreign trade is rapidly expanding, like Israel, Greece and Yugoslavia, and despite the large-scale stagnation of Egypt and Lebanon.

The markets of the Eastern Mediterranean countries represent nearly 40 per cent of the total outlet of this unit, and the Community takes less than half of the exports. The predominance of the Eastern Mediterranean countries is especially marked for Yugoslavia, Egypt and Syria. As for Israel, it is the most diversified country with respect to the destination of its goods (except goods sent to Eastern Mediterranean countries), with substantial sales to the USA in particular.

This group of countries lies at the intersection of the Community's markets on the one hand and the Communist markets on the other, and could expand its sales with either, to the extent that Communist states can be transformed into consumer societies.

Western Mediterranean: The trade of the remaining countries of the Mediterranean is very clearly aimed at the Western world, for less than 20 per cent of the exports go to Eastern Europe, whereas about 60 per cent go to the EEC.

The Iberian peninsula totals 60 per cent of the exports of this Western Mediterranean unit, and if Algerian and Libyan oil are subtracted, is alone responsible for the increase in exports.

It should be noted that despite the recent diversification of their trade flows, almost 50 per cent of Maghreb trade is still conducted with France, whereas Spain and Portugal remain tightly linked with African and Latin American trade, and the traditional Commonwealth relationship can be seen in trade with Malta (the same was previously true for Cyprus).

If oil is omitted, Maghreb exports remain essentially agricultural, whereas for the countries of the Iberian peninsula and Malta more than two-thirds of the exports are made up of industrial products.

Northern Mediterranean: The Northern Mediterranean countries represent two-thirds of the exports from the whole of the area, and the Iberian peninsula nearly half of this percentage. This indicates a greater prosperity for the northern countries (from Portugal to Turkey, including Malta and Cyprus) than for the southern countries, and raises the problem of Mediterranean balance in the possibility of the Northern Mediterranean countries' entry into the Community. If one reflects that Spain on its own could take up the Community's consumption of Mediterranean products, it is easy to see that the various Mediterranean countries do not share the same idea of what is meant by an overall strategy and their respective parts in this framework.

For all the Northern Mediterranean countries, trade with the Community has experienced a very profitable increase, and growth rates in both directions, in the last ten years, have been almost the same as for intra-Community trade. This one aspect of foreign trade shows that the Northern Mediterranean countries have already grasped or are beginning to grasp their new economic opportunities.

One part of the Mediterranean is thus rapidly catching up with the twentieth century and acting thus as an example to the other countries of the area whose performances are less satisfactory.

Southern Mediterranean: The countries of the southern Mediterranean export only a third of the Mediterranean total. Furthermore, their earnings from tourism and the money sent home by migrant workers are lower than in Northern Mediterranean countries, their dependence on foreign countries for services is greater and their private investments are less significant.

If in addition, one subtracts from the Southern Mediterranean Israel, whose economic and political characteristics are quite different, the southern countries, which can be roughly described by the term 'Arab states', represent from the point of view of trade only one-quarter of the Mediterranean area, divided one-eighth for the Maghreb and one-eighth for the Middle East (including Libya, but excluding Israel). Oil exports at the present time are of real concern to only two of these countries, Algeria and Libya, and except for oil it can be observed that all other exports are stagnating and include very few industrial products apart from some textiles. This feeble export capacity does not augur well for the development of the Arab states of the Southern Mediterranean which, in addition, are having to shoulder the burden of a population growth too high for the new jobs that it is possible to create in present-day conditions. The only country free of population problems and with financial resources is Libya. With the exception of this country, then, the Southern Mediterranean is not in a position to finance development with what it earns from exports.

Europe must face the question whether, without directly or indirectly damaging its own interests, it can allow a serious imbalance in the Mediterranean to get any worse.

Description of the Agreements Reached Between 1963 and 1973

Pre-entry Associations

The agreements with Greece and Turkey can be understood only if they are placed in the context of the time at which they were negotiated – that is, at a time when the Cold War was at its height and the Soviet push towards the Mediterranean, especially the Near East, was beginning to assume frightening proportions. These agreements, moreover, were encouraged, if not exactly instigated, by the USA, because they formed part of their defensive strategy against Soviet influence and might also lead to a fairer share-out of defence costs.

As European countries, Greece and Turkey have a theoretical obligation to seek entry. The agreements were therefore drawn up in such a way as to facilitate their inclusion in the Community. As a way in, they foresee the progressive setting up of a Common Customs Tariff (CCT), the free circulation of goods, and common decision-making procedures, especially with a view to bringing about necessary harmonisations. In addition, financial assistance must encourage the development of competing economies able to blend with the Community's economy. Lastly, the agreements set up associations, based on Article 238 of the Treaty. They are heterogeneous acts in the sense that included in them are the Community, for all matters in its jurisdiction, and the member states (for all decisions concerned with their sovereignty, such as labour forces and financial aid).

The desire to take up the mechanisms of the Common Market, the obligation to respect the rules of the General Agreement Tariffs and Trade (GATT), and the need to take account of the uneven development of fellow members resulted in the adoption of a time-table for the establishment of a customs union spreading over twenty-two years (thus greatly exceeding all estimates in both economic and political fields); and it has been left to the Council of Association to decide on all the measures to do with the progressive realisation of economic union. These could not be settled in advance because some of them were not yet decided even for the Community itself.

This construction was indeed a sort of carbon copy of the Treaty of Rome. It is imbued with considerable legal conformism, and it constitutes a highly theoretical and unimaginative formulation of the relationship between the Community and the Mediterranean countries.

The experience of agreements with Greece and Turkey has enabled us to see the illusory nature of excessively long-term engagements. It can of course be very useful to fix in advance all the stages of an economic *rapprochement* whose intention is to prepare the partner of the Community progressively for the desired integration. However, in a world of rapid changes, it is almost impossible to guard against unforeseen circumstances which inevitably arise, such as those that forced the Community to limit the application of the agreement with Greece to mere administration. Similarly, doubts can be felt about the possibility of Turkey becoming a full member of the Community at any date which can be forecast in advance.

The agreements with Greece and Turkey have therefore provided, *a contrario*, a telling lesson in pragmatism, and this was taken into account when the cases of Malta and Cyprus had to be considered.

Indeed, the agreements reached with these countries leave open the question of entry into the Community. Similarly, the possibility of setting up a customs union is postponed to a later stage. The only pledges made were for a set period during which an appropriate dismantling of obstacles to trade is carried out on both sides. For agricultural produce, only *ad hoc* solutions are allowed in case of need, apart from any attempt at harmonisation. The Council of Association has no decision-making powers and, although the legal basis is Article 238, the contents of the agreement are strictly commercial and the Community alone arranged the settlement.

The agreement lays down arrangements only for the length of its applicability (five years for Malta and four years for Cyprus, with an eye to synchronisation), and thus rests on the idea that only the experience derived from an initial stage will enable them, with full knowledge of the facts, to determine the terms of a subsequent attempt at economic *rapprochement.*

The ultimate decision about entry would be reached only with full knowledge of the facts. It would be carried into effect in only a few years and would thus eliminate the risks of long-term procedures.

The Development Associations

Chronologically, the agreements with Morocco and Tunisia occurred after the agreements with Greece and Turkey, and before the agreements with Israel, Spain, then Malta, Cyprus, Egypt and Lebanon. In fact, they were the first attempt at a pragmatic approach following on the more ambitious Greek and Turkish projects.

The problems raised by the relations with Morocco and Tunisia were very delicate ones, first of all because they involved considerable Community agricultural interests. Recalling the mishaps experienced in applying the agreement with Greece, and because of the fact that in the case of Morocco and Tunisia there was no intention of entry later, it was not a matter of settling these problems by institutional solutions or at the price of some sort of harmonisation. Concrete solutions had therefore to be found, and this was made even more difficult by the unfinished state of some market organisations. In addition, any concession granted solely to the Maghreb countries seemed dangerous to some member states because of the imbalance that it might create in the relations between the Community and the rest of the Mediterranean, especially Spain and Israel. Finally, some member states did not wish to get involved in financial co-operation with the Maghreb at that stage of the evolution of the Community's foreign relations and after the breakdown of the United Kingdom's entry negotiations.

This explains why, after exploratory talks in 1963 and 1964, and as a result of a very incomplete first mandate in 1965, followed by a brief negotiation, in 1966 everything was still at the preparatory stage.

The situation of Morocco and Tunisia on the one hand and of Algeria on the other inevitably appeared paradoxical, in the sense that Morocco and Tunisia would have been in a hurry to reach an agreement and to benefit from advantages similar to those arising from the Yaoundé Convention, but had not been able to go in this direction as long as the Algerian conflict remained unresolved, whereas Algeria, still enjoying the position it reached on obtaining independence, could afford to play a waiting game.

Now, from 1966 onwards it became very obvious that if projects of the Yaoundé or Greece–Turkey variety were not dropped, there would still be long delays before completion, which would not suit Moroccan or Tunisian impatience. However it could be seen at that moment that it was already possible to reach a relatively substantial agreement, if account were taken of the fact that the regulations concerning olive oil and fruits and vegetables in particular had already been decided. On Moroccan and Tunisian initiative, the idea was therefore put forward of negotiating commercial agreements of a partial nature whose advantage would lie in getting the association off the ground. These first agreements were therefore reached with the aim of making political engagement into a reality, and they are proof of confidence in the future of mutual relationships.

About 80 per cent of the imports from Morocco and Tunisia are covered by these partial agreements, which can be said to make substantial progress towards the elimination of obstacles to exchanges. Despite this, saying and doing are two different things. The agreements are a first step in the area of privileged relationships, but do not entail any very important advantages, as foreseen.

To be sure, the industrial sector receives from the Community duty-free admission without a ceiling, but it cannot be thought that the limits laid down for the generalised preferences granted to all developing countries would have handicapped Moroccan and Tunisian exports. In addition, the industrial sector is undeveloped in these countries whose economic and political climate is not always very encouraging to foreign investors, despite the efforts made to attract them. These agreements, then, do not as yet provide industry with any really concrete advantages.

As for the Community's agricultural concessions, they represent a transposition of the situation already obtaining on the bilateral level with France rather than new preferences, the emphasis having been placed more on market balance and the stabilisation of product prices than on the increase of sales outlets. The concessions that for their part Morocco and Tunisia have granted the Community have been extremely cautious, *erga omnes* on the part of Morocco which did not denounce the Act of Algeciras, and directly extrapolated from the agreement made by Tunisia with France. This is clearly only the early days of associations.

In the time-table of relations between the Community and the countries of the Mediterranean basin, the agreements with Morocco and Tunisia have acted as detonators. They have done so from the political angle first; on the one hand the preferential relationships with Arab states have encouraged other Arab states to seek *rapprochement* with the Community, and on the other Israel could not be discriminated against. Next, from the economic standpoint, the similarity of interest of various Mediterranean countries (especially in agriculture) meant that solutions had to be found to preserve the balance of their trade relations with the Community.

With this in mind it must be recalled that the granting of concessions for oranges in the agreements with Morocco and Tunisia led the Community to make simultaneous provision for corresponding advantages for Israel and Spain, firstly notwithstanding Article XXV of GATT and secondly in the framework of preferential agreements.

Although at the end of 1973 no agreement has yet been signed with Algeria, it is worth while trying to characterise the relationship between the Community and this country, more especially with respect to Morocco and Tunisia. Firstly, Algeria was part of the Community until its independence (February 1962) and benefited from a dynamic *status quo* that enabled it to take partial advantage of the concessions which member states granted one another up to that date, and since then it has benefited from a simple *status quo* (subject to the setting up of market organisations). Furthermore, it has always been recognised that the protocol maintaining the customs arrangement applicable by France to Morocco and Tunisia, and the declaration concerning the association of these countries, had to be extended, *a fortiori*, to Algeria, for the obvious political reason that Algeria could not be penalised for obtaining independence at a later date.

In the same spirit, the Community would have wished to be able to 'globalise' on the scale of the Maghreb the solutions found for Morocco and Tunisia, and has always shown a tendency to seek an identical settlement for the three countries.

On the other hand, Algeria is fond of emphasising the exceptional nature of its relationship with the Community and of reminding everyone that it was once an integral part of the Common Market. It must also be borne in mind that with the predominance on the one hand of oil exports in the industrial sector and on the other of wine in the agricultural sector, Algeria's problems are much more restricted in scope than those of its neighbours. In addition, its prosperity derived from oil and its tougher political stance make it a difficult negotiator, which will probably rely on Magrahine solidarity only in so far as this will strengthen the negotiating position of the three Maghrahine countries with respect to the Community.

Preferential Trade Agreements

Although there is a difference in the historical facts (the existence of preferential links with a member state) and the legal basis (Article 238) of the agreements with Morocco and Tunisia, the agreements first with Spain and Israel and later with Egypt and Lebanon are directly based on them. The commercial content is similar, the reciprocities achieved are very slight, the powers of the administration are non-existent, the rules of origin are, with a few exceptions, identical. It is, in fact, the same concept of a partial agreement, but the Community did not want to grant these agreements the name of association by reason of the customary identification (which, though wrong, has become almost official) of the idea of association with the idea of pre-entry (in the case of a European country) and of co-operation or development (in the case of a non-European country). It was about Spain and Israel that agreement was first reached within the Community on the possibility of basing a preferential agreement on Article 113 of the Treaty.

At first sight, Spain and Israel appear very dissimilar and it is surprising to see them put into the same category. The reasons for this comparison need therefore to be explained. The first similarity stems from the political difficulties that, for various reasons, the member states experienced in linking themselves preferentially with countries which could not be treated as friends either because of their internal regime or because of their relations with non-member countries. In both cases these links were accepted only because they were defined as being strictly commercial. Secondly, Spain and Israel both stand out in the Mediterranean by reason of the high level of national income and the importance of their industrial sectors. In addition, for both countries the United Kingdom market is of special importance and poses similar problems in the context of the enlargement of the Community. Finally, as they do not have the same support within the Community, Spain and Israel have come together in the same manœuvrings at every stage of the preparation and carrying out of the negotiations and the agreements.

The scope of the agreements in question is characterised not only by the extent of the tariff reductions granted by the Community, but also by the fact that at the time of the negotiations the Community showed little interest in the real economic content of what it should demand in return from its partners.

Deliberately biased in favour of Spain and Israel, because of the obvious vulnerability of their economies at the time of the negotiations, the 1970 agreements were therefore drawn up as the first stage of an economic *rapprochement* with no defined political objective.

The political impetus afforded by the example of other Mediterranean countries, the attraction of the great zone of prosperity represented by an expanding Common Market, the urge to alter the balance of the excessive influence of the USSR and the USA by means of links with Europe, led to requests for negotiation from Egypt and Lebanon, in a movement of 'Eurotropism' affecting all the Mediterranean countries except Libya, Syria and Albania.

Anxious on its own behalf to preserve a balance among the countries of the Near East, the Community had agreed to take part in negotiations with Israel only on the condition that a positive reply would be made to the Egyptian and Lebanese requests. In point of fact, only the difficulties connected with the shaping of a *modus vivendi* that would preserve boycott legislation while safeguarding the principle of non-discrimination between firms and individuals of the contracting parties have introduced an important difference between the time-table of negotiations with Israel on the one hand and with Egypt and Lebanon on the other.

The agreements with Egypt and Lebanon are a straight copy of the preferential trade agreements concluded with Spain and Israel, both for the general principles of the agreement and for its operation and contents. The few existing adjustments correspond to the special characteristics of the countries in question: thus, in the case of Egypt, account had to be taken of the need, quite exceptional for the Mediterranean, to consider rice exports and to grant them special conditions.

It is a case, then, of preferential trade agreements of relatively limited scope, which take on their full significance only in connection with later developments that Community partners expect from them.

Non-preferential Trade Agreement: the Case of Yugoslavia

Yugoslavia is one of the Mediterranean countries whose trade with the EEC has developed most. It is the second Mediterranean market after Spain; its industry is also one of the most advanced in the whole area. It is hardly surprising, therefore, that the Community and Yugoslavia have a great interest in each other, and that Yugoslavia has experienced a kind of rivalry in the face of the rapid spread of preferential links between the Community and the countries of the area.

Whatever attraction it might feel, Yugoslavia could still not repudiate its links with Eastern Europe by asking the Community for a preferential agreement which would hardly be compatible ideologically with the choice of a socialist regime and, on the practical level, with the continuance of a state-controlled trade.

The only possible solution lay in a non-preferential trade agreement. And this is in fact the type of agreement reached by Yugoslavia and the Community. This agreement includes tariff concessions *erga omnes*, which are still selective enough to give priority to the parties to the agreement. It also lays down elements of co-operation, with arrangements allowing for discussions on manpower problems. The Association Council, in addition, can propose resolutions with a view to undertaking co-operation likely to contribute to the development of trade between the parties. Lastly, and independently of the agreement, Yugoslavia benefits from generalised preferences to a very large extent, given its relatively high level of industrialisation. In these conditions and at this stage, the relations between the Community and Yugoslavia can be considered reasonably satisfactory.

Mediterranean Agreements and the Enlargement of the Community

Problems Created by the Enlargement

The conditions of entry had specified that new member states were bound by the Community's contractual obligations, which applied to them fully and immediately subject to necessary transition periods and taking account of the corresponding arrangements of the conditions of entry. This automatic nature of the acceptance of the Community's contractual obligations was furthermore to entail essential technical adjustments, from the legal and technical point of view (in certain cases, the geographical definition of the Community was to be modified, or else quantitative or tariff quotas had to be adjusted). Inevitably, then, all the arrangements ratifying the extension of agreements to an enlarged Community had to be translated into special protocols.

In the case of mixed agreements (Greece, Turkey), these protocols had to be concluded by the Community and the member states, and in the case of Community agreements (all other Mediterranean agreements, whether based on Article 238 or Article 113) by the Community alone. In the case of mixed agreements, national ratifications would take place, if necessary, in accordance with the Constitution of each member state.

However, such protocols could be concluded only for agreements signed before 31 December 1972, and this restriction nearly created a problem in the case of Cyprus (as the negotiations with this country were unexpectedly protracted). However, nothing stood in the way of their being decided after entry.

This flexibility was welcome, because no additional protocol, without exception, was decided before 31 December 1973, for the practical reason that the Community's Mediterranean partners were exclusively concerned with the economic change of balance of the agreements, a matter that the Community was not in a position to settle.

However, from 1 January 1973 there was, therefore, a legal gap with respect to the conditions of application of the agreements to new member states. In this vacuum, three arguments were in fact put forward. The first (backed by the Commission's legal experts) maintained that the Community section of the agreements was immediately and totally applicable by new member states, without transition, from 1 January 1973, in every case where the agreements contained no geographical definition of their restricted application: in these conditions, all concessions appearing in the agreements with Morocco, Tunisia, Spain, Israel and Malta (agreements reached before 1 January 1973) would be applied from 1 January 1973 by new members to these countries, who had only the 'Community' to acknowledge and to which the entry conditions were not opposable. In return, the concessions granted to the Community had to be simultaneously extended completely to new member states.

The second argument, put forward by the Council's legal experts, held that, in the absence of additional protocols, agreements within the jurisdiction of the Community alone and not entailing any restrictive geographical definition of the Community would be immediately applicable between Mediterranean countries and new member states, bearing in mind the timetables and transition procedures mentioned in the entry conditions.

A third argument (put forward without any consistent legal submissions) concluded in favour of the non-extension of agreements to new member states in the absence of additional protocols.

This last argument has proved *de facto* to be the best one, for no economic operator has been willing to run the risk of a wastefully expensive legal wrangle, and no concrete case has led to a trial in the Court of Justice which might have enabled this legal tangle to be sorted out.

At the economic level, one could talk endlessly but to no avail about the advantages of a wider preferential market, or on the disadvantages of greater competition. On the other hand, the indisputable fact is that for a certain number of products, mainly agricultural ones, the existing agreements contained no concessions, whereas the import system for the United

Kingdom before entry was very generous, and on the other hand the common customs tariff and the agricultural market organisations are admittedly rather protectionist. This is the situation particularly for a large quantity of early vegetables and also for many processed fruits and vegetables. Now, if for all the other countries except Spain and Israel these new market conditions create problems only for potential exports, for those two countries very substantial trade currents are at stake, amounting for certain products to about one-third of the total outlet.

In these conditions, there should be no surprise, therefore, that Spain and Israel have refused to negotiate additional protocols that settle only the legal and technical aspects of the adjustment of the agreements to the situation created by enlargement, whereas the economic consequences of expansion were not taken into consideration for very important products the trade in which was under threat. This refusal of additional protocols in 1973, from the point of view of Spain and Israel, is all the more justified as the first tariff *rapprochements* of the new members towards the CCT did not take effect until the end of 1973.

That is why, in order to settle the legal problem without pre-judging the solutions which might be found for the economic problem, Spain and Israel finally agreed to a protocol which specified that for the year 1973 the commercial arrangements of the agreements would apply only to their relationship with the Community as originally constituted.

The success of the adaptation of the agreements to the situation created by the enlargement took on some importance precisely because of the fact that the first agreements (except those with Greece and Turkey) had no great economic consistency, and from the political angle their main value was as a pledge to do better next time – that is, after a five-year period, which is the one generally laid down for these partial agreements. The enlargement of the Community, which had come about in the meantime, shortened this waiting period and required the political goodwill of the Community to be 'put to the test' earlier than expected.

This event might have appeared all the more alarming as, when the enlargement came, the difficult question of how to treat the other EFTA countries had been settled on the whole quickly and in a relatively satisfactory fashion. It would have been quite serious if the efficiency with which the Community solved the problems of EFTA had had to be compared with its inability to find satisfactory adjustments for the Mediterranean agreements.

A failure in this area might mean that the regional policy in the Mediterranean would be queried and might disappoint the Mediterranean countries to such an extent that they would be led to conclude that, in wagering on the future of their relationship with the Mediterranean on the occasion of the first agreements that their chief value lay in the commitment that they represented, they had committed a serious political mistake. The politicians in the Mediterranean countries who favoured a *rapprochement* with Europe might thereby have lost all credibility for a long time.

Adaptations of the Mediterranean Agreements

In the course of 1971, the Commission had suggested that the Council should adopt the agreements which were being worked out without modifying their length of application, and that the Community should agree to a few additional concessions mainly in the agricultural sector, to take account of the problems created by the continuation of certain trade currents, mainly between the United Kingdom on the one hand and Spain and Israel on the other. These proposals were studied by the Council in 1971–2 without any result being achieved. That was a big setback for the Commission and for the Mediterranean policy, in a period when, on the other hand, negotiations with EFTA countries were being carried out with great speed.

About the middle of 1972, it became obvious that the year would be out and the entries would become effective without any substitute solution having yet been discovered.

Amongst the reasons that explain why a pragmatic approach should have failed, these are worthy of note:

the absence of political pressure: the Community was too much involved in its own enlargement to concern itself unduly with the consequences of this enlargement, other than by appropriate procedures – the Mediterranean was thus seen as a problem 'to be solved at a later date';

the desire of certain member states to play for time, to have done with legislative elections, and meanwhile to avoid antagonising a peasant electorate which needed to be treated carefully;

the understandable fear of having to make concessions without any reciprocal arrangements to adjust the agreements, and then of having to grant still more after the initial stages (that is within a relatively short time): the whole operation might well be concluded in a single effort;

lastly, the desire for clarification on the internal and external levels about the numerous, seemingly disparate agreements, which created increasing problems for member states both in their relations with their own pressure groups and with other important non-member countries, and for GATT.

Definition of an Overall Strategy

At the end of the first term in 1972, the Commission was therefore invited by the Council to suggest proposals concerning an overall strategy based on a renegotiation of all the agreements (except for those with Greece and Israel, which were conceived on a permanent basis).

This global conception of relations between the Mediterranean and the Community was in accordance with the long-term views of the Commission's services. However, these had put off drawing one up because the period of an enlargement of the Community did not seem a suitable moment for the launching of ambitious proposals; only a Community that had already achieved a certain level of economic and monetary integration might be capable of shouldering the responsibilities, and the burdens, of an overall strategy in the Mediterranean; lastly, it seemed to be an unsuitable time for imposing on new member states any more than the assumption of obligations already agreed to by the Community and for asking them to accept even more considerable engagements.

There is no doubt that if the Commission had proposed an overall strategy a year earlier, it would have been rejected straight away by the Council. It was only by allowing the dossier to gather a lot of dust that the Council was able to decide on a new direction.

On the basis of reports made by the Commission, the Council of the Communities met in advance in its enlarged format on 6 and 7 November 1972 and defined the directions of an overall strategy. They can be summed up as follows:

this approach would concern all the countries bordering on the Mediterranean, as well as Jordan;

the objective of the agreements would be the setting up of free-trade zones;

free trade would also involve the main part of agricultural trade, in a progressive way, taking account of the situation in the Community and with the prospect of successive 'agricultural get-togethers';

steps would be taken concerning co-operation and labour forces, in a manner appropriate to each agreement, and with priority given to the cases of the Maghreb and Malta.

Perspectives

Bearing in mind the internal and external limits and constraints imposed on the Community, the effort it has put into securing mandates of negotiation during the first term of 1973, by reason of the political importance it attaches to its relations with Mediterranean countries, deserves to be emphasised. When this has been said, however, the results obtained will be inevitably and not unreasonably judged by the Community's partners as inadequate. Second rounds of negotiation, which presuppose modifications in the first mandates, will be necessary.

As foreseen by the first mandates, these agreements would include a definite element of imbalance. Let us leave aside the imbalance, inherent in the volume of trade, which ensures that with the Maghreb countries, and especially Spain and Israel, the Community exports in absolute value more than it imports. More important than that is the relative imbalance of the concessions envisaged, which stems from the fact that the Community aims to set up industrial free trade (which affects most of its exports) and foresees only limited concessions in the agricultural sector (which remains an important part of the exports of the Community's partners).

It is obvious that in these conditions a total industrial free trade, set up on a permanent basis, would be to the advantage of the Community, and the Mediterranean countries would lose all bargaining powers for the ultimate granting of additional concessions in the agricultural area.

This remark obviously is of major importance to Spain and Israel above all, for these are countries from which reciprocity is strictly expected.

These countries, then, will definitely demand either a shift of balance in the industrial sector, or that the completion or the improvement of free trade in both the industrial and agricultural sectors will be carried out in a second phase of the projected agreement.

It is likely that this question of the balance over time of the agreements will be the central subject of future negotiations. From the standpoint of the Maghreb countries, an additional factor will be the definite wish to link the duration of trade agreements to those of co-operation agreements (especially technical and financial), with the obvious intention of getting a satisfactory revision of the latter.

At the centre of the negotiations with Spain there will be, in addition and more especially, the questions of administrative control of the agreements, especially as regards fiscal non-discrimination both for imports and exports, and the operation of state-controlled trading. All these questions are definitely as important as, if not more important than, the schedules for the lifting of tariff or quota restrictions.

Beyond these future agreements, which can already be guessed in outline, there are the basic problems of the development of the Mediterranean area:

Will Europe on the one hand and the governments of the Mediterranean countries on the other be able to grasp the opportunity offered them of leading the Mediterranean into the twentieth century?

Will the Mediterranean governments and their peoples be able to place progress and optimism at the top of their list of collective concerns? Will an ideology of success win the day? Will a climate favourable to investments be created?

Will a psychological revolution enable the rural masses of the Southern Mediterranean countries to take their place in the twentieth century and to overcome their population problem?

Will the Mediterranean countries develop intra-Mediterranean co-operation, and will they be able to find solutions, if not collectively then at least without conflict, for their problems of development?

Finally, it is indeed a matter of civilisation, and furthermore it is a matter of finding out whether the Mediterranean will be for Europe a zone of friendship, of fraternity, or rather of misunderstanding and hostility. Whichever way these questions are answered, the answer must be favourable.

Statistical Appendix

The following remarks concern trade flows between the European Community and the Mediterranean countries. The indices are calculated on the basis of statistics drawn from OECD publications.

1. Exports from the EEC

See Table 1 *Distribution by Country of Origin*

(*1*) The Mediterranean outlet (i.e., bordering countries, plus Portugal and Jordan) for the Community represents (in 1971) about 10 per cent of the total exports (intra and extra), which is a considerable amount. The market is more or less equal to that of the USA, eight times bigger than the Japanese or Soviet markets, and two-and-a-half times bigger than that of the whole of Latin America.

(*2*) The relative importance of the Mediterranean outlet is greater for the Six than for the Three, and each of these units is about 20 per cent higher or lower than the average calculated for the Nine. The relative importance of the USA and Japan is greater for the Three than for the Six.

(*3*) Italy and France are the countries most affected by the Mediterranean outlet. Equal second are the United Kingdom and Germany; then come the group of Belgium, Holland and Denmark, and last of all Ireland.

TABLE 1 Percentage distribution of EEC exports to the Mediterranean countries and relative size to exports to other areas (1971)

	W. Germany	Benelux	France	Italy	Holland	The 6	U.K.	Ireland	Denmark	The 3	The 9
Albania	0·1	*	*	0·45	0·5	*	*	–	*	*	0·1
Cyprus	1·2	0·7	0·6	1·35	1·6	1·0	3·7	3·2	2·3	3·7	1·5
Spain	20·6	23·7	23·2	15·45	29·6	20·9	22·6	48·2	23·4	23·0	21·3
Greece	15·2	13·0	7·6	12·00	15·1	12·4	9·7	6·1	10·5	9·7	11·9
Malta	0·2	0·5	0·2	1·6	0·9	0·7	3·0	1·8	1·5	2·9	1·0
Portugal	9·1	9·7	6·1	5·4	7·5	7·4	14·3	4·7	15·2	14·2	8·7
Turkey	7·2	5·7	3·2	6·75	3·3	5·7	5·1	1·4	3·7	5·0	5·5
Yugoslavia	23·5	11·7	6·1	24·3	10·0	17·2	8·4	3·6	10·6	8·5	15·5
N. Mediterranean	77·1	65·0	47·0	67·3	68·5	65·3	66·8	69·0	67·2	67·0	65·5
Algeria	4·0	6·6	21·8	5·8	5·3	9·6	3·7	–	4·6	3·8	8·5
Egypt	3·2	1·6	3·0	3·0	3·3	3·1	2·7	1·5	5·6	2·9	3·0
Israel	6·7	14·9	4·2	4·35	7·9	6·1	14·8	25·1	7·2	14·2	7·7
Jordan	0·3	0·5	0·1	0·35	1·3	0·1	1·2	0·4	2·5	1·2	0·6
Lebanon	2·7	3·9	3·1	3·65	3·7	3·2	3·5	2·5	4·3	3·5	3·3
Libya	1·9	1·5	4·1	9·6	3·4	4·4	3·9	0·7	2·6	3·8	4·2
Morocco	1·8	3·6	9·4	2·35	3·3	4·4	1·7	–	2·0	1·8	3·8
Tunisia	0·8	1·1	5·6	1·85	1·4	2·5	0·7	0·4	1·7	0·7	2·1
Syria	1·5	1·3	1·7	1·75	1·9	1·3	1·0	0·4	2·3	1·1	1·3
S. Mediterranean	22·9	35·0	53·0	32·7	31·5	34·7	33·2	31·0	32·8	33·0	34·5
Mediterranean	100·0	100·0	100·0	100·0	100·0	100·0	100·0	100·0	100·0	100·0	100·0
USA	122·0	163·0	48·0	81·5	99·0	92·0	142·0	505·0	218·0	153·0	104·0
Japan	17·0	14·5	7·0	6·4	13·4	11·3	20·6	35·0	23·0	21·2	13·1
USSR	15·0	12·4	11·0	16·2	8·2	13·5	11·4	1·8	19·5	11·8	13·1
Latin America	49·0	45·0	24·0	33·0	48·5	38·2	45·0	23·0	68·0	46·0	40·0
World	1,270·0	2,400·0	885·0	830·0	2,480·0	1,220·0	1,250·0	4,520·0	2,770·0	1,400·0	1,250·0

Notes: *Negligible. – No Trade. *Source*: OECD trade statistics.

(*4*) For the Nine, the whole group of northern bordering countries represents an outlet twice as important as the southern group (from Morocco to Syria inclusive). This proposition is more or less the same for the Three as for the Six. The preponderance of the northern area holds for all the member states, except France, for which the southern countries' outlet is more important than the northern one (53 per cent as against 47 per cent), by reason of its historic links with the Maghreb and its sales to the Arab states.

Spain, Greece and Yugoslavia are the most important outlets for the Community of Nine, and this remark applies to both the Three and the Six. Those three countries represent nearly 50 per cent of the total Mediterranean outlet. This shows the greater dynamism of the European countries of the Mediterranean.

(*5*) The sales of the Three to the Mediterranean are marked, in addition, by the special importance of the Portuguese outlet (EFTA), which is relatively twice as important as for the Six. Malta, Cyprus and Israel hold a more important place in the trade of the Three than in that of the Six (for historical reasons). North Africa, on the other hand, plays a relatively insignificant part in the export trade of the Three.

Bearing in mind the important volume of United Kingdom trade in relation to Irish and Danish exports, the structure noted for the Three corresponds in fact to that of the United Kingdom. On the other hand, the data assembled indicate that for Ireland the Mediterranean does not form a whole unit. Only the Spanish and Israeli markets have any real consistency: these two countries on their own represent nearly 75 per cent of the total Mediterranean outlet of Ireland.

On the other hand again, Denmark shows a trade structure fairly similar to that of Benelux or Holland, indicating a great diversification of Mediterranean interests, within a total economic interest in a Mediterranean policy.

(*6*) Germany's interests lie clearly in the northern Mediterranean for the most part (77 per cent), with Yugoslavia, Spain, Greece and Portugal being of special importance. Turkey in the north and Israel and Algeria in the south provide nonetheless a not inconsiderable volume of trade.

In the northern area, Spain is France's most important market. But the predominance of the southern area, especially the Maghreb countries, must be pointed out.

Italy has very diversified Mediterranean interests, with its neighbour, Yugoslavia, being of significant importance.

For Benelux, one should note the economic predominance of politically unpopular countries, Spain, Greece and Portugal, which, with Yugoslavia, form the main outlets. Benelux has quite a good diversification of sales over the Mediterranean as a whole, with Israel in the south, a relatively dynamic market, holding a special place.

Table 2 *Development of Outlets*

(*1*) The index of the global exports of the EEC of the Nine towards the Mediterranean countries reached the level of 249 in 1971 (1960 = 100); this represents an annual growth rate of about 8·5 per cent.

By way of comparison, the trade index of exports (excluding intra-Community trade) of the Nine for 1963–72 was 197, which represents an annual rate below 8 per cent. Table 2 lists the figures containing for the World, the intra- and extra-trade of the EEC (index 306 for the period 1970–1). It can be deduced that EEC exports to the Mediterranean have developed less quickly than intra-Community trade, but more quickly than the total foreign trade. Table 2 shows that although EEC sales have progressed less than those towards Japan and the USA, they have experienced a growth much greater than the progress of exports to the USSR (1·27 quicker) and to Latin America (1·59 quicker).

(*2*) Paradoxically enough, the sales of the Three to the Mediterranean have developed more quickly than the sales of the Six. This stems exclusively from the losses in French exports to Algeria and from their mediocre success in the rest of the Maghreb, as the previous exclusive relationships could not be continued.

(*3*) It is significant that the Community's exports have developed more quickly with the northern Mediterranean countries (index 412) than with the southern countries (index 139). Amongst the southern countries, only sales to Israel and to Libya (index 430 and 403 respectively) have had a growth similar to that of EEC exports with the northern Mediterranean countries.

(*4*) The record for increase in exports is held by Spain (index 612), followed by Yugoslavia and Greece. These countries also represent the largest sales in absolute value.

(*5*) Leaving aside Ireland (whose percentage progress is not significant for the small volume involved), it is Italy that has performed best, both towards the south and the north, thus confirming its Mediterranean aptitude.

Germany comes in second place, thus proving its export dynamism. The results of the Benelux countries, the United Kingdom and Ireland are comparable for the Mediterranean as a whole, with better progress made

TABLE 2 Development of the EEC exports to the Mediterranean area; 1960–71 (1960 = 100)

	W. Germany	Benelux	France	Italy	Holland	The 6	UK	Ireland	Denmark	The 3	The 9
Albania	1,660	∞	82	400	∞	376	300	–	∞	400	380
Cyprus	296	144	235	312	285	273	192	450	200	198	232
Spain	617	554	630	800	725	650	495	745	557	505	612
Greece	485	296	495	537	454	451	332	57	300	316	429
Malta	–	–	–	–	–	–	–	–	–	–	–
Portugal	264	137	262	465	256	260	276	144	1,040	388	290
Turkey	194	232	235	198	139	209	195	*	192	196	206
Yugoslavia	562	645	462	420	510	500	375	*	323	370	486
N. Mediterranean	420	223	442	462	442	425	370	325	417	377	412
Algeria	910	970	46	1,000	272	70	740	–	240	680	76
Egypt	90	87	244	179	115	128	90	400	330	98	99
Israel	315	755	340	400	352	368	620	7,000	270	602	430
Jordan	93	93	212	97	188	117	126	*	400	141	126
Lebanon	219	145	207	261	237	218	47	140	159	51	129
Libya	294	410	885	525	384	500	201	*	350	206	403
Morocco	298	216	109	198	134	137	203	–	78	197	140
Tunisia	284	300	104	296	240	134	159	*	400	166	136
Syria	128	87	136	222	137	145	242	*	170	240	155
S. Mediterranean	223	301	79	342	214	132	186	950	214	190	133
Mediterranean	355	290	128	405	331	240	278	410	317	283	249
USA	420	232	276	382	307	348	250	460	270	281	328
Japan	102	312	565	741	344	450	478	∞	620	500	465
USSR	252	35	221	370	178	216	196	∞	155	192	194
Latin America	197	148	232	216	147	180	104	158	113	105	156
World	342	326	335	399	302	337	225	310	245	230	306

Notes: *Negligible. – No Trade. ∞Infinity. *Source*: OECD trade statistics.

in the north than in the south. France's results, excellent with the northern countries and mainly with Spain, are negative for the south by reason of the drop in sales to Algeria. Nevertheless, excellent results with the Arab states of the eastern Mediterranean should be noted.

Table 3 *Distribution by Country of Destination*

(*1*) The Six are responsible for 81 per cent of the exports from the EEC of the Nine towards the Mediterranean. This percentage is not basically different from the Six's share in the total trade of the Nine (78·8 per cent).

It can be concluded, then, that the interest for the Six and for the Three of the Mediterranean market is shared equally.

(*2*) The distribution between the Six and the Nine of their total exports to the northern and southern Mediterranean is fairly similar, with a little above 80 per cent in both cases for the Six.

(*3*) The major supplier for the Mediterranean is Germany, with 30 per cent, followed by the Mediterranean countries France and Italy. It should, however, be noted that, scoring on a level with Italy, the United Kingdom is giving material proof of its trade interest in the Mediterranean area.

(*4*) It should be noted that Germany plays a relatively more important part in trade with the north (35·2 per cent), whereas France has the most important share of the trade with the south (34·3 per cent). The outlets of the other member states for the Mediterranean countries are balanced more equally between north and south, with very similar percentages for north and south for each of them.

(*5*) These facts should be noted, for each member state:

Germany's special interest in Yugoslavia, Turkey and Greece;

the major part played by France in the Community's exports to Algeria (57·5 per cent), Morocco (55·8 per cent) and Tunisia (60·1 per cent), and the relative weakness of its suppliers to Israel (because of the continuance of traditional relationships on the one hand, and political impact on trade on the other);

the balanced distribution of Italian interests over the area as a whole (a very diversified Mediterranean aptitude);

the relative importance of United Kingdom sales to Cyprus (45 per cent), Malta (50 per cent), Israel (33·6 per cent) and Portugal (28·6 per cent), for historical reasons similar to the French case.

TABLE 3 Percentage distribution of EEC exports by country of destination, 1971

	W. Germany	*Benelux*	*France*	*Italy*	*Holland*	*The 6*	*UK*	*Ireland*	*Denmark*	*The 3*	*The 9*
Albania	21·3	0·6	9·0	54·3	12·2	97·4	2·0	–	0·6	2·6	100·0
Cyprus	16·4	2·4	10·2	17·4	5·6	52·0	45·0	0·7	2·3	48·0	100·0
Spain	29·2	5·5	24·2	12·9	7·6	79·4	18·6	0·6	1·4	20·6	100·0
Greece	39·0	5·7	14·3	18·2	7·2	84·4	14·3	0·1	1·2	15·6	100·0
Malta	7·4	2·7	4·9	27·6	4·9	47·5	50·0	0·4	2·1	52·5	100·0
Portugal	31·8	5·6	15·8	11·0	4·8	69·0	28·6	0·1	2·3	31·0	100·0
Turkey	39·8	5·2	13·1	21·6	3·3	83·0	16·2	*	0·8	17·0	100·0
Yugoslavia	45·6	3·8	8·7	27·9	3·6	89·6	9·5	*	0·9	10·4	100·0
N. Mediterranean	35·2	5·1	16·1	18·3	5·8	80·5	17·8	0·3	1·4	19·5	100·0
Algeria	14·5	0·3	57·5	11·8	3·4	91·5	7·8	–	0·7	8·5	100·0
Egypt	32·9	2·6	22·9	17·6	6·0	82·0	15·7	0·1	2·2	18·0	100·0
Israel	26·3	9·8	12·4	10·0	5·7	64·2	33·6	0·9	1·2	35·8	100·0
Jordan	20·6	4·8	9·5	11·9	11·7	58·5	36·0	0·1	5·4	41·5	100·0
Lebanon	24·4	6·3	21·8	20·6	6·4	79·3	18·8	0·2	1·7	20·7	100·0
Libya	13·9	1·7	22·3	40·6	4·5	83·0	16·1	*	0·9	17·0	100·0
Morocco	15·1	4·8	55·8	11·2	4·8	91·7	7·6	–	0·7	8·3	100·0
Tunisia	11·7	2·8	60·1	95·7	3·6	93·9	5·1	–	1·0	6·1	100·0
Syria	25·4	5·5	19·2	25·0	8·4	83·6	13·9	–	2·5	16·4	100·0
S. Mediterranean	20·0	5·2	34·3	17·1	5·0	81·6	17·0	0·2	1·2	18·4	100·0
Mediterranean	30·1	5·15	22·4	17·85	5·5	81·0	17·5	0·25	1·25	19·0	100·0
USA	35·1	8·0	10·2	13·9	5·2	72·4	23·7	1·3	2·6	27·6	100·0
Japan	38·4	5·5	11·4	8·5	5·6	69·6	27·5	0·7	2·2	30·4	100·0
USSR	34·1	4·9	18·9	21·8	3·3	83·0	15·1	*	1·9	17·0	100·0
Latin America	37·4	5·8	13·5	14·6	6·7	78·0	19·7	0·1	2·2	22·0	100·0
World	30·2	10·5	15·7	11·6	10·8	78·8	17·4	1·0	2·8	21·2	100·0

Notes: *Negligible.
–No trade.
Source: OECD trade statistics.

2. *EEC Imports*

Table 4 *Distribution by Country of Destination*

(*1*) The Mediterranean countries taken as a whole represented in 1971 6 per cent of the total import trade of the EEC (intra and extra), which is equivalent to about 13 per cent of the Community's external trade.

This volume represents about twice the imports from Latin America and corresponds, all in all, to the total sales of Japan, the USSR and Latin America to the Community.

The Mediterranean is a supplier relatively less important (5 per cent) for the Three than for the Six (6·5 per cent). The ratio is however the same, in percentage, (from 6 to 7 per cent) for Italy (7·2 per cent) as for France, Germany and the United Kingdom (6 per cent). The relative importance is less for the Netherlands (4·2 per cent), the Benelux, Denmark, and lastly Ireland (for which the percentage is lower than 30 per cent of the trade of each country (intra and extra)).

(2) The Nine's imports from the south are slightly more important than those from the north (54 per cent as against 46 per cent), but this proportion is inverse for the Three (47 as against 53 per cent) by reason mainly of Portugal's contribution.

(*3*) Not surprisingly, the north's share is mainly important for France and Italy, but also for Holland (oil).

(*4*) Amongst the northern Mediterranean countries, Spain's predominance as the major supplier is very marked, except for Italy (Yugoslavia). Portugal has a special importance for each of the Three (because of its geographical position and EFTA).

(*5*) Amongst the southern countries, Libya (which is the chief supplier amongst all the Mediterranean countries) and Algeria owe their position to oil: they represent 70 per cent of the value of the deliveries from all the southern Mediterranean countries. This predominance affects the Six and the United Kingdom, excluding Ireland and Denmark (for reasons peculiar to the trans-national trade of the oil companies).

The relatively greater share of Israel on a supplier of the Three than of the Six (for tariff and historical reasons) should also be noted.

Table 5 *Development of Imports*

(*1*) The EEC's imports from the Mediterranean have developed at a rate higher than the total imports of the EEC (intra-trade included). The mean

TABLE 4 Percentage distribution of EEC imports from the Mediterranean countries by country of destination and relative size to imports from other areas, 1971

	W. Germany	*Benelux*	*France*	*Italy*	*Holland*	*The 6*	*UK*	*Ireland*	*Denmark*	*The 3*	*The 9*
Albania	*	–	*	0·5	*	0·1	–	–	–	–	0·1
Cyprus	0·7	*	0·5	0·3	0·8	0·4	3·8	3·0	1·1	3·4	1·1
Spain	16·4	18·9	24·0	13·5	23·2	18·6	24·8	32·6	26·2	27·4	19·7
Greece	8·4	6·4	4·2	4·6	4·7	6·0	2·4	2·0	3·1	2·4	5·2
Malta	0·1	0·4	*	0·1	0·3	0·1	1·2	0·5	0·5	1·1	0·3
Portugal	3·2	8·9	3·5	1·9	4·9	3·5	14·1	14·3	26·2	15·0	5·7
Turkey	5·9	5·9	4·4	4·0	4·1	4·8	1·6	4·8	14·7	2·5	4·5
Yugoslavia	13·8	5·5	3·9	17·6	5·0	11·0	3·1	0·8	5·2	2·6	9·4
N. Mediterranean	48·5	46·0	40·5	42·5	43·0	44·5	51·0	58·0	77·0	53·0	46·0
Algeria	11·8	11·6	15·2	4·7	4·5	10·3	2·8	2·0	0·3	2·5	8·8
Egypt	2·0	2·4	2·0	3·1	5·6	2·6	2·4	0·5	1·9	2·3	2·6
Israel	4·2	8·5	3·2	2·8	3·9	3·9	8·1	14·8	5·7	8·1	4·9
Jordan	*	–	*	*	*	*	*	–	–	*	*
Lebanon	0·4	2·4	0·2	0·6	27·9	1·2	0·6	6·9	2·3	0·9	1·2
Libya	28·2	20·7	21·0	39·3	22·9	28·2	32·1	–	8·4	29·8	28·2
Morocco	2·4	7·5	14·6	1·8	2·9	5·5	2·6	16·3	3·2	3·0	5·0
Tunisia	1·7	0·7	2·9	3·0	0·4	2·1	0·3	1·5	0·6	0·3	1·9
Syria	0·8	0·2	0·4	2·2	8·9	1·7	0·1	–	0·6	0·1	1·4
S. Mediterranean	51·5	54·0	59·5	57·5	57·0	55·5	49·0	42·0	23·0	47·0	54·0
Mediterranean	100·0	100·0	100·0	100·0	100·0	100·0	100·0	100·0	100·0	100·0	100·0
USA	149·0	201·0	118·0	95·0	254·0	144·0	179·0	396·0	340·0	197·0	153·0
Japan	30·0	34·0	18·0	13·0	37·0	24·0	33·0	200·0	20·0	36·0	27·0
USSR	15·3	25·0	17·0	20·0	11·0	17·0	19·0	18·0	27·0	20·0	18·0
Latin America	58·0	84·0	32·0	32·0	72·0	54·0	52·0	70·0	95·0	55·0	54·2
World	1,449·0	3,160·0	1,385·0	1,380·0	2,580·0	1,550·0	1,645·0	4,558·0	4,070·0	1,910·0	1,620·0

Notes: *Negligible.
–No trade.

Source: OECD trade statistics.

TABLE 5 Development of EEC imports, 1960–71 (1960 = 100)

	W. Germany	*Benelux*	*France*	*Italy*	*Holland*	*The 6*	*UK*	*Ireland*	*Denmark*	*The 3*	*The 9*
Albania	1,100	–	∞	2,100		2,000	–	–	–	–	2,140
Cyprus	85	37	238	109	565	117	258	200	200	255	180
Spain	246	299	570	286	650	336	187	260	216	206	280
Greece	286	990	595	400	500	380	150	125	500	152	370
Malta	–	–	–	–	–	–	–	–	–	–	–
Portugal	210	316	420	210	340	266	400	570	575	425	320
Turkey	195	236	400	165	480	222	72	210	156	96	192
Yugoslavia	585	450	550	323	388	435	97	100	300	108	399
N. Mediterranean	294	340	575	272	520	334	210	273	266	226	293
Algeria	1,070	2,380	45	1,030	1,530	119	124	62	57	120	119
Egypt	156	189	298	161	320	190	180	66	210	179	191
Israel	405	262	1,470	370	370	425	282	545	233	284	365
Jordan	300	–	∞	400	–	300	150	–	–	150	266
Lebanon	835	155	240	232	143	160	163	400	520	216	167
Morocco	109	215	112	100	154	113	97	3,200	92	105	115
Tunisia	1,090	465	65	284	20	135	31	300	88	40	122
Syria	730	65	90	∞	520	740	3	–	100	4	151
S. Mediterranean	860	505	114	873	390	420	328	266	260	322	354
Mediterranean	445	490	167	450	435	350	248	270	264	260	300
USA	236	209	242	267	245	239	165	301	216	172	216
Japan	1,070	670	1,652	590	900	1,050	410	930	156	415	710
USSR	270	360	274	235	148	235	128	332	107	130	220
Latin America	157	194	142	270	240	174	64	198	125	70	133
World	340	324	334	338	328	334	187	191	156	199	293

Source: OECD trade statistics.

growth rate noted is of the order of 10·5 per cent per year as against less than 8 per cent for the external trade of the Community.

The progress observed is 2·2 higher than that by Latin America, 1·4 higher than that by the USA, and the USSR.

(2) The Mediterranean's sales to the Six (index 350) are higher than those made to the Three (260). But the ratio of total trade (Six: 350/334 = 1·04, and Three: 260/199 = 1· 3) shows that the relative progress of sales to the Three has been larger than for the Six.

(*3*) The performances recorded on the market of the Six have been in fact weakened by the relative stagnation of French imports. For the other member states of the Community the index 1971/1960 is over 400.

(*4*) The results obtained by the southern countries are better than those achieved by the northern countries taken as a whole; these results are due to oil, especially from Libya. But Israel has also achieved excellent results. Among the non-oil-producing countries the best results have been achieved by Yugoslavia, Greece, Israel, followed by Portugal and Spain – Portugal's results being mainly obtained on the market of the Three.

(*5*) The overall stagnation of the Maghreb countries, due mainly, for Algeria and Tunisia, to the drop in sales to France, should also be noted.

Table 6 *The Structure of Trade by Country of Origin*

(*1*) The relative shares of the Six and the Three in their total imports from the Mediterranean (respectively 80 and 20 per cent) are not so very different from the distribution of the Nine's world imports (the Six taking 76·5 per cent and the Three, 23·5 per cent). These figures indicate, all the same, that the Mediterranean is slightly more important for the Six than for the Three.

(2) In addition, it can be noted that the Southern Mediterranean countries find a relatively more important outlet with the Six (82·5 per cent of the Community) than the Northern countries (77 per cent).

(*3*) Germany is the main outlet (29·6 per cent of the total), and France, Italy and the United Kingdom are markets of more or less equal importance (18 to 19 per cent).

(*4*) These facts should be noted:

the predominance of Germany as an outlet for Greece, Turkey, Yugoslavia and Algeria (ahead of France);

France is still in the lead for Morocco and Tunisia, and is on an equal footing with Germany and the United Kingdom for Spain;

TABLE 6 Percentage distribution of EEC imports by country of origin, 1971

	W. Germany	*Benelux*	*France*	*Italy*	*Holland*	*The 6*	*UK*	*Ireland*	*Denmark*	*The 3*	*The 9*
Albania	13·0	–	5·0	82·0	1·0	100·0	–	–	–	–	100·0
Cyprus	18·6	0·2	7·0	4·0	5·2	35·0	62·0	1·0	2·0	65·0	100·0
Spain	24·7	4·7	23·2	13·1	8·3	74·0	23·0	1·0	2·0	26·0	100·0
Greece	47·0	6·2	15·2	16·2	6·4	91·0	7·9	0·3	0·8	9·0	100·0
Malta	13·7	5·3	1·5	9·8	5·7	36·0	61·0	1·0	2·0	64·0	100·0
Portugal	16·3	7·9	11·5	6·3	6·0	48·0	44·0	2·0	6·0	52·0	100·0
Turkey	39·0	7·0	18·0	17·0	7·0	88·0	7·0	1·0	4·0	12·0	100·0
Yugoslavia	43·0	3·0	8·0	36·0	4·0	94·0	5·9	*	0·1	6·0	100·0
N. Mediterranean	31·0	5·0	17·0	18·0	6·0	77·0	20·0	1·0	2·0	23·0	100·0
Algeria	40·0	8·0	32·0	10·0	4·0	94·0	5·9	0·1	*	6·0	100·0
Egypt	23·0	4·8	15·0	23·6	15·6	82·0	16·5	0·5	1·0	18·0	100·0
Israel	26·2	9·2	13·3	11·4	5·9	66·0	31·0	1·4	1·6	34·0	100·0
Jordan	18·4	–	12·4	25·0	6·2	62·0	38·0	–	–	38·0	100·0
Lebanon	10·0	10·8	4·0	9·6	50·6	85·0	9·3	3·0	2·7	15·0	100·0
Libya	29·3	3·7	14·2	26·1	5·7	79·0	20·6	–	0·4	21·0	100·0
Morocco	14·7	7·7	54·6	6·8	4·2	88·0	9·5	1·6	0·9	12·0	100·0
Tunisia	27·0	2·0	32·3	33·0	1·3	95·6	3·5	0·4	0·5	4·4	100·0
Syria	15·7	0·9	7·2	29·2	45·0	98·0	1·4	–	0·6	2·0	100·0
S. Mediterranean	28·2	5·2	21·2	20·3	7·6	82·5	16·5	0·4	0·6	17·5	100·0
Mediterranean	29·6	5·1	19·1	19·0	7·0	80·0	18·2	0·5	1·3	20·0	100·0
USA	29·0	6·8	14·7	11·7	12·0	74·2	21·3	1·4	3·1	25·8	100·0
Japan	33·8	6·6	12·8	9·4	9·9	72·5	22·5	4·0	1·0	27·5	100·0
USSR	26·1	7·5	18·4	21·0	4·8	77·8	19·5	0·5	2·2	22·2	100·0
Latin America	32·2	7·9	11·4	18·3	9·6	79·4	17·5	0·6	2·5	20·6	100·0
World	26·5	9·9	16·2	12·4	11·5	76·5	18·5	1·5	3·5	23·5	100·0

Notes: *Negligible.
– No trade.

Italy is characterised by the diversification and balance of its network of suppliers;

the United Kingdom is the main outlet for Cyprus, Malta and Portugal.

Special Remarks

Farm Produce

(*1*) The Northern Mediterranean's agricultural deliveries to the Community increased from 1960 to 1971 (index 200), whereas those from the south fell back (85).

In 1960, north and south shared half each the Community's market. In 1971, the north took more than 70 per cent of the Mediterranean outlet on the Community.

(*2*) The overall progress of the Mediterranean as supplier of farm produce to the Community is less than that of imports from the world, the USA and Latin America (Mediterranean: index 139 as against world: 201, USA: 163 and Latin America: 156).

(*3*) For the Northern Mediterranean countries, the progress is generalised and affects them all as a whole.

As for the southern countries, only Israel, Morocco and to a lesser extent Egypt have achieved progress.

The drop stems mainly from Algeria. When the statistics for this country are subtracted, the south's progress, in this hypothesis, would remain less than that of the north (index 158 as against index 200).

Non-agricultural Products

(*1*) In volume, the Northern Mediterranean countries export 60 per cent of the total non-agricultural products sold by the Mediterranean to the EEC (1971).

Since 1960, the southern countries have nevertheless made greater progress than the northern ones (index 660 as against 405), mainly because of oil.

For the Mediterranean as a whole (index 465), the overall results are excellent (a rate of 15 per cent per year).

(*2*) The Mediterranean's textile exports to the Community have developed even more rapidly (610 as against 465) than total non-agricultural products.

The index for the south (710) is slightly higher than for the Northern Mediterranean (590).

For the south the biggest developments are those of Israel, Egypt, Morocco and Tunisia.

For the north, Portugal, Yugoslavia and Greece have achieved the best results.

(3) However, it is in the oil sector that the best results have been achieved (1971: index 1310 for the Mediterranean, whose share of supplies to the Community rose from 6 per cent in 1960 to 23 per cent in 1971).

Libya and Algeria are obviously responsible for this improvement.

14

Mediterranean Policy in the Context of the External Relations of the European Community: 1958–73

STANLEY HENIG

1. Introduction; the Bases of External Policy

A critical motivation of the post-war drive for European unification was the desire to change the bases for Europe's relations with the rest of the world in an era of dominance by extraneous continental super-powers and of the decolonisation of its own nineteenth-century empires. The strategy adopted after the collapse of the European Defence Community (EDC) of concentrating on economic integration, and assuming that its inevitable success would facilitate political unification, left the European Communities with few instruments for the pursuit of external policy. Even within the economic sphere joint methods of policy formation have only fully superseded the national institutions in the fields of commerce and agriculture. Limitation of competence is demonstrated by the provisions of the European Economic Community (EEC) Treaty dealing with external relations: beyond the notion that democratic, economically advanced states in Europe should all be members of the Community (namely, Article 237) and a declaration of intent for the benefit of erstwhile colonies (Part Four and so on),[1] there is a doctrinal vacuum, particularly as concerns association (Article 238) and trade agreements (Articles 111–14).

The striking economic success of the Community has acted as a magnet for large numbers of third countries. At first their reactions were generally negative, arising from fears of the discriminatory effects of the Common External Tariff (CET) and Common Agricultural Policy (CAP), but subsequently the demonstration of the potential gains from free trade coupled with the global increase in Community imports from all sources has exercised a more positive attraction. Even before enlargement, the Com-

1 This notion was originally adumbrated to ensure that the United Kingdom could not aspire to any halfway house short of full membership. Once British membership was assured, the Community was prepared to relax the 'rule' and grant preferential trade agreements to the various EFTA non-candidates.

munity was the biggest single export market for a large number of third countries, including many in the Mediterranean regions. Purely trading motivations led to a large number of countries seeking some form of special privileged relationship with the Community, and this polar attraction has been further increased by enlargement.

A number of broad considerations determine the initial Community response to requests for bilateral agreements. Evidently, the scope of such agreement is conditioned by the Community's own competences, arising formally from the treaties, from subsequently established common policies or just conceivably from an *ad hoc* pragmatic decision to undertake some additional common action – such as the granting of financial aid – purely to facilitate an agreement. Formally the Community's motivations should be purely economic – to correspond with its competences – but here a major problem intrudes. Although the Community may be the major, or a very important, trading partner for countries such as Greece, Spain, Israel, Morocco, Nigeria, Tanzania and so on, none of these can be of equally great actual or even potential importance to the Community. To take one example, in 1956 almost half Greece's exports went to the Six and in 1961 the figure was still more than thirty per cent. Even though the Community enjoyed a balance of trade surplus with Greece throughout the period, exports to that market could never have anything like the same proportional importance for the Europeans. This lack of economic and psychological balance in any negotiations is yet further reinforced if one considers other possible items on the agenda. Financial assistance may well be of critical importance for poor, developing countries: possible reciprocal demands to ensure a kind of Most Favoured Nation treatment for capital exports cannot have the same degree of significance for the rich developed country. It is difficult to avoid the conclusion that, on purely economic criteria, the amount of time expended by the Community on reaching bilateral agreements has been misspent, granted also the involvement in general worldwide efforts to lower barriers to trade by the General Agreement on Tariffs and Trade (GATT) and United Nations Conference on Trade and Development (UNCTAD). In fact the only real motivations for these bilateral agreements are political. Given that the Community cannot yet aspire to a common foreign policy, an argument demonstrated rather than contradicted by recent events, the only discernible principle underlying apparently motiveless acts of external policy lies in the desire to show the *bona fides* of the Community by demonstrating international goodwill. It is almost an item of faith that the reaction to any request should be positive in principle, even if there is no obvious substantive content for a potential agreement. In practice, however, this very negative analysis must be tempered by a related set of considerations.

The functioning of the Community institutions is not fully autonomous from the political process of the member states even in spheres where they are competent. In the external field in particular, the role of the Commission as policy initiator has been strictly limited by member governments which still aspire to promote national foreign policies and often attempt to use the common institutions as an instrument for this end. Thus individual member states may seek to promote or prevent agreements with individual third countries.[2] It may be of interest to students of the so-called spill-over process that the usual result of confrontations in these cases is often different external agreements rather than none at all.

The Community is today linked by a plethora of bilateral agreements with individual third countries, and it is committed to many more. The vast majority of these agreements are based on preferential trade arrangements, invariably granting the partner country easier access on a global basis for its industrial exports to the Community market and considerably less generous treatment for agricultural produce – all this normally against some kind of reciprocity, more or less substantive. Now, a loaf of bread, even one in process of organic automatic growth, can only be split so many ways, and it is possible to argue that the greater the number of such bilateral agreements the less valuable their contents to the third countries in question, especially when the Community's multilateral trade diplomacy in GATT and UNCTAD is also taken into account. At the time of enlargement, the Community had entered into preferential trade agreements with thirty-one countries (eighteen in the Yaoundé agreements, plus Mauritius, a new adherent); three by the Arusha agreement; and nine in the Mediterranean by individual arrangements). The initial or impact effects of enlargement brought with them eight further agreements – the European Free Trade Association (EFTA) and Cyprus – plus a commitment to offer similar arrangements to sixteen additional British Commonwealth countries. On the assumption that the long-running saga of negotiations with Algeria ultimately reaches a successful conclusion, the Community will have

2 Thus France championed Greece and Spain; the Netherlands and Germany championed Israel; Italy effectively held up the Austrian negotiations over the question of terrorism in the Tyrol. The mandate system often means that real negotiations take place in the Council in the formal absence of the third country. The Commission is messenger boy rather than negotiator.

special, privileged trade relations with some sixty non-members.[3] For good measure, it has also been proposed to include those few African countries not otherwise covered, and Britain is currently reminding her partners of the existence of Asia. The spectrum of external policy can be completed by reference to non-preferential agreements with Iran, Yugoslavia and some South American countries, the multilateral trading concessions granted to more than eighty developing countries as a result of UNCTAD, and a major, worldwide lowering of all tariffs, primarily for the benefit of developed countries, in the Kennedy Round.

Characterising the Community's external policy as broadly liberal with a concentration of diplomatic and economic efforts on certain areas, particularly Africa and the Mediterranean, it is possible to pose a number of questions. To what extent are a liberal trading policy and concentration on special economic relations with particular third countries in fact compatible? How desirable is it to divide the world with the other economic super-powers into spheres of influence, with Africa and the Mediterranean as our choice and an opting away from Asia and South America? Finally, is there any residual danger that the progressive whittling away of the trading privileges of actual Community membership might weaken the drive towards European unification?

The bulk of this chapter will be concerned with evolution of Community policy towards the Mediterranean. In one sense the policy is very different from that towards Africa, where the Community inherited a legacy and an outline policy in the shape of Part Four of the treaty. In contrast, Mediterranean policy has entirely evolved since 1958 and represents a Community achievement. Unfortunately, given the parameters affecting external policy as a whole, and the rampant pragmatism of the policy makers, the fundamental questions referred to above have never been posed, and much less answered, even by the Commission. Like Topsy, Mediterranean policy, and indeed the whole of bilateral external policy, has just grown; and each stage is claimed as a success by its progenitors. In reality it is extremely difficult to measure this success in the general absence of defined goals. The remainder of this chapter will be devoted to an analysis of the evolution of Mediterranean policy and an extremely tenuous effort to evaluate its achievements together with some speculations about the future course of general external policy.

3 As well as a number of remaining colonial territories of which some (e.g. Surinam and the Antilles) now have agreements under Article 238.

2. The Origins of Mediterranean Policy

The centre of the ancient world has become the crucible for moulding the external policy of the Community. In this area are situated a large number of those countries for whom economic relations with Western Europe are critical. Traditionally, Western Europe has been a major market for Mediterranean agricultural produce as well as being an obvious source for the requirements – particularly capital – of economic development. The early stages of industrialisation are frequently characterised by the ability to produce relatively unsophisticated manufactures for which economically more advanced countries may offer an obvious market. In general terms – but with one striking exception – the economic interest of this area to the Community is much smaller. Even in the long term only two countries can offer important markets – Spain and Turkey – and these are geographically eligible for full membership when their political and economic circumstances permit, thus ultimately excluding them from the scope of external policy. Two member states – France and, more particularly, Italy – produce similar agricultural goods to those of many other Mediterranean countries, and they are unwilling to sacrifice domestic production in the hope that geographic contiguity will allow them to make economic gains in other sectors. Even on the assumption that France and Italy have a natural interest in the possibility of joint production and marketing arrangements for these commodities, this would be far outweighed by the advantages of Community membership and the CAP.

The major exception to this picture of economic imbalance in relations between the Community and the Mediterranean concerns oil. A limited number of countries in the region contain oil in sufficiently abundant deposits to be able to produce it more cheaply than anywhere else in the world. Joint action by the suppliers can force up the price of oil to the economic disadvantage of the Community. Supply and demand patterns may change from time to time, but given the continuing rise in world oil consumption and the lack of availability for the present of sufficient supplies from alternative sources, conventional forms of economic action even by a united European Community seem unlikely to have much impact on price levels in the face of current Organisation of Petroleum Exporting Countries (OPEC) policies and the relative solidarity of Arab producers. The strategic implications of dependence on Middle Eastern and Mediterranean oil involve political considerations falling well beyond the limited economic competences of the European Community. Indeed, on the political plane the imbalance of interests between the members of the Community and the Mediterranean almost match those apparent, but in the opposite direction, in the economic sphere. Historically, the Mediterranean was particularly important because of its position in relation to Europe's major trade routes. Today, the Community has an obvious interest in preventing any threat to fuel supplies either by countries within the area or by potentially hostile outside powers. In fact, political instability coupled with a dispute between Israel and the Arab countries, which has proved quite incapable of local settlement, has provided the occasion and excuse for ever-growing military involvement by the super-powers, posing a continually growing threat to Europe's security. Although two of Europe's middle-ranking powers have long Mediterranean coastlines, that sea is now totally dominated by two extraneous navies, one of which is presumably considered hostile by at least those seven Community members that participate fully in the North Atlantic Treaty Organisation (NATO). In addition, control of the oil by one side to the Middle East dispute has now made possible the threat of withholding it altogether as a means of enlisting European support. However, in general terms the Mediterranean countries have little political interest in Europe. The abilities of the two sides in the local conflict to maintain their positions now largely depends on the respective super-powers who jointly control also the international setting relevant to the bases and conditions for a possible settlement. The prospect of Europe's replacing the super-powers in either context does not seem to be on the agenda, and there has been no reaction whatsoever in the area to the notion of 'honest broker'.

In such a situation the political options open to the states of Western Europe are extremely limited even if acting jointly. Use of the economic instrumentalities of the Community offers one of the few possibilities – real if limited – of independent action. The argument runs along the following lines. Political instability, which facilitates the extraneous penetration and the use of war as a tool to distract from internal discontents, is occasioned by economic backwardness. Economic advance would lead to greater political stability and also the possible emergence of consumer-orientated societies in which oil boycotts and wars would alike be inadmissible for the self-inflicted economic damage they would cause. On this argument the Community has strong reasons of self-interest for pursuing an active economic policy, comprised of measures for trade and aid, aimed at increasing the rate of economic advance throughout the area. This kind of Mediterranean policy is a substitute for, rather than a precursor of, a joint foreign policy.[4]

4 See for example Wolfgang Hager: 'The Community and the Mediterranean' in

The minutiae of Mediterranean policy – different tariff rates for citrus, and so on – may seem far removed from such global considerations, which are themselves to some extent abstractions from the actual motivations of day-to-day policy. Nonetheless, this analysis does offer a framework in which Mediterranean policy can be sensibly placed and its achievements possibly measured. Although in the early years Mediterranean policy simply spread pragmatically on a case-by-case basis, there have been subsequent attempts to establish doctrinal coherence. The input from the member states into the policy-making process has increasingly arisen from these general political considerations.

3. Mediterranean Policy – Phase One

The first period of Community Mediterranean policy – up to 1965 – was virtually synonymous with general bilateral policy. Indeed, the first five agreements with non-member countries – Greece, Turkey, Iran, Israel, Lebanon – were all within the *broad* Mediterranean region. Although no Mediterranean country, apart from France and Italy, could conceivably be considered for immediate full membership, such a relationship could be a legitimate long-term aspiration for any country on the north littoral. Any agreement with Greece and Turkey – the first two suitors – could be placed in this context, thus circumventing for the moment the problem of establishing a long-term doctrinal basis for relations with non-members. The procedures would in all cases have to follow those of Article 230 dealing with association or Article 111 dealing with trade agreements. Whereas the latter article permitted, according to Community rules, either preferential or non-preferential trade agreements, the regulations of GATT – to which all Community members belonged – precluded any discrimination save in the context of a customs union or free-trade area on Article 111: such far-reaching economic arrangements implied association or full membership. However, it was also widely held that association implied a political relationship usually acceptable in the cases of potential full members or erstwhile colonies, but very much more doubtful in, say, the case of Israel – another early suitor.

The earliest application for association was by Greece, although this was

Kohnstamm and Hager, *A nation writ large* (Macmillan, 1973). He argues, 'The present ambiguous neutrality, which allows France to keep friends, and Germany to do its duty towards Israel, is certainly preferable to a joint Community stance, which, without being politically effective, would play havoc with the diplomacy of the member countries. If there is to be a common stance, it should be a joint commitment to resist Arab attempts to export, the conflict through threats of boycott, etc., in retaliation for dealing with Israel.'

shortly followed by Turkey. Possible parallelism in negotiations was prevented to the distinct advantage of Greece by the upheaval in Turkey occasioned by the anti-Menders *coup*. In the immediate aftermath of the breakdown of the Organisation for European Economic co-operation (OEEC) wide free-trade negotiations and the emergence of EFTA, the Community was anxious for diplomatic success. Greece's choice of the Six rather than the Seven was hardly surprising in view of its trade links, but it did give the Community a chance to demonstrate for the first time its international goodwill. During the negotiations Greece was able psychologically to exploit its own economic weakness, and there was strong US pressure on the Community to give assistance to an exposed NATO member – an interesting contrast to later criticism as Mediterranean policy unfolded. The basis of the agreement was to be a customs union and the progressive integration of Greece into the economic system of the Community to the point when full membership might be considered. The essential balance was struck between Greece's immediate gain of virtual intra-community treatment for all exports plus a measure of multilateral financial assistance against its own much slower rate of tariff disarmament (up to twenty-two years for 40 per cent of imports) and an implied loss of economic independence inherent in accepting the doctrine of harmonisation. To clinch the agreement, the Community actually allowed Greece certain rights of veto for a limited period over changes in some items in the CET, immediately asserting that neither this nor indeed the general nature of the arrangements could be considered a precedent. Community opinion was soon to come round to the view that harmonisation in the context of association was unenforceable and therefore unworkable. Long before the colonels' *coup* placed the whole agreement in something of a state of suspended *rigor mortis*,[5] the Commission had resolved not to endeavour any repetition.

The argument that the Greek agreement be not taken as a precedent immediately clashed with Turkey's claim for similar treatment. Given Turkey's even greater economic backwardness as well as the cooler approach to 'diplomatic successes for the Six', the Community would have preferred a much simpler agreement concentrating on specific measures of trade and aid to help prepare the Turkish economy for a full association. However, for two of

5 The trade provisions continued to be applied, but financial assistance was unilaterally ended as a result of Commission action, and the political institutions have hardly functioned. Political developments in Greece during 1974 are likely to lead to a reactivation of the association.

Turkey's major exports, tobacco and raisins, there were also other major suppliers who could gain something for nothing in the event of a Most Favoured Nation reduction.[6] In addition, these were two of the products where tariff changes would require Greek approval. To evade the limitations of the Treaty of Athens, the Turkish agreement had to be an association, whilst to keep in conformity with GATT, it had to be dressed up as a free-trade area – although the lack of any detailed time-table constituted at least a technical infraction of the rules of the wider organisation.

Despite the dressing, the Turkish agreement was limited and specific in content for an initial preparatory period, but it was to be sufficiently successful for agreement to be reached by the end of the 1960s on commencement of a new, transitional phase of the association.

The Community thus acquired two cadet members, but meanwhile Israel had tabled an application for negotiations to establish a closer relationship – to spare Europe's blushes not specifically for association. On purely economic criteria Israel was in a much better position to accept the implications of an association characterised by any kind of 'balance between rights and obligations'. Once this was precluded on political grounds, thus ruling out a customs union or free-trade area, the Community could only offer a non-preferential Most Favoured Nation agreement. The problem was that for its major exports affected by Community tariffs Israel was not the major supplier. Israel's citrus products competed with those of Italy and other Mediterranean countries likely in the future to be negotiating with the Community: any general concessions were precluded at this stage. On the industrial front, Israel – a precursor for other developing countries – exported a wide range of goods for which it was a virtually insignificant supplier.[7] The agreement reached in 1964 consisted for the most part of a series of technical manipulations, some of only temporary effect, in Community tariffs with only one really substantive concession – on grapefruit. Interestingly, the Community did undertake – in a slightly bizarre exchange of unpublished, private but non-confidential letters – to take the greatest amount of Israeli interests in the Kennedy Round of GATT negotiations.

6 That is, tariff reduction extended to all other parties to the GATT and any other country with whom the Community might have a similar non-discrimination arrangement. The concept of Most Favoured Nation usually implies that non-preferential tariff concessions are negotiated only with the biggest supplier.

7 With the exception of industrial diamonds, for which Israel is a major supplier. Trade is not affected by the CET and gross exports are far larger than the real net figure because of the high import content.

During the protracted negotiations with Israel, Iran[8] presented an application for a trade agreement, which was dealt with very much more speedily. Like Turkey, Iran was only really interested in four products, and in all these cases it was a major supplier likely to draw most benefit from non-preferential concessions. Even so, for one product – raisins – the Community again ran into difficulties of its own making, for the concession had to be severely restricted to avoid having to request prior Greek approval. The contents of the agreement were real if limited involving Most Favoured Nation tariff quotas for four products, but it did represent a list of achievements for bilateral policy under Article 111. Finally, to complete this survey of the first phase of Mediterranean policy, mention should be made of the 1965 agreement with Lebanon, which laid down the principle of Most Favoured Nation treatment between the parties and made provision for Community technical assistance – like financial aid to Greece and Turkey, an example of increased competences arising from the practical exigencies of a negotiation rather than *a priori* principles.

4. Assessment and Reorientation

The mid-1960s were a time for stock-taking in Community external and, more specifically, Mediterranean policy. The Six could claim real but rather limited achievements. However, the course of succeeding negotiations, the recurrence of a number of specific problems related to particular products and the evident interactions between the economic needs of various countries in the region all pointed to the desirability of seeking to establish an overall policy framework as a basis for future agreements. Clearly, any attempt to achieve this would throw into relief the potential clash between the needs of third countries and the domestic interests of member states: a single pragmatic concession might be more readily acceptable than the establishment of a broad, liberal doctrine as the basis for external commercial policy. In this situation, one catalyst was a memorandum submitted to its partners in 1964 by the Italian government, dealing with broad underlying principles for a Mediterranean policy.

Italy was the Community member whose economic interests were potentially most affected by developments in the Mediterranean trades. Although others might have an interest in some of the products – particularly processed goods, such as cigarettes and tinned fruit juice – it was Italy that had

8 It is worth referring to Iran at this point, although not a Mediterranean country, in view of the products involved and also to contrast with the Israeli case.

the largest domestic production which was directly competitive with exports of other Mediterranean countries. Italy considered that successive agreements with Mediterranean countries had whittled away some of its advantages that should accrue from Community membership.[9] Although all might share the benefits of any opening of Mediterranean markets to industrial products, the price of securing these gains was unevenly distributed.[10] The Italian memorandum also established a link between the Community's active Mediterranean policy and the French veto on the negotiations for British entry: the whole direction of external policy had been distorted in one direction, altering the balance between the interests of different members inherent in the Treaty of Rome itself. Italy, therefore, proposed a new framework for future Mediterranean policy. For European countries in the Mediterranean, membership was the only acceptable permanent relationship: association could be only a transitory relationship. The interests of non-European states could best be met by trade agreements, but these must not jeopardise the special advantages of Community members. Any trade privileges must, therefore, fall short of general intra-Community treatment. Although this did not preclude preferential agreements, Italy did indicate a preference for dealing with the problem of the region as far as possible through worldwide tariff negotiations like the Kennedy Round.

Multilateral and bilateral diplomacy constantly interact. Later in the 1960s, UNCTAD and general preferences were sometimes postulated as the catch-all for third-country problems. Earlier, 'waiting for Kennedy' was equally in vogue, but in reality this was an opportunity for delaying any systematic thought about the nature of bilateral external policy. No outcome of the Kennedy Round – which was after all essentially a bargain between the most developed countries – would lead to a substantial diminution of requests for special, bilateral relations. That there would be some kind of positive Community response was determined by both the continuing vague, platitudinous declarations of goodwill and the now more specific political attitudes at least towards the Mediterranean.

The Italians were to an extent rationalising on past events, but their

9 At that time the enormous gains made by Italian industry from the Community were much less apparent than subsequently. It was widely assumed that if the Six were able to increase exports to the Mediterranean, Germany would gain the greatest benefit.

10 Italy had not forgotten the last stage of the Greek negotiations when the Commission, without its consent, made a concession on tobacco imports going beyond the maximum Italian position in order to secure agreement.

arguments also reacted with the Israeli syndrome. For political reasons the Community needed to discover an intellectual basis for divorcing special economic relations from organic, institutionalised political links. The Italian doctrine did not preclude this, but it did imply that concessions for Israel or any other country, not eligible or immediately acceptable as an ultimate full member, must fall short of full free trade. In the second phase of Mediterranean policy, the bizarre juxtaposition of Spain and Israel – alike persistent suitors, championed and bitterly opposed by differing combinations of member states and both raising major political issues – provided a pragmatic basis for evolving a new overall policy. For the moment, Community policy was conditioned by four sets of limiting factors – continuing bilateral requests from Mediterranean countries, domestic producer interests in member states, broad political considerations as well as pieces of lingering national foreign policies, and the rules of GATT. An effective policy could only be achieved through change in one or other of these factors.

5. Mediterranean Policy – Phase Two

Two countries, Spain and Israel, and one product, oranges, played crucial roles in determining the shape of this second phase. Such was Israeli dissatisfaction with the first agreement that it made no request for its renewal when it expired in 1967: unwilling immediately to negotiate wider arrangements, the Six unilaterally kept the concessions in force.[11] The juxtaposition with Spain partly revolved around the dictates of Gaullist foreign policy. Well before the Six Day War France had given Israel little reason for encouragement in its approach to the Community, but after its major policy *volte face* France was implacably hostile. In the wake of the veto on the British negotiations France had already begun to encourage the notion of Spanish involvement, with some tacit support from the German Christian Democrat government, although a formal request only arose sometime later. In each case, France's major opponent on political grounds was the Netherlands, whereas Italy was opposed on economic grounds to far-reaching agreements with either. Progress through an overall package deal only be-

11 Given Israel's position in May and June 1967 and the overwhelming support it then enjoyed from European public opinion, the Community probably felt it could do no other. The 'concessions' were now worth even less than hitherto with the imminent coming into force of the CET after the transition period. Those concessions based on national accelerations towards a lower CET were thus voided of content. The tariff suspension on grapefruit had been consolidated in the Kennedy Round.

came possible when Germany, with the Social Democrats now included in government, rallied strongly to the pro-Israeli camp, whilst the Dutch worked out an economic compromise with the Italians.

The criteria determining policy had their starkest effects in these two cases. Both Israel and Spain were major citrus producers in competition with Italy, neither could be helped by a non-preferential agreement and both were questionable on political grounds – the one through fear of damaging relations with the Arab world, the other because of the history and nature of its internal regime. In the circumstances, the weak link in the chain determining policy was the rules of GATT. The Community decided to base extensive preferential arrangements on Articles 111 or 113[12] with nominal commitment to full free trade but no automatic method of reaching it. Bringing free trade into effect slowly would preserve the primacy of relationships based on membership or association, whilst the Community could claim that the ultimate commitment to free trade was sufficient to compensate for any technical infraction arising from the lack of a detailed timetable. Given that the agreements also gave little indication that there would ever be free trade in agricultural products – a major part of both countries' exports – this argument was juridically somewhat shaky, but on a political basis the Community was secure: it could submit such agreements to GATT under Article 24 of the latter, knowing that they could only be turned down by a two-thirds majority vote of all members. As a practical compromise this reconciled all kinds of Community interests. Notably, the Netherlands – on record as being strongly opposed to continuous derogations to and exceptions from GATT – much preferred this to the opposing alternatives of association for Spain or nothing at all for Israel.

Trade in the critical product, oranges, is the most important in the citrus group, but over a long period the Community market has been virtually static. Although Italy is self-sufficient, the other five import 95 per cent of their needs from non-Community sources. Only 15 per cent of the imports of these five come from non-Mediterranean sources – usually at times of the year when those countries are not producing. For Spain, Israel and Morocco, arrangements for oranges would be a vital part of any agreement with the Community, and they were also a useful export for Tunisia and Algeria. In reality, tariffs are not the sole or even perhaps the major determinant of trade in such a product, but real concessions for any one Mediterranean producer would to some extent be at the expense of others. A simple general reduc-

12 Article 111 applied up to the end of the transitional period of the Treaty of Rome; Article 113 thereafter.

tion in the Community tariff might conceivably redistribute some marginal financial resources towards the supplier countries, but was ruled out by Italian opposition. The final solution was to lay down a series of regulations aimed at protecting Italian production through the imposition of certain price requirements on all imports and within this framework to grant a variety of tariff preferences to different producers. Community and Greek produce circulates free of all tariffs; Morocco and Tunisia (and presumably ultimately Algeria) receive a reduction of 80 per cent in the tariff; Israel, Spain, Turkey and Cyprus (and presumably any other interested Mediterranean producer) receive a reduction of 40 per cent. Finally, in face of criticism from the USA (under pressure from its own producers), the Community has made a general tariff reduction of 40 per cent for the period of the year when there is little or no Mediterranean production.

'Orange policy' was established well in advance of the agreements with Spain and Israel. When the Community reached its agreements with Morocco and Tunisia, it simultaneously granted the pre-arranged concessions on a unilateral basis to Turkey, Spain and Israel. This necessitated approaching GATT for a waiver and led to a protracted institutional farce. Under GATT Article 25, the Community needed a positive two-thirds majority, and it was soon evident that there was no hope of attaining this. In reality, the opinion of GATT was irrelevant, because the concessions would shortly form part of the bilateral trade agreements which would be presented as free-trade areas and so could only be condemned by an absolute majority the other way – an almost equally unlikely contingency. Having withdrawn the request for a waiver, the Community then considered a Commission proposal that for the period up to the coming into force of the bilateral agreements, the general tariff on oranges should be suspended by 40 per cent on a Most Favoured Nation basis. Italy objected, but agreed to accept a decision by qualified majority in accordance with Community rules. To this procedure France – champion of unanimity – objected, presumably on the grounds that a vital Italian national interest was involved. Finally, the Council put into effect a little-known but apparently 'established' procedure for withdrawing the concession. This involved consultation of the European Parliament and was duly completed by the end of the major Mediterranean producing season. The bilateral agreements were expected to be in effect for the next season!

During the second phase of Mediterranean policy the Community reached bilateral agreement with nine countries as well as establishing with Turkey the bases for a further development of the association. When the Algerian negotiations are concluded, the Community will have bilateral arrangements with all Mediterranean countries except Albania, Libya and Syria. Of the nine new agreements, four are based on Article 238 and five on Articles 111 and 113 – of which latter group the agreement with Yugoslavia is alone non-discriminatory. If one considers the other eight agreements, the real dividing line cannot be based on purely juridical considerations arising from the article used. It is possible to establish a continuum based on the degree of closeness of economic relations with all eleven partners in the Mediterranean with Greece very much at one end and Morocco, Tunisia and Turkey also receiving better treatment than the other seven. Greece had the good fortune to be first: the terms granted to Turkey, Malta and Cyprus – just as eligible for full membership – are clearly inferior. In fact, a distinction can be drawn in the second phase between the treatment given to the Maghreb countries, based on the declaration of intent in the EEC Treaty, and all other cases.

In general, the Community grants substantial measures of tariff reductions for industrial goods. Morocco and Tunisia, as well as Greece and Turkey, receive intra-Community treatment: the others do not, and reductions vary from 70 per cent for Malta and Cyprus to 50 per cent for Israel. For agricultural goods, only Greece receives intra-Community treatment on certain conditions, although Morocco and Tunisia are again treated much more favourably than any of the others. However, none of the agreements concluded in the second phase looks forward to free trade in agricultural produce. All agreements in both phases embody the principle of reciprocity:[13] bilateral commercial policy is kept quite distinct from aid policy and only Greece and Turkey receive financial assistance. However, the margin of reciprocity varies enormously, with Morocco and Tunisia standing out from all the others. In all other cases there is some kind of balance in the agreement. Greece and Turkey are committed ultimately to granting free entry, whereas counter-concessions by Cyprus, Israel, Lebanon, Malta, Spain and Egypt usually involve various lists of products to be affected by different rates of concessions with an average rate of around 35 per cent (rather less in the case of Israel). Any detailed assessment of the economic impact of this exchange of preferences must depend on the structure of trade, various elasticities and existing tariff levels, but it is worth making the point that a high rate of concession on a low tariff may well be less valuable than a low rate of concession on a high tariff, since

13 See footnote 5.

the partners to the agreement are not only lowering their domestic rates of protection but are also giving each other advantages vis-à-vis other countries. In contrast to these finely balanced agreements, Morocco and Tunisia have taken advantage of the wave of sentiment in UNCTAD against reverse preferences. Tunisia does grant a few trade preferences on a limited range of products, but Morocco's obligations extend only to some Most Favoured Nation reductions. In contrast even to the Yaoundé countries, Morocco and Tunisia make no commitment whatsoever to free trade in both directions. Finally, it is worth briefly mentioning the agreement with Yugoslavia, the first with a state trading nation. Although non-preferential, this makes use of tariff manipulations to give Yugoslavia some practical assistance in exporting cows and beef to the Community – particularly the Italian – market.

6. Towards a Third Phase

Although the Community had established by the time of enlargement a broad framework within which to negotiate and reach agreement with Mediterranean countries, the policy could not be considered multilateral. Individual negotiations took place for individual agreements with each applicant, invariably resulting in a bilateral institutional framework. The Community is now involved in a series of Councils of Association and special Joint Committees with supervisory and consultative status. Even the Councils of Association are far more circumscribed than the institutions of the Community in further developing areas of co-operation, whilst the Joint Committees (in the context of trade agreements) cannot function as a vehicle for any kind of renegotiation. Some of these institutional links commit the Community to prior notification of new membership or association agreements, whilst enlargement has necessitated some degree of renegotiation in all cases. It is hard to resist the conclusion that, to an extent, the Community has institutionalised a great deal of the diplomatic commerce which is carried out rather less formally in traditional inter-state relations.

Renegotiation has proceeded by various stages. During the late 1960s, the agreements entered into were normally limited to a duration of five years, on the twin assumptions that the partner countries would subsequently seek some form of evolution and that by then the Community itself might have new members. During 1974, a major re-assessment of Mediterranean policy was inevitable, because the Israeli and Spanish agreements would have to be renegotiated or a decision made simply to continue with them in their present form. In fact, the trade implications of enlargement could have begun to affect Mediterranean countries from April 1973, by which time the Community was hardly ready to complete a major renegotiation. The countries likely to be most affected were again Israel and Spain which faced the possibility of an imminent increase in the tariffs on their agricultural exports to the United Kingdom. As a result, various standstill arrangements were negotiated on the assumption that by the end of 1973 they would be superseded by wider agreements between the Nine and various Mediterranean countries. But it became clear well before the end of 1973 that the projected time-table would not be met, occasioning various institutional problems and leaving certain Mediterranean agreements in a somewhat undefined position during 1974.

Work had begun during 1971 on formulating the bases for a new phase in Mediterranean policy. Underlying assumptions in the Commission's thinking were that the agreements had been economically and politically useful and should be extended as far as was consistent with the preservation of basic Community producer interests. At the same time, the Commission recognised the problem of limited competences and resolved that the new agreements should not be as limited as hitherto to purely trading considerations. Broadly, the Council agreed that the Phase Three agreements be based on the concept of industrial free trade between the Community and each partner country (thus hoping to remove some of the international criticism of the previous contraventions of GATT), with extended provision for special arrangements on the agricultural side and development of financial and other forms of co-operation. In principle, the Community would remove all tariff barriers on industrial imports by the end of 1978, but the degree of reciprocity would be conditioned by the degree of economic development of the partner country, Israel and Spain giving the most, the Maghreb countries, the Egypt and the Lebanon the least. A series of broad principles was also laid down for lowering Community barriers on agricultural imports with the intention that concessions should cover 80 per cent of each country's exports under these heads to the Community. However, these concessions would not normally amount to free entry, and there would be no question of any additional reductions in agricultural levies. By one means and another the prime position of Community suppliers would be maintained. Finally, economic co-operation seems posited as the growth area in the agreements with the possible provision of low interest loans, technical assistance such as worker training, rules for non-discrimination as regards migrant labour and joint ecological schemes.

7. Assessment – Fifteen Years in the Mediterranean

In no area of the world does the Community have as developed an external policy as it does towards the Mediterranean. It has gone to the limits of its own competences in laying down a framework within which it can develop close economic relations with all countries in the region. The Community now possesses a network of agreements in the Mediterranean that give real, if sometimes limited, economic benefit to the countries involved. That the policy is ultimately not fully satisfactory reflects the lack of competence rather than inability of the Commission fully to appreciate the scope of the problems. So long as Community agricultural interests are strong enough to secure the continuance of an agricultural policy which is intellectually geared to the notion of self-sufficiency, the scope for close commercial relations with important producers to the south must be severely limited. So long as Western Europe remains a major producer of the agricultural goods it consumes, then Mediterranean countries will have one additional reason for desiring to diversify and re-orient their economies, a course more appealing to some – notably Greece and Israel – than to others. Re-orientation and economic development can be facilitated by the Community, and on a positive interpretation this seems to be the intention of the co-operation provision of the putative Phase Three. So far, despite a great deal of lip service, there have been few achievements in this sector – technical assistance and financial aid have been used extremely sparingly in the Mediterranean. Undoubtedly, one problem is the unwillingness of the Mediterranean countries to group themselves into something like the old OEEC. It would be grossly unfair to accuse the Community of divisiveness in its approach to the Mediterranean, but it is hard to discern the kind of statesmanship that epitomised the US approach to Western Europe in the late 1940s.

Phase Three does indicate a way ahead, but it also incorporates the ultimate limits of the present approach. Further trade concessions will become increasingly difficult, and the benefits of those granted during the first three phases may themselves be whittled away, as Community policies towards other parts of the world are developed. On the assumption that the Community will want to continue with special close relations with the Mediterranean, then future phases of policy will have to be based on a qualitatively quite different approach. Here it may be possible to criticize a certain lack of imagination in the Commission's approach. New competences do not only arise from formal decisions in advance of policy formulation: they may also be occasioned by the practical exigencies of a given situation, as has already happened with several Mediterranean agreements – Greece, financial assistance; Israel, national accelerations to the CET; Lebanon, technical assistance. The working documents for Phase Three do represent a considerable step forwards, but the Commission seems generally unwilling to risk the consequences of the kind of boldness that characterised some of its earlier endeavours: in external policy it still resembles a technical secretariat rather than a political innovator.

Mediterranean developments cannot be considered in isolation from general external policy. The Community has been under increasing pressure from the USA over issues of trade discrimination as the latter's own economic problems have mounted. The general response has taken a number of forms – denial that there is any discrimination (a dubious argument enshrined in the Commission memorandum of September 1972 that formally launched Phase Three); undertakings that the policies will not be repeated elsewhere; and assertions that the economic policies are determined by political considerations that the USA itself understands. On the latter score, it is noticeable that the US attitude has changed strongly during the last decade; ten years ago there was no worry about discrimination when association for Greece was being encouraged. During that period, the Community has become an economic super-power, whereas the USA has faced all kinds of short-term trade and financial problems. In addition, whether or not Community policy is ultimately successful in terms of its own current political motivations, in the short-term nothing can be achieved. Since the mid-1960s, Europe's political role in the area has declined still further, external military – especially Soviet – penetration has increased, the Middle East dispute has worsened and, finally, the long-feared threat to the price and availability of oil has at last materialised. Given the USA's world commitments, Community Mediterranean policy can look like a series of irrelevant pinpricks.

It is possible to argue that the underlying conception of Community external policy simply does not match up to the kind of role that Europe ought to be playing in the world. Working out joint policies towards Upper Volta or Malta may be an advance on what has happened in the past, but this hardly represents an enormous challenge to European statesmanship. The whole future of the transatlantic relationship, within and without its own area, is a very much larger question but it has occasioned little statesmanship in recent years. Arguments over Mediterranean oranges are not in themselves fundamental, but they do illustrate the increasing tensions over much larger issues. Given that one motivation for trying to bring about European unification was an endeavour to change the basis for relations with the rest of the world, it is an interesting reflection that whereas economic success has in reality changed that basis, Europe seems temperamentally unwilling to recognise the implications in terms of the necessity for evolving a common foreign policy.

At one level it can be argued that the spreading of bilateral agreements and the increase in derogations from the CET and even from the CAP pose in themselves a threat to the cement binding the Community. From one point of view the twin notions of a tightly organised Europe and a loose, worldwide, liberal trading system stand eyeball to eyeball for the first time since the 1950s. So long as the overall scope for common action remains limited, external policy can in this way threaten the existence of the whole notion of community. From another point of view though, these considerations are increasingly academic.

The European Community has a sufficient history now to be accepted within and without Europe as a full actor on the international scene. Already, according to this view, the ties of Community are more than strong enough to withstand diminution of the original mutual trade advantages on which it was based. The future of Europe now depends on its reactions to the external world – the pressures of the transatlantic relationship, the detente, oil boycotts and so on. Mediterranean policy is again relevant in this context. Whereas as an exercise in endlessly splitting the loaf of bread its achievements can be easily measured – positive, limited and perhaps slightly dangerous – as a forerunner for a European foreign policy it can realistically be measured against some of the criteria outlined in section 2. At first sight the apparent inability of the Community to determine political conditions in any way in the Mediterranean may seem to suggest failure, but ultimately this is not the acid test. The current trend in the Arab world of limiting oil sales to Europe introduced a totally new situation. This is a clear example of the external threat which, it was assumed, could be better handled through unity. In the last analysis, the external world – in the form of Arab boycotts or even a fresh, agonising re-appraisal by the USA – may decide whether the Community breaks up or moves towards political union. Perhaps the final verdict on the Mediterranean will remain for the moment open – a part of a coherent attempt to come to terms with the world or a time-consuming and slightly frivolous escape from the real problems.

15

The European Community's Mediterranean Policy in a World Context

DAVID ROBERTSON

Development of the European Community's Mediterranean policy has been discussed mainly in terms of the direct interests of the European countries and Mediterranean countries that are parties to these bilateral agreements. The contents of these agreements, however, have much wider implications for the whole system of international trade and payments.

Grave uncertainty has arisen about the international system of trade and payments because of the many new problems and changes that have occurred in the world economy in recent years. The development of chronic inflation and serious commodity shortages in the early 1970s – culminating in the energy crisis of 1973–4 – exacerbated weaknesses that had been exposed in the 1960s in the institutional framework provided by the International Monetary Fund (IMF) and the General Agreement on Tariffs and Trade (GATT). The balance of economic power shifted during that decade as a result of the full recovery from war devastation and the rapid economic growth experienced in Western Europe and Japan in the 1950s. In consequence, the institutional system formulated after World War II to establish economic order, which was based on a non-discriminatory equilibrium trade system, involving strict reciprocity under fixed exchange rates, came under assault from Western European countries that had always favoured a preferential system based on trade controls.[1] The weakening of international discipline that has resulted is especially dangerous in present circumstances.

The General Agreement was founded on twin pillars: the principle of non-discrimination, operating through the Most Favoured Nation principle as equal treatment, and a procedure for the gradual removal of tariffs through negotiated reciprocal reductions among the contracting parties.

1 See H. Corbet, 'Commercial diplomacy in an era of confrontation', and G. Curzon, 'Crisis in the international trading system', both in *In search of a new world economic order*, H. Corbet and R. Jackson, eds. (London: Croom-Helm, 1974).

The principles of non-discrimination and reciprocity were supported by a body of rules providing for exceptions under particular circumstances and provisions for multilateral consultations. The first assault on the basic principles of the GATT by the West European countries involved the use of the exception to the Most Favoured Nation clause provided by Article 24 on customs unions and free-trade areas;[2] this exception was included by the founders of the GATT in the belief that it would foster trade liberalisation. But, then, the European Community chose to extend its preference system beyond the 100 per-cent preferences permitted under Article 24, and proceeded to create a system of multiple trade discrimination which contravenes the undertaking in Article 1 of the General Agreement that no new trade preferences should be introduced.

The Mediterranean policy of the European Community is a constituent part of this system of multiple trade discrimination. It consists of a network of bilateral preferential trade agreements that has been built up through a series of separate negotiations carried out, fitfully, over many years. Whether these individual bilateral agreements are mutually consistent is in some doubt, but the proposed 'global' Mediterranean policy is presumably intended to ensure mutual consistency in trade dealings with the disparate countries of the Mediterranean region.

A more fundamental question, however, is whether such a system of multiple trade discrimination, which undermines the international institutions supporting the world trade and payments system, is appropriate in the present uncertain economic circumstances. The General Agreement was, after all, intended to prevent the proliferation of bilateralism that had virtually destroyed the multilateral trading system in the 1930s. This body of rules was strongly supported by small countries, including countries numbered among the less developed, because they had suffered in the pre-war period from the superior bargaining strength of the economically powerful countries.[3] If the present difficulties that beset the world economy are not to cause degeneration into similar bilateralism and protectionism, it will be necessary to restore order to the international system of trade and payments. This can only be done if the major countries support the system. If major entities in world trade continue to flout the rules, the system must

2 General Agreement on Tariffs and Trade. Basic instruments and selected documents (GATT Secretariat, Geneva, 1969).

3 See Karin Kock, *International trade policy and the GATT 1947-67* (Stockholm: Almquist and Wiksell, 1969); and G. Curzon, *Multilateral commercial diplomacy* (London: M. Joseph, 1965).

break down. This requires the European Community to accept its responsibilities for the operation of the system and its responsibilities to the small and weak nations whose interests are best served by an orderly, multilateral trading system. In order to fulfil its role, the European Community must evolve a broad strategy on trade relations. And within that strategy the Mediterranean policy, among other things, must be evaluated.

Some Questions

A number of serious questions must be raised about the Community's Mediterranean policy; questions which have perhaps not received sufficient consideration.

How, for example, does the Mediterranean policy reflect the economic self-interest of the Community, and its member countries? It is widely recognised that the urge to establish a Mediterranean policy is based on political rather than economic considerations.[4] These are, however, rather difficult to define. Italy and France are the only founder members of the Community having traditional political ties with the Mediterranean region, although Britain has maintained a military interest. Strategic considerations, connected with security of oil supplies and the defence of the southern flank of the North Atlantic Treaty Organisation (NATO), have increased in importance in recent years (although the actual burden of patrolling has fallen largely on the US Sixth Fleet). An economic dimension is often added by asserting that the Community's policy, by fostering economic development in the region, will underpin its political stability. However, the miserly attitude adopted towards financial and technical assistance and the niggardly trade concessions included in all the bilateral agreements with the Mediterranean countries (as revealed in the country chapters) belies the sincerity of this claim.

Even if these political aims are worth while, it is still necessary to ask, what economic price should be paid for their achievement? The European Commission is adept at using economic instruments to achieve political aims, and it is assisted in this by the institutional confusions over the defined competences of different directorates in the Commission, and their relationships with the Council of Ministers. The economic consequences of such policies should be assessed, though, in order to permit the Community members to decide whether they are prepared to pay the price for these common policies.[5]

4 See Henig, above, p. 305.

5 H. G. Johnson has sketched a theory that incorporates non-economic objectives

It is also questionable whether the Community's proposed 'global' Mediterranean policy serves the best economic interests of the less developed countries in the Mediterranean region. There are alternative means by which the Community's interest in the Mediterranean could be pursued, which might bring greater benefits to the Mediterranean countries. These alternative policies should be explored. At the same time, the consequences of the Community's 'global' Mediterranean policy for third countries, especially non-associated less developed countries, should be assessed. This is not entirely altruistic, either. The consequences for third countries have repercussions, indirectly, on the European Community through the interdependence of national economies.[6]

Ultimately, it becomes a question of whether a policy of 'regionalism', pursued through discriminatory trade agreements, should be the preferred policy for the Community? Or, would a return to a 'multilateral' trading system be a more effective and profitable approach, seeking to avoid discrimination in trade and to stimulate economic development in less developed countries without favouring one group of countries (the Associated African countries) over others on the basis of tenuous historical links. The controversy over 'regionalism' versus 'multilateralism' is a fundamental problem facing the Tokyo Round of GATT trade negotiations.[7] The Community's Mediterranean policy represents one aspect of this problem and its effects require careful examination.

These questions about the Mediterranean policy of the Community are not easily answered. But they must be confronted. An attempt will be made in this chapter to consider the following questions. First, how far has the Community's Mediterranean policy lived up to its aims? Second, what are the economic effects of the bilateral trade agreements between the Community and the Mediterranean countries? Third, what alternative policies might the Community employ to foster economic development in the Mediterranean area? And, finally, how should the Community's Mediterranean policy fit with its responsibility, by virtue of its size and importance in world trade, for the management of the international system of trade and payments?

into the determination of trade policy. See H. G. Johnson, 'An economic theory of protectionism, tariff bargaining, and the formation of customs unions, *Journal of Political Economy* (June 1968).

6 The Rey Report, *Policy perspectives for international trade and economic relations.* Report by the OECD High Level Group on Trade and Related Problems (Paris: OECD Secretariat, September 1972).

7 See Rey Report, *op. cit.* chapter 5; T. Geiger, 'Towards a world of trade blocks', *The Atlantic Community Quarterly* (1971–2).

An Untidy Collection

The European Community's relations with the Mediterranean countries evolved somewhat absent-mindedly over the period 1962–72. The agreements with ten countries signed in this period were pragmatic. Only towards the end did they begin to show certain common features. Yet it was not until this collection of heterogeneous bilateral trade agreements with a very disparate group of countries had been drawn up that any collective attention was given by member governments of the Community to the question of evolving a so-called global policy towards the Mediterranean countries. There have always been many difficulties and delays in discussions to develop common approaches to negotiations with the Mediterranean countries, because of the often completely opposing views of some member countries on particular issues (for example, in French and Dutch attitudes towards trade agreements with Spain and Israel). In the latest attempt to arrive at a 'global approach', the deadline set for January 1974, was passed without any sign of accord on the major issues.

The Community's first agreements with Greece (1962) and Turkey (1964) were association agreements which provided, ultimately, for full membership of the European Community. Both agreements covered not only trade but also included provisions for financial aid from the European Investment Bank (EIB). Because the Community adopted a pragmatic approach towards difficult issues in these two association agreements, other Mediterranean countries felt encouraged to seek commercial agreements with special exemptions. These put the agreements outside the provisions of the GATT and in contravention of the Most Favoured Nation principle – a matter that the Commission and others in Europe have treated with indifference but that has far-reaching implications for world trade.

Disagreements among the member countries delayed the European Commission from reaching any more agreements for several years. The relevant country chapters contain details of the commercial agreements, and show the substantial differences between them. Five-year commercial agreements were reached with Tunisia and Morocco in 1970. Similar five-year agreements with Malta (1971) and Cyprus (1972) represented the first stages of association, with options to seek membership of the Community at a later date. The trade agreements with Spain and Israel, signed in 1970, followed ten years of political wrangling among the Community's members. The agreements were very similar in their contents, and were based on Article 113 of the Treaty of Rome. Finally, in 1972, five-year trade agreements were signed with Egypt and Lebanon that followed closely the commercial content of the agreements with Spain and Israel.

Agricultural Content of the Mediterranean Agreements

Like most outside countries dependent on exports of agriculture-based products, the Mediterranean countries became concerned as the Common Agricultural Policy (CAP) of the Community took shape in the early 1960s. The concept of 'organisation of markets', so strongly advocated by French spokesmen, was given full scope; trade, in particular, was to be regulated as a residual to the interests of the Community's farmers. The Community has taken the view that its agricultural policy benefits developing countries because of the stability that its pricing and marketing policies provide. In answer to demands that less developed countries should be granted improved access to developed countries' markets for their agricultural exports, the Commission has responded that uncontrolled access to the Community might benefit other developed countries rather than less developed countries' suppliers. The economic case for protection of this kind is unfounded over any reasonable period of years, if other developed countries are more efficient producers than those in the Community.[8] It is, then, a question of economic adjustment in the Community's agriculture. But agriculture is deemed by the Community to be different from other industries.[9] Moreover, even in products in which reduced protection for the Community would benefit *only* producers in less developed countries, the Commission has been unwilling to act to change the CAP, as the bilateral agreements with the Mediterranean countries have shown.

The experience of the Mediterranean countries showed the Community most unwilling to grant even limited preferential access to some developing countries if it meant interfering with the delicate internal balance of member countries' interests in the CAP. Yet preferential agreements were welcomed in industrial products. Because of the importance of agricultural exports to the Community from Mediterranean countries, discussions on agricultural trade have always been at the forefront of their negotiations for bilateral trade agreements. Only minor concessions were, however, wrung from the Commission.

The association agreement with Turkey provided an early example of the Community's unwillingness to grant free access for agricultural products

8 The basis for this statement is to be found in any elementary textbook on international trade. For example, D. Robertson, *International trade policy* (London: Macmillan, 1972).

9 See Rey Report, *op cit.* chapter and Comment; and 'Development of an overall approach to trade in view of the coming multilateral negotiations in GATT', Supplement 2/73 *Bulletin of the European Communities*.

from the Mediterranean. Quota restrictions were imposed on Turkish exports of tobacco, raisins, hazel-nuts and dried figs, which together in 1967 accounted for 40 per cent of total exports to the Community. In the first few years of the agreement, these quotas are thought to have restrained, rather than stimulated, trade with the Community.[10] A specific example of EEC protectionism is provided by hazel-nuts. Apparently Turkey has a virtual monopoly in world exports of hazel-nuts, and that country's exports to the Community were more than double the agreed annual quota in the period up to 1968. Yet, when the transition phase of the association agreement was negotiated, quotas were retained on hazel-nuts.

Trade in citrus fruit has provided the most difficult problems in connection with the trade agreements with Mediterranean countries. Most of these countries have some interest in exporting citrus fruits – fresh, preserved or juices. In the Community, Italy has been anxious to protect its producers' markets, although they account for less than 10 per cent of total sales in the Community. The Maghreb countries, Spain and Israel were the main suppliers. The Maghreb countries had privileged access rights because of their links with France. Spain and Israel were accorded less generous preferences in their agreements. Thus, a whole spectrum of preferential rates was established, later to be complicated by the introduction of reference prices for all imports of citrus fruits into the Community. Each preferential rate is jealously guarded in the trade agreements.

Where concessions on agricultural imports have been granted to less developed countries, they have been mostly reserved for the Associated African States. Yet the investigation by Professor Kebschull (chapter 4) shows that preferences on agricultural commodities appear to have brought few identifiable benefits overall to these countries. Some redistribution of markets has occurred in as much as sales to Community countries other than France have risen. Generally, however, the effects of other factors have swamped the effects of preferences. Similar results were obtained by Ouattara.[11] These studies suggest, perhaps, that preferences on agricultural trade in agreements with the Community should not be overvalued.

Enlargement of the European Community has brought added concern to a number of Mediterranean countries. Before accession, trade barriers

10 See J. Bridge, above, p. 161.

11 A. D. Ouattara, 'Trade effects of the Association of African countries with the European Economic Community', *International Monetary Fund Staff Papers (July 1973)*.

(tariffs and quotas) on agricultural imports from some Mediterranean countries into the three new members, and especially Britain, were considerably lower than those of the Community. Under the 'global' Mediterranean policy, Spain and Israel both face substantial rises in tariffs and other restrictions on their exports of citrus fruit (fresh and preserved) and other fruits and vegetables into Britain; and Cyprus faces new restrictions on exports of wine to Britain. Moreover, the CAP system of variable import levies means that any attempt to cut prices to remain competitive against internal producers is frustrated. This increase in effective protection in north European countries serves no purpose but to raise prices to the consumer, because there are no marginal producers within the Community capable of raising significantly their output of citrus fruit and semi-tropical produce to meet the demand. If demand for this produce is price-elastic, the consequences of reduced sales for producers in less developed countries in the Mediterranean could be considerable. In this case, the Mediterranean policy would positively harm economic development in the region, as well as reduce consumer welfare in the new Community countries.

Although a major reason why Mediterranean countries have sought bilateral trade agreements with the Community has been to preserve or to expand markets for their agricultural exports, the actual concessions obtained have been quite small. On balance, it would appear that the Mediterranean countries are probably worse off as a result of these agreements with the Community than they were under the independent commercial agreements with the individual members. In other words, the development of a common commercial policy for the Community in this region has not brought benefit to the separate Mediterranean countries, as far as agricultural trade is concerned. And, moreover, it seems highly likely that consumers in some Community countries may also lose from greater restrictions on agricultural imports from the Mediterranean.

Progressive Discrimination

It is apparent from a cursory examination of the chronological development of bilateral trade agreements between the European Community and separate Mediterranean countries that there has been a progression away from 'association' agreements that were compatible, at least in general terms, with Article 24 of GATT, and towards exclusive preferential trade agreements that cannot be reconciled with the fundamental principles of the GATT. Once the first infringement of the conditions for the establishment of free-trade areas under Article 24 had occurred in the association agreements with Greece and Turkey, it seems to have been viewed by the European Commission as proving a licence to enter into any kind of preferential agreement, however limited the magnitude of the tariff reductions or the proportion of trade covered. It is ironic that the United States, for political and strategic reasons, supported the granting of waivers in the GATT to permit the association agreements with Greece and Turkey. As has been noted elsewhere, these agreements were the starting signal for pressures from many other Mediterranean countries to seek unique, and increasingly exclusive, bilateral trade agreements with the Community.

After the Greek and Turkish agreements had been signed, there was a considerable lapse of time before the next agreements were reached. The reasons were to be found in the difficulties and disagreements among the EEC countries caused by the pressures from the Mediterranean countries. Throughout the 1960s it was apparent that the European Commission was 'leading from behind' in encouraging the negotiation of these agreements, which were one of the few areas in which the Commission had power to act under Article 113 of the Treaty of Rome, and in the absence of a will among the member governments to establish a common foreign policy. In this power vacuum, the Commission was able to pursue an external commercial policy by negotiating bilateral agreements within a confused institutional structure. (Reference to the methods by which the agreements were drawn up are made in chapter 13 by Papa and Petit-Laurent.) As successive agreements were reached and published, the pressure for similar agreements or comparable concessions from neighbouring countries increased.

By 1972, ten bilateral agreements with Mediterranean countries were in existence, and several other agreements were under discussion. The problem of reconciling different interests of individual Mediterranean countries, and of preserving their separate interests when reaching further trade agreements, must have become formidable. Common elements were developed and embodied in the agreements; a marked similarity exists, for example, in the agreements with Spain, Israel, Egypt and Lebanon. Pragmatism resulted, therefore, through an iterative process, in the creation of a general framework, which could be adapted to meet special problems.

The next step was for the Commission to seek to simplify the complex, separate bilateral agreements by creating a 'global approach' for the Community with the whole Mediterranean area. The difficulty of resolving the many disparate interests in the Mediterranean countries of the nine member governments has been illustrated by the failure to achieve a 'global policy' by the deadline set by the Council of Ministers for January 1974; and that concerned only policy towards six Mediterranean countries: Spain, Israel, Tunisia, Algeria, Morocco and Malta.

A 'Global' Policy

The achievement of a 'global' policy for the European Community towards the Mediterranean countries is expected to simplify trading regulations, and thus it has obvious attractions for the European Commission. It must be doubtful, however, whether the different political attitudes towards, and economic links with, individual Mediterranean countries that exist in the European countries could ever be reconciled a meaningful global policy. And the wide political and economic differences among the Mediterranean countries themselves also suggest that any kind of global policy, which must represent the lowest common denominator, will be a very sketchy framework. In these circumstances, there must be a question whether the level of political effort involved in obtaining a global approach is warranted by the economic results.

Before any attempt can be made to assess the viability and value of a global Mediterranean policy, some attempt must be made to measure the effects of the present bilateral trade agreements for the Mediterranean countries. What have been the economic benefits? How do they compare with the probable effects of alternative trade policies, especially the generalised preference schemes and GATT trade negotiations? What have been the losses for the Mediterranean countries, and for third countries, of the bilateral agreements? And these material questions apart, what of the imponderables, the stake of small countries in a multilateral framework of rules and principles, to which they must look for their interests to be protected.

There must also be doubts whether the Mediterranean policy really serves the economic interests of the European Community. It seems unlikely that a global policy will provide for association agreements with the Community that will meet the conditions for a free-trade area as defined in Article 24 of the GATT, in which case, the global policy for the Mediterranean countries would represent another violation of the non-discrimination principle – and another step away from the multilateralism embodied in the GATT. The European Community should really consider the position of discriminatory commercial relations with the Mediterranean countries in the broad context of its world trading strategy. How does it relate to commercial policy with the other industrial countries, with the

Associated African States, with countries that are applicants for association ('the Associables') and with the non-aligned, less developed countries? And it is also relevant to ask how a global Mediterranean policy relates to the Community's negotiating strategy for the promised Tokyo Round of trade negotiations in the GATT?

Effects of Preferential Trade Agreements

Bilateral trade agreements embodying tariff preferences result in trade creation and trade diversion, in the same fashion as 100 per cent tariff preferences result in a customs union. Trade creation occurs where low-cost production in one country substitutes for higher-cost production in the other country, when its tariffs are reduced under the agreement. This leads to a re-allocation of production and consumption towards lower-priced output and increased economic efficiency. Trade diversion, on the other hand, occurs where imports from the partner country displace lower-cost imports from third countries, because of tariff discrimination against the latter. This lowers economic efficiency in the countries that are a party to the trade agreement, and causes a deterioration in the terms of trade of the importing country.

The main burden of adjustment under such discriminatory trade agreements falls on third countries. The benefits of trade creation accrue to groups inside the agreement, whereas the harmful effects of trade diversion fall mainly on outside countries. To some extent these trade effects on countries within the agreement may spill over through multiplier effects and ameliorate the burden on outsiders, but those compensations are likely to be small. For example, in as much as trade diversion raises income levels in the country enjoying increased exports, there may be an induced increase in imports from third countries. But this offsetting trade is likely to be very small compared with the initial loss of exports by outsiders caused by the tariff discrimination; moreover, the distribution of these trade effects among third countries must be considered, too.

Possibilities for trade creation between the industrialised countries of the European Community and the developing countries of the Mediterranean basin are obviously limited. Only Spain and Israel among these countries have made any real progress towards industrialisation. In these cases, static customs-union theory states that economic gains will occur from a re-allocation of production and consumption towards the lowest cost source of supply within the area of the trade agreement. Spain and Israel, however, have been seeking to develop domestic industries by import substitution policies behind considerable trade barriers. The discriminatory removal of tariffs, and possibly other trade barriers, in favour of the European Community involves reversing this policy. Presumably, the import substitution policy represented a conscious social choice on the part of those countries, and the social costs of trade protection were an acceptable burden in order to establish viable industries. If producers in the European Community are able by means of tariff preferences to make inroads into the domestic markets of these adolescent industries, the past investment in these industries by these countries in the form of consumption forgone, will be sacrificed and the domestic industries may never reach maturity. In the absence of alternative employment, the development process would be slowed. The number of industries in Israel and Spain that could withstand intense competition from producers in the European Community must be few. The granting of trade preferences, therefore, involves critical social choices in these countries.

Preferential access to the Community market for exports of industrial goods means very little to Mediterranean countries where industrialisation is only just beginning. The competitive effect, therefore, on the Community's industries will be trivial. The only area in which Mediterranean countries could provide serious competition for the Community producers is in certain types of agricultural products, especially fruit and vegetables (fresh and preserved). Here, as it has been seen, there are major difficulties. Most of the bilateral agreements with Mediterranean countries provide for only limited access for particular agricultural products. Generally, these concessions represent no more than security for a country's previous share of the market, and often fall short of that.

Trade diversion, then, by means of so-called reverse preferences, is likely to be the major trade effect of these bilateral trade agreements with the Mediterranean countries. In any preferential trade agreement, third countries face double discrimination against their exports. Third country exporters are discriminated against in Mediterranean markets in favour of exporters from the Community; and in the European Community markets, preferential access is granted to Mediterranean countries' exporters. As it has been seen, the latter is comparatively unimportant.

Reverse preferences, however, raise more serious issues.

Trade preferences for less developed countries' exports have become accepted as means for encouraging economic development. It is difficult to see, however, how reverse preferences make any contribution to economic development. It has been noted above that granting preferential access for Community exports may undermine development policies based on import substitution. Because many developing countries have high levels of tariff protection, the preference granted may be large and may have serious distortive effects on trade flows. The United States' and the European Community's exporters, for example, often compete directly in developing countries' markets for manufactured goods. In this context, a tariff preference for the Community's exporters puts the US exporters at a serious disadvantage, and may lead to real economic losses to the preference-granting country if higher f.o.b. import prices have to be paid.

Moreover, reverse preferences discriminate against imports from *all* third countries, including suppliers from developing countries. This applies especially to the Community's bilateral agreements with the Mediterranean countries. Associated African States are permitted under the Yaoundé Convention to enter preferential trade agreements with other developing countries. This provides an escape, although in practice it is seldom used.

Reverse preferences have caused tensions between the United States and the European Community, as Professor Kreinin has explained (chapter 3 above). The volume of trade covered by these preferences in Mediterranean countries is not large at present, and for this reason the European Commission tends to belittle charges of unfair discrimination from third countries. (If similar preferential trade agreements were reached with the oil-producing Arab countries of the Near East, however, the trade impact would become much more significant.) But this misses the real point of United States' objections to these bilateral agreements. The main charge is that these preferences undermine the principles of the multilateral trading system, which form the basis of international relations in peacetime. This fundamental charge has not been answered by the European Community, or its member governments.

Professor Kreinin, in chapter 3, points out the dangers to the preference-granting countries of these bilateral agreements. Although the preferences apply to all the Community countries, in many cases one supplier may pre-empt the market and establish a monopoly position. (In the case of former French colonies in North Africa, French suppliers have an obvious advantage.) In this position, the monopolist is able to collect the whole economic rent provided by the tariff protection he has against other suppliers. By charging a price equal to the world market price plus the full tariff, the monopolist is able to add the tariff preference he receives to his general profit. In this way the consumer in the importing country is paying a transfer to a supplier in a European country. Professor Kreinin puts forward some empirical evidence to support these suggestions as far as Associated African States are concerned. A similar potential for exploitation seems to exist in the Mediterranean countries.

Semi-industrialised countries, such as Israel and Spain, may obtain certain gains from preferential access to a large rich market like those in the European Community. Portuguese experience in the European Free Trade Association (EFTA) supports this case. The product groups, however, in which such gains may be achieved are probably limited. In terms of economic welfare, a key issue is what price is paid for this preferential access to the Community market, in the form of granting reverse preferences to their home market? This aspect of the problem appears not to have been stressed in analyses of the trade agreement with the Mediterranean countries. One reason for this is that the Israeli and Spanish agreements are comparatively recent and so little is known about their effects. Professor Kreinin concludes that the effects of reverse preferences on the Mediterranean countries will vary from one country to another. He anticipates that they will be most adverse in the least developed countries, and least adverse, and may be even beneficial on balance, in the semi-industrialised states.

A Multilateral Alternative

The preceding section showed that there are several reasons to doubt whether discriminatory trade agreements bring economic gains to the participating, less developed countries. As Lipsey stated, '. . . the customs union is more likely to bring gain, the greater is the degree of overlapping between the class of commodities produced under tariff protection in the two countries'.[12] This applies to any preferential trade agreement. The production patterns of the European Community and the Mediterranean countries are broadly complementary, so that trade diversion is likely to outweigh trade creation. Even if economic gains occur as a result of a preferential trade agreement, it is by no means certain that the gains will be distributed evenly between the two participants. One may lose and the other gain. Because the Community has granted few concessions on agricultural imports, where the Mediterranean countries have comparative advantage, it seems likely that the less developed countries will lose. It is also apparent that third countries are likely to lose from these bilateral trade agreements.

12 R. G. Lipsey, 'The theory of customs unions; a general survey', *Economic Journal* (September 1960).

Empirical studies of the effects on less developed countries of association agreements with the European Community have shown few gains from this preferential access.[13] Where gains have occurred in certain product groups, they have usually been the counterpart of market losses by other less developed countries. Similar results have arisen also from other preferential agreements, such as the system of Commonwealth preference.[14]

In view of the uncertainty of the advantages to be had from bilateral preferential trade agreements, it would seem worth while for the Mediterranean countries to consider alternative ways of obtaining preferential access to the Community market.

One possibility that has been mooted in Commission circles would be to establish fully-fledged free-trade areas between the Community and individual Mediterranean countries, along similar lines to those applied to individual EFTA countries. This would require the mutual elimination of all tariffs and other trade restrictions in a stipulated period. Mediterranean countries seeking to industrialise their economies would have objections to this. It would also require changes in the level of access to agricultural markets in the Community, which is unlikely to be acceptable. Because of these problems the Commission's 'global' policy towards the Mediterranean countries reverted to a preference scheme, involving partial removal of trade barriers.

Another possibility concerns the generalised schemes of preferences, in which all the Mediterranean countries are eligible to participate. The European Community's scheme provides for duty-free entry for most manufactures and semi-manufactures, but it is heavily circumscribed with quota ceilings on imports of 'sensitive products'. A study by Professor Cooper has shown that the quota ceilings are highly restrictive of the Community's imports from less developed countries.[15] Indeed, the quotas are so restrictive that Murray has suggested that the Community's generalised scheme of preferences offers little or no incentive to manufacturers in less developed countries.[16] The Mediterranean countries might, therefore, apply their negotiating efforts to making the generalised scheme of prefer-

13 Ouattara, *op. cit.*

14 J. Maranjo and R. C. Porter, 'The impact of the Commonwealth preference system on the exports of Latin America to the United Kingdom', *Journal of Development Studies* (1973).

15 R. N. Cooper, 'The European Community's system of generalised tariff preferences: a critique,' *Journal of Development Studies* (1972).

16 T. Murray, 'How helpful is the generalised system of preferences to developing countries?' *Economic Journal* (1973).

ences more liberal. This implies operating within a non-discriminatory system for all less developed countries. But if attention were directed towards extending the range of imports from less-developed countries covered by the Community's scheme, to include processed agricultural produce, and towards expanding the quota 'ceilings' on textiles and other manufactured goods exported from Mediterranean countries, considerable benefits would be obtained. Unfortunately, to be effective such lobbying would require a co-ordination of policies among the Mediterranean countries which seems unlikely in view of the competitiveness of their exports and the political differences that separate them.

Both these alternatives face the same basic difficulties as have faced the Mediterranean countries when negotiating bilateral trade agreements with the Commission. The European Community will be able to offer more generous concessions on imports from less developed countries – bilaterally or multilaterally – only when it takes steps to encourage internal economic adjustment to change competitive conditions, and ceases to oppose such competitive forces through trade protection. At present, any sudden surge of imports is met by introducing restrictive measures under safeguard clauses. These may be according to escape provisions in the General Agreement, or according to specific safeguard clauses in bilateral agreements, or according to the safeguards provided in the generalised scheme of preferences. As long as competetive pressures are avoided by using safeguards and not encouraged as a means to bring about industrial adjustments to new market conditions, it will be difficult for less developed countries to gain secure access to developed countries' markets. Secure markets for exports are the basis for economic development. But the quota ceilings in the Community's generalised preference scheme so restrict access at the preferential rate that high cost production in less developed countries receives no encouragement.

Adjustment to changing market conditions, whether on the demand or the supply side, is a normal and continuing process of economic development, and the need for adjustment arising from an increase in the competitiveness of imports or reductions in trade barriers are usually met without government interference – as was the case when tariffs were dismantled in the European Community. To be able to commit themselves to programmes to reduce trade barriers, however, governments demand 'safeguards': that is, agreed rules according to which such programmes can be postponed or delayed where unrestrained growth in imports exceeds the adjustment capacity of the corresponding domestic industries. In order to be effective, these temporary safeguards should be accompanied by domestic adjustment policies which will eventually permit the programme of trade liberalisation to be restored. Recent experience has shown that smooth adjustment can be made to foreign competition; the Swedish and British cotton textile industries have adjusted gradually to competition from low-cost producers in the Far East.[17]

Problems of international adjustment at the microeconomic or industry level are a major topic for the Tokyo Round of GATT trade negotiations.[18] This refers to circumstances in which individual industries or regions may be forced to adjust relatively to the rest of the national economy. The present GATT articles offer safeguard provisions involving the introduction of import restrictions for as long as necessary (Article 19). But these provisions do not require that remedial measures need be taken; so, they merely provide an excuse for imposing trade restrictions, and they can be used to invalidate reductions in trade barriers under international agreements.

Most recent studies of the international trading system have recommended that changes should be made in the safeguard provisions in order to make them effective as an instrument for international economic adjustment. Safeguard provisions are essential in order to allow strict economic agreements to be negotiated, because the circumstances of their operation cannot be fully anticipated when they are signed. But safeguards must recognise not only the right to emergency protection but also the obligation to trade partners, which must be backed by adequate procedures. To achieve the correct balance three conditions must be met. First, a maximum period should be set for emergency protection. Within this period, such protection should have a diminishing impact. Second, protection of this kind must be accompanied by appropriate domestic economic adjustment. Third, there must be international supervision.[19]

If a more effective multilateral safeguard system were to be established, developed countries, including the European Community, might become more willing to offer improved access to their markets for exports of less developed countries. If the need for economic adjustment to changed market

17 S. Mukhorjee, *Free trade is good but what about the workers? trade liberalisation and adjustment assistance*, PEP Broadsheet (March 1974); and D. Robertson, 'Changing the pattern', *The Guardian*, 28 May 1974.

18 D. Robertson, *Safeguarding national interests in international trade agreements*, Trade Policy Research Centre, Thames Essay, 1974.

19 See Rey Report, *op cit.* chapter 5.

conditions became accepted, the market opportunities for less developed countries would expand. All less developed countries, therefore, have an interest in a successful agreement to reform the safeguard provisions in the GATT in the Tokyo Round, to make it a truly effective mechanism of international economic adjustment.

Unfortunately, the European Community does not have a good record for encouraging internal adjustment to changing market conditions, and it has always shown a preference for trade restrictions in cases of market disruption. The Commission was unwilling in 1973 to relax the very rigid safeguard provisions in member countries' bilateral trade agreements with Japan in drawing up a new Community-wide agreement. And the final version of the Community's 'Overall approach to the forthcoming trade negotiations in GATT', agreed by the Council of Ministers on 26 June 1973, shows much less willingness to revise safeguards than the earlier versions.[20]

A Worldwide Strategy for Trade

The Community has built up a system of multiple trade discrimination, of which the agreements with the Mediterranean countries are only part. When the Community was enlarged from six to nine members in 1973, by the accession of Britain, Ireland and Denmark, bilateral free-trade agreements were introduced with the non-applicant EFTA countries. Towards less developed countries a hierarchy of tariff preferences had developed over the years, involving varying degrees of generosity. The stages range from the most generous arrangements covering trade and financial and technical assistance under the Yaoundé agreement, through less generous concessions on trade only under the Arusha agreement, down to the uneven and patchy agreements with the Mediterranean countries.[21] These different degrees of trade discrimination cause frictions with non-aligned countries receiving Most Favoured Nation treatment (or is it 'least favoured nation' treatment?). But they also create tensions among countries receiving different degrees of privileged access to the Community market. John Pinder has shown how the Associated African States defend their position at the top of the hierarchy, aided by the French government's vigilance in the corridors of the Commission.[22] And the striving for position among the Mediterranean countries has already been mentioned.

20 Robertson, *op. cit.*

21 J. Pinder, 'The Community and the developing countries: associates and outsiders', *Journal of Common Market Studies* (1973).

22 Pinder, *op. cit.*

This hierarchical structure is about to become even more complex following the enlargement of the Community, because twenty Commonwealth countries are eligible for associated status. Association offers the most complete commercial access to Community markets for these countries, but it also involves a political commitment which independent Commonwealth countries may not be prepared to undertake. Renegotiation of the Yaoundé agreement, coupled with negotiations for a 'global' Mediterranean policy, seem certain to result in further complexities being added to the Community's system of multiple trade discrimination. Differences of opinion and commitment among the nine member countries and the existence of separate pressure groups to support each type of agreement seem to ensure a continuing multiplicity of preferential trade arrangements.

The system of multiple trade discrimination that the Community has evolved is a disjointed and inharmonious policy, in which little attention has been given to either internal consistency or compatibility with international commitments embodied in the GATT. There are grave dangers in dismissing the last point too lightly, as Mr Henig has done in his paper. Ignoring or destroying the international commercial order established by GATT, following the chaos of the 1930s, would be foolhardy. Perhaps in some ways the GATT provisions are honoured more in the breach than in the observance, but they provide a basis for international discussion and negotiation that is vital if a retrograde move back to protectionism and bilateralism is to be avoided. The ever-widening net of discriminatory trading agreements being cast by the Community endangers the whole fabric of GATT, and, if other major countries disregard the principle of non-discrimination, it is quite possible that the Community, as the world's largest trading entity, would be the greatest loser.

It seemed possible that the Commission's memorandum, 'Development of an overall approach to trade in view of the coming multilateral negotiators in GATT' (April 1973), would form the basis for a co-ordinated strategy on international trade relations. In the end, however, the Council of Ministers emasculated the document by removing or qualifying its more liberal passages. It remains to be seen how exactly this document will be shaped into a negotiating mandate, now the US Trade Reform Bill has been enacted. The 'Overall approach' does not truly represent a broad strategy for trade relations, however, because it pays little regard to the structure of the Community's preferential trade agreements. It is to be feared that the Community still prefers a piece-meal approach to trade matters. Only for formal international negotiations, where the Commission is empowered to negotiate, such as the Tokyo Round, is there any attempt to derive a co-ordinated approach to trade matters. Yet, it has been indicated above, there may be substantial economic costs from an unco-ordinated approach to advances from outsiders seeking a privileged position.

Some of the internal difficulties of the Community regarding discriminatory trade agreements could be resolved in a successful outcome to the Tokyo Round. The chances of this depend on the climate in which the negotiations take place, and in the willingness of the participants, including the Community, to seek complete solutions. One particular issue concerns revisions to the safeguard provisions in GATT, to make them a genuine mechanism for international economic adjustment. As the system of multiple trade discrimination expands, as the Commission apparently intends, the competition faced by Community producers from 'privileged' imports will increase and the need for effective economic adjustment will increase too. An effective international safeguards mechanism in GATT would give a multilateral solution to which no trading partners could legitimately object. If, instead, the Community is forced to introduce unilateral safeguard protection, or use safeguards in bilateral agreements, it will be open to accusations of favouring one trading partner against another, according to the hierarchy of preferential agreements.

The GATT ministerial declaration from Tokyo, in September 1973, announced that priority should be given in the negotiations to the trade needs of developing countries; wherever possible, special and more favourable treatment should be provided for less developed countries. The question of UNCTAD schemes for generalised preferences and the vexed issue of reverse preferences are certain to become involved in the negotiations. A placatory attitude on these questions by the Community would enable it, on a multilateral level, to eliminate some of the complexities in its dealings with less developed countries, if it so wishes. There is a suggestion in the *overall Approach* (Chapter 5) that the Commission would be prepared to improve its generalised preferences.

The centre-piece of the Tokyo Round negotiations will, of course, be reductions in tariffs and non-tariff barriers. Here the mandate given to the Commission's negotiators will be a crucial factor. At the annual GATT Council session in Geneva in September 1972, Japan proposed that the elimination of industrial tariffs should be a working hypothesis for the negotiations; a proposal supported at the time by Sweden and the United States. The 'Overall approach' in its final form rejected the suggestion that tariffs should be eliminated on trade between industrial countries. Indeed, in chapter II of the 'Overall Approach', it is specifically stated that there should be a minimum level of tariffs below which no reduction would be required. As a consequence of this, the United States' authorities modified their position too. The alternative negotiating procedures will prolong the Tokyo Round but they still offer scope for substantial reductions in trade barriers. There are still doubts, however, whether the Community is willing to reduce its common external tariff (CET) because of the cement it provides for the common market that has been created. This appears to express little confidence in the institutions of the Community, never mind the spirit of European unity, but it is clearly implied in the Explanatory Memorandum to the 'Overall Approach'.[23]

At the end of July 1974, the Council of Ministers finally agreed on the form of a 'global' Mediterranean policy to be put to six countries; Spain, Israel, Tunisia, Algeria, Morocco and Malta. This appears to require preferential reductions in trade barriers on imports from these countries by some members, but considerable increases in trade restrictions on some products by other countries, especially the three new members. It is difficult to judge whether on balance the Community or the Mediterranean countries stand to gain much from this 'global' policy. What is clear, however, is that this policy represents another stage in the Community's multiple trade discrimination; and further stages will follow as the second half of the 'global' policy for Egypt, Lebanon, Syria and Jordan, is developed. No specific mention of the policy towards the Mediterranean countries is made in the 'Overall approach'. Yet the 'global' policy has been announced before this policy statement for the GATT negotiation is even implemented. This shows once again the absence of an overall strategy for the Community in its trade relations. A common commercial policy can hardly be established successfully in a vacuum. The Community's Mediterranean policy typifies the piecemeal and unco-ordinated character of the Community's external economic policies.

Division of Interests

It is important to recognise the very different interests of the individual member countries of the Community in the Mediterranean region, in order to appreciate the difficulties of achieving a 'global' policy towards this very

23 Final version of *The development of an overall approach to the forthcoming multilateral trade negotiations in GATT*, European Communities, Luxembourg, 29 June 1973 (1/135/73 [Comer 42]).

disparate group of countries to the south. France and Italy were the first members to suggest that a common policy should be evolved towards the Mediterranean countries. Their main interests were political, arising out of their geographical location and colonial links. Germany and the Benelux countries were, on the whole, unmoved by these arguments. Enlargement of the Community to include Britain, Ireland and Denmark swung the balance further towards the views of the northern group. Nevertheless, the impetus imparted to the Commission's activities by the earlier moves was not to be denied.

Discussions in Brussels about the 'global' Mediterranean policy have exposed the divergence among the views of the northern and southern members of the Community. France and Italy remain keen to achieve a 'global' policy for political reasons, but they are worried about the economic costs to their farmers from increased imports of wine, fruit and vegetables from the Mediterranean countries. On the other hand, the northern countries find attractive the prospect of lowering the Community's trade barriers and importing cheaper agricultural produce from the Mediterranean; they are less concerned about the political aspect.

Britain is in an extreme position among the northern group. The prospect of discriminatory reductions in trade barriers against agricultural imports from the Mediterranean, which appeals to most of the northern members of the Community, means little to Britain. Paradoxically, because Britain has had barriers as low as zero against imports of fruit and vegetables (fresh and preserved) and wine from several Mediterranean countries, in harmonising to the new level of preferential tariffs under the 'global' Mediterranean policy Britain will have to raise trade barriers against imports from countries like Cyprus, Spain and Israel (although not as high as would be required under the present bilateral agreements). This will involve welfare losses to the British consumer forced to pay higher prices for this produce. Moreover, in implementing the Mediterranean policy Britain will be introducing new preferences to replace the Commonwealth preferences relinquished on entry to the Community. Without a quantitative analysis of the effects of this new policy on Britain's trade and economic welfare, it is difficult to be entirely certain about the overall effects. But on first impressions, and bearing in mind the inconvenience and frictional effects of changing trading conditions, there would seem to be substantial economic disadvantages to Britain in the adoption of the Mediterranean policy. Britain's previous policy of zero tariffs would have offered greater benefits to the Mediterranean countries, too.

The other northern countries in the Community are, presumably, in a similar position to Britain. That is, they would stand to gain more from a minimum of restrictions on agricultural imports from the Mediterranean. Until agreements are finally reached with the individual Mediterranean countries, there is, presumably, the possibility of changes in the 'global' policy as defined by the Council of Ministers. The room for manœuvre, though, is small.

Concluding Comments

Development of the Community's Mediterranean policy has demonstrated how political objections may transcend economic considerations in the determination of the Community's external commercial policy. Very little attempt appears to have been made to ascertain the economic implications of the complex series of piecemeal bilateral trade agreements established with the Mediterranean countries. Without such an evaluation, however, how are we to know whether the economic 'price' of the policy is worth paying? Some attempts have been made in the earlier chapters of this book to measure the economic effects of the separate bilateral trade agreements. The effects are generally small and the periods of operation of the agreements too short to give conclusive results. A more comprehensive and vigorous exercise should now be undertaken to quantify the economic effects of the proposed 'global' Mediterranean policy on the Community as a whole, as the individual member countries, or on the Mediterranean countries.

In the end, however, the full significance of the Mediterranean policy of the Community's system of multiple trade discrimination can be properly assessed only in terms of its consequences for the international system of trade and payments. Are the uncertain economic benefits and the obscure political aspects of this policy worth causing further weakening of the international system of trade and payments? If the Community must have a Mediterranean policy it would seem preferable to seek to support its economic development through financial and technical assistance rather than through trade preferences. So far, financial and technical assistance has played only a minor role in agreements with the Mediterranean countries.

The absence of a broad strategy for international trade relations, including a viable framework for the international system of trade and payments, leaves the European Community vulnerable to inconsistent and costly policies under a piecemeal approach to problems. Discontinuities may occur between the Commission and the member governments in the formation of trade policy that enable political objectives to be achieved by means of economic instruments, without due regard for the economic consequences. The problems associated with the Community's Mediterranean policy emphasise the weakness of pursuing discriminatory trade policies and of failing to establish a comprehensive strategy on international trade relations.

INDEX